JUL 2 0 2015

Self and Salvation
Being Transformed

Ford's publications include *Barth and God's Story: Biblical Narrative
and the Theological Method of Karl Barth in the Church Dogmatics* (1981),
Jubilate: Theology in Praise (with Daniel W. Hardy, 1984), *Meaning and
Truth in 2 Corinthians* (with F. M. Young, 1988), *The Modern
Theologians* (editor, second edition, 1997), *The Shape of Living* (1997)
and *A Long Rumour of Wisdom: Redescribing Theology* (1992).

Cambridge Studies in Christian Doctrine

Edited by
Professor COLIN GUNTON, *King's College London*
Professor DANIEL W. HARDY, *University of Cambridge*

Cambridge Studies in Christian Doctrine is an important series
which aims to engage critically with the traditional doctrines of
Christianity, and at the same time to locate and make sense of
them within a secular context. Without losing sight of the
authority of scripture and the traditions of the church, the books
in this series subject pertinent dogmas and credal statements
to careful scrutiny, analysing them in light of the insights of both
church and society, and thereby practise theology in the
fullest sense of the word.

Titles published in the series

1. Self and Salvation: Being Transformed
   DAVID F. FORD

2. Realist Christian Theology in a Postmodern Age
   SUE PATTERSON

3. Trinity and Truth
   BRUCE D. MARSHALL

4. Theology, Music and Time
   JEREMY S. BEGBIE

5. The Bible, Theology, and Faith: A Study of Abraham and Jesus
   R. W. L. MOBERLY

6. Bound to Sin: Abuse, Holocaust and the Christian Doctrine of Sin
   ALISTAIR McFADYEN

7. Church, World and the Christian Life: Practical-Prophetic Ecclesiology
   NICHOLAS M. HEALY

8. Theology and the Dialogue of Religions
   MICHAEL BARNES SJ

9. A Political Theology of Nature
   PETER SCOTT

Titles forthcoming in the series

Remythologizing Theology: Divine Action and Authorship
KEVIN J. VANHOOZER

A Christian Doctrine of Knowledge
PAUL JANZ

Worship as Meaning: A Liturgical Theology for Late Modernity
GRAHAM HUGHES

Georges Rouault, *Ecce Homo*, 1953.

Self and Salvation
Being Transformed

DAVID F. FORD

CAMBRIDGE
UNIVERSITY PRESS

CAMBRIDGE UNIVERSITY PRESS
Cambridge, New York, Melbourne, Madrid, Cape Town, Singapore, São Paulo

Cambridge University Press
The Edinburgh Building, Cambridge CB2 8RU, UK

Published in the United States of America by Cambridge University Press, New York

www.cambridge.org
Information on this title: www.cambridge.org/9780521416078

© Cambridge University Press 1999

First published 1999
Reprinted 2000, 2002, 2003

A catalogue record for this publication is available from the British Library

Library of Congress Cataloguing in Publication data
Ford, David, 1948–
Self and salvation: being transformed / David F. Ford.
        p.   cm.
(Cambridge studies in Christian doctrine; 1)
Includes index.
ISBN 0 521 41607 8 (hardback)
ISBN 0 521 42616 2 (paperback)
1. Salvation. 2. Self. I. Title. II. Series
BT751.2.F68   1998
234–dc21   98–14398 CIP

ISBN 978-0-521-41607-8 hardback
ISBN 978-0-521-42616-9 paperback

Transferred to digital printing 2008

Unless otherwise noted,
all biblical extracts
are adapted from the
New Revised Standard Version

To DEAREST DEBORAH

Contents

List of illustrations x
Acknowledgements xi
Introduction 1

I Dialogues: Levinas, Jüngel, Ricoeur

1 Facing 17
2 Enjoyment, responsibility and desire: a hospitable self 30
3 God, others and substitution: a self without idols 45
4 Language, love and testimony: a worshipping self 73

II Flourishings

5 Communicating God's abundance: a singing self 107
6 'Do this': a eucharistic self 137
7 Facing Jesus Christ 167
8 The face on the cross and the worship of God 191
9 Love as vocation: Thérèse of Lisieux 216
10 Polyphonic living: Dietrich Bonhoeffer 241
11 Feasting 266

Bibliography 281
Index of scriptural references 287
Index 291

Illustrations

Georges Rouault, *Ecce Homo*, 1953, Private Collection, Paris. *frontispiece*
Raphael, *The Ecstasy of St Cecilia with Sts Paul, John the Evangelist, Augustine, and Mary Magdalene*, Pinacoteca Nazionale, Bologna. *page 273*

Acknowledgements

During the period spent writing this book I have accumulated gratitude to innumerable people and institutions.

Cambridge has been home for most of that time. I am deeply grateful to colleagues in the Faculty of Divinity for their warm welcome and generous support. The Faculty has been going through a major transformation, and without the extraordinary dedication, not only of colleagues such as Graham Davies, Morna Hooker, Nicholas Lash, Julius Lipner, Rosalind Paul, Janet Soskice, Fraser Watts and especially David Thompson, but also of the Development Committee chaired by Lord Runcie, and of other members of the University and its Development Office, there would not have been the time and energy to complete this work. It has also been a delight to be a Fellow of Selwyn College, and I have greatly appreciated being welcomed back to St John's College, where I was a student for five years, and joining the Foundation of Trinity College. Cambridge University Press, especially through Alex Wright, Ruth Parr, Kevin Taylor and Joanne Hill, has been most supportive throughout the book's preparation.

Senior Seminars in Systematic Theology and New Testament in the Faculty of Divinity have responded helpfully to early drafts of several parts of the book. Colleagues have been most helpful in conceiving, developing and testing ideas – especially Jeremy Begbie, Markus Bockmuehl, Graham Davies, Morna Hooker, William Horbury, Tim Jenkins, Nicholas Lash, John Milbank, Nick Sagovsky, Janet Martin Soskice and Margie Tolstoy. Above all, Dan Hardy has been the theological midwife of the book, and I owe him the greatest gratitude for his friendship, generosity and wisdom. My graduate students too have contributed much to my thinking over these years, and I thank especially for their direct assistance with this book Michael Barnes SJ, Mike Higton, Paul Murray, Ann Nickson and Ben Quash. Beyond the Faculty, I especially thank Jeremy Maule for his contributions on Thomas Traherne, and a range of Cambridge and visiting academics for a diverse set of influences. Yet this essay has by no means been shaped only through academic life in Cambridge, and the worshipping communities of Holy Trinity Church and St Bene't's Church have been particularly significant.

Before my coming to Cambridge this work was conceived in Birmingham, and my fifteen years there were of crucial importance to it. I am deeply indebted to Frances Young for her friendship and theological collaboration. Our five years working on 2 Corinthians together has left marks throughout this book. Also formative were fifteen years worshipping in St Luke's Church, Bristol Street. Reaching further back, I recall with gratitude a semester spent living as a guest in the home of Eberhard Jüngel in Tübingen, which began the interest in his theology which is a theme of this book. Even further back, while I was studying in Yale in 1972, Henri Nouwen introduced me to the work of the philosopher who pervades these pages more than any other thinker, Emmanuel Levinas.

In 1993 I was privileged to spend some months as a Member of the Center of Theological Inquiry in Princeton when Dan Hardy was its Director. Among the highlights of that time were intensive engagement with Al McFadyen, who is author of the forthcoming volume on sin in this series; and inspiring conversation with Robert Gibbs and Peter Ochs. Other academic institutions have also been venues for an array of papers and discussions, and I thank especially the Shalom Hartman Institute in Jerusalem, the Roehampton Institute, and the Universities of Dublin, Durham, Leeds, Oxford and Toronto. I am also immensely grateful to the Society for the Study of Theology, which has been a valued intellectual community for over twenty-five years and in particular discussed an early version of the chapter on the eucharist.

From 1990 until 1996 I was a member of the Archbishop of Canterbury's Urban Theology Group. Grappling with issues relating to urban deprivation and 'God in the city' in the aftermath of the *Faith in the City* report deeply affected everyone in our mixed group of academics and those engaged 'on the ground'. The questions we wrestled with only rarely appear in this book, but have accompanied it throughout, and I want to thank the group warmly: Tom Butler, Alan Davis, Laurie Green,

Susan Hope, Ruth McCurry, Al McFadyen, Gill Moody, Michael Northcott, Novette Thompson, Margaret Walshe and above all the chairman, Peter Sedgwick.

The theology of this study tries to relate to churches as well as to academic fields and contemporary society, and it has been most valuable to test its ideas in many different church settings. These have included parishes, small gatherings of laity and clergy, various 'special interest' groups, Lee Abbey in Devon, and several dioceses of the Church of England – Birmingham, Canterbury, Chelmsford, Chester, Coventry, Ely, Lichfield, Lincoln, Sheffield and Wakefield.

In addition there is a host of other friends and dialogue partners to whom I am indebted: Donald Allchin, Brother Anselm SSF, Jim Buckley, Sister Carol CHN, Rachel Christophers, Sarah Coakley, the late Murray Cox, Ingolf Dalferth, Imogen Ecclestone, Ed Farley, Peter Harvey, Werner Jeanrond, Greg Jones, Graham and Ali Kings, Bob Kruger, Morny Joy, Tim Naish, John and Margaret Philpott, Mark Santer, Bryan and Dorothy Scrivener, Peter Selby, Stephen Sykes, Alice Theilgaard, Iain Torrance, David Tracy, Jean Vanier, Rowan Williams, Haddon Willmer. Sirscha Nicholl has given exemplary secretarial assistance. The editors of the series, Colin Gunton and Dan Hardy, have been both patient and supportive. They are joined, in that special category of those who have read and commented on the whole typescript, by Peter Ochs and by Micheal O'Siadhail. Micheal's contribution to my theological thinking (and so much else) during the past thirty years is inexpressibly immense. There is also a special debt to my god-daughter Hannah Knights who has been faithfully supportive even when her godfather has been out of touch with her.

A few portions of this book are based on or derived from material published elsewhere, as follows: parts of chapters 3 and 4 in 'Hosting a Dialogue' in *The Possibilities of Theology: Studies in the Theology of Eberhard Jüngel*, ed. John Webster (T. & T. Clark, Edinburgh 1994) and in 'On Substitution' in *Facing the Other. The Ethics of Emmanuel Levinas*, ed. Sean Hand (Curzon, Richmond, Surrey 1996); parts of chapter 6 in 'What Happens in the Eucharist?' in *Scottish Journal of Theology* vol. 48 no. 3, 1995; and parts of chapter 9 in 'Before the Face of Christ. Thérèse of Lisieux and Two Interpreters' in *The Way*, vol. 37, no. 3, July 1997. I am grateful to St. Vladimir's Seminary Press, Crestwood, New York 10707 for permission to quote from *Saint Ephrem. Hymns on Paradise*, Introduction and Translation by Sebastian Brock (1990).

Finally, there is my family, gratitude to whom is daily and immeasurable: to my children, Rebecca, Rachel and Daniel, to my mother Phyllis and to my parents-in-law Perrin and Dan Hardy. And the dedication of the book to my wife Deborah is a small recognition of all I have to thank her for during the book's preparation.

Introduction

'Health' is the root sense of the word 'salvation', and this has an immense range of meaning. Health can be physical, social, political, economic, environmental, mental, spiritual, moral and so on. If it is understood to have to do with a God of creation then none of its dimensions can be ignored. That is the first problem in undertaking a single volume on salvation in a series on Christian doctrine. How can the topic be made manageable? Salvation is not really one doctrine at all in most works of Christian theology. It is distributed through treatments of God, creation, human being, sin, Jesus Christ, the Holy Spirit, atonement, justification, sanctification, vocation, church, ethics and politics, worship, sacraments, spirituality, ministry and eschatology: in fact, through all topics. This all-pervasiveness gives it a potentially integrating role, but also risks overwhelming vastness.

I make what David Tracy[1] calls a 'journey of intensification' through all this. This book can be seen as an 'articulated essay'. Years of teaching and writing systematic theology have fed into it, and it tries to be true to that discipline in its rationality and in its alertness to the ways in which each major topic in theology is interrelated with the others. But its form is not in line with other systematic monographs, let alone textbooks. It is custom-made for the journey it takes, and later in this introduction I will give a guide for the reader. My hope is that it will attract readers who want, not a variation on previous systems and dogmatics, but something gentler, more suggestive, and more inviting into the urgencies, perplexities and joys of the task of working out an understanding of salvation today.

---

[1]. *The Analogical Imagination: Christian Theology and the Culture of Pluralism* (SCM, London 1981), pp. 125, 175.

Writing the book over eight years has helped to change my own thinking considerably, and the form of it has been conceived partly in order to allow the reader to go through a comparable learning experience. Several of those from whom I have learnt most over a far longer period of time make major contributions. I have been engaged for over twenty years with Emmanuel Levinas, Paul Ricoeur, Dietrich Bonhoeffer, Thérèse of Lisieux and Eberhard Jüngel, and even longer with the Bible and the eucharist. I am also fascinated by the way in which form and content go together, and by the challenge to match theological thinking and imagining with the appropriate genre. So another reason for the unfamiliar 'essay' form of the book is that it articulates together various theological genres: meditation, critical dialogue with philosophers and theologians, biblical exegesis and hermeneutics, practical theology, historical and doctrinal discussion, theological biography, and poetry.

The interrogative field

Theology, like other intellectual disciplines, is pervaded by the interrogative mood. The deepest questions are rarely satisfactorily answered, but there is impoverishment if they are not continually being pursued. It is the questions behind this essay on salvation that give it its most obvious coherence. There are six interconnecting questions.

1. The heart of Christian identity?
One basic question has been: can this theology of salvation go to the heart of Christian identity? Another way of posing that might be: how can an approach to salvation act as a focus for the gospel story in its biblical setting while also having universal implications? The definiteness yet openness of the gospel and of Christian identity both need to be affirmed. 'Identity' as a term tends to be more associated with definiteness, and concern to do justice to this runs through the book. One name, Jesus Christ, indicates the face at the heart of this vision of salvation. Yet that face is understood to be turned to all human beings and in that sense to be universal. The dynamics of Christian life are explored primarily through the worship of God and the transformation of the self before God, and the most illuminating interpretations of Christian identity are found in particular lives marked by joy and sacrificial responsibility.

2. An accessible salvation?

A second basic question, leading on from the openness of the gospel and of Christian identity, asks: can this theology of salvation be widely accessible today, and related to imaginative, intellectual, emotional and practical concerns? Because the range of salvation is as broad as creation itself, I have had to be very selective. The main access is through discussion of the self in transformation, drawing as much as possible on the experience of ordinary life in enjoyment, responsibility, desiring, suffering, communicating and worshipping. The dialogue partners are chosen partly for their breadth of engagement with the problems and possibilities of human existence, and their willingness to wrestle with practical, aesthetic and intellectual questions. There is no attempt to be exhaustive; but this may be an advantage, since the reader's own context-specific improvisations on the themes of the book may be helped rather than hindered by the themes not being overspecified.[2]

3. A key image?

Is it possible to focus on self and salvation through a few symbols, images or metaphors, or even have one which is primary? A theology of salvation needs intensity and gripping power. It needs to have the capacity to go to the depths, to help interrogate yet also integrate selves and groups in vision and in living, and to relate strongly to our situation.

In Christianity the death of Jesus is the central example of this. It is striking how the most powerful ways of thinking about the death of Jesus have generally been shaped by one primary image. I have in mind imagery taken from the religious cult (sacrifice), the law court (guilt, judgement and justification), warfare (victory), the marketplace (exchange, redeeming slaves or prisoners), the family (parent–child relationships, adoption), medicine (healing, saving), history (exodus, exile), politics (satisfaction in relation to the honour of a superior, liberation from oppression), friendship (laying down life) and nature (light and darkness, seeds dying and bearing fruit). Many of these have been followed through with great intensity in imagination, thought, feeling and practice.

2. I once heard Nigel Swinford, Director of the New English Orchestra, respond to a paper by Jeremy Begbie on doing theology through music. Swinford told of experiments with his orchestra in encouraging them to improvise together. He found that he usually overestimated the length of theme he needed to give the musicians. It went much better if he gave a shorter theme and trusted them to develop it.

There are theologies which take a rather superior attitude to this range of imagery and make a virtue of the way in which they assess the advantages and disadvantages of each. That can be useful, but it often misses a vital point. There is something about the reality of salvation that resists an overview. Attempting to deal evenhandedly with all the approaches can even seem distorting if it does not risk involvement in the depths of one of them. How can justice be done to the definiteness, specificity and urgency of Christian salvation? 'For an idea to stick', says Peter Brook, 'it is not enough to state it: it must be burnt into our memories.'[3]

Undoubtedly the image that has gone deepest and is most pervasive in this book is the subject of the meditation in chapter 1, facing. It is not a usual focus for salvation, but I hope that it emerges by the end of the book as worthy to play at least a minor role alongside the others in the tradition. At least it is scriptural, widespread in the Christian and other traditions, relevant to everyone, and a focus for some fascinating contemporary discussion. It interweaves through the book with two other key images, those of abundance (linked mainly with flourishing, joy, blessing, thanks, overflow, love, infinity, singing, polyphony and feasting) and substitution (linked mainly with responsibility, love and sacrifice), and all of them converge in the book's leading concept, the worshipping self.

4. Conceptual richness?

How conceptually rich is this understanding of salvation? Can the work's concepts help in interpreting the Bible, tradition and life as a whole, in relating the range of doctrines to salvation, and in linking various fields of study to this topic? Can these concepts have heuristic value, inspiring a diversity of investigations and discussions, acting as a framework for creativity, encouraging a new look at familiar problems, ambiguities and dilemmas, and opening fresh lines of dialogue with other soteriologies? Meeting all those expectations is unimaginable, but the questions do at least orient the mind and underline the need for hard conceptual work in this most practical of areas.

Ricoeur has written, 'the symbol gives rise to thought',[4] and my key images of facing, abundance and substitution are conceptualised in

---

3. Peter Brook, *The Shifting Point. Forty Years of Theatrical Exploration 1946–1987* (Methuen, London 1989), p. 54.
4. *The Symbolism of Evil* (Harper and Row, New York 1967).

various ways. I coin some concepts, and borrow others from theologians, philosophers, biblical writers, historians and others, taking advantage of the labour that has gone into developing them. The ones I have found most fruitful include: joyful responsibility; 'oneself as another'; the series of characterisations of selfhood that are found in the titles of chapters 2–6 – hospitable self, self without idols, worshipping self, singing self and eucharistic self; God as 'more than necessary'; substitution; attestation, witness or testimony; analogy; passivity; the logic of superabundance; *parrhesia*, *pleroma* and *praütes* in Ephesians; improvisation and nonidentical repetition; eucharistic time; carnal generality; saintly singularity; the *disciplina arcani*. I hope that the ways they are used go some way towards responding to the expectations of the previous paragraph.

5. Practical fruitfulness?

Does this theology have practical promise of fruitfulness in the three main dynamics of Christian living: worship and prayer; living and learning in community; and speech, action and suffering for justice, freedom, peace, goodness and truth? The concerns of the first four questions – Christian identity, wide relevance and accessibility, imaginative gripping power and conceptual richness – are all taken up into these three interrelated sets of practices. I focus particularly on worship, but with the intention of showing how it shapes and is shaped by the imperatives of loving and learning in community, and of practical realisation in all spheres. Above all, the realisation is seen in the way lives are lived, as exemplified in Jesus, Thérèse and Bonhoeffer. But whether all this amounts to a theology which will actually bear good fruit is not for me to say.

6. A defensible theology?

Finally, are my suggestions defensible against diverse attacks, and are they able to anticipate and deal with the main criticisms and alternatives? Self and salvation is a topic where deep divisions, passionate debates and strong prejudices are normal. There are obvious and not so obvious massive differences between the various worldviews, religions and ideologies. There is no possibility of doing justice to even the objections among fellow Christian theologians to my positions, let alone the critiques that the other main religions, worldviews and philosophies might apply to my suggestions. Recognising this impossibility, my strategy has been fivefold.

First, there is a range of explicit debates running through the book. But they are only the tip of the iceberg.

Second, there are all those discussions which implicitly feed into every decision as regards dialogue partners, sources, line of argument, field of imagery and so on. It is impossible (or extremely pedantic) to make all these explicit.[5]

Third, my choice of dialogue partners has borne in mind the need for justification on many fronts. The main partners are thinkers who have entered into wide-ranging debates and with whom, on the topics of most concern to me, I have a large measure of agreement. I have not attempted to rehearse again debates to which Levinas, Ricoeur, Jüngel, Dalferth, Bonhoeffer or some other partner has, in my judgement, contributed a convincing case.

Fourth, the infinite regress that would be required to meet all objections is well known to any thinker alert to the questions. One becomes especially aware of the increasing shift to second and even third order discourse so as to try to justify what one is saying in first order statements. That is legitimate, but the trouble is that the second and third orders are parasitic on the first, and we need to risk contemporary first order statements as well. It is usually safer in academic theology and religious studies to discuss such matters as method, epistemology, hermeneutical theory, contextual relativity, and the ways in which all sources and thinkers are conditioned and even compromised by their particular interests and biases.

It is riskier to come up with a constructive position, an attempt to design a habitable contemporary dwelling. At every step in the process one is aware of the immense power of the demolition experts with flourishing businesses, of the overcautious insurance and lending companies, of those who protest at one's building going anywhere near their own, of those who claim authority to make the regulations for this district, and those who seem quite content that no actual dwellings be built at all if they cannot meet their own impossibly ideal specifications.

This book is trying to make first order statements so as to offer a habit-

---

5. In the field of twentieth-century Christian theology the horizon of questions and debates within which I have been thinking is sketched in the second edition of David F. Ford (ed.), *The Modern Theologians. An Introduction to Christian Theology in the Twentieth Century* (Basil Blackwell, Oxford 1997).

able conception of self and salvation in a time of housing shortage. This inevitably limits the amount of justification that can be offered, but I hope that in relation to major problems there are sufficient hints indicating what the strategy of response might be. My main concern is that the design be 'good enough' as regards the second order concerns, and then to get on with the building.

Fifth, this is only one volume in the Cambridge Studies in Christian Doctrine. Many of the questions that can be raised about my position come more directly within the scope of other volumes in the series. I have been particularly helped by A. I. McFadyen who has been writing the volume on sin; by my Cambridge colleagues Daniel W. Hardy and Jeremy Begbie, who have been writing respectively on the church and on theology through music;[6] and by an early draft by Bruce Marshall for his volume on the Trinity. Each of those works is closely related to mine, and it has been encouraging to know that work congenial to my own is being prepared for companion volumes, which will address many of the questions left hanging by mine.

Such, then, is the interrogative field within which this work has been conceived. Those massive questions can never be answered satisfactorily, but perhaps it is better to fail trying to do something worthwhile rather than set one's sights too low in the first place.

A guide to the book

Part I, 'Dialogues: Levinas, Jüngel, Ricoeur', begins with a meditation on facing which opens up the theme of self and salvation in a way that engages mind and imagination together. The self, as one key contemporary locus of identity, crisis and transformation, is symbolised by the dynamics of human facing. The aim of the meditation is to evoke the multifaceted nature of human selfhood as it touches on biology, the five senses, history, ethics, gender, communication, politics, institutions, the arts, sin, evil, salvation and God. There is complexity and subtlety but also simplicity, and any attempt at definition is overwhelmed by the abundance which is expressed at the end of the meditation through Ephrem's poetry.

The rest of Part I develops, through dialogue with Levinas, Jüngel and Ricoeur, an understanding of self that is both philosophical and theolog-

6. On the latter cf. chapter 5 below.

ical. Is it possible to conceive self and salvation in a way which learns from leading twentieth-century philosophers and critically develops their thought in doing constructive theology? That is the leading question in these dialogues and I see it as a vital inquiry if theology is to have appropriate rigour and relate intelligently to other areas. It cannot, of course, mean that I construct a whole philosophical theology. Rather, I take just two philosophers, Levinas and Ricoeur, who engage broadly with the tradition of Western philosophy and in particular develop Husserlian phenomenology in ways which are hospitable to Judaism and Christianity respectively. As a catalyst between them I introduce Jüngel in order both to help work out what theology is and also to give to the emerging idea of self and salvation a content that is more explicitly theological while still being philosophically informed.

These aims are pursued in three chapters. Chapter 2 introduces the multifaceted description of human existence offered by Levinas, especially in his book *Totality and Infinity: An Essay on Exteriority*. He relates ethics to the 'appeal in the face of the other', and I interpret his account of enjoyment, responsibility and desire in terms of a 'hospitable self'. Chapter 3 takes up his later work, which is more extreme in its concept of responsibility as sacrificial and substitutionary. This is brought into dialogue with Jüngel, and they are both seen as concerned to save us from the idolatries which get us in their grip. Can theology itself be justified? Where is God? How might a non-idolatrous self be conceived? What about death, love and substitution? The engagement between Levinas and Jüngel is continued in chapter 4, the major suggestion being that Levinas's extreme notion of responsibility be combined with Jüngel's extreme notion of joy. This is worked through in relation to God-language and love, and opens up the possibility of a 'self without idols' being also a 'worshipping self'.

Neither Levinas nor Jüngel offers a satisfactory account of the worshipping self, so at this point Paul Ricoeur's philosophy, which takes some account of both of them, is introduced in order to develop the pivotal concept of 'oneself as another'. He offers a philosophy which mediates between a centred, self-positing subject and a decentred, shattered subject. The 'other' (a concept which need not for him only signify other people, but is also open to various accompanying construals – our bodies, the interiority of conscience, and even God) is integral to selfhood. The mode of truth appropriate to this self is attestation, testimony or witness, which does not require certainty and also can resist pervasive suspicion and doubt. Ricoeur suggests that his philosophical account of the self is open to being intensified and transformed through biblical faith, and that is what I attempt in the later parts of chapter 4, taking up the main determinations of self in his *Oneself As Another* and pressing them towards a fuller theology than is hinted at in his religious writings. The result is my work's central idea: the worshipping self, before the face of Christ and other people, in an 'economy of superabundance'.

The dialogues in Part I may at times be rather difficult to follow for those not immersed in the writings referred to. Each thinker is in his own way complex and sophisticated, as is appropriate to the subject matter they treat. I hope my prose is more accessible than any of the three and that these chapters may even act as an introduction to aspects of their thought for readers not acquainted with them. Yet inevitably the task of trying to do justice to them means that there will be readers who find some sections heavy going. One option is to start with Part II, which should be far more immediately comprehensible and familiar, especially for those already at home in Christian thought and practice. But I would urge returning to Part I later because those dialogues are intrinsic to the Part II discussions and are, I hope, worth the labour of wrestling with them.

Part II, 'Flourishings', follows the exploration's journey of intensification through some of the richest areas for Christian understanding of the worshipping self: the singing of an early Christian community, the Lord's Supper (or eucharist, holy communion or mass), and the lives of Jesus and two modern Christians. The aim is to do theology in places where Christian selfhood has been most profoundly shaped – a biblical text, a sacrament, the person and work of Jesus Christ and the specific histories of two very different 'saints'.

The biblical text studied is the Letter to the Ephesians, which chapter 5 takes as testimony to God's 'economy of superabundance' being worked out in the ordinary life of an early Christian community. The letter's injunction to sing is taken seriously as a transformative practice of self, and it is linked to the transformation of communities and institutions. The quality of communication and living represented in this letter to a worshipping community is seen as a complex portrayal of salvation which can help to inspire improvisations on similar themes today.

The eucharist is the ritual which is probably most participated in and discussed in human history. What sort of self is shaped through participation in it? The self described in chapter 6 embodies a multi-dimensional 'habitus', formed through repeated celebration of the eucharist and interweaving that with the rest of life. I unite a social anthropological account of practice and apprenticeship with a theological account of imperatives, incorporation and time. The eucharist can enable us to face death, and participation in its prophetic drama can transform our ordinary lives, relationships and sense of time. As it is 'non-identically repeated' at different times of our lives and of the church year, and in different company and settings, the abundance of the eucharistic self is generated through being blessed, commanded, placed and timed.

The most distinctive mark of the eucharistic self is that it is oriented towards Jesus Christ and other people. Understanding it therefore requires understanding them. This is the reason for the next four chapters, which explore these 'others' who are part of the constitution of a Christian worshipping self.

Jesus Christ as worshipper and worshipped is at the heart of this book's idea of the worshipping self, leading to a reconception of notions of worship, of God and of self. How can one person be related as God is to creation, history and the transformation of people? How does the God whose desire is for human flourishing face and bless people through Jesus Christ? These are the leading questions of chapters 7 and 8.

Dalferth's christology is the starting point for exploring the meaning and truth of facing Jesus Christ. What does it mean to recognise the face of Christ? What about the 'risen and glorified' face and the 'historical' face? Is visual representation of his face appropriate? Is the focus on this face not dominating, imperialist and exclusivist? The answers to those questions lead directly into chapter 8's opening focus on the dead face of Jesus on the cross. This is intensively reflected upon, and I reach back from the psalms quoted in the Gospel accounts of the crucifixion to explore the theme of the face of God in the Old Testament as a rich approach to self and salvation. Then the dead face of Jesus is seen as pivotal for transformed understandings of power, responsibility, worship and God. The culmination is a discussion of whether this face is being idolised by Christians. It involves above all an account of the significance and truth of the resurrection of Jesus, whose 'logic' is: God acts; Jesus appears; the disciples are transformed. It is an event which changes the meaning of worshipping God, and is critical for understanding how Jesus Christ is significant for human flourishing.

How can anyone cope with being loved by the God of Jesus Christ? Chapters 9 and 10 answer that question by examining two 'saints'. Instead of doing a theology of self and salvation under such usual headings as justification, sanctification and vocation, I engage in the theological issues through the lives and thought of the saints. Edith Wyschogrod's Levinas-influenced 'hagiographic ethic' is the provocative starting point. I then examine Thérèse of Lisieux in her devotion to the 'Holy Face' and in her vocation of love. Her practices of facing, formed largely in relationships with women, are especially significant, embodying her 'little way'. Chapter 10 draws Dietrich Bonhoeffer into the discussion. I suggest that their diverse embodiments of joy, sacrificial responsibility, reserve, love and wisdom not only recapitulate many of the themes of my exploration but are also prophetic for our time. Bonhoeffer's life and wisdom can inspire an interrogative, worshipping faith which emerges disciplined and enriched from the Middle Ages, Renaissance, Reformation, Enlightenment, nineteenth century, and the changes and traumas of the twentieth century.

Both Thérèse and Bonhoeffer exemplify revelling in the abundance of the God of joy, which is the main note of the concluding meditation on feasting in chapter 11. The horizon for this feasting is sketched through a few paragraphs on aesthetics, ethics, metaphysics and hermeneutics. Then there are just three courses to conclude. The 'joy of the saints' is glimpsed through Raphael's *The Ecstasy of St Cecilia with Sts Paul, John the Evangelist, Augustine, and Mary Magdalene*, which in classic high Renaissance mode recapitulates centuries of spirituality and theology. Then, at the genesis of the sort of modernity associated with the Enlightenment, Thomas Traherne responded to massive religious, political, scientific and other changes by daring to stretch his thought to conceive the 'infinite felicity' of God. Taking account of those transformations of the seventeenth century, he testified to an embracing transformation by joy, and his style gives a taste of the 'infinite communicativeness' which that inspired. Finally, two poems by Micheal O'Siadhail celebrate the musical testimony to heaven in jazz. It is suitably open-ended, allowing for future variations on the theme of self and salvation.

What sort of theology?

The final introductory issue is: what sort of theology is this? By that I do not mean to begin a description of the whole field of contemporary theology within which this work is situated,[7] but rather to ask how this book's particular approach is conceived. For the most part that should emerge in reading it, but a few pointers at this stage might also help the reader.

My strongest desire has been to write a theology of self and salvation that responds to God as adequately as possible in the polyphony – and cacophony – of contemporary living. The sketch of the interrogative field above has given some sense of the range of concerns this opens up, but the outline of the work which followed will have shown how constricted the actual treatment is.[8] Some readers' most urgent questions about self and salvation will not be treated in what follows.[9] Yet I hope that the exploration might nevertheless be helpful as a learning process, offering ideas and approaches which can be employed more widely than in dealing with the topics which are explicitly discussed.

What might be learnt in this process? I hope that something of the joy and responsibility of doing theology itself is communicated. I hope too that an example is given of how to draw on various theological and other disciplines and genres without becoming stuck in any one – a feature of some theology and religious studies is that they are inhibited from pursuing fascinating and appropriate questions by the fear of transgressing boundaries which are often quite arbitrary. More specifically, I hope that

7. I have grappled with this question elsewhere in: *A Long Rumour of Wisdom. Redescribing Theology* (Cambridge University Press, Cambridge 1991); 'Concluding Reflection: Constructing a Public Theology' in *Dare We Speak of God in Public? The Edward Cadbury Lectures, 1993–94*, ed. Frances Young (Mowbray, London 1995), pp. 151–61; 'On Being Theologically Hospitable to Jesus Christ: Hans Frei's Achievement', review article of Hans Frei, 'Types of Christian Theology' in *Journal of Theological Studies*, ns, vol. 46, pt 2, October 1995, pp. 532–46; 'Introduction to Modern Christian Theology' and 'Christian Theology at the Turn of the Millennium' in *The Modern Theologians*, pp. 1–15, 720–8; 'Theology and Religious Studies at the Turn of the Millennium: Reconceiving the Field' in *Teaching Theology and Religion*, vol. 1, no. 1, February 1998, pp. 4–12.
8. A fuller treatment of Christian living is given in a less academic mode in my book *The Shape of Living* (Fount/Harper Collins, London 1997). There many of the themes of the present study are worked out in relation to such matters as vocation, character, secrets, disciplines, leisure, work, bereavement and celebration.
9. This is true of some burning issues for me too. Five topics in particular have been frequently on my mind but have not been discussed at any length: Christianity in relation to other religions; gender in relation to self and salvation; physical and psychological healing; the politics and economics of self and salvation; and, perhaps most insistent of all, the Shoah, or Holocaust. Each figures at various points but none is done justice, although there are implicit positions on each.

the fruitfulness of thinking theologically in dialogue with phenomenological and hermeneutical philosophy is confirmed, especially when the theology is willing to go on to engage closely with specific texts, practices and persons. I even dare to hope that some readers might be grasped (or grasped afresh) by the desire to be transformed before the face of Jesus Christ.

I

Dialogues: Levinas,
Jüngel,
Ricoeur

1

Facing

We live before the faces of others. Some are there physically, others in memory or anticipation. We have been formed face to face from our earliest days, deeper than conscious memory. A baby is welcomed – amazed gratitude, hugs and kisses, feeding, anxious oversight, eyes meeting, the first smile, accompanying singing and speaking, friends and relatives come to see. It is a face exactly like no other, mark of individuality and uniqueness, constantly moving and changing. But who is it like? It is part of genetic history, features formed by race and family, a one-off that constantly displays its origins, the very type of continuity with novelty.

Already too it is part of cultural history, has been involuntarily taken into a particular family, society and period. What meanings are already played out in these first encounters? How is this particular baby received and understood? What are the habits and customs, the codes and influences, which are distilled into communication with this new person? What does it mean to be firstborn? Or female?

We may never unravel the dense weave of these early meetings and patterns of interaction, and the same is true for the other participants over the generations. We find ourselves in the midst of them, a nodal point where strands are entwined, where many dimensions of life (genetic, linguistic and cultural, psychological, religious and so on) converge in ordinary face to face behaviour. We are recognised and rejected, welcomed and ignored. Language is learnt here and facing others remains the main location of speech. All the emotions are registered – fear, anger, shame, scorn, joy and pain – or indifference. They show in smiles, tears, frowns and other endlessly nuanced expressions, accompanied by words and other gestures or not. We meet cold and hard faces,

faces that turn away, blush, laugh, and are attentively still. There are beauty and ugliness, compassion and hatred.

This is a 'micro-history' at the heart of our lives, but most of it is missed by any historian. Who can ever tell the full story of one good afternoon with an old friend? All accounts are abstractions from the intimate particularity, the layers of meaning, the look in the eyes. It is in such face to face meetings, deeply resistant to adequate description, that many of the most significant things in our lives happen, in love and enmity, in education, business, committee meetings, law courts, marriages, families, groups of all sorts. The dynamics of such meetings illustrate the contingencies of life as well as anything in nature. A word, a glance, an instantaneous interpretation, a confrontation, a dissimulation, a misconstrual, an indirectly conveyed attitude – these can be turning points, moments of insight, decision or shame.

No wonder this is the realm of life most usually rendered in the dominant media of our time – films, television programmes, magazines, cartoons, novels and other stories, songs and musicals. So we are continually in the midst of projections of face to face relationships that invite our responses and identifications. Hundreds of scenarios are presented, with characters, events and settings which offer images of self and others. Minds and homes are filled with the images of those who act, entertain, rule, suffer, fight, advertise, comment, and otherwise get publicity.

Our imaginations are therefore the scene of innumerable rehearsals of life with real or fictional characters. This is a major concern of our 'inner life'. Who are our own chief characters? What are our plots and sub-plots, settings and points of view? There are layers of memory, deposits and interweavings of narratives and more fragmentary images, and often the focus for memory is a face. A face is a distillation of time and memory. Think of the face of someone important to us and it conjures up past events, stories and associations, a world of meaning. It can reach into the future too, with plans, hopes and fears. Imaginatively, we rehearse our lives and intentions before the faces of those we respect, fear, love or otherwise take special notice of or want to impress. What faces do we have habitually in our hearts? Might that be one of the best clues to our identity? Pleasing our parents, bringing up a child, impressing our peers, asserting ourselves against those who threaten or compete, together with many more complex and nuanced motives and desires, are linked to people deeply imprinted on our memories. We perform our lives before them, consciously or not.

1.1 Faces and selves

How are you related to your face? Why does that sound a rather odd question? Partly because it does not ring true in separating face and self. Yet it would also seem odd to identify face and self. Obviously you are more than the outside of part of your head. Yet that last phrase is clearly inadequate as a description of the face. To meditate on the face is to find an approach to a range of key questions about the self. The face often seems to be a pivotal 'interface' between two aspects of the self.

We are given our faces. We have no choice about them, and inheritance together with social formation determines much about them. Yet we seem to have some freedom with them and perhaps in the long run significantly form them through our habits of living. Kierkegaard spoke of 'historical beauty' in faces shaped by a lifetime of good living.

Each face is uniquely individual yet it is also a primary locus for relating to others and the world. The face as relating, welcoming, incorporating others is fundamental to social life. It is possible to have a glimpse of the fact that individuality and sociality need not be in competition by thinking of the way in which faces can interanimate each other and at the same time each seem to become more fully and distinctively itself. This leads on to the relation of private to public spheres. Developed still further, it is possible to see the polarity of particularity and universality mediated through the face. The particular face has a capacity to relate to others that is in principle universal. This is clearly a principle appreciated as much by emperors and dictators as by religions.

All the senses are active through the face, or closely connected with it – smell, touch, taste, sight and hearing. It is also the site of speech. So it acts as the most intensive locus of human communication. But what of the interior side of all this communication, the processing of information, thinking, remembering and so on? Clearly there are complex neural networks and the phenomena variously called mind/brain, soul, psyche, ego, spirit, heart. If one does not subscribe to a dualistic (matter/spirit) account of these, then the terms in which they will be described are as matter organised on different levels in a dynamic order of energy and information. This links the dynamically ordered, communicating and responsive face much more intrinsically into the self than could happen in a dualistic account. There can be no simple picture of a mind, soul or will causing a face to be expressive in certain ways, but a much more complex open system of energy and information in which the face is a vital aspect of the embodied self, crucially mediating between what is 'external' and 'internal'. It is especially vital to the 'punctuation' of self and world – those many ways in which the self shapes and is shaped by communication and other exchanges while maintaining a distinct identity. Those 'other exchanges' are not to be ignored. They include kissing, eating, drinking and breathing, and are a reminder that the embodied self is material, the face is flesh.

The uniqueness of each face does not conflict with it being describable within various categories. There are family resemblances and, perhaps most important in our culture, race and gender. What about race? Skin colour and other typical characteristics in faces allow easy identification of difference and therefore compartmentalisation, stereotyping and unjust discrimination. One way societies may respond is to level all the differences and affirm 'equal rights' for all human beings, making the human race into the inclusive compartment. But can that, if it is followed through consistently, avoid a destruction of 'good' differentiation? Is one root of unjust discrimination not the failure to recognise each person as transcending any of our overviews? Is there not a pluralism that is most clearly seen in faces? There is no synthesising of faces, they embody otherness and particularity. Might it even be that justice is rooted in the face to face, in what Levinas calls 'the appeal in the face of the other'?

What about gender? The face is a revealing indicator of gender formation, in which hormones and culture both participate. Is even to talk about 'the face' a way of ignoring gender differences? Should we not speak of male and female faces? But here the particularity invoked in relation to race is again significant. It is not that there are not differences along gender lines or major issues of inappropriate discrimination. The face can help to relativise the gender categories in ways which both intensify the challenge to injustice and also make sure that personhood is appropriately affirmed. The appeal in the face of the other is more fundamental than any identification of that face by gender.

1.2 Surface, depth and representation

But is all this about the face still too much on the surface, only skin deep, missing out on any significant engagement with the depths, too vulnerable to mere appearances? 'There's no art to find the mind's construction in the face' (Shakespeare). This is another interface, between surface and depth. There are many questions in current thought about the ways such metaphors are used, their presuppositions about self and world. Why play down surfaces? Why make a sharp dichotomy between appearance and reality? We talk of gazing deeply into the face of another. There is a concept of depth that does not separate it from the face. There are faces in the memory, in the heart. In mutual joy or grief it is as if the whole self in its heights or depths strains to appear in the face and accompanying words and behaviour, and 'superficiality' would be a ridiculous description. It seems rather that face to face behaviour can embody depth or shallowness.

The Shakespearean dictum in its context in *Macbeth* raises the related question of simulation and dissimulation, deceit and masking. Besides the 'bright mystery' of the inexhaustibility of the face of the beloved and the infinity of hiddenness and revelation glimpsed through the amazement of adoration (Dante and Beatrice are perhaps the supreme example in literature), there is the 'dark mystery' of the lying face, deceptive communication. The possibility of this (and it is sometimes desirable) also says something important about the self in its capacities for differentiation, many-levelled communication, ambiguity, ambivalence and contradiction. There are of course many modes of being deceptive, but the role of the face in both sincerity and deceit lets it be a suggestive way into these fundamental matters.

The truthfulness of communication leads into two questions of representation. First, there is the representation of the self through the face. The self is far too complex and multidimensional to be adequately represented in face to face communication. The notion that it is a presentation that corresponds to some internal state is inadequate – that oversimplifies the interplay of 'inner' and 'outer', 'body' and 'mind'. All the dimensions of the face already discussed could be gathered here to conceive the self more adequately – through early and later face to face relationships, input from the media and other cultural sources, our inner life performed before significant others, our inherited physical features and their shaping over time, the significance of family, race and gender. Once we have rejected a correspondence theory of face and self we can let it play its part in a more adequate social, communicational and ethical understanding. It is only a part, but one which is pervasively important in the 'ecology of self'. It is also one which has been ignored, neglected or suppressed in much modern Western thought or culture. Indeed, one might argue that the Enlightenment and its aftermath tended towards a 'faceless self' and that many of the challenges to the Enlightenment suffer from the same defacing of people. Yet there are many resources for a recovery of the face and for conceiving a more adequate notion of self.

The second question about representation is closely linked to the previous one. In a complex communicational ecology of self the modes of representation are vital, in words, symbols, pictures, sounds, gestures and other behaviour. Words have their primary context in faces. They can also try to describe them, evoke them, reflect on them. The resonances of the notion of face are wide-ranging. It enters into countless tropes. Objects and buildings have faces or façades; we face the future; we lose face, save face, outface, aboutface, deface, surface, interface; we countenance and discountenance; bureaucracies can be faceless. Not only that but every part of the face generates metaphors – of nose and smell, eyes and sight, lip, mouth, ear and sound, cheek, brow, chin, beard and complexion. From the concrete particularity of your face, for which the appropriate word is your name, the resonances spread out through metaphor, analogy, synecdoche, metonymy.

What about the visual representation of the face? Art surrounds us with faces of other centuries and our own. Artists might be seen as tutors in seeing each other and ourselves. There is no 'innocent eye': our seeing has a history and representation has a history. Seeing is a complex process of recognition, attention, interaction and integration. To be just in our seeing requires a long apprenticeship, learning from those with practised eyes, and alert to the ways in which our vision is laden with interests, theories and many-levelled associations. Artists can draw us into the complexities of this apprenticeship. We can begin to appreciate the diverse interrelationships of 'finding' and 'fashioning', 'matching' and 'making'. How does a Cézanne portrait relate to its subject? Any notion of copying or exact likeness is inadequate, but so is sheer invention. It is a witness to the sitter that innovates on a long tradition of portrait painting and in doing so can be an event in our own seeing that affects how we see faces. Its testimony becomes embedded in our habitual seeing and no face is ever quite the same again because each is now somehow in relation to this portrait. It is one of our 'faces in the heart'. But caricatures too, humorous or malicious, can enter the heart. And much twentieth-century art has been iconoclastic – defacing, distorting or fragmenting the human face. We see each other through those images too.

The number of represented faces that the history of art offers is as nothing compared to the inundation of faces encountered today through image technologies – photography, cinema, television, video, computer.

We are overwhelmed with images mediated by various instruments. No civilisation has ever been through anything like this before. In an average day we can see hundreds of people from around the world and from various periods of history, participants in events and entertainments. We may view far more actors than 'real' people. Always it is viewing edited by those who select programmes, finance films, point cameras, decide on the day's headlines for newspapers or television, write scripts, publish CD-ROMs, magazines and books and advertise products. It is also often optional viewing, with an endless variety of choices. Our meetings with people in our daily life are interwoven with these 'quasi-meetings' within a global horizon. Our sense of time and space is formed in relation to all this material. How do we cope? How can our habits of 'facing' and 'being faced' be shaped appropriately? How can we habitually discern among the abundance of testimonies through which reality is probed, constructed, enhanced, ironised, distorted, caricatured, manipulated and so on? Is it possible to find or enable 'communities of the face' which do not succumb to confusion or distraction and do more than just cope with all this?

1.3 Facing, community and God

The main focus of this meditation so far has been on the face, but the dynamics of 'facing' has been perhaps even more fundamental. 'Facing' helps to avoid the wrong sort of fixations on the face as an 'object'. It embraces the face in activity and passivity, purpose and temporality, loneliness and reciprocity. It can be a joint conception – facing something together. Or it can refer to interiority, facing oneself, one's past, present and future. At its most general it can refer to environments, institutions, nations or even civilisations 'facing' situations, challenges or possibilities.

It is in such extended uses that the connection with a human face may seem most tenuous, to the point of being dead metaphor. Yet might it be helpful, on the analogy with the 'quasi-meeting' mentioned above, to think of 'quasi-facing' in such a way that the force of the earlier part of this meditation is significant in distributed ways? The links to particular human faces might be indirect and mediated through institutional polity and policy, vast political, economic, cultural or environmental forces and many levels of abstraction. Yet it might be the most crucial thing of all to recognise and strengthen those links. 'Communities of the face' might be the niche in this vast ecology whose flourishing is intrinsic to the flourishing of all the others in just and sustainable ways, and which act as the best test for the health of institutions, trends and policies. To have a primary concern with such communities and the quality of facing is by no means to be unconcerned about quasi-facings at other levels. On the contrary, it is to be passionately motivated to deal with them in their demanding complexity and to travel often long and dangerous detours in order to get their 'ecology' right. To see a new baby is to be accountable before a face whose future is bound up with that flourishing. Each face is an interrupting summons to justice and peace, with endless ramifications for economics, politics, institutions and other structures.

Communities of the face are vital but they can hardly be described in general terms. Like the face itself they cry out for content in particular ways. Above all, the quality of facing is inseparable from who is facing and being faced, and from the complex history of that over time. And because 'the corruption of the best is the worst' the deformations of facing are likely to be most terrible where the fullest facing is risked. That has certainly been so in the community which is mainly at issue in this book, the Christian church. It might be described as being concerned with the transformation of facing before the face of Christ. If there is a key text for this book it is Paul's second letter to the Corinthians, and it is worth meditating on two verses from that.

> And we all, with unveiled face, beholding [*or* reflecting] the glory of the Lord, are being transformed into his likeness from one degree of glory to another; for this comes from the Lord who is the Spirit. (2 Cor. 3.18)

> For it is the God who said, 'Light will shine out of darkness', who has shone in our hearts to give the light of the knowledge of the glory of God in the face of Christ. (2 Cor. 4.6)

Those verses describe being faced by God. There is the ultimate 'quasi-facing' of God's word which creates light as the environment of facing and warns us against ever finally disconnecting anything from such facing. The scope is universal. There is the focussing of the light, knowledge and glory of God through one particular face, that of Jesus Christ. This face 'has shone in our hearts', fundamental to our identity in community. All of that might be seen as the 'transformational grammar' of what is said in 3.18: the dynamics of salvation in a community of the face.

Christianity is characterised by the simplicity and complexity of facing: being faced by God, embodied in the face of Christ; turning to face Jesus Christ in faith; being members of a community of the face; seeing the face of God reflected in creation and especially in each human face, with all the faces in our heart related to the presence of the face of Christ; having an ethic of gentleness (*praütes*) towards each face; disclaiming any overview of others and being content with massive agnosticism about how God is dealing with them; and having a vision of transformation before the face of Christ 'from glory to glory' that is cosmic in scope, with endless surprises for both Christians and others.

This salvation, or health, is about full hospitality and full worship. The facing is fulfilled in feasting, and that is the movement from this opening meditation to the one which concludes this book. But for the joy of that celebration to be holy it needs to have come by way of sharing food with the hungry and being liberated from the idols that distort the dynamics of our praising, knowing and desiring.

Perhaps the greatest poem of Western Christianity is Dante's *Divine Comedy*. In its final canto a long journey of face to face encounters culminates in a vision of God. At the heart of the vision is the face of Christ. It is the ultimate transformation, as imagination is overwhelmed and desire and will are moved by

the Love that moves the sun and the other stars.[1]

In the linguistic home of Jesus nearly a millennium earlier, St Ephrem the Syrian – perhaps the greatest theologian poet before Dante – led communities in worship with his Hymns on Paradise, daringly evoking an intensity of transfigured existence. He constantly prompts questions that are likely to be suggested by the following chapters of this book. Is this too much? Might God be this generous? Dare we be so joyful? Is such delight the open secret of life? Here is a taste of his feast:

> Such is the flowing brook of delights
>   that, as one tree takes leave of you,
> the next one beckons to you;
>   all of them rejoice
> that you should partake of the fruit of one
>   and suck the juice of another,
> wash and cleanse yourself
>   in the dew of a third;

1. Dante Alighieri, *Paradiso*, translated with an Introduction by Allen Mandelbaum (Bantam Books, New York 1986), Canto XXXIII, line 145, p. 303.

anoint yourself with the resin of one
and breathe another's fragrance,
listen to the song of still another.
Blessed is He who gave joy to Adam! ...

Breezes full of discernment
nourish the discerning;
this breeze provides you with nourishment in abundance,
that one delights you as it blows,
one causes your countenance to shine,
while another gives you enjoyment.
Who has ever experienced
delight in this way,
eating, without employing his hands,
drinking, without using his mouth?
As both cupbearer and baker
do these delightful breezes act ...

Instead of bread, it is the very fragrance of Paradise
that gives nourishment;
instead of liquid,
this life-giving breeze does service:
the senses delight
in its luxuriant waves
which surge up
in endless variety,
with joyous intensity.
Being unburdened,
the senses stand in awe and delight
before the divine Majesty ...

But if you are greedy
Moses will reproach you;
he took no provisions
as he ascended to the mountain summit;
he was richly sustained because he hungered,
he shone with much beauty because he thirsted.
Who has ever beheld
a famished man
devour a vision and grow beautiful,
imbibe a voice and be sustained?
Nourished with the divine glory
he grew and shone forth.

All that we eat
    the body eventually expels
in a form that disgusts us;
    we are repelled by its smell.
The burden of food debilitates us,
    in excess it proves harmful,
but if it be joy
    which inebriates and sustains,
how greatly will the soul be sustained
    on the waves of joy
as its faculties suck
    the breast of wisdom.

Torrents of delight
    flow down through the First Born
from the radiance of the Father
    upon the gathering of seers:
they indulge themselves there
    upon the pasture of divine visions.
Who has ever beheld the hungry
    find satisfaction,
fare sumptuously and become inebriated
    on waves of glory
flowing from the beauty
    of that sublime Beauty?

The Lord of all
    is the treasure store of all things:
upon each according to his capacity
    He bestows a glimpse
of the beauty of His hiddenness,
    of the splendour of His majesty.
He is the radiance who, in His love,
    makes everyone shine
– the small, with flashes of light from Him,
    the perfect, with rays more intense,
but only His Child is sufficient
    for the might of His glory.

Accordingly as each here on earth
    purifies his eye for Him,
so does he become more able to behold
    His incomparable glory;

accordingly as each here on earth
    opens his ear to Him,
so does he become more able to grasp
    His wisdom;
accordingly as each here on earth
    prepares a receptacle for Him,
so is he enabled to carry
    a small portion of His riches.

The Lord who is beyond measure
    measures out nourishment to all,
adapting to our eyes the sight of Himself,
    to our hearing His voice,
His blessing to our appetite,
    His wisdom to our tongue.
At His gift
    blessings swarm,
for this is always new in its savour,
    wonderfully fragrant,
adaptable in its strength,
    resplendent in its colours.

Who has ever beheld gatherings of people
    whose sustenance is the giving of praise?
Their raiment is light,
    their countenance full of radiance;
as they ruminate
    on the abundance of His gift
there burst forth from their mouths
    springs of wisdom;
tranquillity reigns over their thought,
    truth over their knowledge,
reverence over their enquiry,
    and love over their offering of praise.

Grant, Lord, that I and those dear to me
    may together there
find the last remnants
    of Your gift!
Just the sight of Your Dear One
    is a fountain of delight;
whoever is worthy
    to be ravished thereby

will despise ordinary food;
   all who look upon You
will be sustained by Your beauty.
   Praises be to Your splendour![2]

2. St Ephrem the Syrian, *Hymns on Paradise*, Introduction and translation by Sebastian Brock (St. Vladimir's Seminary Press; Crestwood, NY 1990), Hymn IX, pp. 138ff. Reproduced by kind permission of St. Vladimir's Seminary Press, 575 Scarsdale Rd., Crestwood, NY 10707, USA.

2

Enjoyment, responsibility
and desire: a hospitable self

30   The meditation on 'facing' has tried to evoke some aspects of selves and others – the complexity of many levels and dimensions in play simultaneously, but also the familiarity of it in common experience. In order to move ahead with a conception of self and salvation which takes facing in that sense as pivotal it is desirable to be clearer about how the human self is being understood. This chapter and the two which follow to complete Part I take one route through the vast and immensely contentious literature on the self in order to develop key concepts and categories.

The present chapter, in the form of an appropriation of and dialogue with the thought of Emmanuel Levinas, considers the self in terms of enjoyment, responsibility and desire, culminating in the concept of a 'hospitable self'. The overriding aim is to serve the constructive theological purpose of this study, and the theological significance should become clearer in succeeding chapters.

Why have a dialogue with Levinas? It is worth mentioning some of the considerations that weighed in choosing him as a partner, especially as his influence is present throughout this book, even when it is not explicit.

First, as a Jew and a philosopher, he has had a long and deep engagement with the Hebraic as well as the Hellenic traditions.[1] He has taken account of many of the main contributions to thought about the self – ancient, modern and postmodern – that figure in Western academic

---

1. Cf. Robert Gibbs, *Correlations in Rosenzweig and Levinas* (Princeton University Press, Princeton 1992), chapter 7; Jacques Derrida, *Writing and Difference* (University of Chicago Press, Chicago 1978), chapter 4.

debates, and at the same time he has grappled with the questions of God and atheism.

Second, he has been through and thought deeply about some of the most terrible events of our century. Levinas (1906–95) was a Lithuanian Jew who settled in France and became a philosopher there. He was especially influenced by Husserl and Heidegger, but became increasingly critical of the latter. Levinas himself was imprisoned in France and did forced labour; many of his family died under the Nazis. His biography is, he writes, 'dominated by the presentiment and the memory of the Nazi horror'.[2] After the war he continued as a philosopher, later becoming a professor at the Sorbonne, and he also studied the Talmud more deeply and worked for the renewal of Judaism. His major works, *Totality and Infinity: An Essay on Exteriority*[3] and *Otherwise Than Being or Beyond Essence*,[4] are philosophical and prophetic statements which put forward ethics as 'first philosophy', in which responsibility for the other is primary and is the pivot of a radical critique of that Western tradition which has culminated in this century of violence and mass death. Levinas therefore is speaking out of the experience of the Shoah and is testifying to peace and goodness in a civilisation which he sees as drastically distorted. He is engaging with some of the deepest questions that an understanding of salvation has to deal with, and he will be relevant to the theme of salvation beyond the question of the self. But for now his particular value is that he has put the question of the good at the centre of his thought on the self, and he has offered both a concept of the human person that has faced up to the worst this century has done and also a critique of the 'totality' through which he sees not only the Shoah but also much more 'ordinary' evil happening now.

Third, specifically for a Christian theology he is a most significant 'other'. Judaism is an important (perhaps the most important) set of traditions with which Christian traditions need to engage. I do not see Levinas as a representative Jewish thinker – he is too controversial within Judaism for that. Nevertheless, a sophisticated Jewish position which deals with God, ethics, peace, justice, the self and much else of relevance to salvation, and which has also wrestled with the Western philosophical tradition and the horrors of the twentieth century, is likely to fulfil at

2. 'Signature' in *Difficult Freedom. Essays on Judaism* (Johns Hopkins University Press, Baltimore 1990), p. 291.   3. Duquesne University Press, Pittsburgh 1969.
4. Martinus Nijhoff, The Hague/Boston/London 1981.

least partially the need to take account of the present significance of Christianity's 'elder sibling'. He serves as a resource and inspiration, dealing with many common themes; but he also tests Christian theology profoundly. He is strongly critical of Christianity and dismissive of theology (as the next chapter will discuss). If Christian theology is convinced that it has to be submitted, among other tests, to thorough engagement with the richest and most rigorous contemporary thought about its major themes, then Levinas is an ideal partner. The series to which this book is a contribution is especially concerned to produce Christian theology that has been tested in this way, and my experience is that Levinas is incomparable in the way he combines being a profound critic and a copious source for theological thinking.

Fourth, there is Levinas's role in relation to philosophy. Phenomenology has not only been one of the richest philosophical movements of the twentieth century, but has also had great influence on theology and religious studies. Levinas engaged deeply with the greatest phenomenological philosopher, Edmund Husserl, and also married his critical appropriation of Husserl with Jewish thought, especially that of Franz Rosenzweig. That move through and beyond phenomenology, opening it to the God who is not categorisable as a phenomenon, is very important to this study. Another dialogue partner in Part I, Paul Ricoeur, also takes both phenomenology and God seriously. My aim is to engage with both of them in the interests of offering a post-phenomenological theology of the worshipping self such as none of them attempts.

Finally, having been fascinated by Levinas's thought for the past quarter of a century, his philosophy has been woven into my own thinking in ways too pervasive to trace. Having lived with his writings, and with those of many who have engaged with him in expository and critical modes, I am acutely aware that it is not possible to recapitulate even the relevant parts of all that discussion in this book. I have made a few minor contributions to it,[5] but on the whole must assume that those who want to enter into the major debates lying behind practically every contention in what follows will be able to pursue them in Levinas's works and the vast secondary literature on them. The alterna-

---

5. Frances M. Young and David F. Ford, *Meaning and Truth in 2 Corinthians* (SPCK, London 1987; Eerdmans, Grand Rapids 1988); David F. Ford, 'Hosting a Dialogue: Jüngel and Levinas on God, Self and Language' in *The Possibilities of Theology: Studies in the Theology of Eberhard Jüngel*, ed. John Webster (T. & T. Clark, Edinburgh 1994), pp. 23–59; David F. Ford, 'On Substitution' in *Facing the Other. The Ethics of Emmanuel Levinas*, ed. Sean Hand (Curzon, Richmond, Surrey 1996), pp. 21–43.

tive would be an endless regress of ramifying discussions. I am presenting what I have found to stand up to diverse testing in academic and wider contexts.

Before engaging with his philosophy of the self (which might more properly be called a philosophy of 'the other'), a word about his style is appropriate. One striking thing about his vocabulary is how many resonances there are with ordinary living. This is partly due to his distinctive way of using and developing a phenomenological approach, but also to a remarkable style which somehow achieves an academic rigour (and considerable difficulty) at the same time as using common terms and experiences in a dense and evocative way. The face, enjoyment, breathlessness, restlessness, insomnia, home and hospitality, the caress, teaching, saying, sincerity, witness, patience, desire and many other such terms contribute to a vocabulary which aims to open up normal philosophical discourse to the sphere of the 'non-philosophical'. The result is a rich description of human existence which connects well with my book's aim of expounding self and salvation mainly through the dynamics of ordinary human relationships.

How does he describe it? That at once poses the problem of summarising or paraphrasing a philosophy whose style is so intrinsic to its message. If even a good book-length introduction, which engages closely with texts of Levinas, often seems strangely disconnected from the vitality and impact of Levinas's own words[6] then a very brief account such as that which follows can only offer pointers to it as a resource for appreciating what it is to be human. Moreover, the selection of pointers serves the particular purposes of my theology and so has even less claim to being an adequate introduction. But in fact, of course, such assimilation of one text into another, with transformations, is an essential part of intellectual and literary life, and Levinas himself is a good example of one who is continually drawing thoughts from others and giving them new and often surprising life in his own text.[7] I will summarise and discuss his thought in my main text and I will also put into notes some further summaries,

---

6. I refer to Adriaan Peperzak, *To the Other. An Introduction to the Philosophy of Emmanuel Levinas* (Purdue University Press, West Lafayette, IN 1993).

7. Perhaps the most notable example is his use of Descartes's idea of infinity from the *Third Meditation*. Levinas claims to retain 'only the formal design of the structure it outlines' and then develops it in ways that question much of Descartes's philosophy. See 'Philosophy and the Idea of Infinity' in Emmanuel Levinas, *Collected Philosophical Papers* (Kluwer Academic Publishers, Dordrecht/Boston/London 1993), pp. 47ff. and Peperzak, *To the Other*, chapters 2, 3 and 4 for an excellent analysis of this key paper.

quotations and comments. Yet I am well aware that by abstracting and extracting in these ways I am risking doing more disservice than service to a writer whose prose has something of the integrity, distinctiveness and difficulty more often associated with poetry.

2.1 Enjoyment

Levinas is at pains to affirm the separateness of the self. His whole philosophy resists any subsuming of selves into a totality, and even talk of relationality (so much in vogue in recent decades as an antidote to 'individualism') has to be purified by a rigorous affirmation of separation. There are two fundamental concepts through which separation is understood: enjoyment and the face. To follow the development of each in turn is to be led through the central theses of *Totality and Infinity*. It is also to open up issues that recur in later chapters of this book, such as joy, responsibility, God, gentleness, time, language and freedom.

'The personality of the person, the ipseity of the I, which is more than the particularity of the atom and of the individual, is the particularity of the happiness of enjoyment [*bonheur de la jouissance*].'[8] Enjoyment is more fundamental than intending, representing, reasoning, freedom, theory and practice, or any psychological state: 'enjoyment is the ultimate consciousness of all the contents that fill my life – it embraces them'.[9] We do not know 'being' first in some neutral state, or as needed for living, but rather through joy or pain, as object of enjoyment or not. 'Life is love of life, a relation with contents that are not my being but more dear than my being: thinking, eating, sleeping, reading, working, warming oneself in the sun.'[10] So enjoyment is given a quite basic role in the constitution of the self, and it is one which even is said to be 'beyond ontology'.[11] Being itself is exceeded and overflowed by this exaltation at the dawn of the self, this jubilation beyond simple being. It breaches any totality that tries to embrace it – reason or other forms of representation, biological or sociological categories, any notion of necessity or utility or finality. 'To enjoy without utility, in pure loss, gratuitously, without referring to anything else, in pure expenditure –

8. *Totality and Infinity*, p. 115.
9. Ibid., p. 111. Levinas's linking of consciousness with enjoyment in this way gives a clue as to why he dissociates the latter so sharply from responsibility. In later chapters my linking of responsibility with joy does not confine the latter to the contents of human consciousness and relates it to a God of joy.   10. Ibid., p. 112.   11. Ibid.

this is the human.'[12] It is also, as sensibility, more fundamental than any split between body and spirit or mind. Levinas's philosophy of enjoyment is as radical and intense as his philosophy of responsibility. In later chapters I will appropriate both of them while connecting them together in a way somewhat different to his.

What about the enjoying self? For Levinas enjoyment is uniquely my own, individuating; it produces the radical separation of an ego at home with itself, with interiority and solitude. Its essence is to be nourished and invigorated from outside by 'the transmutation of the other into the same',[13] to be 'the very pulsation of the I',[14] an egoism that lives from the world in enjoying it. 'Subjectivity originates in the independence and sovereignty of enjoyment.'[15] This extreme notion of the self's separation and autonomy excludes any intrinsic relating with other people or with God (Levinas calls it an 'atheism').

It cannot, of course, be completely independent, as it is open to and dependent on the world it enjoys, including other people. The self must go beyond the immediacy of enjoyment in order to sustain itself in its 'happy dependence' of enjoyment. Enjoyment has its insecurity and requires to be secured. This leads into what Levinas calls the sphere of 'economy' within which enjoyment happens: representation and recollection, things as implements and possessions, the arts, labour, habitation and the home. The home is where the separation of enjoyment becomes more secure, where 'familiarity and intimacy are produced as a gentleness that spreads over the face of things [*une douceur qui se répand sur la face des choses*]'.[16]

When, in *Otherwise Than Being*, he returns to the topic of enjoyment as he develops an idea of responsibility which is, as we will see, more extreme than *Totality and Infinity* in its identification of suffering and sacrifice with the responsible self, he is even more insistent on both the enjoying self as the indispensable condition for responsibility and the implication of corporeal satisfaction with ethics.[17]

In the formation of selfhood through enjoyment ('only in enjoyment does the I crystallize'[18]), hunger satisfied by eating is the paradigmatic case of immediacy – taste in contact with food – but none of our other activities and passivities have to do with a neutral 'reality' either. All are encompassed by enjoyment (which of course can also turn into

---

12. Ibid., p. 133.   13. Ibid., p. 111.   14. Ibid., p. 113.   15. Ibid., p. 114.
16. Ibid., p. 155.   17. *Otherwise Than Being*, pp. 72ff.   18. *Totality and Infinity*, p. 144.

pain[19]). The continuity of time is ruptured by the gathering of life into knots of enjoyment, 'the marvel of the good time standing out from the continuity of the hours'.[20] The pervasiveness of enjoyment in constituting the separated self and its interiority acts as a resistance to attempts to conceive the self primarily in other terms, while yet allowing for those terms to be taken into account.

Levinas can even say that 'at the origin there is a being gratified, a citizen of paradise';[21] and, 'To be I, atheist, at home with oneself, separated, happy, created – these are synonyms.'[22] What does that mean? It sees 'creation' as *ex nihilo*, radically separate, signifying a good, happy being. There is no intrinsic link with the divine or the infinite, and lack does not define humanity. Rather 'jubilation'[23] does. This apparent paradox of a self both created and atheist will be explored theologically in the next chapter, where Eberhard Jüngel's concept of God as not necessary but 'more than necessary' will be understood to make a similar point. That will prepare for the development of a somewhat different idea of jubilation in later chapters. Critical to the difference from Levinas will be a modification of his principle that enjoyment is maintained by assimilating to myself what is other. Rather, it is possible to conceive of an enjoyment which honours and delights in and is responsible before what is other without necessarily assimilating it, such as can happen in worship.

Already in this phenomenological philosophy of enjoyment Levinas has not only drawn on ideas of atheism and creation *ex nihilo* but has also offered a radical critique of the main modern Western ways of understanding and explaining the self. Any such way – biological, sociological, economic, intentional, utilitarian, idealist, Heidegger's *Sorge*, and others – is broken open by this fundamental reality of enjoyment. They are exposed as potentially reductionist and threatening to human flourishing.[24] Positively, enjoyment and jubilation constitute the dynamic of self.

---

19. See ibid. On enjoyment as covering also 'the "defective modes" of what one ordinarily counts as enjoyment' see John Llewellyn, *Emmanuel Levinas. The Genealogy of Ethics* (Routledge, London 1995), p. 78.
20. *Totality and Infinity*, p. 148.   **21.** Ibid., p. 144.   **22.** Ibid., p. 148.   **23.** Ibid., p. 144.
24. Edward Farley, *Good and Evil. Interpreting a Human Condition* (Fortress Press, Minneapolis 1990) proposes a theology influenced by phenomenology to respond to reductionist positions on human selfhood which appeal to the natural and human sciences and to various modern philosophies and ideologies. His careful engagement with actual representatives of such positions is a necessary complement to Levinas's meditative assertions. However, I find Farley's heavy reliance upon notions of freedom and courage less convincing than a theological modification of Levinas's approach to selfhood through enjoyment and responsibility.

2.2 The face

Levinas finds something even more radical cutting across this enjoyment in which separation is maintained by assimilating to myself what is other. This is an otherness which cuts across enjoyment, questions the self, and is unassimilable. 'The way in which the other presents himself, exceeding the idea of the other in me, we here name face.'[25] In the approach of the other in the face Levinas finds the concretisation of Descartes's idea of infinity: an idea which is greater than its own thought and which comes from beyond the self. The face is an 'epiphany', a 'revelation'. What matters is not its 'phenomenality', its particular form and features which might be represented in an image, but its appeal, its expressing, its signifying.[26] It is primarily an ethical relation in which I find myself summoned to responsibility for the one who appeals to me.

It is also an asymmetrical relation – I am summoned to a responsibility that is not dependent on reciprocity or equality but on 'looking up' to the other. There is a 'curvature' of intersubjective space in which the other comes as 'a separated – or holy – face . . . This "curvature of space" is, perhaps, the very presence of God.'[27] The separation of the face to face is never subsumed in a totality. There is no overview or adequate idea of 'the face to face, the irreducible and ultimate relation';[28] there is an unsynthesisable plurality, and the idea of the infinite means relationship without totalisation.[29] This critique of 'totality' in a way which is oriented to the other person, which resists containment in embracing philosophical, political or other concepts and also mentions God opens the way for my account of a 'self without idols' in the next chapter.

How are the selves related in the pluralism which resists totality? The main way is by language, which can relate across the 'abyss of separation'[30] and at the same time confirm the separation. Levinas even says that 'the epiphany of the face is wholly language'.[31] Language is not first of all about a content to be communicated but is rooted in the orientation to the other, in sincerity and frankness, and in responsibility answerable to the other. 'The face opens the primordial discourse whose first word is

---

25. Ibid., p. 50.   26. Cf. ibid., pp. 199ff.
27. Ibid., p. 291. In his ethical notion of the face Levinas makes a critical break with phenomenology, while yet drawing on its characteristic language and concepts. The extent of the break is measured by the reference to God.   28. Ibid., p. 295.
29. Cf. ibid., p. 216: 'Multiplicity in being, which refuses totalization but takes form as fraternity and discourse, is situated in a "space" essentially asymmetrical.'
30. Ibid., p. 295.   31. 'Philosophy and the Idea of Infinity', p. 55.

obligation which no "interiority" permits avoiding.'[32] So the essence of language is seen to be ethical, prior to all its uses in representing reality, universalising thought or informing particular actions.

Reason too has its being in this ethical context. It is about being taught, being questioned before others, being called on for answers that justify statements or actions. 'The other is not for reason a scandal that puts it in dialectical movement, but the first teaching.'[33] It might seem that rational objectivity is not related to ethics, since there is a massive insistence on the separation of 'facts' from 'values' in much modern Western thought, with scientific rationality often seen as the authoritative mode of discourse about 'facts'. Levinas, on the contrary, sees objectivity as one way of offering the world to the other in language that can be justified by certain criteria, and so, without contradicting scientific methods, he grounds all the sciences in the ethical. He refuses them the sort of autonomy which might let them forget that the very rationality which allows them to develop is to be referred ultimately to the face to face and responsibility. It is here that intelligibility is born through speaking, and rational discourse is about bearing responsible witness and guaranteeing that witness before others.[34] Witness, attestation or testimony will in later chapters of this book emerge as a pivotal concept in understanding the dynamics of self, community and worship. Ricoeur in particular will be drawn on in order to refine it and relate it to scriptural interpretation and Christian faith, and its culmination will be in the discussion of lives which embody radical witness to truth. That embodiment in costly action and suffering is also at the heart of Levinas's idea of witness.

Besides language and reason, freedom is also given a distinctive, ethical interpretation by Levinas: in face of the other my free spontaneity is called into question. He finds that most Western thought fails to question the fundamental of spontaneous freedom – where freedom is found to be limited this is perceived as a defect or tragic.[35] This freedom is closely tied to a consciousness which strives to represent and comprehend reality in theory. Levinas is not denying the legitimacy of freedom or theory, he is relativising them by reference to the face of the other. The priority of the other means that ethical critique is more fundamental than ontology or epistemology.

> The freedom that can be ashamed of itself founds truth . . . Shame
> does not have the structure of consciousness and clarity. It is oriented

32. *Totality and Infinity*, p. 201.   33. Ibid., p. 204.   34. Ibid., p. 201.
35. Cf. ibid., p. 83.

in the inverse direction; its subject is exterior to me . . . Morality
begins where freedom, instead of being justified by itself, feels itself to
be arbitrary and violent.[36]

In line with this critique of freedom[37] Levinas's notion of the will is as
belonging to one who is summoned to assume responsibility.

> The will is free to assume the responsibility in whatever sense it likes;
> it is not free to refuse this responsibility itself; it is not free to ignore
> the meaningful world into which the face of the Other has introduced
> it. *In the welcoming of the face the will opens to reason* [original italics].[38]

The will is thus subordinated to responsibility, language and reason.
Our free will is not an absolute beginning: it always finds itself already
summoned, obliged, called to responsibility before the other. The heteronomy is sharpened in the notion of judgement. Levinas sees the
judgement of God concretely brought about through the accusation 'in
the face of the Other – whose very epiphany is brought about by this
offense suffered, by this status of being stranger, widow, and orphan. The
will is under the judgement of God when its fear of death is inverted into
fear of committing murder.'[39]

Moreover – and here Levinas indicates a dynamic that will be of special
importance in the present book – the responsibility of the will to which
the judgement gives rise is infinite. There is in responsibility a dynamic
of excess, of overflow, which means that it increases in the measure that it
is assumed. 'Duties become greater in the measure that they are accomplished. The better I accomplish my duty the fewer rights I have; the
more I am just the more guilty I am . . . This is termed goodness. Perhaps
the possibility of a point of the universe where such an overflow of
responsibility is produced ultimately defines the I.'[40] That insight is, as
we shall see, carried yet further in *Otherwise than Being*. It is an extreme
conception of ethical selfhood for which the other before whom one is
responsible is definitive.

2.3 Desire

There remains one further aspect of Levinas's account of the self up to
Totality and Infinity which is of great importance in this and later chapters:
desire. Levinas opens *Totality and Infinity* with a section on 'desire for the

---

36. Ibid., pp. 83f.
37. The critique also raises questions about Farley's use of freedom as his fundamental
concept in *Good and Evil*.   38. *Totality and Infinity*, p. 219.   39. Ibid., p. 244.
40. Ibid., pp. 244f.

invisible'. This is the inner dynamic of responsibility. It is a desire that is not motivated by need or lack. That would be to see the self as oriented to assimilation of what is other and would be a form of nostalgia, a longing for return, for a lost completeness, for what we sense really belongs to us. The resonance is with Abraham setting out for a promised land rather than Odysseus returning home. It is desire for what is genuinely other, 'for a land foreign to every nature',[41] for something more than completeness, for what can never satisfy it. 'The Desired does not fulfil it, but deepens it.'[42] This desire for the absolutely other, which is experienced as infinite responsibility, has as its meaning 'the alterity of the Other and the Most-High',[43] the disinterestedness of goodness. The intentionality of desire is Levinas's alternative to other accounts of humanity in terms such as need, anxiety, thinking, knowing, willing, feeling or imagining. It is an orientation to the invisible, whose trace appears in the face of the other, and the consequences are utterly radical: 'to die for the invisible'.[44]

Enjoyment and responsibility can be seen as related through desire in a way which preserves their distinctness on separate planes. Enjoyment is essential for responsibility in the sense that there must be this separated self to be appealed to by the face of the other. Desire is not derived from enjoyment but presupposes it.[45]

Perhaps the richest of the ways in which Levinas explores the relationship between enjoyment, responsibility and desire is through the home, dwelling, habitation. The insecurity of enjoyment requires labour and the security of a home to sustain life. These involve other people, language and representation, and the creation of an 'extraterritoriality in the midst of the elements of enjoyment with which life is nourished'.[46] There can be intimacy and 'a first revelation of the Other'.[47] Gentleness, a theme that will be taken up again in chapter 5 below, is the phenomenon that Levinas especially remarks upon here. He says:

> This extraterritoriality has a positive side. It is produced in the gentleness [douceur] or warmth of intimacy, which is not a subjective state of mind, but an event in the oecumenia of being – a delightful 'lapse' of the ontological order. By virtue of its intentional structure

---

41. Ibid., p. 34.   42. Ibid.   43. Ibid.   44. Ibid., p. 35.
45. Cf. ibid., p. 148: 'Egoism, enjoyment, sensibility, the whole dimension of interiority – the articulations of separation – are necessary for the idea of Infinity, the relation with the Other which opens forth from the separated and finite being. Metaphysical Desire, which can be produced only in a separated, that is, enjoying, egoist, and satisfied being, is then not derived from enjoyment.'
46. Ibid., p. 150.   47. Ibid., p. 151.

gentleness comes to the separated being from the Other. The Other precisely *reveals* himself in his alterity not in a shock negating the I, but as the primordial phenomenon of gentleness . . . The welcoming of the face is peaceable from the first, for it answers to the unquenchable Desire for Infinity.[48]

The home[49] is therefore a pivotal locus where enjoyment and the desire for infinity come together. Yet Levinas does not derive responsibility from the intimate 'I–thou' of the home any more than he sees it springing from the separated self's enjoyment.[50] The home is a consolidation of enjoyment and contentment and can remain closed. It is the home opened in hospitality to the hungry and strangers that is ethical in Levinas's sense. The appeal in the face of the other cuts across the home as it does the individual, and it awakens the desire which leads into responsibility. 'Recollection in a home open to the Other – hospitality – is the concrete and initial fact of human recollection and separation; it coincides with the Desire for the Other absolutely transcendent.'[51] The face of the other comes primarily from outside the home, as one who speaks, commands and teaches, and in response I learn to give what I possess, to be a hospitable self.[52]

So in Levinas's idea of hospitality there is a convergence of enjoyment, responsibility and desire. Yet at the same time the very associations of the word hospitality suggest some doubts about his insistence on insulating responsibility from being derived from enjoyment, and also about his separation of desire for the infinite or for 'the Other absolutely transcen-

---

48. Ibid., p. 150.
49. For a perceptive discussion of Levinas on enjoyment, the home and the feminine see Llewellyn, *Emmanuel Levinas*, chapter 7.
50. Cf. *Totality and Infinity*, p. 155.   51. Ibid., p. 172.
52. Cf. ibid., pp. 170f.:

> But in order that I be able to free myself from the very possession that the welcome of the Home establishes, in order that I be able to see things in themselves, that is, represent them to myself, refuse both enjoyment and possession, I must know how *to give* what I possess . . . But for this I must encounter the indiscreet face of the Other that calls me into question. The Other – the absolutely other – paralyses possession, which he contests by his epiphany in the face. He can contest my possession only because he comes not from outside but from above. The same can not lay hold of this other without suppressing him. But the untraversible infinity of the negation of murder is announced by this dimension of height, where the Other comes to me concretely in the ethical impossibility of committing this murder. I welcome the Other who presents himself in my home by opening my home to him.
>
> The calling in question of the I, coextensive with the manifestation of the Other in the face, we call language. The height from which language comes we designate teaching . . . Teaching is not a species of a genus called domination, a hegemony at work within a totality, but is the presence of infinity breaking the closed circle of totality.

dent' from other desires. There is a tension between, on the one hand, a Kantian tendency to detach ethical imperatives from pleasure, interest and desire (which in chapter 4 below will be taken up in discussing Ricoeur's modification of Levinas which appeals to both Aristotle and Rosenzweig), and, on the other hand, what I take to be the logic of his conceptions of enjoyment and desire. Why should enjoyment in some form not be intrinsic to the derivation of responsibility? What is the relationship of gentleness to responsibility? Might there be the possibility of joy in the invisible as well as desire for the invisible?

These questions are intensified by the intriguing final section of *Totality and Infinity* entitled 'Beyond the Face'. There Levinas discusses erotic love in its ambiguity as both need and desire, concupiscence and transcendence, and introduces the child, or fecundity, as a 'new category', though one not confined to biological fecundity. Fecundity relativises the categories of knowledge and power,[53] neither of which is adequate to describe the relation to one's child.

> Transcendence, the for the Other, the goodness correlative of the face, founds a more profound relation: the goodness of goodness.
> Fecundity engendering fecundity accomplishes goodness: above and beyond the sacrifice that imposes a gift, the gift of the power of giving, the conception of the child. Here the Desire which in the first pages of this work we contrasted with need, the Desire that is not a lack, the Desire that is the independence of the separated being and its transcendence, is accomplished – not in being satisfied and in thus acknowledging that it was a need, but in transcending itself, in engendering Desire.[54]

One might see welcoming the child as the transgenerational mode of hospitality, in which a new face is born, a new multiplicity in the self is engendered, the basic face to face community of the family (and its non-biological analogues) is realised, and time is structured through the discontinuity of new births, the welcoming of new strangers. Here if anywhere is a sphere where joys and responsibilities are inextricable.

Levinas even sees the discontinuous time of fecundity, with its ever new recommencements, as signifying 'pardon as constitutive of time itself'.[55] In a pregnant series of phrases he speaks of 'the discerning in

---

53. Cf. ibid., p. 277.   54. Ibid., p. 269.
55. Ibid., p. 283. The preceding paragraph reads: 'Pardon in its immediate sense is connected with the moral phenomenon of fault. The paradox of pardon lies in its retroaction; from the point of view of common time it represents an inversion of the natural order of things, the reversibility of time. It involves several aspects. Pardon refers

pardon of a surplus of happiness, the strange happiness of reconciliation, the *felix culpa*, given in an everyday experience which no longer
astonishes us'.[56] Here the reality of discontinuous newness has its
deepest meaning in a conception of life as a drama in which pardon can
happen and which includes, despite and even through the wrong,
happiness. The formal structure of this is that 'death and resurrection
constitute time', and the presupposition of it is 'the relation of the I and
the Other, and, at its basis, fecundity across the discontinuous which
constitutes time'.[57] This prepares for the enigmatic final paragraph in
which not death but 'messianic time' is said to be the completion of
time, and 'the dream of a happy eternity' is 'not a simple aberration'.[58]
The concepts and the imagery might be adapted to the messianic
hospitality which, in a Christian mode, will be the culmination of this
book. But Levinas ends his essay on a characteristic interrogative note:
'Is this eternity a new structure of time, or an extreme vigilance of the
messianic consciousness? The problem exceeds the bounds of this
book.'[59]

2.4 Conclusion

This chapter has been drawing from Levinas elements that will be developed and woven into succeeding chapters. I have left to others (and to
Levinas himself in extensive parts of his writings) the examination of the
genealogy of his thought and response to its critics. Yet my own inter-
pretive and very selective redescription of *Totality and Infinity* will seem
controversial to many who read that text differently. Far more debatable

to the instant elapsed; it permits the subject who had committed himself in a past instant
to be as though that instant had not passed on, to be as though he had not committed
himself. Active in a stronger sense than forgetting, which does not concern the reality of
the event forgotten, pardon acts upon the past, somehow repeats the event, purifying it.
But in addition, forgetting nullifies the relations with the past, whereas pardon conserves
the past pardoned in the purified present. The pardoned being is not the innocent being.
The difference does not justify placing innocence above pardon; it permits the discerning
in pardon of a surplus of happiness, the strange happiness of reconciliation, the *felix culpa*,
given in an everyday experience which no longer astonishes us.'   56. Ibid.
57. Ibid., p. 284.
58. Ibid., pp. 284f. The paragraph reads: 'But infinite time is also the putting back into
question of the truth it promises. The dream of a happy eternity, which subsists in man
along with his happiness, is not a simple aberration. Truth requires both an infinite time
and a time it will be able to seal, a completed time. The completion of time is not death,
but messianic time, where the perpetual is converted into eternal. Messianic triumph is
the pure triumph; it is secured against the revenge of evil whose return the infinite time
does not prohibit. Is this eternity a new structure of time, or an extreme vigilance of the
messianic consciousness? The problem exceeds the bounds of this book.'   59. Ibid.

will be the following chapter in which I draw on him for more explicitly theological purposes and bring him into dialogue with a contemporary theologian, Eberhard Jüngel.

The main outcome of this engagement with Levinas has been the rendering of a 'hospitable self'. That is my phrase, not Levinas's, but it helps to focus the distinctive features of how he presents the self in *Totality and Infinity*. Hospitality combines and distinguishes enjoyment and responsibility, it allows for the notes of abundance, celebration and even extravagance and excess which he sounds, and it counters any tendency to separate body and spirit or to play down corporeality and materiality. It helps to imagine an ethic of gentleness and to affirm the fundamental place of language, and, of course, the centrality of being faced. It also opens on an idea of the infinite in terms of responsibility, involving reference to God.

All of those elements will enter into what follows and be taken up into a theology very different from anything Levinas would want to support. But there too I hope that the image of hospitality is apt in that it requires not so much agreement as continuing respectful conversation. Some of the topics in that conversation have already been raised, especially about the analysis and interrelation of enjoyment, responsibility and desire. But the sharpest questions have yet to come, as two new dialogue partners, Jüngel and Ricoeur, each of whom has engaged explicitly with Levinas's thought, join the table.

3

God, others and substitution: a self without idols

The conception of salvation which this book is offering is of people in full worship of God, with the main concentration on ordinary living. Levinas was drawn on for a description of ordinary life in terms of enjoyment, responsibility and desire, and some hints given of the ramifications of this for other aspects such as reason, freedom, language, the home, family and economy. The interim description of what emerged was of a 'hospitable self'. I only touched on another pervasive aspect of Levinas's thought which intensifies after *Totality and Infinity*: his radical 'hermeneutic of suspicion'. To be immersed in Levinas's writings is to be interrogated with a rigour hardly matched by other modern masters of suspicion such as Marx, Nietzsche, Freud or Foucault. It is an interrogation all the more effective for being gentle, being increasingly exercised on his own discourse, and including an insider's devastating critique of religion. I will interpret this as anti-idolatry, portraying Levinas as a twentieth-century prophet against idolatry. His critique deals above all with language itself, the most developed human form of representation and therefore a place of immense idolatrous potential.

Of the various discourses, Levinas is especially critical of theology as an attempt to thematise God inappropriately. I will take one Christian theologian, Eberhard Jüngel, and see if Levinas's general points about theology are applicable to him. I will explore the similarities and differences in their thought and will particularly focus on their answers to the question, Where is God? and on how they conceive the self in relation to death, love and substitution. The engagement with them is intended not so much to try to resolve all their deep differences as to develop the idea of a 'non-idolatrous self'.

Idolatry can be a self-righteous concept, easily used to label those who have different basic orientations from oneself. Both Levinas and Jüngel are rigorous critics of orientations which in their judgement are not towards the goodness of God, and Levinas in particular offers a wide-ranging critique of Western civilisation and its philosophy because of their tendency to totalise and reify reality in ways which close them to the appeal in the face of the other. But the profundity of what I call their anti-idolatry is in recognising that its most insidious and subtle dangers are found at the heart of their own strongest affirmations and convinced practices. It is exactly in the course of answering the question, Where is God? that they need to be most alert against temptations to domesticate God, wrongly identify God, reify or objectify God, use language inappropriately of God, or relate God inappropriately to ethics and to creation. So the central thrust of each is oriented critically on his own answer to that question. Levinas constantly 'unsays' and 'resays' his 'sayings' in exposed vulnerability as he tries to avoid idolising the traces of the infinite in the approach of the other. Jüngel faces the presence and absence of God in the crucified Jesus Christ and wrestles with the complexities of a 'more than necessary' God, of the differentiation of God from humanity, of love defined through the crucifixion, and of how thinking and knowing are related to God. For both of them the way of non-idolatrous relation to God is inseparable from concepts and practices of self, and they will be brought into critical dialogue with each other about these. The culminating discussion will be about substitution, which is where key issues of the presence and absence of God, language, death, love and responsibility converge. It is the substitutionary self that relates non-idolatrously to the world, other people and God.

That discussion will lead to the threshold of the next chapter's discussion of the self in worship.

3.1 Against idolatries

To read Levinas with the prophets of biblical Israel in mind is to be reminded of two of their main themes which are inseparably interwoven: rejection of idolatry and passionate concern for right living with other people. Levinas comes as near as possible to identifying the two, and his 'ethics as first philosophy' is a rigorous critique of the way in which 'idols' of various sorts have so fascinated and dominated the Western intellectual tradition and the civilisation which it has helped to form that the result has been a devastating propensity for violence, murder and war.

His is a critique that does not stay with relatively superficial ways of absolutising some aspect of reality, such as money, power, knowledge, pleasure, beauty, a race, a nation or whatever. He probes the ingrained habits of a civilisation whose influence has an unparalleled global scope. From the Archimedean point of infinite responsibility before the face of the other he diagnoses what has gone most fundamentally wrong.

The embracing form of diagnosis is as 'totality', with the totalising self being seen as the main problem. Here the great 'idols'[1] are good capacities which have been absolutised and become autonomous, embracing reality in their orbit without doing justice to the face of the other. The basic recurring pattern is the reduction of the other to 'the same'. This refers to the ways in which, through enjoyment, through representation in words, images or other expressions, through autonomous freedom, through reason, concepts and theory we attempt to master reality by surveying it, grasping it or acting towards it as if its being were assimilable by such means. It is not that any of the capacities are bad, but that they are only healthy when they acknowledge in their operation their own relativity to the ethical and the infinite which breaches the totality.

The symptoms of a civilisation in the grip of totalitarian dynamics are multifarious. There are 'allergic' relations between people – we see others as threats to our freedom and the normal state of life as war or compromises between people and groups in tension rather than seeing human subjectivity as welcoming the other in hospitality and peace. There is widespread violence, not only as injury and murder of people but as 'making them play roles in which they no longer recognize themselves, making them betray not only commitments but their own substance'.[2] Individuals receive their meaning from the totality and lose confidence in any sense of identity or responsibility that appeals beyond the verdict of history in which the violent and unjust are often successful. Whole systems of philosophy, economics, government, organisation and activity are created which are inimical to the pluralism of the face to face and

1. It is not Levinas's habit to use the language of idolatry in his philosophy, but it does appear occasionally (for example in the course of two important discussions in *Otherwise Than Being*, pp. 44, 150; cf. also the note on p. 199 which perhaps most clearly confirms the thrust of my interpretation) and is understandably more prominent in his explicitly Jewish writings. See for example his description of Judaism in 'A Religion for Adults' in *Difficult Freedom*, pp. 11–23. My interpretation of aspects of his thought in terms of the exposure of idolatries is a theological one which yet claims to be in line with what Levinas says. The issue of Levinas's view of theology will be discussed later. For a perceptive theological discussion of *Totality and Infinity* in relation to Kierkegaard which sees idolatry as a key concept see Merold Westphal, 'Levinas, Kierkegaard and the Theological Task' in *Modern Theology*, vol. 8, no. 3, July 1992, pp. 241–61.   2. *Totality and Infinity*, p. 21.

whose best efforts at justice are continually distorted by their idolatries. In reaction, there are often protests in the name of a unique human subjectivity which itself easily becomes idolatrous, since the subject is not seen in the relation of responsibility to the other. One way of looking at the unusual style of Levinas, spiralling around fundamental thoughts, is as a form of teaching that is trying to immerse the reader long enough in a different way of conceiving self and reality in order to allow the dimensions of the problem to dawn and the surprise of the 'revelation' of the infinite in the face of the other to initiate a new normality.

But how does Levinas see himself avoiding some form of idolatry? How can he claim not to be affected by what he sees as a nearly universal flaw in the discourses and practices of Western civilisation? He does not claim this, but responds to the threat by trying to build into his text ways of minimising the danger that what he says might become yet another form of totality, a 'thematising' which embraces the other in the same. The effort to do this is especially intensive in *Otherwise Than Being* and it is no accident that there he is also more explicit about how God enters into his philosophy. It is as if his main fear is of what he says being frozen into an idol which subverts what he is saying, reducing it to 'sameness', to inclusion in the self's knowing or imagining, and compromising the transcendence of the other, of judgement, of the infinite.[3] He strains for ideas which will express what he wants and give some safeguard against reversion into 'totality'.

His talk of God is a dazzling and enigmatic mixture of eloquence, elusiveness and polemic.[4] He often seems to 'unsay' what he has said so that it may be hard to see why he talks of God at all; yet God is intrinsic to the main ethical point that he wants to make in his philosophy. Radical ethical content is given to theological terms such as creation (especially through the notion of absolute passivity), election,[5]

---

3. On the transition from *Totality and Infinity* to *Otherwise Than Being* see the dense and illuminating final paragraph of 'Signature' in Levinas, *Difficult Freedom*, p. 295.

4. The eloquence and elusiveness are scattered through his philosophical works and through his Jewish writings and are concentrated in his essay, 'God and Philosophy' in *The Levinas Reader*, edited by Sean Hand (Basil Blackwell, Oxford 1989), pp. 166–89. The essay also appears in English in *Collected Philosophical Papers*. For the French version, see *De Dieu qui vient à l'idée* (Vrin, Paris 1982). It is based on versions of a lecture delivered to six different audiences, under Catholic, Protestant and Jewish auspices.

5. E.g. in *Totality and Infinity* p. 279 creation and election are invoked in discussing the relation of father to son, specifically in the context of ethics. In *Otherwise Than Being* creation is invoked to indicate the absolute passivity of the summons to responsibility, which is a goodness beyond being: 'Western philosophy, which perhaps is reification itself, remains faithful to the order of things and does not know the absolute passivity, beneath the level of activity and passivity, which is contributed by the idea of creation.

incarnation,[6] inspiration,[7] and many others. The ethical relation to God is lived as a social relation to other people, and this gives Levinas a criterion for rejecting an array of what he sees as religious errors.[8]

The error I want to discuss now is that of engaging in theology. Any theological appropriation of Levinas has to tackle his repeated distancing of himself from the whole enterprise of theology. It is especially relevant in the present chapter because many of the ways in which he dismisses theology amount to an accusation that theology contributes to what I have been discussing as idolatry.

3.2 Theology as idolatry?

To discuss how Levinas's philosophy might relate to the whole range of theologies would be an enormous undertaking. My shorter way will be to bring him into dialogue with one Christian theologian, Eberhard Jüngel, whose thought will also be taken up in later chapters.[9] First, I will outline Levinas's case against theology.

Philosophers have always wished to think of creation in ontological terms, that is, in function of a preexisting and indestructible matter' (p. 110). A note to this passage explains further: 'This freedom enveloped in a responsibility which it does not succeed in shouldering is the way of being a creature, the unlimited passivity of the self, the unconditionality of a self' (p. 195). As so often, Levinas, having made an ethical point by using theological language, then undercuts any more usual theological use of the point: 'The active source of this passivity is not thematizable' (p. 111). For a perceptive account of the way Levinas 'correlates' (a term used in a special sense) his ethical philosophy and his theological terminology see Gibbs, *Correlations in Rosenzweig and Levinas*, chapters 7 and 9, especially pp. 210f.

6. E.g. in *Otherwise Than Being*, p. 50 on the exposure of the self in 'saying' and substitution: 'It has the form of a corporeal life devoted to expression and to giving. It is devoted, and does not devote itself: it is a self despite itself, in incarnation, where it is the very possibility of offering, suffering and trauma.' Incarnation in Levinas does not, of course, signify what Christian doctrine means by the term: for Levinas, all people are incarnate in the literal sense of being physical, 'in their skin'.

7. Cf. *Otherwise Than Being*, p. 111 on inspiration as the subjectivity of 'the other in the same' in responsibility, and pp. 140ff. on inspiration and witness.

8. In a condensed statement in *Totality and Infinity* he criticises a formidable list: 'the violence of the sacred'; religious experience of the numinous; 'union with the transcendent by participation' and the immersion in myth which that signifies; objectification of God; 'captivation by the Transcendent'; theology, and thematisation of God or of God's attributes by analogy; any 'allegedly direct comprehension' of God; any view of the Other as the incarnation of God; and, finally, any view of salvation which implies that many people are unwittingly taking part in a drama through which mysterious designs are being worked out (*Totality and Infinity*, pp. 77–9).

9. I have discussed the relationship of Levinas to Jüngel in two articles already cited, portions of which are repeated in revised form in this and the next chapter: 'Hosting a Dialogue' in *The Possibilities of Theology*, pp. 23–59; 'On Substitution' in *Facing the Other*, pp. 21–43. They are far more detailed in their discussions and in reference to primary and secondary literature than this book, and should be consulted if further explanation of points is needed.

One striking feature of Levinas's work is his innovative philosophical reworking of the sense of such classical theological terms as incarnation, inspiration, election, hypostasis, soul, creation, expiation, vocation or redemption. Yet he also consistently rejects any implication that in doing so he is doing theology.

His objections to theology are various. Theology,[10] he says, thematises or objectifies what it should not; it is mythological, or suggests that there is a divine drama in progress in which people are participants, often unwittingly; it suggests that it is possible to participate directly in or have cognitive access to the life of God; it finds intrinsic links between human nature and the divine; it tends to confuse creation with causality or to conceptualise creation in ontological terms;[11] it makes ontology absolute, with God as the supreme being, and therefore inevitably totalitarian;[12] it argues analogically from the world to God; it signifies God in terms of presence, action, efficacity in the world; above all its alliance with ontology conspires against doing justice to an ethics which resists the assimilation of the other person to oneself and one's overview, and which finds in the face to face the trace of an unsurpassable, imperative directness and immediacy.

There are many variations on these themes, with *Otherwise Than Being* going further than earlier works. In a note at the beginning of that work, Levinas suggests that the main purpose for the book is 'to hear a God uncontaminated by Being', and through the text theology emerges as a discourse that colludes with the contamination.[13] Philosophy, on the other hand, has a potential for resisting the contamination. The contrast between the two is clearest on pages 149–62. There theology is seen as a betrayal of the 'witness' to God in its thematisation which 'introduces it into the system of language, in the order of the said'.[14] Yet there has to be thematisation, and philosophy's task is to reduce the betrayal that this expression involves.[15] This anti-idolatrous role of philosophy is developed into one of preserving the ambivalence of all talk of God in the interests of its ethical significance.[16]

The crucial distinction here is between 'saying' (*le Dire*) and 'the said' (*le Dit*). 'The signification of saying goes beyond the said.'[17] In saying there is a relation to the other which is the condition for all speech and which is not exhausted by anything said. The great danger is that the said

10. Cf. the 'religious errors' in note 8 above.   11. *Otherwise Than Being*, pp. 110ff.
12. See also ibid., pp. 94ff.   13. Ibid., pp. 93ff., 145–62.   14. Ibid., p. 151.
15. Ibid., pp. 151f.   16. See especially ibid., pp. 161f.   17. Ibid., p. 37.

comes to dominate the saying, to suppress the living transcendence of the relation to the other. The said synchronises[18] language in an ontology, a totality,[19] a synopsis, and constantly threatens to absorb the speaking subject.[20] Here one might see the question of idolatry going to the heart of Levinas's own discourse. He has seen language as the primary relating of self and other outside any totality, and the appeal in the face of the other as a saying that is prior to any particular thing said. This allows his philosophy to act as an instrument of extraordinary vigilance against idolatries in language, behaviour, structures, orientations and world-views. Yet Levinas's own risk of idolatry is likely to be in this area. His whole philosophy is something 'said' which is yet testifying to something which can never be said. He rejects theology and its talk of God because he sees it inevitably reducing God to the said, but what about his own 'said'?

His 'said' is needed in order to communicate, and its positive, ethical meaning is in its contribution to a society in which there can be responsibility and justice.[21] Yet his comprehensive critique of all representation calls for 'unsaying' (dédire) which attempts to witness, through the ambiguity of everything said, to the 'one-for-the-other'. Saying is witness in which there is 'a proximity that is possible only as an openness of self, an imprudent exposure to the other . . . that, as responsibility, is

18. For Levinas the temporal mode of totality is 'synchrony', simultaneously gathering being in an overview, in memory and recollection, in systematic interrelation or in projection. The present is the privileged time, and thought is continually tracing realities back to their principles, beginnings, *archai*. 'Diachrony' is Levinas's term for a non-totalitarian time, of which there can be no overview and through which there is no continuity that can be thematised. He talks of an 'anarchy' and an 'anachrony', of thinking back to a time that is not in linear sequence with the present and cannot be remembered as ever present (*Otherwise Than Being*, p. 38). It testifies to a radical otherness, to being elected, called, summoned from a time that we can never synchronise with ours, that is not to be characterised ontologically but is 'otherwise than being'. He frankly admits to abusing language in order to indicate this apparently contradictory concept. One word for such a time from which we are radically but not purely negatively separated is creation. His abusing of language has the purpose, in my terms, of iconoclastically challenging all those notions of the self which do not allow for transcendence and whose implicit or explicit absolute is a particular concept of time. This has far-reaching consequences for relativising accounts of the self in terms of genetic origins, history, social sciences and any pattern of linear causality.
19. Levinas does not often use the concept of totality in *Otherwise Than Being*, just as other key earlier terms such as exteriority and separation are rarely mentioned. Peperzak suggests that one partial reason is the different perspective of the later work: 'In *Totality and Infinity* the central place was taken by the Other and its visage; in *Otherwise Than Being* Levinas meditates on the "position" and the meaning of the subject; of the self who meets the other' (*To the Other*, p. 212). But significantly for the present discussion Levinas does talk of totality and of God together as he wrestles with the relation of saying to said in *Otherwise Than Being*, pp. 153ff., especially p. 155.   20. *Otherwise Than Being*, pp. 134ff.
21. Ibid., p. 45.

signification itself, the-one-for-other. It is the subjectivity of the subject that makes itself a sign . . . [which] bears witness to the glory of the Infinite.'[22] The unsaying of each representation has its positive form in the witness to responsibility, and its aim is to point to the trace of transcendence in each statement.[23] What results is a fresh saying, a saying again (*redire*), which needs to undergo the same process of 'unsaying' in order, despite its inevitable ambiguity, to continue to witness. It is an invitation to unending critique or prophecy, but one which is in the service of the other by repeatedly subverting the ways in which 'the glory of the Infinite' is lost. It is an iconoclasm which searches out idolatry even in the way the words which expose idolatry themselves betray their inspiration from the other.

It is not a critique which is a technique to be learnt. The phrases above about imprudent exposure and the subjectivity of the subject making itself a sign hint at the implications. This is anti-idolatry which can only be sustained by a self which is vulnerable to the other in such an unreserved way that Levinas uses words such as substitution, hostage, expiation and sacrifice to describe it. This is the pivotal point of *Otherwise Than Being* and it explains why the issues of language and discourse (further discussed in the next chapter) are inseparable from those of God and the self around which this chapter revolves. The non-idolatrous self as a substitionary self is Levinas's extreme conclusion. It will also be the culminating issue in this chapter between Jüngel and Levinas.

Jüngel also ties language, self and God closely together and I will bring him into dialogue with Levinas about each of them. That engagement will be the true test of Jüngel's theology in the face of Levinas's dismissal of the discipline, but first it is worth responding from Jüngel's point of view to the above case against theology.

3.3 Jüngel's response

It is now time to introduce Eberhard Jüngel (born 1934) as a dialogue partner.[24] He has produced many types of theology – dogmatics (or systematics), New Testament theology, commentary, sermons, ethics,

---

22. Ibid., p. 151.   23. Cf. ibid., p. 152.
24. John Webster is the most comprehensive commentator on Jüngel in English. See especially *Eberhard Jüngel. An Introduction to His Theology* (Cambridge University Press, Cambridge 1986); and 'Eberhard Jüngel' in *The Modern Theologians. An Introduction to Christian Theology in the Twentieth Century*, 2nd edn, ed. David F. Ford (Blackwell, Oxford 1997).

political theology and editorial work of various kinds. He has been a mediator between the theologies of Karl Barth and Rudolf Bultmann which often polarised the field of European Protestant academic theology during the middle two quarters of the twentieth century. His main thrust has been towards understanding both God and humanity in relation to Jesus Christ, a classic Christian concern which he has pursued in intensive dialogue with both theologians and philosophers.

His deep theological involvement with philosophy makes him especially suitable as a dialogue partner with Levinas, and the interests of the two intersect at many points. Each has engaged with the themes of God, language as address or testimony, the self, presence and absence, similarity and difference, freedom and responsibility, suffering and death, thought and reason, revelation and the rejection of natural theology, creation and eschatology, vulnerability and weakness, necessity and what is beyond necessity or more than necessary, substitution, and desire. Jüngel also has a habit of giving (though only sporadically in comparison with Levinas) vivid, intensive and often difficult phenomenological portrayals of human experience – of love, faith, joy, speaking or thinking. Levinas has championed 'ethics as first philosophy'; Jüngel might be seen as proposing in a comparable way 'soteriology as first theology'[25] – his 'obsession', matching Levinas's ethical appeal in the face of the other, being the doctrine of justification by God through the death of Jesus Christ.

In their philosophy they meet most fully in their fascination with and criticism of Martin Heidegger, but they also share a thorough immersion in other modern and ancient philosophers. In particular they come together in their Heidegger-influenced critique of much Western metaphysics and of the theology that has been shaped by it, which is sometimes summed up under the label 'ontotheology'. But where Levinas's constructive alternative is a philosophical ethics in accord with a contemporary tradition of Talmudic Jewish interpretation and practice, Jüngel's is uncompromisingly theological along rethought Christian trinitarian lines. Jüngel's focus on the crucifixion of Jesus Christ, understood (in a distinctive way) as the death of God, sharply raises questions discussed above under the heading of idolatry. His 'protocols against

---

25. E.g. Eberhard Jüngel, *God as the Mystery of the World* (Wm. B. Eerdmans, Grand Rapids 1983), Section 22 on 'The Crucified Jesus Christ as the "Vestige of the Trinity"', pp. 343ff., and on p. 94 the praise for Hegel in this regard. In his other writings, the doctrine of justification is a fundamental concern – see Webster, *Eberhard Jüngel*.

idolatry'[26] include, as we will see, many ingredients which do not fall foul of Levinas's critique of theology. Its main feature, however, is its understanding of God as Trinity. For Jüngel the main problem with modern atheism from the standpoint of Christianity is that it is not rejecting the Christian God when it thinks it is: the God it rejects is not the Trinity but a human construct – an absolute of some sort which is, in my terms, an idol. The positive side of this analysis is that the God who is identified by Jüngel through the Gospel testimony to Jesus Christ is most appropriately construed as the Trinity. Here there is, of course, a radical difference from Levinas, but in the light of the arguments which will follow I hold that it is not a difference which can be explained by Jüngel's engaging in the sort of discourse Levinas dismisses as 'theology'. Rather it is a difference which deserves the fuller discussion which I offer.

I will first respond from Jüngel's point of view to Levinas's case (as stated above) against theology, and will then proceed to the more important test of Jüngel's theology and Levinas's philosophy by bringing them into dialogue on God, self and language, three terms which are very closely related in the thought of each.

For my purposes, there are five main points which Jüngel might make to show that his theology does not fit Levinas's stereotype, especially as regards the main contention that theology embraces God within 'being' in thematisation. These points also lay the basis for the succeeding discussions of God, self and, in the next chapter, language.

First, there is Jüngel's concern for the unobjectifiable mode of address, the event of continual 'coming', which has much in common with Levinas's ideas of 'proximity' and 'approach' and which runs throughout Jüngel's treatment of God. 'The address function of language [die Anredefunktion der Sprache], even though address can at times be merely a means to an end, is no less inherent to the essence of language than the signal character [Signalcharakter]. It is the address character of language which first makes it humane [menschlich].'[27] Jüngel makes language at least as central to his theology as it is to Levinas's philosophy, and the distinction here between address and signal recalls that between saying and

---

26. The phrase is from Nicholas Lash, *Easter in Ordinary. Reflections on Human Experience and the Knowledge of God* (SCM, London 1988), p. 261. Lash's discussions of the nature of theology, the doctrine of the Trinity, the ethical dimension of theological knowing, and the pervasive danger of idolatry are subtle and persuasive. He also conducts an exemplary debate with another Jewish thinker, Martin Buber, which tries to take account of Jewish 'corrective pressure' (p. 218) on Christian trinitarian belief.
27. Jüngel, *God as the Mystery*, p. 11.

said in Levinas. For Jüngel, address gives priority to the other who addresses; our thought is thought in response to being addressed, and 'the word of address affects not only the consciousness of the person addressed but his whole being'.[28] Jüngel speaks of this as a language event (*Sprachereignis*) which transcends representing, imagining and comprehending[29] and allows something to happen between addresser and person addressed.

Second, and closely linked to that, is the refusal of any overarching concept of being. The suspicion that such a concept is a false absolute which in fact replaces God gives genuine theological impetus to the rejection of 'ontotheology' as idolatrous.[30] Jüngel is as much against any 'natural theology' as Levinas. There is to be no moving deductively or inductively, rationally or experientially, from the world to God. Perhaps Jüngel's most forceful conceptualisation of this is in terms of the non-necessity of God with which he begins his book on God.[31] He sees modern atheism as right in finding God not to be within the world's horizon and so not to be necessary in any worldly sense.[32] Contrasting his own approach with other theologies (notably that of Wolfhart Pannenberg), Jüngel says that 'the following investigations will proceed on the basis that theology is, in fact, being confronted with a truth when the worldly non-necessity of God [*die weltliche Nichtnotwendigkeit Gottes*] is asserted'.[33] Levinas's practical, ethical rejection of the necessity of God might be seen by Jüngel as essential to an adequate notion of human responsibility.[34] Likewise, Jüngel is sympathetic to Levinas's connection of a necessary God with totality, violence and 'the deification of domination'.[35]

Jüngel's alternative to a God who is not necessary is a God who is 'more than necessary' (*mehr als notwendig*).[36] For such a God, relationship in the mode of address, self-revelation, free and gratuitous communication, is characteristic. The parallels with Levinas on infinity, gratuity, non-erotic desire, disinterestedness and excess are sufficient to exempt Jüngel from Levinas's dismissals of theology and to allow them to proceed to a more fruitful debate.

---

28. Ibid.   29. Cf. ibid., p. 9.

30. It is quite another matter whether the suspicions are in fact justified – I suspect that many classical theological thinkers accused of this sort of ontotheology are not guilty as charged.   31. Jüngel, *God as the Mystery*, pp. 14–35.   32. Ibid., p. 16.

33. Ibid., pp. 17f.   34. Ibid., p. 20.   35. Ibid., p. 23.

36. Ibid., p. 24. Jüngel acknowledges the logical problems in this phrase, comparable to many of Levinas's formulations, but suggests that 'it may be an appropriate way to draw attention to the uniqueness of God, which cannot so easily fit into the logic of modality'. He examines the concept of necessity at length in the following pages.

A third reason for the inapplicability of Levinas's strictures is in Jüngel's sustained critique of the sort of notions of 'presence' that both Levinas and other critics of 'ontotheology' also reject. In contrasting ways, Levinas and Jüngel both include a radical notion of absence in their concepts of God. Levinas does it by the notion of a trace of the infinite which was never present, an 'anarchic', 'diachronic' reality which cannot be represented or correlated with our being synchronically present to it.[37] Jüngel does it by his interpretation of the crucifixion as the death of God and of the 'word of the cross' as indicating a reality beyond the alternative of presence and absence.[38]

Fourth, that 'word of the cross', the pivotal matter for Jüngel's whole theology, acts as the event through which he both deconstructs and reconstructs ideas and tendencies of which Levinas is critical. This does not necessarily mean a convergence of meaning, but it does call for a further stage of debate between the two. Above all, Levinas's critique of union with God by participation is deflected by Jüngel's notion of faith in a God who both identifies with humanity and at the same time radically differentiates himself through the crucifixion and resurrection of Jesus.

Fifth, to return to the topic of language, Jüngel's concept of analogical talk of God, strongly critical of much previous theological talk of analogy, also escapes the suspicions on which Levinas bases his dismissal of analogical predication in theology.[39] Can there be any correspondence at all between our language and God? Jüngel's 'analogy of advent' avoids Levinas's critique while at the same time challenging Levinas's extreme scepticism about the possibility of any language event of correspondence. Levinas's talk of God is interminably enigmatic, 'abusive' and equivocal; even so, it is talk of God. Jüngel has 'mystery' (*Geheimnis*, *musterion*) at the heart of his theology, but this is a mystery that is eminently 'speakable', that continually issues in fresh speech events and above all is informed by the crucifixion and resurrection of Jesus. The cross destroys any fixed idols in words and concepts as much as in images: it suggests a parallel to Levinas's 'unsaying', just as the fresh speaking has echoes of Levinas's ever-new 'saying' and 'resaying' in proximity to the other.

The above attempt to show that, at least where Jüngel is concerned, Levinas is attacking a stereotype of theology which need not be taken as definitive, is, by extension, part of the justification of my own theological

---

37. Cf. above note 18.   38. Jüngel, *God as the Mystery*, chapter II.
39. Ibid., sections 17 and 18. Cf. below chapter 4 for more on analogy.

engagement with Levinas and others who take similar lines on theology.[40] It is also a further step towards conceiving a non-idolatrous self with the aid of both thinkers. In order to develop that theme further I will discuss some of what they each say about God, self and language.

3.4 Where is God?

A key perception of Jüngel in *God as the Mystery of the World* is that the most important form of the question about God has changed in modernity from being about the existence or the nature of God to the problem of the location of God: where is God?[41] That might imply a despairing giving up on the possibility of offering any convincing answer in a world of such suffering and evil, so that God is pronounced dead. Or it might, as with Jüngel, lead to rethinking God in the aftermath of modern atheism.[42] If this second way is taken then the risks are increased: to locate God would seem to be basic to idolatries.

Jüngel's answer to the question about where God is is: in God's Word, understood through the event of Jesus Christ. 'The place of the conceivability of God is a Word that precedes thought.'[43] Here is 'prevenience'; here is found the character of human being as addressable and responsible, and a concept of self that does not try to secure itself in certainty but lives freely in faith; here one particular existence, that of Jesus Christ, is perceived as essential to the being of God and any separation of essence and existence is ruled out; here 'God is present as the one absent in the word';[44] here 'God on the cross as our neighbour'[45] is revealed; here, above all, we face the stark choice to renounce the thinkability of God or to transform our understanding of God in line with the man Jesus, who died. The word of the cross becomes the pivot for thought of God. This means thinking God and 'perishability'[46] together, in a way rejected by the classical thought of God. Both God and perishability need to be rethought in the process.[47] As regards the latter, perishing is recognised as radically serious, but it does not end all possibilities,[48] it does not mean annihilation. As regards God, his being is involved with nothingness by

---

40. Jüngel too tends to stereotype Levinas in his criticism of his philosophy. See Ford, 'Hosting a Dialogue', pp. 33–5.   41. *God as the Mystery*, chapter II.
42. E.g., ibid., pp. 53ff.   43. Ibid., p. 155.   44. Ibid., p. 166.   45. Ibid., p. 183.
46. 'Perishability' is not a very satisfactory translation of '*Vergänglichkeit*', but 'transience' or 'transitoriness' are perhaps too weak.   47. Jüngel, *God as the Mystery*, p. 202.
48. Ibid., p. 213: '... the thesis which is fundamental for everything which will follow: that which is ontologically positive about perishability is the possibility [*das ontologisch Positive der Vergänglichkeit ist die Möglichkeit*]' (original italics).

taking it into himself in identifying with the dead Jesus.[49] This identification is also a differentiation, so that 'the thought which follows faith is not to distinguish between the essence and existence of God, but rather between God the Father and God the Son. In unity with the man Jesus, God differentiates himself from himself, without ceasing to be the one God in this self-differentiation.'[50]

That paragraph summarises a great deal of detailed discussion and argument by Jüngel, whose main point is that if the starting point is the gospel of Jesus Christ as witnessed to in Christian faith then it makes sense radically to rethink God with reference to the crucified Jesus and to avoid idolatry through a trinitarian understanding of God in self-differentiation.[51]

Levinas seems to be in sympathy with the diagnosis of a change in the fundamental question about God. He too talks of the death of God in ways which do not lead to a simple negation of the idea.[52] Like Jüngel, he is not so interested in following the road of 'metaphysics' (Levinas would call it ontology[53]) but is intensely interested in the location of God in relation to good and evil. The contrast, of course, is in the nature of the location. Each is 'most concrete' and each finds God in what is human. Each also offers a positive answer which is 'beyond the alternative of presence or absence';[54] but for Jüngel this is in the crucified and risen Jesus, for Levinas it is in the trace of the infinite in the face, or saying, of the other person.

The culminating two pages of *Otherwise Than Being* (pp. 184–5) can be read as Levinas's summary constructive statement as well as a refusal of Jüngel's Christian theological path. Levinas evokes a reality of rich particularities, an abundance of singularities beyond any human expression, and they are all related to the conception of a God who speaks to each person.

> The caress of love, always the same, in the last accounting (for him that thinks in counting) is always different and overflows with exorbitance the songs, poems and admissions in which it is said in so many different ways and through so many themes, in which it

---

49. Ibid., p. 219.
50. Ibid., p. 221. He adds: 'We shall have to dwell in greater detail on the trinitarian implications of this content later.'
51. For more on this see Lash, *Easter in Ordinary*, especially chapters 14, 15 and 16.
52. E.g. *Otherwise Than Being*, pp. 123, 185.
53. Their use of these two terms tends to be weighted in opposite ways: Jüngel usually mentions 'metaphysics' negatively but does use 'ontology' positively; Levinas usually does the reverse.   54. Jüngel, *God as the Mystery*, p. 55.

apparently is forgotten. According to the word of Jehuda Halevy, with his eternal word 'God speaks to each man in particular'.[55]

Here we have Jüngel's 'Word that precedes thought', but there is no question of it being focussed through the event of Jesus Christ. There is in this vision a generous ethical universality (often using the same scriptural language as that which Christians apply to Jesus Christ) embodied in varied particularity. It must count as an attractive alternative to Jüngel's Christian 'scandal of particularity' centred on the crucified Jesus Christ. It is a vision comparable to some of the approaches currently being canvassed in order to live with pluralisms of various sorts, stressing both ethical convergences and respect for otherness. In this complex of responsibilities, what worries Levinas most about the cross-centred position identified with Jüngel is that somehow Christianity involves a shifting of responsibility on to that man on the cross, and an infinite pardon which encourages irresponsibility.

The critical positive point is that each human person is 'virtually a chosen one, called to leave in his turn, or without awaiting his turn, the concept of the ego, its extension in the people, to respond with responsibility: *me*, that is, *here I am for the others*, to lose his place radically . . .'[56] The 'place' of responsibility to the point of substitution, or being a hostage, is seen as a sort of utopia, a non-site; but Levinas has already said that 'there is no need [*necessité*] to refer to an event in which the non-site, becoming a site, would have exceptionally entered into the spaces of history'.[57] That is the critical negative point and is the massive, simple difference from Jüngel. Its implications for God are the topic of the enigmatic final paragraph of the book:

> After the death of a certain god inhabiting the world behind the
> scenes, the substitution of the hostage discovers the trace, the
> unpronounceable inscription, of what, always already past, always
> 'he', does not enter into any present, to which are suited not the nouns
> designating beings, or the verbs in which their essence resounds, but
> that which, as a pronoun, marks with its seal all that a noun can
> convey.[58]

Jüngel's response might be that there is indeed 'no need' to refer to an exceptional event of substitutionary responsibility in history, but yet he trusts a particular testimony[59] to such a happening. How can Levinas so confidently rule out this 'non-necessary' event? Perhaps Jüngel's idea of

---

55. *Otherwise Than Being*, p. 184.   56. Ibid., p. 185.   57. Ibid., p. 184.   58. Ibid., p. 185.
59. See chapter 4 for further discussion of testimony.

the 'more than necessary', to which Levinas too has analogies, should open Levinas at least to the possibility of the truth of Jüngel's tradition.[60] Jüngel's critical counter-question for Levinas is whether the imperative of infinite responsibility for others is actually sustainable by anyone at all. Levinas seems to say that it does not have to be; Jüngel is speaking from trust in testimony that it has been.

Here is the contrasting simplicity of their positions. There is no doubt that they differ profoundly; but they do so by offering to the question, 'Where is God?' answers which are rooted in the biblical God and yet take fully seriously the critiques of theism. Each has a variation on the approach of the other in address or 'saying'. The most obvious contrast is between Jüngel's christological particularism with trinitarian universality and Levinas's face to face particularism leading to a God-related universalism of responsibility. We see here a form of Christian theology confronting, without much prospect of agreement, a form of philosophy in harmony with some traditions of Judaism. Yet both have resources for a critique of idolatries and it is possible to draw further on both in order to conceive of a non-idolatrous self.

3.5 The non-idolatrous self and God

The self according to Levinas is 'atheist' in its enjoyment as it maintains its separation by assimilating to itself what is other; but it is also 'obsessed' by infinite responsibility for the other, whose dynamic is a 'desire for the invisible', for a goodness that relativises death. Levinas is quite clear how mad this 'demented pretension to the invisible'[61] seems in a century like ours. He knows that there is by definition no 'proof' of it – any proof itself is a justification before others and assumes (even if it forgets) the ethical relation. What then is the status of his claim? Two linked categories that he uses (especially in his later work) are prophecy and witness.[62] Levinas's claim is an address by him which testifies to 'the other in the same',[63] and vulnerably exposes his own psyche in this extravagant attestation. And the self that witnesses is described in terms of 'substitution', being a hostage for the other, responsible even for the other's responsibility.

60. Despite statements which seem to reject the incarnation *a priori* Levinas has said in private interview that that is not his position. See Steven G. Smith, *The Argument to the Other* (Scholars Press, Chico, CA 1983), p. 289 for an account of the interview and Smith's plausible interpretation of Levinas's position in line with that of Michael Wyschogrod.
61. *Otherwise Than Being*, p. 185.   62. See chapter 4 below.
63. *Otherwise Than Being*, p. 149.

Jüngel in *God as the Mystery of the World* makes important statements about the self which are strikingly resonant with what Levinas says. The most basic point is that his self too is in a sense atheist – God is not necessary or intrinsic to the world but comes freely in an interrupting revelation. The ego 'is always defined by a word which lays claim to it',[64] and speaking leads to reason and thought.[65] Faith[66] is 'the ego's going out of itself unceasingly' in response to the interruption of the addressing word.[67] There is then no way back: the self is 'taken along' in a way which is distinguished from reflective and representational thought[68] and comparable with Levinas's notion of the 'non-recurrence' of the self to itself in responsibility. The distinction between faith and thought

> consists of the fact that faith does not desire anything for itself. It does not return to itself but rather remains with that which is believed. In contrast, thought, when it arrives at its content, always returns to itself: in essence, it is reflection, a reflexive form of 'being taken along'. In the act of reflection, the ego remains independent of the fact that it is being taken along.[69]

The thinking of faith 'sets reason in movement',[70] but without any certainty that is self-grounding. 'The certainty of faith is of significance chiefly because it shifts the ego into another position from that of securing itself.'[71] There is an appropriate certainty of trust which deprives one of security and makes one vulnerable. Faith's liberation from the compulsion to ground oneself is the 'emergence of freedom',[72] and the sources of false security from which we are set free are among what this chapter identifies as 'idols'. In addition, faith's essential passivity[73] is linked to responsibility for others in a way reminiscent of Levinas on desire, passivity and responsibility.

Because of their very different ways of conceiving 'the other' – Levinas through the other person and through God as 'the other than the other, transcendent to the point of absence',[74] Jüngel through Jesus Christ and the Trinity – they are testifying very differently. But it is possible to see each being enriched by mutual engagement. I will first explore just a few of the questions that Levinas might raise if he were wanting to enhance Jüngel's conception of the self.

First, what might Jüngel learn from Levinas on separation and otherness? An essential component in Jüngel's terminology is that of 'event'

---

64. *God as the Mystery*, p. 171.   65. E.g. ibid., p. 254.

66. Not a key term for Levinas, but there is considerable overlap with his notions of desire and passivity.   67. Jüngel, *God as the Mystery*, pp. 165–7.   68. Ibid., p. 166.

69. Ibid., p. 167.   70. Ibid.   71. Ibid., p. 170.   72. Ibid., p. 164.

73. E.g. Ibid., pp. 176, 179, 340ff.   74. 'God and Philosophy', p. 179.

and its cognates. Levinas is very wary of such language, seeing it as part of a history-centred totality, and one which tends always to subsume persons within a dynamic of 'the same'. Jüngel goes to great lengths to expound the event of the crucifixion as differentiating between God and humanity and establishing the proper otherness of humanity. Death itself is not even conceived as an event – it is 'eventless, a non-event [*Das Tote geschieht nicht. Es ist ereignislos*]'[75] and only in the light of the resurrection is it possible to say that something took place in this death: 'in this death God himself was the event that happened'.[76] That, in both positive and negative senses, gives immense weight to event language, and it could do with some conceptual iconoclasm as taught by Levinas. Levinas's 'face' is a very different sort of concept from event, as he himself is acutely aware. In his hands it has greater potential for resisting 'totality' than more narrative-based notions. What might Jüngel's theology look like if the face of Christ were as integral to it as the death of Christ?

Part of the answer concerns the way death figures in his theology. Death can be seen as one of the great idols: we are tempted to think of it as absolute, as being the ultimate event, as requiring in homage the best energies of individuals and societies who strive for survival, and as dominating our lives in multifarious conscious and unconscious ways. A non-idolatrous self is one that is not dominated by death, and both Jüngel and Levinas resist the sovereignty of death in conceiving the self. Jüngel does it through the death and resurrection of Jesus Christ which is the divine answer to the threat that there could be nothing at all rather than something.[77] Levinas does it through ethics in relation to the infinite, and concepts such as creation, election and the radical passivity of the call to responsibility refuse to permit death to be definitive of humanity. This does not make goodness intrinsic to humanity in the way Jüngel fears – that would be to include it as a category within being. For Levinas, the basic issue is not ontological, why there is anything at all, but ethical, why there is good at all – and goodness is 'otherwise than being'.

This priority (though he has various ways of making it more radical than 'priority' suggests, as in his concepts of diachrony and anarchy[78]) of ethics over ontology means that events of death are inadequate means of differentiation for Levinas: true pluralism requires a differentiation which is utterly and uncompromisingly ethical. Levinas's claim regarding *Otherwise Than Being* is:

75. *God as the Mystery*, p. 363.   76. Ibid.   77. See ibid., pp. 30ff.
78. Cf. *Otherwise Than Being* p. 140 and above note 18.

This book has exposed the signification of subjectivity in the extraordinary everydayness of my responsibility for other men, the extraordinary forgetting of death or the being without regard for death.[79]

Put bluntly, it seems as if Jüngel's ontological notion of death could draw the reply from Levinas: you have not given goodness its proper priority, you are repeating a fundamental error of the Western philosophical and theological traditions, and the consequences of giving a pivotal position to death rather than goodness means that you have compromised ethics. A more nuanced appraisal might be in terms of each thinker's response to Heidegger's conception of 'being towards death'. That is rejected by Jüngel by reference to the death and resurrection of Jesus but he leaves death as a functioning ultimate, the irreducible differentiator even in the being of God. Levinas rejects Heidegger's notion and dethrones death by an infinite which allows that 'extraordinary forgetting of death'. 'Contrary to the ontology of death this self opens an order in which death can be not recognised.'[80] He even sees the relation with God as one which 'survives the "death of God"'.[81]

One of Levinas's most fruitful ideas here is his particularising of death:

The approach, inasmuch as it is a sacrifice, confers a sense on death. In it the absolute singularity of the responsible one encompasses the generality or generalization of death. [En elle la singularité absolue du responsable englobe la généralité ou la généralisation de la mort.][82]

It is arguable that the idolatrous power of death is linked to its faceless generality. It is thought of as a universal power affecting everyone indiscriminately. But Levinas allows one to think of each death differently, to transcend the totality of death face by face. Jüngel's *God as the Mystery of the World* could be seen as encompassing the generality of death in the absolute singularity of the death of Christ, with loving sacrifice intrinsic to that.[83] But for that to be sustained in line with Levinas, Jüngel's notion of love would need to be critically rethought. I will now begin to do this,[84] the ultimate theological aim being to further the suggestion above that in soteriology the face of Christ should be as integral as the event of his death.

79. Ibid., p. 141.
80. Ibid., p. 115. Levinas's many references to death in this crucial chapter on substitution (pp. 108f., 123, 126, 128) can be read as an ethical critique of Heidegger, refusing the centrality of death in relation to substitution.   81. Ibid., p. 123.   82. Ibid., p. 129.
83. See, e.g., Jüngel, *God as the Mystery*, p. 364, but note the negative appraisal of the 'demand' of the law on the following pages.
84. There will be further discussion of love in the next chapter.

3.6 Love

Jüngel says:

> Formally judged, love appeared to us as the event of a still greater
> selflessness within a great, and justifiably very great self-relatedness.
> Judged materially, love was understood as the unity of life and death
> for the sake of life ... We shall proceed on that basis of the full form of
> love ... in which a loving I is loved back by the beloved Thou.[85]

Later, this is further conceptualised in terms of 'a dialectic of being ...
an ontological dialectic defined by an unsurpassable inner rationality ...
the dialectic of being and non-being which reigns in the essence of love'.[86]

It is instructive to ask why Levinas could not have written that and
whether Jüngel has anything to learn from that inability. Even though
the specificity and difference of the other who is loved is stated by
Jüngel,[87] Levinas would suspect that there is here an integrating through
the notions of event, unity and dialectic which amounts to a 'totality' that
loses radical separation and ethical otherness. Event and process seem to
be the comprehensive categories, but to measure them by whether they
do justice to what Levinas intends, for example, by 'the face' or 'the good
beyond history', is to question their adequacy.

Levinas's questioning of this conception of love might ask whether
Jüngel has questioned Hegel critically enough as regards this understanding of self and love. Jüngel's fundamental thrust in *God as the Mystery
of the World* is to follow through Luther's christology with a critical
appropriation of Hegel's philosophy of the death of God. The main criticism he makes of Hegel is in line with Levinas: Hegel fails to differentiate
God and humanity sufficiently.[88] So Jüngel constantly insists that the
event of the death of Jesus Christ involves the differentiation of humanity
from God. Levinas's persistent question is whether, without a more
fundamental rethinking of his categories in ethical terms, this differentiation is adequate. The danger is that both the otherness of God and
the pluralist otherness of human beings are compromised by concepts
which are in need of Levinas's iconoclastic probing.

Levinas would also probe the notion of mutuality in Jüngel's 'full
form of love'. Levinas takes the Hebrew scriptures seriously when, in
divine–human and interhuman relationships, they give a massive pre-
ponderance of concern to justice, righteousness and mercy, the Torah

---

85. *God as the Mystery*, p. 317.   86. Ibid., p. 320.   87. E.g. ibid., p. 318.   88. Ibid., pp. 94ff.

being intrinsic to this. Love needs to subsume all that, and in the New Testament it could be argued that it is indeed always presupposed. Is some of the weight of that presupposition lost in Jüngel's definition of love? Levinas criticises Buber's I–Thou as failing to do justice to the dimension of 'height',[89] the 'curvature' of intersubjective space, and proper separation.

A thoroughly ethical constitution of the self in face of the other and in relation to God challenges Jüngel to relate the 'unity of life and death for the sake of life' to – what? A 'unity of good and evil for the sake of good'? That is just what he does in his own concept of substitution: 'God has then identified himself with the Jesus who made himself sin for us as our substitute.'[90] He even sees Jesus's conception of the law as a 'pure demand' for which he dies.[91] That in context seems very similar to Levinas on obligation to the point of substitution, with the usual proviso about Jüngel's christological particularism. But what Levinas would press throughout is the question of the relation of the ethical to the ontological and the danger of a theology undermining its own explicit statements if it is conceived, as is Jüngel's definition of love, in a way which risks the appropriate otherness being subsumed.[92]

This section on love and the previous section on the non-idolatrous self and God have now led to the sharpest issue between Levinas and Jüngel relevant to this topic, that of substitution.[93]

3.7 Substitution

Substitution has emerged as central to Levinas and Jüngel in different ways and this gives rise to a clash of extremisms between them which it is fruitful to explore.

Levinas's mature thought on substitution has already been introduced as the radicalising of his idea of responsibility. If the notion of hospitality with which I summarised *Totality and Infinity* on the self perhaps suggests something rather comfortable and domestic, then *Otherwise Than Being* explodes such associations with its use of obsession, persecution, expiation, sacrifice, kenosis and hostage.[94] The exposure

---

89. *Totality and Infinity*, p. 155.   90. *God as the Mystery*, p. 367.   91. Ibid., p. 366.
92. See further chapter 4 below on love and language.
93. For a more expansive treatment of Levinas and Jüngel on substitution see my essay, 'On Substitution' in *Facing the Other*.
94. Even less in tune with the later work are the hints of happiness quoted from *Totality and Infinity* at the end of chapter 2 section 2.3 above.

and vulnerability of the responsible self are evoked in extreme terms. Crucial to this is a depth of passivity. 'The self as an expiation is prior to activity and passivity.'[95] Levinas questions himself as to whether he has done justice to this deep passivity of 'the persecuted subjectivity' and tries to do so by invoking the idea of creation, and by again dissociating what he is doing from his idea of theology.[96]

Levinas conceives subjectivity as so radically passive that it is not possible to conceive of a time when it was not under an absolute obligation. It is a self 'obsessed' by something distinct from all that can be represented under the category of 'being'. Levinas reaches for terminology that can express the drastic discontinuity between, on the one hand, this 'election' to responsibility and, on the other hand, 'being'. The discontinuity is so radical that it is wrong to subsume both sides of it under the discourse that most Western philosophy takes as unsurpassable, that of ontology. He suggests his agreement with the judgement that ontological thought has a 'theological context' (sometimes labelled 'ontotheology'). But the idea of creation *ex nihilo* is detached from that context in order to signify a discontinuity ('anarchy' and 'diachrony' are also concepts that try to suggest this discontinuity in relation to notions of beginning, sovereignty and time) that allows for an absolute passivity, what the previous section had called 'the infinite passion of responsibility'.[97]

Levinas goes on to describe the self in terms of this dynamic of responsibility in a passage which brings together many of his key terms – essence, accusation, persecution, passivity, hostage, proximity, alterity, recurrence, substitution, summons, inspiration and incarnation:

> Responsibility for another is not an accident that happens to a subject, but precedes essence in it, has not awaited freedom, in which a commitment to another would have been made. I have not done anything and I have always been under accusation – persecuted. The ipseity, in the passivity without arche characteristic of identity, is a hostage. The word *I* means *here I am*, answering for everything and for everyone . . . This passivity undergone in proximity by the force of an alterity in me is the passivity of a recurrence to oneself which is not the alienation of an identity betrayed. What can it be but a substitution of me for the others? It is, however, not an alienation, because the other in the same is my substitution for the other through responsibility, for which I am summoned as someone irreplaceable. I exist through the other and for the other, but without this being alienation: I am inspired. This inspiration is the psyche. The psyche can signify this

95. *Otherwise Than Being*, p. 116.   96. Ibid., pp. 113ff.   97. Ibid., p. 113.

alterity in the same without alienation, in the form of incarnation, as being-in-one's-skin, having-the-other-in-one's-skin.[98]

Later in the same section Levinas sketches the scope of what depends on this. It amounts to the very quality of daily life:

> It is through the condition of being hostage that there can be in the world pity, compassion, pardon and proximity – even the little there is, even the simple 'After you, sir.'[99]

So that is an extremism of responsibility which yet claims to be pervasively important in ordinary living. Jüngel's christocentric extremism claims a comparable universal relevance. If there is an 'obsessive' concern in his theology it is for justification by faith. Jüngel's treatment of justification draws together fundamental themes of his theology. Justice, righteousness, peace, goodness, ethics and the 'new ordinariness' of life in faith are intrinsic to justification. Substitution is also an essential category for describing it.[100] Creation by God is understood primarily through the event of justification,[101] and creation *ex nihilo* is a critical concept in expressing radical difference and discontinuity between God and humanity.[102] He wants to relativise being and non-being by reference to justification. He also gives a major role to the category of interruption and recognises his own kinship with Levinas in this.[103] The radical passivity of Levinas has an analogy in Jüngel's notion of faith as 'pure passivity'[104] which is the subjective counterpart of the 'new creation' of justification. This, as was noted above, forbids Jüngel to have any 'substantial coinciding of self with self', and like Levinas he works this out partly in critical opposition to modern notions of the 'self-securing ego'.[105]

There is convergence here between Levinas and Jüngel in meeting what I have called the dynamics of idolatry with an appeal to being created, and in linking that intrinsically with being addressed, approached in an asymmetrical way such that the self is defined through what comes through the other. But the tension between the two is all the more extreme because the conceptual similarities make it so obvious. It is most glaring in the following two statements.

Levinas says: 'No one can substitute himself for me who substitutes

98. Ibid., pp. 114f.   99. Ibid., pp. 117f.
100. See especially his essays 'The Mystery of Substitution' and 'The Sacrifice of Jesus Christ as Sacrament and Example' in *Theological Essays II*, edited by John Webster (T. & T. Clark, Edinburgh 1995), pp. 145–90; and *God as the Mystery*, pp. 367f.
101. *God as the Mystery*, p. 218.   102. Ibid., pp. 199–225.
103. *Theological Essays II*, pp. 89ff.   104. *God as the Mystery*, p. 340.
105. Ibid., pp. 169ff.

myself for all'.[106] Jüngel by contrast contests the definition which says that 'I am human, because and to the extent I am there for other people'. He proposes instead:

> ... the humanity of the human ego consists of my allowing someone else to be there for me. Only on the basis of that can I be there for someone else. The main theological point is that *I am human in that I let someone else be there for me.* That can be called trust, and with regard to the 'someone else' who as God has promised himself to us, we must call this trust in God. This is precisely what is meant when we speak of *faith* [original italics].[107]

It might be possible to ameliorate the tension if Jüngel did not affirm one person, Jesus Christ, as the incarnation of God and therefore as the particular one who is there for all others. As it is, the extremism of Levinas seeing 'me' substituting for all confronts Jüngel's extremism of seeing 'Jesus Christ' substituting for all. The fundamental 'witness' of each seems irreconcilably opposed to the other, along the same lines as has already emerged.

I am attempting, in this and succeeding chapters, what must seem impossible: to retain what I see as the heart of both extremes. In other words, I want to argue for a substitutionary self, defined by radical responsibility, and also for Jesus Christ dying for all.[108]

I will begin with Jüngel's resistance to the idea of a substitutionary self. Dietrich Bonhoeffer has a position with many similarities to that of Levinas, linking a radical notion of responsibility with substitution. Jüngel has sympathy with Heinrich Vogel's critique of Bonhoeffer's ethical idea of substitution.[109] Vogel refuses to acknowledge a general anthropological framework of substitution within which Jesus Christ's would make sense, and instead sees the concept of substitution as 'the essence of the uniqueness of Jesus Christ'. Levinas also rejects any general framework – that would be a totalising overview – but, by contrast, allows the conception of substitutionary responsibility as the uniqueness of each ('I am summoned as someone irreplaceable'[110]). Bonhoeffer reaches a similar conclusion about the substitutionary self of each by considering the person of Jesus Christ to whom each self is related. I do not see why this need be rejected by Jüngel.

---

106. *Otherwise Than Being*, p. 126.   107. *God as the Mystery*, p. 180.
108. Here my concern is not to argue against Levinas's Jewish witness so much as for the view that his philosophical position does not necessarily deny the Christian witness.
109. *Theological Essays II*, pp. 153ff.   110. *Otherwise Than Being*, p. 114.

Jüngel has a non-competitive concept of divine and human freedom – in line with the massive insistence on this by twentieth-century theologians such as Barth and Rahner. In addition Jüngel draws on Bonhoeffer for his notion of the worldly non-necessity of God.[111] The latter is what allows Bonhoeffer to match a non-competitive notion of human freedom with a non-competitive notion of human substitutionary responsibility. The logic of the full humanity of Jesus Christ is by Bonhoeffer taken to the heart of ordinary life in a way which should be acceptable within Jüngel's theology. However, it may be that the deepest reason for Jüngel's resistance to the substitutionary self is to do with what I argued above to be his inadequate relating of ethics to death, and so to accept the critique of him on that point would further strengthen the present case. Jüngel fears for the proper differentiation between humanity and God if the human self is substitutionary in constitution; but, in both Levinas's and Bonhoeffer's conceptions, differentiation and otherness are intrinsic to responsibility. Bonhoeffer does not allow death to play a role such as that in Jüngel: he is far closer to Levinas in having a pervasively ethical idea of transcendence. Overall Bonhoeffer relates ethics, selfhood and Jesus Christ in a way that is more in harmony with Levinas's philosophy than is Jüngel's theology.[112]

What of Levinas's ban on anyone substituting themselves for me? His fear is clear: it is of irresponsibility, of shifting obligation from me to another and so corrupting the very 'ipseity' of the substitionary self. For Levinas it is to do with 'me', with my unique 'election', and the asymmetry in relations between me and others.[113] I am responsible for all, but I cannot generalise this or 'require substitution and sacrifice' from others.[114] There is no comparison of myself with others: I am uniquely chosen, 'overwhelmed by the other in proximity'.[115] What if I recognise that someone has, in Levinas's sense, substituted himself or herself for me? What is the significance of someone taking greater responsibility for me? There is a sense in which there is little differentiation among 'others' in Levinas. Robert Gibbs says that Levinas's 'other' is 'strangely undetermined, is almost formal, in its concreteness. This face is anyone we meet, is any other, but it is archetypically a poor person, one who is hungry.'[116] His idea of uniqueness is primarily that of my responsibility in substitution. Yet Gibbs notes that occasionally Levinas also 'grants a

---

111. *God as the Mystery*, pp. 57ff.   112. For more on Bonhoeffer see chapter 10 below.
113. *Otherwise Than Being*, pp. 126f.   114. Ibid.   115. Ibid.
116. *Correlations in Rosenzweig and Levinas*, p. 183.

parallel uniqueness to the other', as in an essay in *Entre Nous*:[117] 'The relation goes to the unassimilable, incomparable, other; to the irreducible other; to the unique other. Only the unique is absolutely other. But the uniqueness of the unique [*l'unicité de l'unique*], that is the uniqueness of the beloved.' Previously Gibbs remarked about Levinas's own teacher: 'Levinas's account of Shushani's influence is so extreme that one might well ascribe to him the source of Levinas's goal of translation, and even of the lived experience of the face.'[118]

The hungry other; the particular beloved; the particular teacher: to begin to differentiate like this helps in conceiving both how one might be extravagantly grateful before one particular face, as Jüngel is, while yet maintaining the witness to substitutionary responsibility, as Levinas does. Gratitude for what has been done, indeed, is for Jüngel the basic movement of the self in faith, and he sees it as energising rather than absolving from responsibility. A general idea of someone taking responsibility for me might encourage me to be irresponsible, but to have before me always the face of Jesus Christ in faith – need that be so?

3.8 Conclusion

The previous chapter discussed Levinas's conception of a hospitable self – enjoying, responsible and desiring. That is a self radically oriented towards others and it is clearly crucial how that orientation is understood and how it can flourish or become disoriented. This chapter has explored and brought into dialogue two ways of conceiving how it can be characterised in the light of radical threats to its well-being. I have described those threats as idolatries that engage the dynamics of self in their compulsions and have the effect of disrupting good other-relatedness.

Levinas analyses in drastic terms[119] the various forms of 'totality' which grip our world and are inimical to relationships of radical responsibility. But he recognises that idolatry's most insidious characteristic is that it is most powerful when it corrupts what is best. So he directs his main efforts against his own philosophy's tendencies to reify its

117. *Entre Nous: Essais sur le penser à l'autre* (Bernard Grasset, Paris 1991), p. 214.
118. *Correlations in Rosenzweig and Levinas*, p. 170.
119. It is not a 'balanced' account any more than is his description of responsibility. The next chapter will draw into the dialogue that most balanced of philosophers, Paul Ricoeur, who will attempt to mediate between the 'paroxysm' of Levinas and less extreme philosophers.

'saying' into a 'said' which can then be misused as a representation that turns the 'other' into the 'same' and 'contaminates God with being'. A side-effect of his rigorous attention to the capacity of his philosophical discourse for subverting and betraying its witness to the other and to 'the glory of the infinite' is his dismissal of theology. It is, however, a blanket rejection which seems to depend on stereotypes rather than on respectful listening to any particular theologian. So I have hosted a dialogue between him and Jüngel, the opening move of which was to show how Jüngel at least fails to fit the stereotypes.

Jüngel's non-idolatrous self resists what Levinas would call the 'totality' of any overarching concept of 'being' through its trust in a God who created being out of nothing and who is in a free, non-necessary and more than necessary relationship with the world. That freedom is exercised in being responsible for the world to the point of being crucified in Jesus Christ. This encounters hearers in 'the word of the cross', an event which transforms the self who trusts in it. It indicates a reality beyond the alternative of presence and absence, mediating a 'presence in absence' which exposes and resists the would-be overwhelming presences and powers of idols. The God to whom the word of the cross testifies is a living mystery, constantly inspiring fresh speech, thought and action. The doctrine of the Trinity is the least inadequate conceptualising of this God who is the self-differentiating 'unity of life and death in favour of life'. It is a doctrine which, among other roles, acts as a critique of idolatries, including those produced by sophisticated modern metaphysicians in their discussions of 'God'. It also strongly differentiates between God and humanity, as is appropriate for a theology which wishes to affirm both the transcendence of God and the incarnation of 'God on the cross as our neighbour'.

Faith in this God secures the self in trust in a way which liberates it from the compulsion to find other good or bad absolutes or inappropriate forms of certainty. The self is 'taken along' in vulnerable faith, defined by the one by whom it is addressed. Its radical passivity in being loved by the God who is love turns into the active gratitude which loves God and fellow human beings in return.

The encounter of Levinas and Jüngel involved each questioning the other. The main concern with Levinas was to question whether the exclusion of Jüngel's theology and the rejection of Jüngel's Christian anti-idolatry were necessary within his philosophy. In other words, while of course recognising major unresolved issues, is it possible to envisage a Levinassian Christian theology? The questioning of Jüngel was more substantial, pressing an ethical critique of his ontology and theology, and finding especially problematic the role which death plays in both.

The last section brought the dialogue to a head. Each has a substitutionary self in the pivotal position of his thought: Jüngel's is Jesus Christ while Levinas's is each responsible 'I'. They converge in their resistance to the dynamics of idolatry, but are also in obvious tension. My constructive proposal, mediated by Bonhoeffer, is to affirm, in non-competitive relationship, both the substitutionary self in radical responsibility and the substitutionary life, death and resurrection of Jesus Christ.

That proposal now requires development more positively beyond resistance to idolatries. In particular the previous chapter's description and questioning of Levinas's ideas of enjoyment and desire need to be taken up again in the context of the self relating to God in worship.

4

Language, love and
testimony: a worshipping self

Living without idols inevitably raises the question of positive worship. This chapter develops an initial understanding of a worshipping
self, a pivotal concept for subsequent chapters.[1]

I begin by continuing the dialogue between Levinas and Jüngel, suggesting how Levinas's philosophy of responsibility might be united with
Jüngel's theology of joy. Two new concepts in particular are proposed: in
relation to language there is the analogy of joyful obligation; in relation
to love there is the unity of joy and substitutionary responsibility for the
sake of joy. They bring us to the verge of worship, but neither Levinas nor
Jüngel take us far enough in conceiving a worshipping self. So another
major dialogue partner, Paul Ricoeur, is introduced. His work focusses
on the self in a way which neither of the others do; his long-term engagement with Levinas and his commendation of Jüngel's theology allow him
to offer a concept of self which might do justice to both; and his tentative
explorations in theology encourage a more thorough theological
development of his thought. In line with my concerns, I draw out two
interrelated themes from his major philosophical work on the self: the
centrality of attestation, testimony or witness; and the critical appropriation of Levinas's philosophy. Ricoeur also throws out the challenge to
attempt a theological version of his notion of self, recapitulating and
intensifying its concepts in a biblically inspired way. I take up that chal-

1. For a fuller theological treatment of worship than is given at any point in the present
work, see Daniel W. Hardy and David F. Ford, *Jubilate. Theology in Praise* (Darton, Longman
and Todd, London 1984; US edition: *Praising and Knowing God*, Westminster Press,
Philadelphia 1985). Hardy has developed that theology further in *God's Ways with the World*
(T.&T. Clark, Edinburgh 1996), and his theology as exemplified in those essays, papers and
sermons has been an important accompaniment to the present study. On worship see
especially chapter 2, 'The Foundation of Cognition and Ethics in Worship', and on
language see chapter 4, 'The Trinity in Language'.

lenge, and the result is a self being transformed in worship before 'the glory of God in the face of Christ'.

4.1 Levinas and Jüngel: an analogy of joyful obligation

In the previous chapter the discussion of Levinas and Jüngel culminated in a substitutionary self which had at its core a notion of radical responsibility but also pointed up the deep differences between the two. In particular Jüngel's definition of love was criticised with the help of Levinas. I now want to open a further dimension by asking a question of Levinas: in his conception of the 'I' separate in enjoyment, vulnerable and suffering in substitution, with the face of the other calling the self from separation to limitless responsibility, what happens if one introduces a conception of joy as extreme as the conception of responsibility?

In *Totality and Infinity* a discussion of Descartes leads to one of Levinas's most eloquent affirmations of God in terms of personal relation with an other who is a 'Majesty approached as a face' and evokes 'admiration, adoration, and joy'.[2] In *Otherwise Than Being* the culminating statement about the exorbitant overflow of the caress of love[3] plays a variation on the same theme, and both works have other hints of joy.[4] But it bears no comparison with the radicality of responsibility. Enjoyment is fundamental to the separated, 'atheist' self,[5] but there is no transformation of this in ethical response to the other. Might it be that that rich conception of enjoyment could, in being opened up to responsibility by the appeal of the other, be transformed into joy in the other?

This need not take away at all from the reality of substitution at the heart of the self. It rather means that the substituting self might, through that very 'passivity', be opened up also to a joy that is as infinite as the responsibility. The 'trace' found in the face of the other might be of an infinite that 'obsesses' me not only with responsibility but with joy too. This in turn would change our notion of the content of the imperative to be responsible. It might then accommodate the biblical command to rejoice. Levinas seems so aware of the manifold misinterpretations and misuses of thoughts of joy that he does not develop them. Or perhaps his

---

2. Levinas, *Totality and Infinity*, pp. 211f.   3. *Otherwise Than Being*, p. 184.
4. Occasionally explicit as in mentioning aspiration to 'the religious order where the recognition of the individual concerns him in his singularity, an order of joy [*ordre de la joie*] which is neither cessation nor antithesis of pain, nor flight before it . . .' (*Totality and Infinity*, p. 242), but more often indicated in other ways: so pardon is 'a surplus of happiness, the strange happiness of reconciliation' (ibid., p. 283); and one can be thankful for the very fact of finding oneself able to thank (*Otherwise Than Being*, p. 10).   5. See above, p. 36.

prophetic message would be diluted if he were to try to testify to everything.

Jüngel might suggest a theological interpretation too. Jüngel's appreciation of joy goes deep. It is of course linked with his faith in the resurrection of Jesus Christ, but his basic theological analysis of it rings true with Jewish traditions of rejoicing in God too. It goes to the root of his conception of the self and of faith:

> The most original attitude of one ego toward another person, an attitude called forth by that other one, completely uncoerced and realised gladly, is *joy*. For that reason, one can say 'joy in God' instead of 'faith'. For faith permits God to be that one who in and of himself *is for us* and *takes us unto himself* so that we do not *want to be* what we are without him. The self-definition for which man is determined in faith can thus be only the immediacy of a defined joy [original italics].[6]

Jüngel's analysis of joy then links it with the fundamental concept of God as 'more than necessary'. Earlier he had summarised what he called 'anthropological and theological truth of the contemporary discovery of the nonnecessity of God' as follows:

(a) Human beings and the world are interesting for their own sake.
(b) Even more so, God is interesting for his own sake.
(c) God makes human beings, who are interesting for their own sake, interesting in a new way.[7]

The first statement (a) is in line with Levinas's concept of the separation of the 'atheist self'.

The second (b), however, is one of the points of greatest tension between Jüngel and Levinas, as the latter's rigorously ethical, practical concept of the infinite rules out what is dismissed as speculation or mythology or objectification or direct comprehension of God.

The third (c) has its parallel in such ideas of Levinas as the call to infinite responsibility and the transformation of the separated self by response to the trace of the infinite in the face of the other. But the quality of newness in the third is critically dependent on the content of the second. It is therefore of vital importance that when Jüngel talks of joy he goes on to connect it with the possibility of rejoicing in God for God's own sake, in the process employing his key concept of the 'more than necessary':

> Joy in God would then be the origin, the source, of the true thought of God, to the extent that joy is that 'existential' in which God is thinkable *for the sake of his own self.* For joy is always joy in something

---

6. *God as the Mystery*, p. 192.   7. Ibid., p. 34 (my adaptation).

for its own sake. Thus, it is indeed the real origin of thought – over against the disquieting *thaumazein* [wonder] at the madness of existence. But regardless of that, whoever does not think God *for his own sake* has not yet begun to think *God* at all. To think God without joy in God is a self-contradiction which must lead even the most logical proof of God to absurdity. All attempts to prove the necessity of God are therefore so distressing as well as paradoxical, because they can arrive at God only at the end of the process and thus can know him only as the 'God at the end'. They cannot *begin* with God, because they do not begin with God for his own sake. But if God is thought for his own sake, on the basis of a joy summoned forth by God himself, then the very act of thinking God is the demonstration of the fact that God is *more than necessary* [original italics].[8]

Jüngel immediately goes on to relate this to Jesus Christ, but one could (and many Jewish thinkers have) read the Psalms, for example, in such a way. Levinas seems so bound negatively by his reaction against 'ontotheology' and its totalising ontology that the only alternative he can confidently pursue is one which is severely practical. He is also responding to the horror of the Shoah. *Otherwise Than Being* is dedicated

To the memory of those who were closest among the six million assassinated by the National Socialists, and of the millions on millions of all confessions and all nations, victims of the same hatred of the other man, the same anti-semitism.

In the face of such considerations it is no light matter to put the case for joy. But the glimpses of it already in Levinas, its presence in one of the primary influences on his thought, Franz Rosenzweig's *The Star of Redemption*,[9] together with the fundamental place that its kindred, enjoyment, has in his account of the constitution of the self, all suggest that there is a possibility here, encouraged by Jüngel, of 'thinking the unthought' in Levinas. It need by no means be in conflict with substitutionary responsibility or with non-totalitarian reason and representation; and it might well be a prophetic witness at least as disturbing and counter-cultural as Levinas's to responsibility.

Is it possible to think together Levinas's responsibility and Jüngel's joy? A critical matter is that of language, because Jüngel's joy in God is inseparable from speaking of and to God, just as Levinas's responsibility is inseparable from 'saying' and witness.

Chapter 4 of *God as the Mystery of the World*, 'On the Speakability of God

---

8. Ibid., pp. 192–3.
9. University of Notre Dame Press, Notre Dame, London 1985.

[*Zur Sagbarkeit Gottes*]', is a *tour de force* of contemporary theological argument about language and God. Its aim is a concept of responsible talk about God which corresponds to God by 'letting him come', letting God be present through human speech.[10] There is a critique of classical theology's insistence on the ineffability, incomprehensibility and inexpressibility of God. At the heart of that tradition he finds the principle that 'God is always greater', which in relation to analogy means that for all the similarity between God and what we say about God there is always an even greater dissimilarity. The mystery of God means that, however near we approach, the distance from the essence of God is even greater. Jüngel challenges this concept of inaccessible mystery with his New Testament understanding of a mystery which is inherently an event of language,[11] which 'must be *said* at all costs and which may under no circumstances be kept silent . . . The public realm belongs . . . to the essence of the mystery.'[12] The mystery allows itself to be known as a mystery. There is a critique of the role which silence has played in much theology. Jüngel then sets out to reconceive analogical talk of God, moving through a historical discussion to his positive proposal, an 'analogy of advent'.[13] The decisive statement about analogy is:

> In that in Evangelical speech God comes close to men, he carries out his divinity's own humanity, in order to make concrete the difference between his divinity's own humanity and the humanity of man. The difference between God and man, which is constitutive of the essence of the Christian faith, is thus not the difference of a still greater dissimilarity, but rather, conversely, the difference of a still greater dissimilarity between God and man in the midst of a great similarity.[14]

Put more existentially, 'analogy is the addressing event of gripping freedom'.[15] The primary linguistic form is that of parable, with Jesus as the parable of God. This hermeneutical perception about the analogy of

---

10. *God as the Mystery*, pp. 226ff. It is a form of presence that does justice to absence – cf. the later definition of revelation as 'the becoming present of an absent one as absent [*Offenbarung als Anwesendwerden eines Abwesenden als Abwesenden ist*]', ibid., p. 349. Cf. above chapter 3, pp. 54ff.
11. Jüngel, *God as the Mystery*, pp. 248ff. Cf. as a definition of this language event p. 289.
12. Ibid., p. 250.
13. Ibid., p. 285: 'One must understand analogy as an event which allows the One (x) *to come* to the Other (a) with the help of the relationship of a further Other (b) to even one more Other (c). The issue is an *analogy of advent*, which expresses God's arrival among men as a definitive event . . . The God who comes to the world (x—a) makes use of the obvious in this world in such a way that he proves himself to be that which is even more obvious over against it. It is all too obvious that one will give everything for the value of the treasure buried in the field in order to have that greater value.'   14. Ibid., p. 288.
15. Ibid., p. 292. (*Die Analogie ist das ansprechende Ereignis fesselnder Freiheit.*)

advent has its ontological counterpart in the being of God as love, which 'realises itself *in the midst of such great self-relatedness as still greater selflessness*' (original italics).[16]

So the dynamics of language in relation to God are linked to love and both are understood in christological and trinitarian terms. Here too Jüngel has maintained his primary difference from Levinas, whose talk of God likewise pivots around a central focus, ethics between people. And here too it is necessary to ask how Jüngel comes through Levinas's critique in terms of ethical otherness.

That can be approached, as before,[17] by asking why Levinas would not be likely to produce such a formula. He would be suspicious of it as implying a dialectical conception in which the primacy of similarity would confirm his doubt about whether it does justice to God's 'transcendence to the point of absence'.[18] A Levinassian alternative might be an 'analogy of obligation', although he would never call it an analogy – that is only conceivable in the light of Jüngel's reformulation of the term. What I call an analogy of obligation in Levinas concerns responsibility which 'increases infinitely, living infinity, an obligation more and more strict in the measure that obedience progresses and the distance to be crossed untraversable in the measure that one approaches'.[19] Here, in the midst of the great and always untraversable dissimilarity there is infinitely expanding obligation.

Levinas is just as hostile as Jüngel to what they both see as the traditional theological concept of analogy leading to a negative, apophatic theology, but he does not entertain Jüngel's singular event of the incarnation through which to construct an alternative. Faith in the event of incarnation (interpreted through the death and resurrection of Jesus Christ) is for Jüngel the source of confidence in the capacitating of our language ever anew in parabolic forms. 'Similarity' for him means the inexhaustible expressibility of the mystery of this event, God genuinely being offered in human expression. Levinas, for all his more agonistic and self-deconstructing language and his refusal to talk of similarity, yet pivots his philosophy around a proximity, a coming near, an approach which is also inexhaustibly fruitful.[20]

---

16. Ibid., p. 298.   17. See above, chapter 3, p. 64.   18. 'God and Philosophy', p. 179.
19. *Otherwise Than Being*, p. 142.
20. Jüngel does not correlate 'sameness' with an ontology of totality, and in this is in line with Ricoeur (see below p. 95), who takes seriously Levinas's ethics but does not see them ruling out an ontology of self. For Jüngel the 'similarity' has an 'advent' at its heart (hence the 'analogy of advent'), just as for Ricoeur there is analogical differentiation in the self which allows him to speak of 'oneself *as* another'.

Might there be yet another alternative? My concern is to offer a Christian development of Jüngel which learns from Levinas. Might an analogy of joyful obligation be conceivable? This would develop Jüngel's 'advent' in terms of facing, substitutionary responsibility and joy. In all the great difference between God and humanity there would be even greater joy in and responsibility towards the other. This would be God's joy and responsibility capacitating that of humanity. It might even lead to a more sympathetic assessment than Jüngel's of traditional theological language's principle that 'God is always greater'. That would be placed in its primary context of the language of worship. Its concept of 'even greater dissimilarity' would be glossed as 'even greater affirmation and celebration of otherness', which gives a more appropriate content to metaphors of 'distance'. This will take some working out, but promises to bring together in a Christian form Levinas's concerns for otherness with Jüngel's for some correspondence of our language to God.

It might even be that the practices of worship could contribute to opening up further conceptions of the analogical use of language in relation to God. One of the perennial features of worship is the complex and changing relation between definiteness (as in scripture, liturgical forms, preaching and teaching doctrine, music, community structures and so on) and innovation or improvisation.[21] There are considerable possibilities for understanding the traditional notions of similarity and dissimilarity in analogical language through thinking about definiteness and improvisation. Each term encourages exploration of the varieties of 'otherness'. Together they also suggest something of the pattern of intensive engagement with the irreducibly particular (Jüngel's word of the cross; Levinas's face or 'saying' of the other) combined with wide-ranging exploration of its implications and applications. Their musical resonances are also helpful in correcting any overemphasis on visual and spatial language. The resulting version of the analogy of advent might affirm that, for all the great definiteness of joy and responsibility in testimony before the God who comes, there is even greater potential for improvisation in praising and loving.[22]

4.2 Love and joy

Language is only part of this and such a view of analogy would have further consequences for Jüngel's concept of love, which the previous

21. For more on this see chapter 6 below on the eucharist, especially the concept of 'non-identical repetition'.   22. This will be taken up again below in chapters 5 and 6.

chapter has already subjected to critique. How might that concept look if improvised upon along these lines? Jüngel's formal definition defined it as 'the event of a still greater selflessness within a great, and justifiably very great self-relatedness'.[23] I have already questioned his dedication to 'event' terminology, and that can be carried further now in relation to the constriction of reference to the richness of love if the dominant formal category for it is that of event. Jüngel's way of concentrating on the word of the cross and identifying that primarily as an event leads him to abstract and project this category too easily.

Nor is the dialectic of selflessness and self-relatedness adequate. It is linked to the conception of the 'full form of love' as a loving I being loved back by the beloved thou. This must not be contradicted, but is it adequately 'full'? Jüngel's own concept of joy might urge him towards some concept of community as the full (and certainly the biblical) form. Joy is perhaps not best seen in terms of selflessness and self-relatedness (though they would be part of the definition), nor in the quantitative language of comparative 'greatness'. Something further is needed which might do justice to the Psalms, to the eucharist, to the arts, to feasting and dancing, and to Dante's *Paradiso*; but perhaps one should refrain from a formal definition.

Jüngel's material definition quoted above in chapter 3 was that love is 'the unity of life and death for the sake of life'.[24] On this one might improvise: love is the unity of joy and substitutionary responsibility for the sake of joy. That has some advantages. It takes account of the Levinassian points made in chapter 3 about the relationship of ontology to ethics and the danger of giving death the role that Jüngel does. It is, in a broad sense, an ethical formulation which can take adequate account of Jüngel's 'life and death'. It refuses to allow death to be the primary differentiator while allowing fully for 'willing victimhood' as a responsible vocation. It is not exclusively event-centred; nor is it in 'I–thou' form – this is a love which allows for the feasting of friends and may find its exemplary embodiment in eucharistic worship. That is, of course, very far from anything Levinas concludes, but he makes a critical contribution to it.

Levinas is himself in turn questioned by this thought. Indeed, having followed Levinas's philosophy through enjoyment, responsibility, desire and the critique of idolatries, the most searching question in relation to this book's theme can now be put to him: Can idolatries be wisely rejected

---

23. Cf. above p. 64.   24. Cf. above p. 64.

if one does not also run the risks of positive worship?[25] Is there not an appropriate retrieval of worship which might accompany this devastating hermeneutic of suspicion? Levinas sympathises with Kant's ethical belittling of worship and is deeply sensitive to the multifarious critiques that can be applied to such practices as the praise, lamentation, thanks, confession, intercession and petition addressed to God in the Psalms. He relentlessly rules out ways in which the ethical purity of responsibility might be compromised or its rigour ameliorated. His concept of prayer in line with his idea of substitution is that of 'Prayer without Demand',[26] and it is here that Levinas's giving exclusively ethical content to theological language is most extreme. He will not even call God 'You': only 'He [Il]' is permitted, and only then on the most severe conditions.

Jüngel notes how Karl Barth was startled by his own conclusion that invocation of God, especially in petition, is the ground of Christian ethics.[27] For Jüngel, as for Barth, God's embracing command is to call on God. Jüngel's ethic is therefore one of commanded prayer. Because this is done in faith, to which joy is intrinsic, it is inextricable from thanks and praise. The logic of excess in relation to the infinite is for Levinas embodied only in responsibility. But might there be another way of maintaining the purity and overflow of responsibility through an excess whose primary dynamic is that of worship? This is the implication of my reformulation of Jüngel's definition of love as the unity of joy and substitutionary responsibility for the sake of joy. The celebratory excess of non-necessary joy in God is part of the 'ecology' of responsibility before God.

That is a very exposed position, not least before the suspicions of Levinas. It deserves in its own way the designation of testimony to the glory of the infinite, given by Levinas to his substitutionary 'saying' which is marked by extreme vulnerability. There might even be a certain defensive security in Levinas's endless enigmatic ambiguity and 'unsaying', especially among sophisticated atheists. Levinas challenges them in many ways, but the joyful witness of worship is not at stake as an issue for either party. I am arguing that responsibility before the other needs to do justice to joy, and may not rule out full worship in faith.

As regards the self, the dialogue between Levinas and Jüngel has now reached a point where another partner is helpful in order to advance the

---

25. This is a question I discuss at the end of my paper 'On Substitution' in *Facing the Other*, on which I draw here without further acknowledgement.
26. See *The Levinas Reader*, chapter 14.   27. *Theological Essays II*, pp. 154ff.

idea of a worshipping self. Levinas has contributed his concepts of enjoyment, responsibility, desire and (in my interpretation) non-idolatry. Jüngel has offered a Christian theological discourse that can respond to Levinas's dismissal of theology, and has done so through rethinking such matters as address, analogy, the location of God, God as Trinity, Jesus Christ, substitution, justification by faith, and joy. What is required is a concept of the worshipping self that can do justice to what I have affirmed in both thinkers, Levinas's prophetic philosophy of responsibility and Jüngel's joyfully risking theology.

4.3 Ricoeur on testimony in Levinas

The third partner is Paul Ricoeur. He was a friend and dialogue partner of Levinas over a long period and has engaged deeply with his thought, while he has also commended the theology of Eberhard Jüngel as one which accords with his philosophy of the self.[28] He parallels Levinas in important ways: he has had a long engagement with the Hebraic as well as the Hellenic traditions; he has grappled with modern and postmodern forms of atheism; he has devoted a great deal of energy to thinking about the self in the contemporary world and has taken into account many of the main contributions to the topic as discussed in Western academic life; and he has related his philosophy to the terrible events of the twentieth century. Unlike Levinas, his career has spanned Europe and America and he has engaged not only with continental European philosophy but also with the largely Anglo-American analytical philosophy. 'Hermeneutical' is the most satisfactory overall adjective for Ricoeur's type of philosophy, and he has been thoroughly interdisciplinary, having contributed to semiotics, structuralism, literary criticism, historiography, political theory, the social sciences and psychoanalysis. He also has a long history of writing in relation to biblical interpretation and Christian theology.[29]

Ricoeur's patient, rational elucidation of many disciplines in a tone of

---

28. Paul Ricoeur, *Oneself As Another* (University of Chicago Press, Chicago and London 1992), p. 25.

29. Many of the most important of his writings on religion are gathered in *Figuring the Sacred. Religion, Narrative, and Imagination* (Fortress Press, Minneapolis 1995). For an appropriation of Ricoeur's thought which is perceptive both philosophically and theologically, and which also engages sensitively with the secondary literature, see James Fodor, *Christian Hermeneutics. Paul Ricoeur and the Refiguring of Theology* (Clarendon Press, Oxford 1995). My discussion complements that in three main ways: by bringing Ricoeur into dialogue with different partners; by concentrating on *Oneself As Another* which receives little attention from Fodor; and by attempting to do constructive theology in contrast to Fodor's largely methodological and programmatic interests.

respectful dialogue is alert to discontinuity, hiatus, aporia, impasse and the frequent need for detours in order to do justice to the diverse pluralism of reality and its discourses. He shares Levinas's interest in otherness, but his style of affirming and exploring it uses many of the methods and sources which Levinas suspects of being irretrievably compromised by a record of suppressing or absorbing the other. Of special importance to the present discussion, he has engaged explicitly with Levinas on the topics of testimony[30] and the self.[31]

Testimony is an appropriate place to begin in continuity with the previous discussion and as a transition to the worshipping self. Jüngel, Levinas and Ricoeur all, in various ways, make testimony a constitutive dimension of selfhood, and it also pervades Christian worship.

In his 1989 essay 'Emmanuel Levinas: Thinker of Testimony'[32] Ricoeur discusses Levinas on testimony in relation to Heidegger and to Jean Nabert in his posthumous *Le Désir de Dieu*. Ricoeur is broadly in agreement with Levinas's ethical critique of Heidegger. Nabert is likewise seen to make an 'ethical break'[33] in relation to Heidegger's ontology, but he also makes a contribution to Ricoeur's critique of Levinas. Nabert suggests a 'métaphysique du témoignage et herméneutique de l'absolu' which is aimed at a critique of false absolutes or false divine names, together with a reception of 'the testimony of certain acts, certain lives, that, despite their radical contingency, their plain historicity, speak in the name of the absolute'.[34] Ricoeur summarises and comments:

> Testimonies are real events whose depths no reflection can plumb. Testimony even divides itself, outside of reflection. There is first the testimony rendered by real acts of devotion up to death. Next, there is the testimony rendered to this testimony by witnesses to its witnesses ... A dialogic structure of testimony is indicated here between testimony as act and testimony as narrative.[35]

This leads further into 'internal testimony, testimony of the third degree' which is akin to Levinas's passivity of being summoned. In addition, the epistemological status of testimony is inseparable from trust:

> Here to believe is to trust. With testimony, it seems to me, the problematic of truth coincides with that of veracity. It is in this sense that testimony is related to and dependent upon a hermeneutics: the believing confidence of a second-order testimony in the first, absolute

---

30. In *Figuring the Sacred*, chapter 6.   31. In *Oneself As Another*, seventh and tenth Studies.
32. *Figuring the Sacred*, chapter 6, pp. 108–26.   33. Ibid., p. 114.
34. Ibid., pp. 115–16. Cf. below chapters 9 and 10 on 'saints'.
35. *Figuring the Sacred*, pp. 116–17.

testimony does not coincide with deductive knowledge or with empirical proof. It stems from the categories of understanding and interpretation. Do we not link up here with Levinas's critique of intentionality and representation?[36]

Yet, for all the proximity of Nabert to Levinas in conjoining ethics and the hermeneutics of testimony, Nabert keeps the connection between his hermeneutics and a philosophy of reflection. Ricoeur sympathises with this and it leads him into his main variation on Levinas with regard both to testimony and to the self. He describes Levinas's strategies for breaking with other philosophies of self, including notions of anarchy, anachrony and unsaying[37] and the use of excessive, hyperbolic, destabilising expressions such as obsession and hostage.[38] His question about these strategies is whether they amount to overkill. He welcomes Levinas's rejection, in the name of the responsible subject not absorbed in being, of three concepts of self – 'the subject absorbed in being', 'the subject at the service of the system' and 'the subject as a speaking that is absorbed in the said';[39] but the question he pushes is about the 'who', the self, required by such responsibility. 'The self is not the ego. Yet it remains that the place of the self is inexpugnable.'[40]

In a string of phrases from Levinas, notably the description of the self as summoned yet irreplaceable, he finds a toehold for his own major distinction between identity as *idem* and identity as *ipse* that is developed in *Oneself As Another*.[41] He concludes by asking: 'is it forbidden to a reader, who is a friend of both Nabert and Levinas, to puzzle over a philosophy where the attestation of self and the glory of the absolute would be co-originary? Does not the testimony rendered by other actions, other lives, reciprocal to the divestment of the ego, speak *in another way* about what testimony, according to Levinas, unsays?'[42]

In the light of that essay one reading of *Oneself As Another* is as a conception of the self which pivots around the notion of testimony and is a crit-

---

36. Ibid., p. 118.   37. These have been introduced by me in chapter 3 above.
38. Ricoeur describes how in Levinas the 'one for the other' of the assignation of responsibility occupies the place of manifestation in Heidegger's ontology. 'The notion of substitution consecrates the break with the Heideggerian version of intentionality as uncovering, *Oneself As Another*, unconcealment' (*Figuring the Sacred*, p. 119). But in his notion of testimony, which he discusses after substitution in *Otherwise Than Being*, Levinas is more concerned with breaking with that reflexive philosophy which affirms 'the primacy of consciousness as master of meaning and of itself' (ibid., p. 121).
39. *Oneself As Another*, p. 123.   40. Ibid., p. 125.   41. See section 4.5 below.
42. *Oneself As Another*, p. 126. I will answer this affirmatively in focussing below in chapters 7–10 on the interpretation of the testimony of and to lives and actions as a contribution to my theology of self and salvation.

ical variation on Levinas. To discuss the book from that angle is important for developing the conception of self that I am suggesting and also
helpful in situating the discussion in a broader philosophical and interdisciplinary context.

4.4 Philosophy and biblical faith: intensification and transformation

At the end of the Introduction to *Oneself As Another* Ricoeur discusses the
relation of the book to Christian theology and biblical faith. He is aiming
at a philosophy that is neither foundational nor 'cryptotheological' but is
open to biblical faith; and he also guards against a biblical faith that is
'cryptophilosophical', 'taking over the henceforth vacant role of ultimate
foundation'.[43] Jüngel is mentioned with approval as proposing 'a faith
that knows itself to be without guarantee'.[44] In terms of chapter 3 above,
Ricoeur's rejection of claims to ultimate foundations while affirming
God might be seen as a way of rejecting idolatries. The distinction and
relationship between philosophy and theology outlined is one that I too
am attempting to put into practice.[45] There are two interwoven lines
suggested by Ricoeur which I wish especially to pursue.

One is that 'Biblical agapé belongs to an economy of the gift, possess-
ing a metaethical character' for which 'love is tied to the "naming of
God"'.[46] This indicates the importance of worship, in which the abundance of God is celebrated in addressing God by name.

The second is what this implies for the self. Hedging it around with
caution, Ricoeur conditionally wonders (but the phrase 'perhaps most of
all' leads me to interpret it as a challenge worth taking up):

> Finally – and perhaps most of all – if, under the title of 'mandated self'
> and 'respondent', the determinations of the self in this work are found
> to be intensified and transformed by the recapitulation that biblical
> faith proposes . . .[47]

What would it be to intensify, transform and, where appropriate,
modify the concept of self that Ricoeur offers? I will begin to answer that
in this chapter. The key notion of 'a worshipping self' will be explored by
moving through the studies of *Oneself As Another*, and then, with the help

---

43. *Oneself As Another*, p. 25.   44. Ibid.
45. It is not my purpose to have a full-scale discussion of this – chapter 3 is the nearest I
come to that. I am more concerned to get the practice right, in the sense of being
philosophically sure-footed while travelling a theological journey.
46. *Oneself As Another*, p. 25.   47. Ibid.

of some of Ricoeur's more theological writings, recapitulating his key concepts with reference to a Christian, biblically oriented theology.

The 'biblical faith' which is at issue here is primarily that of the Psalms (seen as a distillation of all biblical genres),[48] of Paul in his letters to the Romans and Corinthians, of the letter to the Ephesians,[49] of the eucharist,[50] of the Gospels,[51] and of Thérèse of Lisieux[52] and Dietrich Bonhoeffer,[53] and so awaits later chapters for further specification.[54]

Ricoeur in the Introduction to *Oneself As Another* situates his concept of self at equal distance from philosophies of the subject (Descartes, Kant, Fichte, Husserl) and from 'the shattered cogito' of Nietzsche. In philosophies of the subject he resists tendencies to posit the subject immediately (without reflexive mediation through signs, narratives, other people, and other 'detours'), and he challenges definitions of the self which formulate it primarily in the first person as 'I' (whether an empirical or transcendental ego, posited absolutely or relatively).[55] He questions whether such philosophies can do justice 'to the person who speaks, to the I–you of interlocution, to the identity of a historical person, to the self of responsibility'.[56] Nietzsche is seen as taking 'hyperbolic doubt' to its limit, disintegrating the Cartesian cogito and trying out the idea of the self as 'a multiplicity of subjects struggling among themselves'.[57] A shorthand connection of this with my previous chapter on the non-idolatrous self might see the two tendencies as being towards monotheistic and polytheistic idolatries of self. His own way is to posit the self indirectly through a hermeneutics in three movements, followed by a discussion of the ontology of selfhood.

In those four sections there is a recurrence of the themes of the other and of attestation, or testimony, and I will use them as my main focus in continuity with the discussions of Levinas and Jüngel. It is also clear that Levinas and Jüngel are to be situated with Ricoeur at a distance from both the positing and the shattering of the cogito. I consider the three to have made an adequate set of cases for this, and am concerned to work out a theological notion of self in that conceptual space where they engage with each other. In other words, I do not intend to wage again the lengthy

---

48. See further chapters 5 and 8 below.   49. See further chapter 5 below.
50. See further chapter 6 below.   51. See further chapters 7 and 8 below.
52. See further chapter 9 below.   53. See further chapter 10 below.
54. I will not engage much in hermeneutical theory in those chapters, but would be content to assent, on the whole, to the theological appropriation of Ricoeur's hermeneutics by Fodor in *Christian Hermeneutics*.   55. *Oneself As Another*, p. 4.
56. Ibid., p. 11.   57. Ibid., p. 16.

campaigns those three have carried on in order to establish this as a suitable place for philosophical or theological construction.

4.4.1 Who speaks? Who acts? The self in language, action and narrative

I now begin a section with three parts, moving through the studies of *Oneself As Another*, to be followed in sections 4.5 and 4.6 by the theological recapitulation of what preceded.[58]

The first four Studies are concerned with the description of the self, and draw mainly on English-language analytic philosophy of language and of action (Strawson, Austin, Searle, Anscombe, Davidson). By taking that philosophical tradition seriously and incorporating concerns and insights from it into his philosophy of self Ricoeur is also contributing to one of the subsidiary aims of this book, which is to relate Anglo-American and continental European intellectual traditions.

His leading question is 'who?' – who speaks? who acts? He both appropriates the rigour of linguistic analysis and also turns it on itself to show its 'aporias', those places where it needs to go beyond itself to meet problems that are raised within its own terms. He is concerned to resist translating all attributions to persons in terms of attributions to bodies, while also resisting any dualism between persons and bodies. Above all, he disputes descriptions of human agency that subsume human actions under the category of 'impersonal event'.[59] His critical conceptual tools in resisting this subsumption are his distinction between self as *idem* (answering 'what?' and 'why?' questions)[60] and self as *ipse* (answering 'who?' questions),[61] together with the related notion of attestation.

Narrative, which is discussed in the fifth and sixth Studies, is crucial for the relation of *idem* and *ipse*. He finds a dialectic of selfhood and same-

---

58. Material from the studies has at times to be given at greater length than I would prefer in order that the theological recapitulation of what they say might make sense.
59. An important part of his argument here is for the irreducibility of the grammatical persons to any one person – first, second and third persons must each be allowed their integrity, though for particular analytical purposes one may be privileged.
60. *Idem*-identity is therefore concerned with sameness and 'objective' criteria. It is rendered most adequately as persistence in time and so is more fully treated in the fifth and sixth Studies on narration. It is focussed above all in the concept of 'character', summing up a configuration of constant features and habits over time.
61. *Ipse*-identity is about those aspects of self irreducible to the 'what?' and 'why?'. Such aspects distinguish an action from an impersonal event, a motive from a cause, ascription to me from ascription to another. Ricoeur's analytical studies show the inadequacy of attempts to describe the self exhaustively in *idem* terms. *Ipse*-identity too is clearer in a narrative context, and Ricoeur's favourite instance of it is 'keeping one's word' (*Oneself As Another*, pp. 118ff.).

ness over time (exemplified in the relation of character to keeping one's word) which is best rendered in the 'discordant concordance' of emplotment in a narrative. Narrative can portray dynamic personal identity, and, as he argued at length in his three-volume *Time and Narrative*,[62] a hermeneutics of narrative can take account too of semiotic and other analyses of narrative, of historiography which rejects narrative and of the imaginative variations in experimental fiction. He argues for the appropriateness of narrative to configuring and refiguring the many dimensions of action and suffering in a life.[63] So narrative emerges as the crucial genre for description of the self in time.[64]

It also has implications for ethics. In continuity with his conclusions in *Time and Narrative* he shows how narration involves valuation and how the ethical imagination feeds off the narrative imagination.[65] Narrating the self continually problematises it, opening up alternative construals. How is that problematic character of the *ipse* asking 'Who am I?' to be related to the assertive ethical 'Here I am!' of Levinas? Ricoeur's response is crucial for his whole position and underlines the variation on Levinas that he proposes. He concludes the sixth Study[66] with a subtle statement about a double tension in the self.

The first is the discord between the imaginative self ('I can try anything') and the responsible self ('Everything is possible but not everything is beneficial to others and to yourself') which 'the act of promising transforms into a fragile concordance' ('Here I stand!'). The second is the tension between doubts about my identity in all the fragmentation and disturbance of life and that ethical 'Here I stand!' This, suggests Ricoeur,

62. University of Chicago Press, Chicago and London 1984, 1985, 1988. *Time and Narrative* will enter into later chapters.
63. See especially pp. 153ff.
64. In the fifth and sixth Studies Ricoeur stages an illuminating controversy with Derek Parfit in order to show that a hermeneutics of narrative is more adequate than Parfit's elimination of the agent in analysis of action. Parfit's position has strong Buddhist affinities (ibid., pp. 137ff.) and Ricoeur's response to it has implications for the philosophical theology of inter-religious dialogue on the self. Ricoeur by no means rejects Parfit's whole case. He accepts Parfit's notion of carefreeness (Ricoeur compares it to what was 'preached by Jesus in his Sermon on the Mount', ibid., p. 138) and his critique of that egotism which supports an ethic of self-interest. Parfit provokes a crisis within selfhood. In what sense do my experiences belong to me? Ricoeur disputes the elimination of difference between sameness and mineness which allows Parfit to describe the self impersonally without remainder. Ricoeur affirms that one has to belong to oneself in some sense, while positing 'a moment of self-dispossession essential to authentic selfhood' (ibid.). 'Who I am' is a different kind of ownership from 'what I have'. The further point is ethical: 'If my identity were to lose all importance in every respect, would not the question of others also cease to matter?' (Ibid., pp. 138f.)   65. *Oneself As Another*, pp. 163ff.
66. Ibid., pp. 167f.

can be resolved into the 'modesty of self-constancy' whose question becomes: 'Who am I, so inconstant, that *notwithstanding* you can count on me?' He preserves the ethical primacy of the other than the self over the self, but is simultaneously insistent on what he calls the self-esteem which is essential for healthy ethical self-effacement.

His worry about Levinas is therefore that his strategy of excess and hyperbole fails to differentiate within the self adequately, and in particular risks eclipsing the need for self-esteem as an integral part of other-oriented responsibility. Earlier in a revealing footnote he had indicated the ideal he has in mind:

> I shall not conceal the enchantment exerted on me by this passage from the end of Bernanos's *Journal d'un curé de campagne*: 'It is easier than one thinks to hate oneself. Grace means forgetting oneself. But if all pride were dead in us, the grace of graces would be to love oneself humbly, as one would any of the suffering members of Jesus Christ.'[67]

This modification of Levinas in the direction of a more differentiated concept of self embracing both self-effacement and self-esteem also signifies a modification of Levinas's concept of witness. Throughout the first six Studies Ricoeur periodically returns to the theme of attestation. Between the Cartesian quest for guaranteed, foundational certainty and the Nietzschean suspicion of all truth Ricoeur pivots his notion of the truth of the self around attestation. He is not denying methods of verification and falsification, but is saying that they are only definitive if *idem*-identity is all there is to the self. Nor is he denying the value of suspicion; he is rather incorporating it into an epistemology of trust in attestation and recognising that there can be a trust greater than any suspicion. His position lacks the apparent security of claims to impersonal objectivity, and it is always fragile in the face of suspicion, but he makes a cumulative case for it being the conception of truth most appropriate to selfhood. It calls, however, for an appropriate dimension of interiority in line with his differentiation of selfhood, and that emerges in the later Studies in his discussions of conviction and conscience.[68]

---

67. Ibid., p. 24.

68. Another dimension of attestation worth mentioning because of its relevance to the face is its relation to embodiment. The mode of truth of *ipse*-identity is primarily that of attestation, and this comes to a focus in relation to the narrative continuity of embodied selfhood through time. He argues that 'my body's belonging to myself constitutes the most overwhelming testimony in favour of the irreducibility of selfhood to sameness . . . One has only to compare two self-portraits of Rembrandt – it is not the sameness of my body that constitutes its selfhood but its belonging to someone capable of designating himself or herself as the one whose body this is . . . Is my body's belonging to

4.4.2 The ethical self: self-esteem, conviction and recognition

Ricoeur's developed concept of the ethical self is given in his seventh, eighth and ninth Studies. Reading them as a variation on Levinas brings out the features most important for my constructive project. The theme of a self-esteem in which, as suggested by Bernanos, self does not simply mean *my*self but embraces my self and that of others, is a helpful thread.

Ricoeur sets out his position by dialectically relating Aristotle's main concern for the ethical aim of 'the good life' to Kant's primary insistence on obligation to respect the universal moral norm. This dialectic of 'the good' and 'the obligatory' moves towards a description of the ethical self. Ricoeur argues, on the basis of his prior analysis of the ethical implications of narrative, against any dichotomy of 'is' and 'ought'. This implies a distancing from Levinas's definition of 'being' (without denying the ethical thrust of the critique of 'totality') and partly explains why in the tenth Study Ricoeur can conclude his book with an ontology of the self. He gives priority to the ethical aim over the moral norm, but insists that that aim can only be reached by way of the norm. This typical Ricoeurian strategy of mediation between two major traditions is deeply affected in both of its movements by a critical dialogue with Levinas.

The seventh Study discusses the ethical aim of '*the "good life" with and for others, in just institutions*'.[69] It argues for the essential mediating role of other people in realising the good life,[70] and indicates the dialogical content of self-esteem through 'the beautiful name of *solicitude*' (original italics).[71] This is a concept, exemplified in Aristotle's notion of friendship embracing reciprocity and mutuality, to which Levinas is said not to do justice.[72] Yet Aristotle's lack of an adequate concept of otherness is confronted by Levinas's maxim summarised as 'no self without another who summons it to responsibility'.[73] Levinas's notion of the other (in *Totality and Infinity* the 'master of justice', in *Otherwise Than Being* the persecutor) is the source of radical obligation in the sphere of the imperative, the norm. In a crucial move, Ricoeur says:

myself on the order of a criteriology? Does it not come instead within the province of *attestation?*' (Ibid., pp. 128f., Ricoeur's emphasis.) Rembrandt's self-portraits can be seen as testimony to the complex particularity of who Rembrandt was and became, an attestation in which the genius of his artistic imagination and practice are integral to his attempt to do justice to the truth. Ricoeur's distinction and relation between sameness and selfhood can thus be illustrated through Rembrandt's project of concentration on his own face.
69. *Oneself As Another*, p. 172.
70. As Ricoeur says, this is a critical issue on which the fate of political theory depends (ibid., p. 181).   71. Ibid., p. 180.   72. Ibid., p. 183.   73. Ibid., p. 187.

Our wager is that it is possible to dig down under the level of
obligation and to discover an ethical sense not so completely buried
under norms that it cannot be invoked when these norms themselves
are silent, in the case of undecidable matters of conscience. That is
why it is so important to us to give solicitude a more fundamental
status than obedience to duty. Its status is that of *benevolent spontaneity*,
intimately related to self-esteem within the framework of the aim of
the 'good' life. On the basis of this benevolent spontaneity, receiving is
on an equal footing with the summons to responsibility... [I]t
compensates for the initial dissymmetry resulting from the primacy
of the other in the situation of instruction, through the reverse
movement of recognition [original italics].[74]

This is a delicate move, salvaging the ethical priority of the other while
affirming a self-esteem that incorporates benevolent spontaneity,
receptivity and recognition. It is in line with the discussion of Levinas
and Jüngel earlier in this chapter in which I proposed a concept of joyful
responsibility. Ricoeur takes his modification of Levinas further in out-
lining a spectrum of ethical relations to the other. He presses on Levinas
the question: 'But whose face is it?' and roots 'instruction by the face
within the field of solicitude'.[75] At one end of the spectrum is the dissymmetry of Levinas's summons to responsibility coming from the other;
at the other extreme is 'sympathy for the suffering other, where the initiative comes from the loving self',[76] which embodies the different dissymmetry of suffering over against enjoyment; and in the middle is the
symmetry of friendship. In each case, however, Ricoeur argues for a link
of similarity, an analogous form of equality, rooted in an understanding
of self that does justice to the other within self-esteem. There is

an exchange between esteem for myself and solicitude for others. This
exchange authorizes us to say that I cannot myself have self-esteem
unless I esteem others *as* myself... The equivalence between the 'you
too' and the 'as myself' rests on a trust that can be held to be an
extension of the attestation by reason of which I believe that I can (do
something) and that I have worth. [It is] the paradox of the exchange
at the very place of the irreplaceable. Becoming in this way
fundamentally equivalent are the esteem of the *other as a oneself* and
the esteem of *oneself as* an other [original italics].[77]

In a footnote Ricoeur links this with the commandment 'Love thy
neighbour as thyself', and in turn links that with Rosenzweig's sugges-

---

74. Ibid., p. 190.   75. Ibid., p. 189.   76. Ibid., p. 192.   77. Ibid., pp. 193f.

tion that 'the commandment "Love me" addressed by the lover to the loved one in the spirit of the Song of Songs is earlier and superior to all laws'.[78] Here again we connect with the discussion earlier in this chapter which modified Jüngel's definition of love by reference to Levinas. In Ricoeur we find the sort of concept of self required by a definition of love as 'the unity of joy and substitutionary responsibility for the sake of joy'. But we have further to travel before that can be developed into an adequate concept of a worshipping self.[79]

The eighth Study, 'The Self and the Moral Norm', affirms the universality of Kant's ethic of obligation, which has close affinities with that of Levinas. Ricoeur recommends passing through the norm on the way to particular ethical judgements, testing behaviour by reference to the question of whether the maxim of my action is universalisable. The strategy only becomes fully clear in the ninth Study: it aims at 'reawakening the resources of singularity inherent in the aim of the true life'.[80] It wants to do full justice to the rigour, the purificatory power, the rationality and the wisdom of Kant's morality while yet saying that it is not enough. It is summed up in Kant's attitude towards making exceptions to his universal maxims. The only exceptions he considers are those motivated by self-interest. 'But what about the exception made on behalf of others?'[81] Ricoeur wants to test behaviour also through discernment of particular circumstances and consequences. He expresses this in the language of the face. The exception 'becomes a countenance, a face, inasmuch as the genuine otherness of persons makes each one an exception'.[82] This leads on to his own maxim: 'Practical wisdom consists in inventing conduct that will best satisfy the exception required by solicitude, by betraying the rule to the smallest extent possible.'[83]

The route Ricoeur takes to arrive at this critical modification of Kant is full of resonances of Levinas. At key points Ricoeur opens up Kant to this further move towards a face-oriented ethic. He finds implicit in Kant the fundamental and irreducible importance of attestation: Kant's concept of autonomy ultimately depends on acknowledging 'the fact of reason'.[84]

---

78. Ibid., p. 194.
79. The rest of Ricoeur's seventh Study develops the idea of solicitude into that of justice within society and its institutions, where we deal with 'third parties who will never be faces' (ibid., p. 195). The institutional aspects of selfhood will be minor topics in the next two chapters (the concern being not so much to explore this theme as not to ignore it), but it is worth noting that Ricoeur's conclusion brackets his own concept of distributive justice between Levinas's two ideas of the hostage and separation (ibid., p. 202).
80. Ibid., p. 240.   81. Ibid., p. 264.   82. Ibid., p. 265.   83. Ibid., p. 269.
84. Ibid., p. 212. Cf. pp. 280ff. on the theory of argumentation and communication, the renunciation of foundational justifications and the role of attestation in conviction (discussed below).

He also finds implicit in that autonomy and its principle of respect for other people a necessary passivity in relation to others, allowing us 'to doubt the autonomy of autonomy'.[85] Heteronomy need not be conceived as domination by the other, as Kant suggests, but can conceive the other as teacher of justice, facing a disciple rather than a slave.[86] Like Levinas, Ricoeur takes with radical seriousness the threat of evil, and especially of violence, and the need for imperatives and prohibitions of Kantian radicality in order to reply to it. But also like Levinas, Ricoeur wants to pluralise Kant's general notion of humanity. He finds an inadequate notion of otherness in Kant, and the particularising idea of the face responds to this lack. Finally, Ricoeur finds optatives as the required context for Kant's imperatives. In other words, Kant's elimination of desire and inclination is criticised, not insofar as it eliminates selfishness but in its forgetting of the need for purified desire – 'the desire to live well with and for others in just institutions'.[87] This links with Levinas's desire of the infinite in the interest of the other, and, together with the stress on attestation, passivity, heteronomy, imperatives and the irreducible pluralism of faces, it amounts to a Levinassian appropriation of Kant – with one major difference.

The difference concerns the notion of self that emerges, and in particular the development of the concept of self-esteem. By the end of the ninth Study self-esteem has been in dialogue with the 'self-respect' appropriate to Kant's morality, and the result is an enriched ethical notion of self-esteem which Ricoeur calls 'conviction'. That is perhaps best seen as the most fundamental form of attestation. It does not claim any foundational justification. It makes particular affirmations and decisions that take account of universal maxims and of persons. It is part of 'a subtle dialectic between *argumentation* and *conviction*, which has no theoretical outcome but only the practical outcome of the arbitration of moral judgement in situation' (original italics).[88] Above all it is a recognition of responsibility, and the difference from Levinas is in the account offered of recognition at the heart of the self. The recognition of responsibility offers an interiority adequate to Levinas's exteriority and proximity of the face, and it culminates in a concept of conscience, the essence of which is attestation in conviction:

> Recognition is a structure of the self reflecting on the movement that carries self-esteem toward solicitude and solicitude toward justice. Recognition introduces the dyad and plurality in the very

85. Ibid., p. 215.   86. Ibid., p. 276.   87. Ibid., p. 239.   88. Ibid., p. 287.

constitution of the self. Reciprocity in friendship and proportional equality in justice, when they are reflected in self-consciousness, make self-esteem a figure of recognition. What we shall say in the next study about conscience, in the sense of German *Gewissen*, is rooted in these conjunctions of the same and the other in the heart of hearts.[89]

With that the final element of 'oneself as another' is in place. The nine Studies have in various ways attested to selfhood in its inner differentiation (*ipse* and *idem*) and its dialectical relation with otherness. Here that otherness is radically interiorised in the ethical form of conscience 'in the heart of hearts'. There is clear tension with Levinas's 'exteriority', but it is to be heightened further, for Ricoeur has one final Study to come, when he does his own recapitulation in the form of an ontology of self.

4.4.3 Bodies, others, conscience, and the ultimate open question

What is the self's status in reality? How is the mode of reference of Ricoeur's attestation to be understood? How are the basic ontological questions about self and other to be understood? Those are the concerns of the final, tenth Study.

Ricoeur gives an account of being as actuality and potentiality. 'Presence', he suggests, is not as adequate a nexus between oneself and being-in-the-world as a union of actuality and potentiality, and in this he shows affinities with Jüngel's concept of God. Ricoeur gives a complex, critical account of Heidegger's reappropriation of Aristotle on *energeia*, *dunamis* and *praxis* which then is embraced within a brief and tantalising affirmation of Spinoza's conceptions of *conatus* and of God. Human activity, including consciousness, is set within a context of life as power, and God as infinite life understood as acting energy.[90] Ricoeur does not develop the theological implications of this, but recognises that they are there, and in particular that his notion of selfhood does not contradict radical dependence on God.

This opens the way for an account of the self and otherness in which 'passivity becomes *the* attestation of otherness'.[91] It is, however, a 'broken attestation' which comes through a variety of dissimilar experiences. There is a 'polysemy' of otherness, a range of passivities which are related analogically but cannot be unified in a foundation. It remains diverse, vulnerable to suspicion and reliant upon trust. The three passivities

---

89. Ibid., p. 296.   90. Ibid., pp. 315ff.   91. Ibid., p. 318.

Ricoeur discusses are: the flesh of one's own body; other people; and conscience. Together they enable a further specification of my notion of the facing self and prepare for the dimension of Ricoeur's polysemy that opens on worship.

First, in 'my own body' Ricoeur finds an otherness that amounts to an intimate passivity. Through the earlier studies the body had been an obvious location of *idem*-identity and Ricoeur had at several points[92] opened it up to the dialectic of *idem* and *ipse*. The sense of that is seen in a full concept of suffering as not only physical but also involving self-esteem. Suffering is one example of the body as a mediation between an intimate passivity and the external world. The passivity of my flesh precedes the distinction of the voluntary and involuntary. It is an otherness in the heart of the self which is prelinguistic and allows one to think of the self as another. Ricoeur even calls it the 'primary otherness'.[93]

In my terms, what Ricoeur has done here is to offer a conception that can include one's own face and body as primary to an understanding of self while yet giving (as the next two forms of passivity propose) ethical primacy to the other person. My body is not only my own nor is it only part of the world: it is the primary place of their union in differentiation. I see the face as the primary focus of this truth, while of course being inseparable from the rest of the body as in Ricoeur's discussion.

Second, Ricoeur treats passivity before other people. This is Levinas's primary concern, and Ricoeur has prepared throughout *Oneself As Another* for the crucial verdict he now delivers.[94] He affirms Levinas's concern for responsibility but revises his notion of self. The main problem he finds with Levinas is the radical concept of the exteriority of the other person, the 'hyperbolic' separation of the other from the self. Levinas unnecessarily binds the identity of the same (*idem*) to a concept of ontology as totality, he fails to distinguish the 'self' from the 'I', and he therefore ends up with a dissymmetry between self and other which amounts to a lack of relation and to the sterility of interiority. As a corrective Ricoeur sees the other as analogous to 'me' and even intrinsic to my identity through a self-esteem which does not equate 'self' with 'I'. In Levinas there is no return from the other to self-affirmation in the mode of self-esteem and conviction. This converges with my development of Levinas's concept of responsibility so as to embrace joy. Further, in Levinas the conception of separation leads to the accusation that representation (in

---

92. Recapitulated ibid., p. 319.   93. Ibid., p. 327.   94. Ibid., pp. 329–41.

language, art or other forms) is inevitably idealist or solipsistic, a way of assimilating to oneself what is represented. This links with my concern for the language of the self in worship: Jüngel's concept of analogy has been drawn on to open Levinas's ethics towards a worship that is not solipsistic in that way, and Ricoeur's concept of 'oneself as another' now brings a kindred notion of analogy into the heart of selfhood. In terms of language, Ricoeur holds that we internalise the voice of the other through our communication with ourselves, and that involves reciprocity, a dialogue which superposes 'a relation on the supposedly absolute distance between the separate I and the teaching Other'.[95]

The final question to Levinas is about substitution and testimony:

> Who, in fact, is obsessed by the Other? Who is hostage to the Other if not a Same no longer defined by separation but by its contrary, Substitution? I find confirmation of this interpretation of the theme of substitution in the role assigned, under the guidance of this very theme, to the category of testimony. We indeed see to what testimony is given: to the absolute, to be sure, hence to the Elevated, named 'the glory of the infinite,' and to Exteriority, with respect to which the face is like a trace. In this sense, 'there is no testimony ... only of the infinite' (*Otherwise Than Being*, p. 146). But *who* testifies, if not the Self, distinguished henceforth from the I by virtue of the idea of the assignment of responsibility? ... Testimony is therefore the mode of truth of this auto-exhibition of the Self, the inverse of the certainty of the ego. Is this testimony so far removed from what we have constantly called attestation?[96]

The lack of Levinas in the sphere of interiority is then made good by the third passivity, that of conscience.[97] This is the intimate place of testing the veracity of self-attestation through taking account of the most probing suspicions. Through engagement with Kant, Hegel, Nietzsche and Heidegger, Ricoeur integrates a dialectic of selfhood and otherness in this place of the self's constitutive conviction. He eventually arrives at his culminating idea of '*being enjoined as the structure of selfhood*' (original italics).[98] He rehabilitates the metaphor of the voice of conscience as the otherness at the heart of the self. But, in line with his earlier movement through universal morality to the exception represented by every face, the voice of conscience is not just the verdict of a court according to law. Rather he draws again on Franz Rosenzweig to testify to a form of commandment that is not yet law, like the plea of the lover in the Song of

---

95. Ibid., p. 339.   96. Ibid., p. 340.   97. Ibid., pp. 341ff.   98. Ibid., p. 354.

Songs saying to the beloved: 'Thou, love me!' This second person injunction, which unites imperative and optative, is summed up, from the standpoint of the passivity of the self, as 'being enjoined *to live well with and for others in just institutions and to esteem oneself as the bearer of this wish*' (original italics).[99]

Then comes the ultimate question of the book, on the answer to which its most important theological implications depend. Now that otherness has been thoroughly integrated into selfhood through the flesh, other people and conscience, is that all there is to say about that otherness? Here Ricoeur has his final reservation about Levinas. For the latter, the other is unequivocally the other person. Ricoeur, however, sees

> the need to maintain a certain equivocalness of the status of the Other on the strictly philosophical plane . . . Perhaps the philosopher as philosopher has to admit that one does not know and cannot say whether this Other, the source of the injunction, is another person whom I can look in the face or who can stare at me, or my ancestors for whom there is no representation, to so great an extent does my debt to them constitute my very self, or God – living God, absent God – or an empty place. With this aporia of the Other, philosophical discourse comes to an end.[100]

4.5 A worshipping self

The end of his philosophical discourse does not mean the end of what Ricoeur has to say about this aporia. Through *Oneself As Another* there is, as I have described, a wrestling with the thought of Levinas, who likewise sharply distinguishes philosophy from theology; but it is significant for theology that the introduction commends Jüngel and the final pages draw on Rosenzweig. In this way the philosophy is bracketed between two thinkers (Christian and Jewish) who represent the thorough engagement of philosophy in theology.

4.5.1 Beyond the aporia: naming God

Ricoeur himself is more tentative in his theological explorations but in his religious writings he does attest to God as named in the Bible.[101] He does not pretend to have no presuppositions: he risks giving preference to the naming of God in the texts of scripture.[102]

---

99. Ibid., p. 352.   100. Ibid., p. 355.
101. See especially 'Naming God' in *Figuring the Sacred*, pp. 217–35.   102. Ibid., pp. 217ff.

That naming is polyphonic, using many genres.[103] He gives a certain priority to the narrative naming, in dialectical relation with prophecy, prescription, wisdom and other genres.[104] But he can also see worship, and the Psalms as the principal biblical genre of worship, having a privileged position: 'It is the privilege of worship to reactualise salvation, to reiterate the creation, to remember the exodus and the entry into the promised land, to renew the proclamation of the law, and to repeat the promises.'[105] And within all the genres there is 'a dialectic of the Name and the idol'.[106] The worship of this God is appropriate participation in reality, which is attested through the Bible to be an 'economy of the gift'.[107] This operates according to 'a logic of superabundance',[108] which is the logic of love. The primary discourse of love he sees as praise, 'where in praising one rejoices over the view of one object set above all the other objects of one's concern'.[109]

That condensed summary, drawing together strands from various writings and taking up the suggestion from the introduction to *Oneself As Another* that in biblical faith 'love is tied to the "naming of God"',[110] is enough to indicate the appropriateness of using Ricoeur's philosophy in support of a conception of a worshipping self.

What might that worshipping self be like? One way of responding is to take up Ricoeur's other suggestion in that introduction: that biblical faith might recapitulate the determinations of the self in such a way as to intensify and transform them.[111] How might the understanding of the self that has emerged from this chapter so far be intensified and transformed by a biblical understanding of worship? The outline answer given now will only be an introduction to what will be more fully developed in the following chapters.

4.5.2 From being enjoined to being loved and delighted in

The discussion in the first part of this chapter linked Levinas's 'living infinity' of responsibility with Jüngel's joy in a 'more than necessary'

---

103. See Fodor, *Christian Hermeneutics*, chapter 6 for an excellent discussion of Ricoeur's 'pluralistic, polysemic, and analogical notion of revelation' (p. 228).
104. Ibid., pp. 225f.
105. 'Biblical Time' in *Figuring the Sacred*, p. 179. Cf. *Time and Narrative*, p. 334. Fodor, *Christian Hermeneutics*, sees Ricoeur affirming 'the ultimate polarity within the biblical language, the polarity between narrative and hymnic discourse' (p. 233).
106. 'Naming God' in *Figuring the Sacred*, p. 233.
107. 'Ethical and Theological Considerations on the Golden Rule' in *Figuring the Sacred*, pp. 293ff.   108. Ibid., p. 300.   109. 'Love and Justice' in *Figuring the Sacred*, p. 317.
110. *Oneself As Another*, p. 25.   111. Ibid.

God. This led to a concept of love as the unity of joy and substitutionary responsibility for the sake of joy, and to worship of God as the celebratory ecology in which this love flourishes. Ricoeur was introduced to help in exploring more fully a concept of self appropriate to that worship, but he does not work it out. He himself concludes with the idea that 'being enjoined' is the structure of selfhood. This presses towards worship through his use of Rosenzweig: the injunction is most radically understood as the 'command' of the Song of Songs, 'Thou, love me!' And his final insistence on the equivocalness of the status of the other explicitly allows for the otherness of God. In the light of this one might intensify 'being enjoined' and see the structure of selfhood as *'being loved and delighted in'*, as in the biblical blessing that opens the climactic final section of Rosenzweig's *The Star of Redemption*: 'May he make his countenance to shine upon you.'[112]

From this biblical perspective it is now possible to recapitulate and intensify the determinations of selfhood in *Oneself As Another*. Read like this, a worship of God which is alert to its own unceasing need for accompanying critique and suspicion might be understood as the most encompassing and formative 'practice of self' in line with Ricoeur's philosophy.[113] In terms of his own positioning of his project, the worshipping self fits well the space he (and, I have argued, Levinas and Jüngel) opens up between the extremes of Descartes and Nietzsche. Good worship resists any idea of a self-positing of the 'I'. The self is posited by God in community without that necessarily being a dominating heteronomy. Likewise there is no 'shattered cogito' in fragmentation, but there can be a complex gathering of self in diverse relationships (including forms of self-dispossession that require a letting go of control and mastery, often an existential equivalent of shattering) before a God who is trusted as the gatherer of selves in blessing. It is a path between what above I called 'idolatrous monotheisms and polytheisms' and it summons the self into practices of joyful responsibility.

4.5.3 From 'Who speaks and acts?' to 'Who worships?'
In terms of the leading questions of the first half of *Oneself As Another*, 'Who speaks?' and 'Who acts?', the question now is 'Who worships?' The

---

112. P. 418.
113. Ricoeur's own theological development of his concept of self is largely through the prophetic strand of the Bible, focussing on the 'summoned' or 'mandated' self – see *Figuring the Sacred*, chapter 15, 'The Summoned Subject in the School of the Narratives of the Prophetic Vocation', which is drawn on below in discussing Jesus Christ.

'*idem*-identity' over time, rendered most adequately through narrative, is intrinsically related to a particular worshipping community. The character of the Jewish and Christian worshipper is inextricable from communal testimony to God in narrative and other genres. But worship is a present activity which constantly improvises on the past in new situations. In worship there are continual retellings of the past in the face of new contexts and urgencies, with reimagining of the God identified in the past. Ricoeur's championing of fiction as being potentially truthful in its refiguring of reality and its opening of new possibilities of selfhood can be intensified through the convergence in worship of imaginative vision, preaching, prophecy and the reconception of a life after forgiveness. The '*ipse*-identity' exemplified in the keeping of promises is enacted in worship that celebrates above all being in a covenant relationship with God. For the Christian this is a baptised community in which one's word has been definitively given to God and to one's fellow members.[114] The 'Here I stand' of Levinas and Ricoeur is a matter of ethics and now also of worship: 'Here I stand before God.'

4.5.4 From self-esteem to recognition by God

Worship inspired through being loved and delighted in by God also refigures the self-esteem of the worshipper. There is a radical affirmation of self-worth. Deeper than obedience to duty there is at the heart of worship what Ricoeur conceptualises as 'recognition', and active recognition is rooted in the passivity of being recognised. This opens a horizon of worship-related practices in attentiveness, repentance, gratitude, delight, and prophetic discernment. Further, there is the exchange between esteem for myself and esteem for others. Ricoeur speaks of 'the paradox of the exchange at the very place of the irreplaceable. Becoming in this way fundamentally equivalent are the esteem of the *other as a oneself* and the esteem of *oneself as an other*' (original italics).[115] This relating of self and other in a pattern of exchange is taken up and transformed by the dynamics of worship in praise, covenant commitment, sacrifice or eucharist.[116]

Ricoeur's move through Kant's universal norm to the particularity that makes an exception of every face is recapitulated in worship which recognises God as creator of all, legislator for all, and simultaneously in the most intimate relationship of love for each. In worship autonomy is

---

114. Cf. chapter 6 below.   115. *Oneself As Another*, pp. 193f., quoted above p. 91.
116. See chapter 6 below.

not violated by a heteronomy but finds its 'nomos' in desire for God: 'My heart says to thee, "Thy face, Lord, do I seek"' (Psalm 27.8). The 'resources of singularity' are opened up before a God whose relationship with creation is infinitely particular.

4.5.5 Attestation in worship

The intensification of Ricoeur's determinations of selfhood in worship is clearest and most richly polyphonic in the pervasive theme of attestation. The Psalms, the main Jewish and Christian texts for worship, overflow with multifaceted attestation. There are thanks, praise, lament, confession of sin, a vast range of moods, hopes, fears, vows, memories, stories, wisdom, imperatives, exhortations, affirmations of faith, petitions, prophecies, blessings, curses, and so on.

If these are 'true' then the appropriate primary mode in which to conceive their truth is as testimony. The Psalms are shot through with suspicion (generated by enemies, by events and from within the worshipper) as the contrary of testimony. 'Conviction' and 'recognition' in Ricoeur's senses are constant themes, and the Psalms frequently show the fragility and vulnerability Ricoeur associates with attestation.[117] Yet overall, as for Ricoeur, there is a 'trust greater than any suspicion'.[118] More than that, the overwhelming testimony is to an 'economy of superabundance'.[119]

4.6 Being transformed before the face of Christ

Before recapitulating the ontology of self with its threefold passivity of flesh, other people and conscience, let us briefly note one form of Ricoeur's specifically Christian naming of God. In 'The Logic of Jesus, the Logic of God'[120] Ricoeur discusses the fourfold 'how much more' of Romans chapter 5:

> Since, therefore, we are now justified by his blood, how much more shall we be saved by him from the wrath of God. For if, while we were enemies we were reconciled to God by the death of his Son, how much more, now that we are reconciled, shall we be saved by his life. Not only so, but we now rejoice in God through our Lord Jesus Christ, through whom we have now received our reconciliation ... But the free gift is not like the trespass. For if many died through one man's

117. *Oneself As Another*, p. 22.   118. Ibid., p. 23.
119. The self of the Psalmist will be discussed in chapter 5 below.
120. *Figuring the Sacred*, pp. 279–83.

trespass, how much more have the grace of God and the free gift in the
grace of that one man Jesus Christ abounded for many . . . If, because
of one man's trespass, death reigned through that one man, how
much more will those who receive the abundance of grace and the free
gift of righteousness reign in life through the one man Jesus Christ.

He finds in Romans chapter 5 the dialectic of a logic of equivalence
(sin, law, death) with a logic of excess or superabundance (justification,
grace, life) 'from which will emerge the whole theology of an Augustine
and a Luther'.[121] He sees this logic of generosity in the extravagance of
Jesus's parables and the hyperbole of many of his sayings, which encourage an excess of response for which there can be no rules – turn the other
cheek! Give more and more! Love your enemies! Paul sees Jesus Christ
himself as the 'how much more of God', he 'gives a *name*, the name of Jesus
Christ, to the law of superabundance'.[122] Ricoeur's application of his
point in context is to call for an ethics and politics of generosity,[123] but
also at the heart of that passage from Romans is rejoicing in God through
Jesus Christ. What are the consequences of bringing this into the heart of
the self portrayed in the final study of *Oneself As Another*?

We can prepare to answer that by taking a further detour through
what Ricoeur says in one of the lectures that was part of the series upon
which *Oneself As Another* is based. He says:

Recall the dense yet luminous text from the Second Letter to the
Corinthians where Paul says: 'And all of us, with unveiled faces, seeing
the glory of the Lord as though reflected in a mirror, are being
transformed into the same image from one degree of glory to another;
for this comes from the Lord, the Spirit' (2 Cor. 3.18). This text takes on
its full relief if we set it against the background of the Mosaic
prohibition of images, not just those of false gods, or idols, but also of
Yahweh. Is an icon that is not an idol possible? . . . [I]t is to this
reinterpretation of the glory of God figured through the person of
Christ that Paul grafted the extraordinary theme of the
transformation of the Christian into this same image. In this way he
forged the central metaphor of the Christian self as christomorphic,
that is, the image of the image par excellence.[124]

Ricoeur discerns in this 'christomorphic self' the 'heir of the prophetic
"mandated self"', recognising that this is a 'concealed filiation'.[125] But
surely the manifest filiation is the worshipping self in the presence of the
glory of the Lord?

121. Ibid., p. 282.   122. Ibid.   123. Cf. chapter 5 below.
124. 'The Summoned Subject in the School of the Narratives of the Prophetic Vocation' in
Figuring the Sacred, pp. 267f.   125. Ibid., p. 268.

4.6.1 Bodies – transfigured and suffering

Returning to the three passivities of one's own flesh, other people and conscience, how might they be intensified through Paul's testimony in Romans and 2 Corinthians?

The encompassing passivity of 2 Corinthians 3.18 is the theme of this book, 'being transformed'. Here it is embodied in faces turned in worship. The context makes it clear that this passivity is inseparable from comprehensive suffering: 'We are afflicted in every way, but not crushed . . .' (2 Cor. 4.8ff.). Our own flesh (vv. 10, 11) is intrinsic to the transformation.

4.6.2 Others – God and fellow-worshippers

Passivity before others is first of all before the Lord. The substitutionary content of this is made clear soon afterwards: 'For the love of Christ controls us, because we are convinced that one has died for all; therefore all have died. And he died for all, that those who live might live no longer for themselves but for him who for their sake died and was raised' (2 Cor. 5.14f.). The transformation into his image is therefore into a pattern of substitutionary living in love. This dynamic of the Spirit displays the Romans 5 logic of superabundance in transformation 'from one degree of glory to another'.

There are also the others embraced in 'all of us'. This is a dynamic of love between people. There are similar selves being transformed; yet the 'faces' resist collectivisation. It is a picture of intensified community and intensified individuality together, gathered before the one whose love compels (obsesses?) each in joyful responsibility.

4.6.3 The face of conscience

But what of conscience? For a hint we need to look a few verses further on. There is a sense in which the whole of 2 Corinthians is about Paul's conscience and his appeal to the conscience of others: 'We have renounced disgraceful, underhand ways; we refuse to practise cunning or to tamper with God's word, but by the open statement of the truth we would commend ourselves to everyone's conscience in the sight of God' (2 Cor. 4.2). This leads on to the crucial statement of verse 6: 'For it is the God who said, "Light will shine out of darkness," who has shone in our hearts to give the light of the knowledge of the glory of God in the face of Christ.'

There is the heart of the self as it is being transformed. Ricoeur rehabilitates 'the voice of conscience'. That might be intensified by what one might call 'the face of conscience'. There is no need to think of just one face in our hearts: we live before many internalised others. But we do not worship them. Paul's complex naming of God is inseparable from the naming of Jesus Christ as Lord,[126] one in whose face the glory of God is faced, and who is trusted to relate to all other faces too.

4.6.4 Jesus Christ himself as another

The glory of God in the face of Christ is Paul's testimony in response to Ricoeur's final aporia[127] as regards the other who is 'the source of the injunction'. Jesus Christ might be understood under each of the possible descriptions suggested by Ricoeur: 'another person whom I can look in the face or who can stare at me' – whether as the particular one testified to in the stories about him or incognito; an ancestor 'for whom there is no representation, to so great an extent does my debt to them constitute my very self' – one is reminded of the African christologies which develop this theme;[128] 'God – living God, absent God', raising the fundamental questions of divinity, real presence and absence; 'or an empty place', opening up diverse themes of kenosis, death, doubt and the 'empty' Holy of Holies.

It is a response that not only intensifies the determinations of selfhood but also generates new questions.

---

126. For a full discussion of this in relation to 2 Corinthians which takes 4.6 as pivotal see Young and Ford, *Meaning and Truth in 2 Corinthians*, chapter 9.

127. *Oneself As Another*, p. 355.

128. E.g. Charles Nyamiti, *Christ as our Ancestor: Christology from an African Perspective* (Mamba Press, Gweru 1984).

II

Flourishings

5

Communicating God's abundance: a singing self

The understanding of self in the first part of this book has been developed first in a meditation and then in dialogue with three twenti-eth-century thinkers, each of whom has been critically and constructively engaged with the interaction of the Hebraic and Hellenic strands which have been so complexly interwoven, entangled or separated through mil-lennia of history. They have worked to conceive a texture of life which can not only withstand the pressures and rendings of our time but can also sustain human flourishing. They have taken account of contemporary intellectual and spiritual crises and have drawn in particular on the resources of phenomenology, Judaism and Christianity in their responses. I have drawn freely on their hard-won concepts and appropri-ated them under my own headings of hospitable self, self without idols, and worshipping self. The culmination has been worshippers being transformed through facing 'the glory of God in the face of Christ'.

The second part will assume and draw on the understanding devel-oped in the first but will take a different approach. It attempts to become thoughtfully immersed in scripture, in liturgical worship, in particular lives (Jesus, Thérèse of Lisieux and Dietrich Bonhoeffer) and in the figure of feasting. The aim is to explore human flourishing in some of its richest forms, and to do so in a way which invites intelligent and wholehearted appreciation and even participation.

The present chapter takes one text, the Letter to the Ephesians, as a testimony to the quality of transformed life in a worshipping commu-nity. Its horizon for human flourishing is unsurpassably vast: 'the mystery of [God's] will, according to his purpose which he set forth in Christ as a plan for the fulness of time, to unite all things in him, things in heaven and things on earth' (Eph. 1.10). Within that, its special focus is on what it means to have a particular social identity in relation to God and other people.[1] I will choose just one key text as an accompanying hermeneutical key, and examine, with reference mainly to that text, the theme of communication, some of the referents of that communication, and the 'new self' which participates in the face to face dynamics of this community. The intention is, by taking this text as an example, to develop further the theme of this study by examining one vivid, classic articulation of salvation, and also to suggest the sort of theology that could be done in relation to other texts too.

5.1 Ephesians on transformative communication

My key text is Ephesians chapter 5 vv. 18–21:

> And do not get drunk with wine, for that is debauchery; but be filled with the Spirit, addressing one another in psalms and hymns and spiritual songs, singing and making melody to the Lord with all your heart, always and for everything giving thanks in the name of our Lord Jesus Christ to God the Father, being subject to one another out of reverence for Christ.

That is one instance of a pervasive concern in Ephesians with transformative language as a constituent of salvation. Explicit references to speech run through the letter. In chapter 1 the readers' entry into faith in its various dimensions (every spiritual blessing, redemption, the riches of grace, all wisdom and insight into the mystery of God's will, hope in Christ and so on) began with their 'hearing the word of truth', placed in apposition with 'the gospel of your salvation' (v. 13). That is a classically Pauline link between proclamation, faith and salvation. The linguistic consequences of this have in Ephesians chapter 1 been distilled into vari-

---

1. Andrew Lincoln, in his perceptive scholarly and theological treatment of the letter in Andrew T. Lincoln and A. J. M. Wedderburn, *The Theology of the Later Pauline Letters* (Cambridge University Press, Cambridge 1993), takes 'identity' as his leading concept in describing the thought of the letter. He sees the writer's main concern being 'the issue of his readers' identity' (p. 91) and carefully analyses (especially in chapter 7) how this is portrayed and strengthened in the letter. Who are they? – Saints, church, new creation, participants in Christ's exaltation, the body of Christ, the bride of Christ, a holy temple. How did they come to be? – Through believing Paul's gospel about what has happened in Jesus Christ; becoming by baptism part of a community of Jews and Gentiles who have a new relationship to Israel, the Temple, the law and the Jewish scriptures (p. 107); and all of this utterly dependent on God's power, grace, revelation, election and calling. Where are they going? – They are entering more and more fully into an inheritance, for which the Spirit is a down-payment; this involves maturing as a community of love and hope, anticipating and expecting the ultimate unity of all things in Christ. How should they then live? In love, thanks, praise, holiness, submitting to one another, exercising and playing an active role in the cosmic battle against evil.

ations on the formula 'to the praise of God's glory' (vv. 6, 12, 14). The picture is of life supremely realised in being taken up into the dynamic of praise of God, and this includes a continual expression of thanks and intercession for those who are fellow participants: 'I do not cease to give thanks for you, remembering you in my prayers...' (v. 16). Being a singing self in the sense of 5.18–20 is the most obvious realisation of an identity formed through the gospel of the first two chapters.

Chapter 3 makes it even clearer, through its treatment of Paul's ministry, how the process of communication is intrinsic to salvation. The gospel is a 'mystery' (*musterion*) of which Paul is a steward (*diakonos*) by grace, called to 'preach to the Gentiles the unsearchable riches of Christ' and to make all people see what is the 'plan [or 'economy'] of the mystery [*oikonomia tou musteriou*] hidden for ages in God who created all things' (vv. 8–9). The church is part of this communication movement, making known 'the manifold wisdom of God to the principalities and powers in the heavenly places' (v. 10). Here the boundaries of the church are seen as being constituted by communication: by communicating the good news, which relativises all boundaries (between Jews and Gentiles, even between earthly and heavenly creatures); and by giving free communicative access to God through Christ 'in whom we have boldness and confidence of access [*parrhesian kai prosagogen*] through our faith in him' (v. 12), so that participating in this free communication is at the heart of salvation. Chapter 3 ends with an enactment of this in prayer.

Chapters 1–3 might be seen as emphasising and exemplifying the fundamental dynamics of transformative communication in blessing, proclamation, praise, thanks and intercession. Chapters 4–6 are more about the gifts, virtues, habits and distortions of communication in the ordinary life of a long-term community. The gifts of Christ to the church which are mentioned (being apostles, prophets, evangelists, pastors and teachers – 4.11) are largely gifts of communication. They are aimed at building a mature community by 'speaking the truth in love' (4.15) and there is need for continual vigilance about deceit (4.14). The ethics of speech are continually mentioned, both in encouragement and prohibition.[2] The culmination of the general ethics of the letter before it moves

2. E.g.: 'Let everyone speak the truth with his neighbour, for we are members one of another' (4.25); 'Let no evil talk come out of your mouths, but only such as is good for edifying, as fits the occasion, that it may impart grace to those who hear' (4.29); 'Let all bitterness and wrath and anger and clamour and slander be put away from you, with all malice, and be kind to one another, tenderhearted, forgiving one another, as God in Christ forgave you' (4.31–2); 'But fornication and all impurity or covetousness must not even be

on to specific relationships is dominated by the portrayal of transformed communication in everyday life in 5.18–20. Singing is seen as a desirable form of face to face address between members of the community and between singers and God.

Finally in chapter 6 the armour of God which enables the community to stand firm is described in terms shot through with communicational concepts: shared truth, the gospel, faith, the word of God. And the practice that energises all of them is joint prayer: 'Pray at all times in the Spirit, with all prayer and supplication. To that end keep alert with all perseverance, making supplication for all the saints . . .' (6.18). Then, to underline the point, the final plea is to pray for Paul in his ministry of communication: '. . . and also for me, that utterance may be given me in opening my mouth boldly [*en parrhesia*] to proclaim the mystery of the gospel, for which I am an ambassador in chains; that I may declare it boldly [*parrhesiasomai*], as I ought to speak' (6.19–20).

To sum up, the explicit statements of Ephesians describe and encourage an explosion of fresh communication, of *parrhesia* in relation to God, towards the whole world and within the community, a dynamic which is meant to pervade ordinary living, thinking, feeling and action. The most fundamental purpose of the community is fulfilled and enjoyed through this constantly new improvisation of *parrhesia*.

5.2 Genres and *parrhesia*: Ephesians as communication

What Ephesians says on the subject is only a part of its significance for the theme of communication. It is itself an act of communication whose puzzles and complexity have stimulated a lot of discussion. 'Scholars are sharply divided on almost all questions about Ephesians: whether it was written by Paul or someone else, whether it is a letter or not, what situation caused it to be written, whether it does or does not contain liturgical components, whether it is chiefly influenced by Gnostic or by hellenistic Jewish thought, and how it is to be interpreted.'[3]

I will assume that it was probably written in Asia Minor towards the end of the first century by a follower of Paul. Paul's mission had led to the

named among you, as is fitting among saints. Let there be no filthiness, nor silly talk, nor levity, which are not fitting; but instead let there be thanksgiving' (5.3–4); 'Let no one deceive you with empty words . . .' (5.6); '. . . for it is a shame even to speak of the things that they do in secret' (5.12).

3. Kenneth Grayston, *Dying We Live. A New Enquiry into the Death of Christ in the New Testament* (Darton, Longman and Todd, London 1990), p. 142.

first major transposition of Christian faith to the Hellenistic cities of Asia Minor and Greece, where in the syncretistic urban culture it worked out a modified identity. The modifications went on as the communities entered the second generation and faced the usual problems of continuity, adaptation and practical living.

Ephesians seems to be suited to that sort of situation. It is a creative interpretation of Christian faith and life for a reasonably well-established community (or communities) which yet is in need of strong affirmation of its identity. The letter is written out of a matured faith whose language is a distillation of the forms of communication that have shaped the church. It combines a range of genres: liturgical forms such as eulogy, intercession, doxology and hymn; credal and confessional formulae and phrases; kerygmatic, catechetical and other teaching material; and interpretation of scripture (the Old Testament is extensively used) and of the Pauline tradition, both his authentic letters (in particular Romans) and (if it is not by Paul) Colossians. The density and complexity of the letter are partly accounted for by this convergence of genres and sources, and it is no surprise that scholars have differed considerably about how to describe it. It is in epistolary form, but many have considered that to be fairly superficial and have seen it as a theological tract, or a piece of wisdom literature, or a liturgical writing (relating to baptism or eucharist) or a homily.[4]

I am content to see it as a genuine letter addressed to a Christian community or group of communities and concerned to recapitulate the faith for a new context. This involved taking up themes that had been much communicated, prayed through, debated and applied in varied situations, and improvising upon them to make a fresh and probably unprecedented synthesis. It is, in other words, an example of what I would see happening in other classics of Christian thinking down the centuries: immersion in a multifaceted tradition of worship, belief, community living and action helping to generate the continuities and innovations needed for the present and future. Paul had been doing this in his mission; the letter to the Colossians was doing the same (which meant saying something different); and Ephesians does it partly by improvising on Paul's letters and on Colossians. Ephesians eventually entered the

---

4. For a summary of these and other views see Rudolf Schnackenburg, *Der Brief an die Epheser* (Benziger Verlag, Zurich, Einsiedeln, Cologne; Neukirchener Verlag, Neukirchen-Vluyn 1982), pp. 17 ff., supplemented for more recent literature by A. T. Lincoln, *Ephesians* (Word, Dallas 1990).

canonical repertoire of works that have since been continually 'performed' and have helped to shape various Christian identities. I am now trying out yet another improvisatory performance as I interpret it in our late modern or postmodern situation.

I see it as a letter; but that does not say much about its unusual form. Perhaps the best description is as a prose equivalent of the Psalms. By this I mean that just as the Psalms[5] take up most of the main Old Testament genres – narrative, law, prophecy, lament, hymn, liturgy, wisdom, blessing, curse – into an overall movement of praise, so Ephesians interweaves its source genres into a letter whose overall thrust is to shape a community of singers of the glory of God.

Praising God's glory in *parrhesia*, with the confidence of access to God, involves an overflow of well-shaped language. Ephesians does not just encourage this but exemplifies it. The contrast with Colossians is notable here. On many of the above points about explicit communication in Ephesians there are antecedents in Colossians (gospel as word of truth, preached to every creature, mystery made manifest, dangers of delusion and deceit, ethics of speech and singing in the community, the pervasive practice of prayer and thanksgiving). Ephesians develops most of these but above all it might be said to enact the theology of *parrhesia* and church together in a more thoroughgoing way than Colossians. In 3.14–21 there is an extraordinarily daring instance of the *parrhesia* that the writer has just mentioned in 3.12:

> For this reason I bow my knees before the Father, from whom every family in heaven and on earth is named, that according to the riches of his glory he may grant you to be inwardly strengthened with might through his Spirit, and that Christ may dwell in your hearts through faith; that you, being rooted and grounded in love, may have power to comprehend with all the saints what is the breadth and length and height and depth, and to know the love of Christ which surpasses knowledge, that you may be filled with all the fulness of God.
>
> Now to him who by the power at work within us is able to do far more abundantly than all we ask or think, to him be glory in the church and in Christ Jesus to all generations, for ever and ever. Amen.

The first paragraph makes complex use of spatial language (inwardness, rooting, grounding, all the dimensions, surpassing [*huperballousan*], fulness) in an extravagant prayer to be filled with all the fulness of God. One might think that to be filled with all the fulness of God would be the

---

5. For further discussion of the Psalms see chapter 8 below.

ultimate for anyone. But then the second paragraph implies it is not. We have a soteriology of abundance represented in a rhetoric of abundance which in the form of prayer leads us into a spiral of transcendence. The author's understanding of the role of communication in a salvation that is inexhaustibly rich is, as it were, sacramentally embodied in this language. It is a sacrament of fulfilment which changes the meaning of 'full' from implying completeness to an image of ceaseless overflow due to the dynamic abundance of God. The language employs sophisticated metaphorical interplays in order to lead the users, 'with all the saints' in community, in acknowledging the Father, the Spirit and Jesus Christ in petition for something beyond any imagining or knowing. Its logic anticipates Anselm's naming of God as 'that than which none greater can be conceived'.[6]

5.3 To what does the communication testify?

All this talk about communication might cause some uneasiness. It seems to abstract a notion of communication from its actual context in Ephesians. There, it is inextricably associated with substantives such as God, Jesus Christ, the cross, the resurrection, the church, strength and power, Jews and Gentiles, Paul, principalities and powers, and so on. In other words, for all the constitutive power of language and for all the importance of communicative process the question of reference rightly keeps recurring.

The obvious primary reference as regards salvation is to God. This is a theocentric letter in which the primary agent is God. God blesses, chooses, wills, loves, gives, communicates, unites, raises Christ from the dead, sets him over everything, and is constantly glorified – and that is just chapter 1. If I were choosing just one theme to emphasise about the God of Ephesians in relation to salvation it would be that of abundance – the pervasive sense of lavish generosity in blessing, loving, revealing and reconciling. This is a world of meaning in which there is an inexhaustible, dynamic and personal source of abundance and glory with an all-inclusive, universal scope of operation.

If in addition I had to choose just one characteristic term through which to focus this theme it would be *pleroma*, fulness. We have already met it in the prayer to be 'filled with all the fulness of God' (3.19). It is

---

6. This will be taken up below in chapter 8's discussion of the resurrection, using Bonaventure's 'better' as well as 'greater'.

related to all of history and the cosmos in 1.10: '. . . as a plan for the fulness of time, to unite all things in Christ . . . [*eis oikonomian tou pleromatos ton kairon, anakephaliosasthai ta panta en to Christo*]'. In a complex, variously translated verse in 1.23, it is linked to the church as Christ's body, 'the fulness of him who fills all in all [*to pleroma tou ta panta en pasin pleroumenou*]'. And in 4.13 growing towards the measure of the *pleroma* of Christ is seen as the goal of Christian maturity in the church. In Colossians, the closest New Testament parallels to these uses of the term, the two references to *pleroma* are to the fulness of God dwelling in Christ. The author of Ephesians seems to be improvising and enlarging on this theme and weaving together God, Christ, church, Christian living and the whole cosmos into a dynamic soteriology of abundance. It is more integrated and more thoroughly worked out as regards the church than that in Colossians. Its radical culmination for members of the church is in a new location and content of selfhood, as will be discussed below.

The testimony to Jesus Christ in Ephesians pivots, as in the rest of the Pauline tradition, around the death and resurrection of Christ, which will be recurring themes in the later chapters of this book.

The death is seen as 'redemption through his blood, the forgiveness of our trespasses' (1.7). Through that death the readers are told, in a generalising of Paul's doctrine of justification through a phrase which seems to have become a catechetical-type formula, that 'by grace you have been saved through faith' (2.8; cf. 2.5). But more distinctive of Ephesians is the author's daring identification of the *musterion* (mystery, open secret) of Christ with the reconciliation of Jews and Gentiles (3.4–6) and anchoring that in the event of the death of Jesus Christ (2.13ff.). There is an insistence that 'Gentile Christians can have access to God only if they enter into the Jewish heritage of faith. The epistle is a sustained assertion to the effect that Gentiles can benefit from the overwhelming power of God only on these terms.'[7] That reconciliation is further directly linked to the theme of new creation and second Adam, 'that he might create in himself one new human being in place of the two, so making peace [*eis hena kainon anthropon poion eirenen*]' (2.15). It has been preceded by a strong affirmation of the resurrection and exaltation of Christ in chapter 1 and, earlier in chapter 2, by seeing Christians not only 'made alive together with Christ' but also 'raised up with him' and sitting with him (2.5–6) so that the 'immeasurable riches of [God's] grace' (2.7) might be shown in Christ

---

7. Grayston, *Dying We Live*, p. 144.

Jesus. It is succeeded by a picture of the church of Jews and Gentiles being built up as a dwelling place of God in the Spirit, and the essence of the new life is described as access through Christ in one Spirit to the Father.

What is going on here? There has been a complex overlay of interpretations of the death and resurrection of Jesus Christ, coming largely through Paul and the cosmic Christ of Colossians, and prophetically sharpened in relation to the new community of Jews and Gentiles. Two closely related things have happened to the underlying Gospel narrative. First, the emphasis is on its central character, the one new *anthropos*, and what has already happened in him. The narrative sense of decisive, one-off events at a particular time and place in the past is taken up into the decisive, one-off transformation that happened in that person, creating the new *anthropos*. The message of salvation is that there is a new humanity which is already a reality in Christ and that even in relation to the deepest hostility (religious, racial, cultural, etc.) one starts from a situation in which the dividing wall has been removed, giving free access to God together.

The second development is towards a distinctive interrelation of linearity and simultaneity. On the one hand there is a pushing of the Pauline tradition in the direction of what many commentators see as a completed salvation, a realised eschatology: Christians are already seated with Christ in the heavenly places and there is no reference to the parousia of Christ. On the other hand, there is a sense of a community facing up to the long haul, to the need for building up a mature church and engaging in the serious transformation of fundamental social relations between Jews and Gentiles, husbands and wives, parents and children, masters and slaves. One way of seeing the link between these is by the idea of *pleroma* already discussed: an abundance already there but also endlessly generative. In the way this letter talks of completeness there is no sense of a full stop, of ending. It is better conceived through the notion of overflow linked with *pleroma*. In linguistic terms it is found in such notions as blessing, praise and thanks. Thanks is best when it can appreciate something completed; but then the very act of thanks shows that there is more beyond that completion. Likewise praise is best when it is of something perfect; but the act of praise paradoxically perfects perfection. Blessing has a similar dynamic. It is to such highly developed activities, informed by the experience and wisdom of centuries of prayer and worship, that one needs to look for insight into the distinctive sort of completeness indicated by Ephesians. The implied narrative is of a community of worship ('a holy temple in the Lord', 2.21) looking to its living Lord, whose death and resurrection have been a decisive transformation within history, whose purpose is the uniting of all things, and whose present historical embodiment is in this community participating in the purpose and abundance of God towards all. Singing of all this is a realisation of its *pleroma*.

The singing of 5.18–20 is addressed to each other as well as to God, and it displays a further way in which Ephesians accords with the deep thrust of the Gospel narrative traditions. The key perspective of both is that of what Farley calls the 'interhuman' in a 'community of the face'.[8] J. P. Stern calls this the 'middle-distance perspective' of daily living.[9] Just as the Gospels tell the story of Jesus mostly in terms of the interaction of people and events in ordinary situations, so Ephesians testifies to a salvation which is both cosmic in scope and utterly focussed through ordinary living. The daring extravagance of the language strikingly leads to no dilution of the concentration on worship and interpersonal relations in community that are the main concern of Torah. Sitting with God 'in the heavenly places in Christ Jesus' (2.6) does not distract from loving alertness to neighbours, spouses and persevering prayer. Rather, there is an intensification of the virtues and practices required there. That is a notable demythologisation of heaven – 'heaven in ordinarie' (George Herbert). This focus also partly accounts for the continuing accessibility of the text's message over the centuries, for all the differences between then and now – just as the middle-distance perspective of the Gospels

8. Farley, *Good and Evil*, especially chapters 1, 10, 13, 16. The helpful concept of 'communities of the face' will be discussed further in the next chapter.

9. J. P. Stern, *On Realism* (Routledge and Kegan Paul, London 1973), pp. 120ff. For the relevance of this to theological hermeneutics see David F. Ford, *Barth and God's Story. Biblical Narrative and the Theological Method of Karl Barth in the Church Dogmatics* (Verlag Peter Lang, Frankfurt am Main, Bern 1981), chapter 4 and *passim*. My own most concise treatment of the topic is in David F. Ford, 'System, Story, Performance: A Proposal about the Role of Narrative in Christian Systematic Theology' in *Why Narrative? Readings in Narrative Theology*, edited by Stanley Hauerwas and L. Gregory Jones (Eerdmans, Grand Rapids 1989), pp. 191–215. The key definition given there (p. 195) is:

> The middle distance is that focus which best does justice to the ordinary social world of people in interaction. It portrays them acting, talking, suffering, thinking, and involved in institutions, societies, and networks of relationships over time; in general this perspective renders ... 'the detail of how things are'. The perspective and the content go together. If one moves too close and allows the dominant perspective to become, for example, one person's inner world or stream of consciousness, then the middle distance has been supplanted. Likewise, if one takes too broad an overview and subsumes the particular people, words, and actions into a generalization, a trend, or a theory, the middle distance loses its own integrity and becomes, at best, evidence or supportive illustration ... [I]t is a matter of primacy and balance, which writers as diverse as the Evangelists, Iris Murdoch, and Thomas Mann all observe in various ways.

helps them to communicate their story to anyone who has experience of human existence in almost any culture or period.

To sum up on the theme of salvation so far, Ephesians represents a transformation of notions of communication, of event, of human community, of ordinary living and of God.[10] At the heart of it is a focus on the person of Jesus Christ inseparable from his death and resurrection, and the implications of this are primarily in the formation of a face to face community of praise. In this context I will now consider the pivotal matter for my theme of self and salvation: the new, singing selves of Ephesians.

5.4 New selves

Ephesians chapter 1 is perhaps the most daring statement of human identity and worth conceivable – every spiritual blessing; chosen before the foundation of the world; destined in love to be children of God through Jesus Christ; redemption, forgiveness, riches of grace freely lavished; all wisdom and insight into God's purpose; and being part of a process through which 'all things in heaven and on earth' are being united in Christ. There is here a confident dignity and worth due to participation in a reality that embraces each person in love and aims to inspire wholehearted and intelligent response. It is all taken up into that dynamic abundance which I have already described, evoked by the language of wealth, immeasurability, fulness, overflowing, glory, praise, thanks, confident access, inexhaustible mystery, and dimensions of breadth, length, height and depth that surpass comprehension.

I have already quoted Andrew Lincoln's analysis of the letter in terms of 'identity'.[11] Every aspect of his perceptive summary could be expanded upon, but the theme I want to pursue is that of the superabundant self in ordinary life. This takes up the prominence of *pleroma* and *parrhesia* in Ephesians already noted, together with other allied ways of expressing its soteriology of abundance. Participation in this abundance gives a new identity, as outlined by Lincoln. It is a new location of self, most succinctly summed up as being 'in Christ'.

That phrase is a distinctive feature of the Pauline writings which Ephesians characteristically develops further. The best discussion of it as

---

10. It would be a fascinating exercise to develop the implications of Ephesians for the understanding of God. Cf., for the lines on which I would attempt that, Young and Ford, *Meaning and Truth in 2 Corinthians*, chapter 9, 'God and 2 Corinthians'.   11. Note 1 above.

regards my concerns is that of Grayston,[12] who stresses that it is primarily a theological formula about activities by God and by people, and that at the heart of its meaning is the event of the death and resurrection of Christ. Ephesians chapter 1 exemplifies this in statements such as: 'Blessed be the God and Father of our Lord Jesus Christ, who has blessed us in Christ...' (v. 3); 'in him we have redemption through his blood, the forgiveness of our trespasses...' (v. 7); 'we who first hoped in Christ have been destined and appointed to live for the praise of his glory' (v. 12); and '... the working of [God's] great might which he accomplished in Christ when he raised him from the dead...' (vv. 19f.).

But what is the meaning of the 'in'? Grayston, drawing on Lohse, makes two points crucial to this chapter. First, 'Paul is not a mystic, since for him Christ is the *Kyrios* who stands face to face with the believer and is always distinguishable from him.'[13] This irreducible facing relationship clearly rings true with the pervasive theological ethic of Ephesians which I have already discussed. Second, 'in using the preposition in, Paul indicates that humans are shaped at any given time by forces that have power over them. It is not in humans' nature freely to dispose of their affairs in complete independence.'[14] This links up with my discussions of Levinas, Jüngel and Ricoeur on 'passivity' in Part I and with Ephesians' formulaic 'by grace you have been saved' (2.5, 8). Human passivity is graphically expressed in the language of death and resurrection: 'And you he made alive, when you were dead through the trespasses and sins in which you once walked ... But God, who is rich in mercy, out of the great love with which he loved us, even when we were dead through our trespasses, made us alive together with Christ...' (2.1f., 4f.). Yet there is no sense of this divine initiative being in competition with human responsibility – witness Ephesians chapters 4–6.

The distinctiveness of Ephesians lies partly in the more frequent use of 'in Christ' and 'in the Lord',[15] and in a greater bias towards reference to God's activity, both of which are also true of Colossians. But above all I would suggest that Ephesians' use of it expounds its infinite dimensions and its transformation of boundaries. There is an immense spaciousness about this location, qualitatively filled to overflowing by the love and glory of God (3.14–21). At the heart of the transformation of boundaries is the death of Christ. That has broken down the dividing wall of hostility between Jews and Gentiles and created a new communal space 'in Christ'.

---

12. *Dying We Live*, Appendix C, pp. 382–94.
13. Ibid., p. 383.   14. Ibid..   15. For the statistics see ibid., p. 391.

It is space filled with prayer and praise, since it gives 'access in one Spirit to the Father' (2.18). The person who identifies through baptism with this death has his or her boundaries transformed vis-à-vis others – and all people are included under either Jews or Gentiles. The new self is one that has 'learnt' this Christ and therefore lives in a social space in which the barriers of hostility are already down. One is in a situation in which no barrier is to be taken as decisive or final; something more fundamental, more radical than any division has happened, the creation of a new place of love which is infinitely capacious. It is not that a possibility of salvation has been offered: the actuality of salvation is announced in this place. That is where one is sitting with Christ (2.6) and in the face of the powers of evil the main thing to do is to *stand* in this faith (6.11–16). The new boundaries of self in this place are constituted by the exchanges of communication and action already described. Those exchanges are to be radically conformed to the fulness of God enacted in the death of this man: 'Therefore be imitators of God, as beloved children. And walk in love, as Christ loved us and gave himself up for us, a fragrant offering and sacrifice to God' (5.1–2). This is the substitutionary dynamic at the heart of the community of praise.

There are, however, limits to the language of containment 'in Christ' and the letter recognises this by its constant modulation of spatial metaphors. The most obvious is the reversal whereby 'Christ may dwell in your hearts through faith' (3.17). But I want now to explore the most striking image of the second half of the letter, which qualifies 'in Christ' in terms of an interpersonal, institutionalised relationship, that of Christ as husband and the church as wife. There are many dimensions of this, but I will take only one in order to make a point about the new self.

The point is an obvious one: the soteriology of abundance is enacted primarily in loving face to face relationships in daily life which require attention to their supporting institutions, such as marriage. The new self has an other-oriented ethic which is characterised by asymmetry. 'Be subject to one another out of reverence for Christ' (5.21). The death of Christ has introduced a catalyst which generates constant improvisation as regards its implications in particular contexts. One might speculate historically about how it would have changed the institution of first-century marriage for husbands to obey the command to 'love your wives as Christ loved the church and gave himself up for her'. This is the new self in ordinary life, year after year with the same person. Ephesians develops Paul and Colossians in reimagining fundamental relationships.

Marriage is compared to Christ and the church; father–child relationships are recontextualised by the injunction to bring up children 'in the discipline and instruction of the Lord [*en paideia kai nouthesia kuriou*]' (6.4); and slaves and masters are set firmly before Christ, with masters even given that fascinating command to 'do the same to them [*ta auta poieite pros autous*]' (6.9). There is no implication that the riches of the gospel are exhausted in these practical instructions. Rather, given the stress on inexhaustibility and abundance, the corollary is that others coming afterwards need to be comparably daring and improvisatory in their situations. Once an asymmetrical ethic of sacrificial love takes off, with everyone being encouraged to look up to everyone else, who knows where it might lead? Ephesians has a nuptial image for where it does lead: '...that he might present the church to himself in glory [*endoxon*]...' (5.27). The unsurpassable, ultimate image is therefore of joyful face to face meeting and life in love together. It is a short step to the Song of Songs beginning its Christian history as an inspiration to generation after generation attempting to celebrate this relationship.

5.5 A singing self [16]

The most embracing idea of salvation in Ephesians is in 1.10, where God's 'economy' (*oikonomia*) is to unite, or recapitulate, all things in heaven and on earth in Christ. The vast number of aspects of reality which are in need of appropriate interrelation suggests the stupendous dimensions of this vision of what God is about – and also sets an inexhaustible agenda for theology. The obvious areas are those where there are divisions, enmities and evil. But one might also imagine the complexities of the human and natural sciences, the humanities and the arts, economic activities and politics, languages and cultures, relations between humans, animals, plants and matter, the dead and the living, the fragmented interiority of each person, and much else. What might it mean for all these to be interrelated in Christ? Perhaps the greatest artistic attempt to answer that is in Dante's *Divine Comedy*, culminating in his vision in the final canto of the *Paradiso* of how it all comes together. It is

---

16. For this section I am indebted especially to Jeremy Begbie for many discussions and papers. His book for this series of Cambridge Studies in Christian Doctrine will develop many of the themes raised here. I am also grateful to Daniel W. Hardy for discussions on this theme.

no accident that singing and faces play such a prominent part in his poetic evocation.[17] I want now to attempt a recapitulation using Ephesians 5.18–21 as one lens through which to appreciate the letter's implications for self and salvation.

How might those verses be seen as portraying the realisation of a Christian community of the face? 'Be filled with the Spirit' (*plerousthe en pneumati*) is immediately given the content of 'addressing one another in psalms and hymns and spiritual songs, singing and making melody to the Lord with all your heart . . .' 'Filled' has the same root as '*pleroma*' discussed earlier. It invites us to explore what filling with song might mean as a realisation of the soteriology of abundance discussed above. This opens up the fascinating question of the relation of space to song. Sounds do not have exclusive boundaries – they can blend, harmonise, resonate with each other in endless ways. In singing there can be a filling of space with sound in ways that draw more and more voices to take part, yet with no sense of crowding. It is a performance of abundance, as new voices join in with their own distinctive tones. There is an 'edgeless expansion' (Begbie), an overflow of music, in which participants have their boundaries transformed. The music is both outside and within them, and it creates a new vocal, social space of community in song. The *en pneumati* (with/in the Spirit) resonates with the repeated use of the same phrase in Ephesians 2.18 and 22. There the Jews and Gentiles are seen, after the demolition of the dividing wall between them, having access through Christ in the Spirit to the Father. The community is pictured being joined together ('harmonised together' – *sunarmologoumene*) into 'a holy temple', the space which above all is filled with psalms and hymns, 'a dwelling place of God in the Spirit'.

The inclusive, uncrowded space of song therefore embodies a distinctive unity.[18] It is a dynamic, incorporating unity that attracts people into its harmonies. There is no end to its enrichment, and it enables one to imagine how each singer can be valued and have something distinctive to offer while yet being given to the complex unity of the singing. Yet it can also conjure up varied types of participation – silent listening, tentative noises, attempts at innovation, vigorous dancing. There is also the

---

17. Dante, faces and music will recur below in the meditation on feasting in chapter 11.
18. The use of the phrase 'one Spirit' (*hen pneuma*) in Ephesians 4.4 continues that theme, which pervades the whole letter.

fragility of this harmony, its vulnerability to what 'grieves the Holy Spirit of God' (Eph. 5.30). To have the boundaries of the community constituted by the quality of its communication (as suggested above) gives it an exposure to attack which is faced in Ephesians 6.10–20 with a range of disciplines, and there the summary exhortation to 'pray at all times in the Spirit [en pneumati]' (v. 18) can also be linked to the practice of singing.

It is striking that there is encouragement to the members to practise 'addressing one another' in song. This is part of facing each other in the community. One way of understanding it is that one sings a song to another who does not sing. But it can also and more naturally be taken to be about one of the obvious features of psalms and hymns: a large proportion of them do not speak to God directly but address other people or oneself. 'Bless our God, O peoples, let the sound of his praise be heard' (Ps. 66.8); 'O come, let us sing to the Lord' (Ps. 95.1); 'Bless the Lord, O my soul; and all that is within me, bless his holy name!' (Ps. 103.1). For a community of worship, this coming together before God in song is the fullest facing of all, explicitly acknowledging the reality of which they are all part, and adding their energies to enhance it. The specific contribution of music to this building up of community in worship includes its encouragement of alertness to others, immediate responsiveness to changes in tone, tune and rhythm, and sharing in the confidence that can come from joint singing. Singing together embodies joint responsibility in which each singer waits on the others, is attentive with the intention of serving the common harmony.

5.5.1 Being subject

Ephesians 3.21 is very important in this regard: 'being subject to one another out of reverence for Christ'. This much discussed verse can appropriately be given a musical meaning. In context its participial form links it closely to vv. 18–20. The concept of reverence (or fear) is at home in worship. If 'being subject' is interpreted through what goes on in good joint singing, then any notion of domination is neutralised, and this is reinforced by the 'to one another'. The position of 5.18–21 as the introduction to teaching on marriage, family and household matters gives a startling new picture of what being 'in Christ' means in practice for them. We are to imagine singing husbands and wives, singing parents and children, singing masters and slaves.

The main content of that singing is given in v. 20: 'always and for everything (or for everyone) giving thanks in the name of our Lord Jesus Christ to God the Father'. 'Always' suggests a filling of time as well as space. It resonates with Ephesians 1.10 on God's 'plan [*oikonomia*] for the fulness of time [*kairon*]'. Time is transformed by being filled with gratitude in song. Good music can be seen as a redeeming of time. Music obliges us to rethink time:

> [I]t is no longer time for action, achievement, dominion and power, not even time for acquiring ideas (you could misinterpret attending to drama or poetry in these terms). It is simply time for feeding upon reality; quite precisely like that patient openness to God that is religious contemplation . . . A musical event is – whether we know it or not – a moral event, a recovery of the morality of time . . .
>
> If the Christian feels a particularly powerful commitment to music, it's because Christian identity turns so much upon the encounter with God's reality in a narrative, a movement. Each year, the Church renews its understanding of itself and its world in the process, the story, of the Christian year. Above all, in Holy Week and Easter, it takes us inexorably through a series of changing relations, shifting perspectives, that can't be rushed: it leads us through the passion and resurrection of Jesus, which is the centre and wellspring of what we are. We can't do this with selected highlights, saving time; this is a contemplation, a feeding, that requires our flesh and blood, our patience, our passion. It requires that things be done to us, that we allow ourselves to be changed and enlarged.
>
> To listen seriously to music and to perform it are among our most potent ways of learning what it is to live with and before God, learning a service that is perfect freedom.[19]

Rowan Williams, reflecting on much later musical traditions and practices, goes to the heart of the receptive activity which is shaped by musical time. In Ephesians 5.20 the prominence of thanks leads further to the theme of repetition. If given something utterly good and wonderful, a basic response is amazed gratitude. This is characteristically expressed in endless variations on the same theme. If the gift is life in Christ, through whom everything in heaven and on earth is being drawn together, then the gratitude can be endlessly creative 'non-identical repetitions'. I take up this theme of non-identical repetition in the next chapter on the eucharist (which means 'thanksgiving'). For now the key

19. Rowan Williams, 'Keeping Time. For the Three Choirs Festival' in *Open to Judgement. Sermons and Addresses* (Darton, Longman and Todd, London 1994) pp. 248f.

point is that music is very repetitive, with frequent use of the same patterns of notes.[20] There is usually in song a poetic pattern of words, with its own repetitions, blended with the musical patterns. The non-identical repetitions of poetry and music together intensify the meaning, enriching it in ways that can only be hinted at in prose. The significance cannot be abstracted from the melody, rhythm, tempo, assonance and tone.

One practical effect of this intensification is that great energy is concentrated in singing. It characteristically energises singers and hearers. In Ephesians the theme of energy, strength, power and 'dynamism' is pervasive. There is astonishment at 'the immeasurable greatness of [God's] power [dunameos] in us who believe, according to the working of his great might [kata ten energeian tou kratous tes ischuos autou] which he accomplished [energesen] in Christ when he raised him from the dead . . .' (Eph. 1.19f.). There is prayer 'to be inwardly strengthened with might [dunamei krataiothenai] through his Spirit' (3.16). To be filled with the Spirit (5.18) is therefore to be energised and filled with song together. Rowan Williams in the address quoted above rightly makes the link between music and a transformed notion of power which is in tension with domination. Ephesians 5.18–21 invites into a new 'ecology' of power, subjection to one another in singing with gratitude to Christ, 'who loved us and gave himself up for us' (5.2). It is an ethic of truth and love which joins together (harmonises, sunarmologoumenon) a community (4.15f.). One characteristic virtue it promotes is praütes (gentleness, 4.2), as discussed in the final section of this chapter. The picture by the end of the letter is of an energetic, resilient gentleness growing in members of a community who can sing to each other and to God as they resist whatever evils come.

This picture of subjectivity has the advantage that it is intrinsically physical. Singing is about breathing, vocal chords, tongues, lips and ears. More than that, it takes up the whole body into rhythms and movements. The body gives energy to singing and also gains it. Singing can overflow into clapping, other gestures, and dancing. It can integrate the self in a

---

20. A further aspect of repetition is the sort of repetition represented by a new performance of the 'same' piece. All of the world's music before exact notation, and a great deal of it still today, has been passed on 'live' and is learnt in ways that make a certain amount of improvisation inevitable. Even with exact notation there is great scope for interpretation in performance. Sound reproduction by technology enables particular performances to be repeated more precisely, but this may actually encourage later performances to innovate – and the technologies themselves enable many new forms of mixing, dubbing, amending and erasing.

new way. Nor is it just an occasional matter: singing can be developed over time, and practice makes a difference. Bodily habits, rhythms and responses are formed by it. The injunction to be filled with the Spirit and sing is contrasted with 'Do not get drunk with wine' (5.18). That in turn follows on from 5.16 where the exhortation is to 'make the most of the time, because the days are evil'. Drunkenness is a practice that incapacitates people for responsible use of time in line with 'the will of the Lord' (5.17). Singing psalms, hymns and spiritual songs, by contrast, enables a 'sober intoxication' which attunes the whole self – body, heart and mind – to a life attentive to others and to God. It is a practice of the self as physical as drinking – and as habit-forming. One of the main habits formed is that of alertness.[21] There is also the habit of obedience, a word closely connected in many languages with hearing. Singing is a model of free obedience, of following with others along a way that rings true. In this often the body leads the self, and we find ourselves absorbed in a meaning which only gradually unfolds and pervades other spheres. Through all this the content, tone and potential of 'being subject' can be transformed in relation to its meaning not only for the first readers of Ephesians but also, through appropriate interpretation and improvisation, for readers whose conception of subjection, obedience, embodiment, and relations between women and men is very different.

5.5.2 The self of the Psalmist

A further dimension of the 'singing self' of Ephesians is opened up by the reference to 'psalms and hymns and spiritual songs' (5.19). I have already mentioned the relation of words to music. It is worth noting that in that culture there was less distinction between speech and song. Their patterns were closer to each other and the music of speech was more intrinsic to its meaning than it tends to be in the modern West. Song was a heightened speech in which it is probable that usually one word was accompanied by one note.[22] Nor is that the only difference – there is a hermeneutical gap between singing then and now. But my point is not that the church implied by this letter be reproduced today. The situation is rather that that church was itself taking up and innovating on a long

21. Note the conclusion of 6.18: after 'Pray at all times in the Spirit' comes: 'To that end keep alert with all perseverance, making supplication for all the saints . . .'
22. See Donald Jay Grout, *A History of Western Music* (Dent, London 1978), pp. 5, 7. The melody and rhythm of music were most intimately bound up with the melody and rhythm of poetry. The Greek conception was that music was 'essentially one with the spoken word' (p. 7). The same almost certainly applied to ancient Jewish chant.

tradition of community singing before God, represented by the Psalms, and we come after nearly 2,000 years of further improvisation on that tradition in many cultural settings. Much of that tradition has been oral. We have very little of its music and a little more of its words. There can therefore be no recovery of the past even if it were desirable to repeat it. The dynamic tradition of music, above all in song, has pervasively shaped the reality of self and salvation in ways that are largely irrecoverable and unrepeatable. But what is possible is to appreciate its importance and be fully part of its continuation, as Ephesians 5.19 encourages.

The 'spiritual songs' may well refer to 'singing in the Spirit' where a whole gathering joins in, each contributing, possibly in 'tongues', to the overall unrehearsed song. Something like this is today a common practice for hundreds of millions who worship in Pentecostal or charismatic congregations, and it has analogues in variations on plainsong, in 'rounds' and in the music associated with the Taizé Community in France. Such mutual musical dialogue with a degree of improvisation can help form some of the most important and elusive habits in community living. Jeremy Begbie sums this up:

> All the skills which promote undistorted communication – which are
> to characterise the Church considered as persons in active communion
> – are, in the best forms of improvisation, present to a very heightened
> degree: for example, alertness of the whole person, rigorous
> discipline and training that can never be entirely formalised into
> rules, attentive listening and contributing, sensitive decision-
> making, risking, role-changing, resolving conflict, and (often most
> important) keeping silent.[23]

The 'hymns' may be less improvised compositions with a more stable and therefore 'portable' form. The psalms (if, as is probable, this refers to the biblical book of Psalms) have proved the most portable of all, and they can be discussed in more detail. In terms of sheer quantity of use, the Psalms are probably the single most influential book of the Bible in both Judaism and Christianity. To take them as a starting point for investigating the 'singing self' of Ephesians could lead through not only that remarkable corpus but also along its astonishingly diverse paths through history. To begin to appreciate the breadth and depth of the formative power of the Psalms is to glimpse a dimension of the transformation of

23. Jeremy Begbie, 'Theology and the Arts: (2) Music', chapter 34 in David F. Ford (ed.), *The Modern Theologians. An Introduction to Christian Theology in the Twentieth Century*, 2nd edn (Blackwell, Oxford 1997).

selves in song that is rarely done justice to in doctrines of salvation.[24] My brief treatment of this theme now will focus on the 'I' of the Psalms.

Who is this 'I'? Scholars have various hypotheses about who composed the Psalms; the tradition ascribes many of them to David. But he was the king, representing the people, so that even the 'I' Psalms have traditionally been entered into corporately by Israel and the church. And of course individual worshippers have always identified with this 'I' in the most diverse ways. So the Psalmist's 'I' accommodates a vast congregation of individuals and groups down the centuries and around the world today. They are all somehow embraced in this 'I'. A vast array of stories, situations, sufferings, blessings, joys and deaths have been read and prayed into the Psalms by those who have identified with their first person. It amounts to an extraordinarily capacious and hospitable 'I'.

It is a feature of good liturgical texts that they allow large numbers of diverse people to identify themselves through them. The liturgical 'I' suggests a conception of selfhood, in line with earlier chapters, which does not simply see itself as separate from all the other selves and groups worshipping through the same liturgy or the Psalms. Seeing oneself as one among the many who indwell the Psalms by singing them encourages one to consider how the others might be related to oneself. To see (in the flesh or in imagination) the faces of the others who receive and perform their identity through singing the Psalms can lead along the path I have followed through a hospitable self, rejecting idolatries, to a worshipping self for whom the orientation to the face of God and the face of other people is primary. I read Ricoeur's *Oneself As Another* as taking seriously Levinas's emphasis on the exteriority and difference of the other before whose face I am radically responsible; uniting that with an Augustinian (and even Freudian) concern for interiority; and concluding with Rosenzweig's worship-oriented understanding of the Song of Songs, enabling the imperative of love to be at the heart of the self. The 'I' of the Psalms is a singing self that has been commanded to worship and attest to its deepest convictions, and it passes on the command in forms such as: 'Love the Lord, all you his saints!' (Ps. 31.23). It is an 'I' which is (in Ricoeur's terms) neither self-positing nor fragmented, but a self which

24. A rich interpretation of the role of the Psalms in ancient Israel and in the Old Testament is given in Walter Brueggemann, *Theology of the Old Testament. Testimony, Dispute, Advocacy* (Fortress Press, Minneapolis 1997), chapter 23. Brueggemann's use of a Ricoeurian understanding of testimony in his biblical interpretation combines with his appreciation of the role of worship to make an Old Testament theology in line with the main thrust of my book.

has interiorised the imperative, sung testimony of many others, and it lives by passing on that testimony. I sing before the faces of those from whom I have learnt to worship and whom I call to worship. This worshipping self is intrinsically plural, a vivid enactment of 'oneself as another'; it is deprived of any overview of itself, and is constituted through living and singing before these others.

Yet none of that reaches the theological heart of this self. The generously hospitable 'I' of the Psalms is most comprehensively constituted through the activity of God. It acknowledges God's past activity (or laments God's inactivity) and it awaits God's future activity. It is continually opening towards God in appeal, affirmation, commitment, anguish, promise, hope, joy, exclamation, blessing, reminiscence and thanks. It is this rich, polyphonic movement that creates the distinctive hospitality of the Psalms and enables so many others to identify with them. The 'I' has God intrinsic to its identity through worship: the one before whom it worships is the main clue to its selfhood. This God is a refuge, righteous, a guide, faithful, steadfastly loving, gracious, good, blessed, and active in multifarious ways. One way of summarising much of this is through the image of God's facing. The theme of God's face is one that recurs especially with reference to salvation and rejection.[25] The seeking of the face of God in the Psalms is closely related to the Temple and its worship, and to images of refuge, welcome and hospitality.

So the character of God and God's activity is the key factor in the Psalmist's 'I'. It is therefore very important that Ephesians brackets its injunction to sing psalms by references to the Spirit (5.18) and to 'thanks in the name of our Lord Jesus Christ to God the Father' (5.20). There we find the proto-trinitarian pattern of addressing God to which the naming of Jesus Christ is intrinsic. This raises a further specifically Christian dimension of the 'I' of the Psalms: Jesus Christ too is one of those millions who have worshipped through the Psalms. Moreover, according to the Gospels he specifically identified with the 'I', and this was at its most explicit during his crucifixion. "'My God, my God, why hast thou forsaken me?'" (Ps. 22.1; Mark 15.34; Matt. 27.46). "'Into thy hands I commit my spirit'" (Ps. 31.5; Luke 23.46).[26] Yet in the aftermath of the resurrection Jesus himself is named in worship as Lord and saviour. The glory of God is found in the face of Christ. What is sought in worship in the

---

25. E.g. Psalm 27.8f. For further discussion of facing in the Psalms see below, chapter 7.
26. Cf. the use of Psalm 69 in the crucifixion accounts of all four evangelists. Psalms 22, 31 and 69 all refer to the face of God. See further chapter 8 below, pp. 197ff.

Temple is found through him. Here is a pivotal matter for the course of subsequent Christian worship, living and theology, not least with regard to the worshipping self.[27]

Christian identification with the 'I' of the Psalmist is 'in Christ' (in the sense discussed above). One's own self is constituted in relationship to all the others who sing the Psalms, but there is a special relationship to Jesus Christ. Others (notably Jews) may wholeheartedly seek the face of God in praying the Psalms and have a range of responses to the face of Jesus of Nazareth, such as ignoring it, rejecting it, understanding it sympathetically, or acknowledging it as another Jewish face in the image of God. The Christian testimony to the glory of God in that face interprets the hospitality of God through the death and resurrection of Jesus Christ. The coming chapters will develop that thought. For now the main theological implications of Jesus Christ as hospitable 'I' of the Psalmist are threefold.

First, there is the beginning of the tradition of christological interpretation of the Psalms which has been a key formative factor in Christian selves over the centuries. This is implicit in Ephesians 5.20, whose 'rule' for singing the 'I' might be taken as being to regard 'oneself as *this* other'. It is a further intensification of Ricoeur's determinations of selfhood by non-identical repetition of the Psalms 'in the name of our Lord Jesus Christ'.

Second, there are radical implications for a community which faces Jesus on the cross crying out through the Psalms. It has to identify with a face in agony and in death. It has to reimagine God's glory through that. It is a self-effacing glory, even self-distributing (cf. 2 Cor. 3.18). To look in faith towards it is to have one's gaze redirected towards others in the way he gazed at them and with the quality of his responsibility for them. His self-effacing glory shines in order to reveal the glory of God in and for others, face by face.[28]

Finally, Jesus is said to have 'sung a hymn' at the Last Supper before going to Gethsemane (Mark 14.26). But he did not sing on the cross. His 'loud cry' from the cross is the extremity of speech, beyond talk and song. It resonates with the anguished laments of the Psalms and with the cries of sufferers down the centuries. It is one way of relativising the 'singing self', guarding it against any sense of sentimentality or lack of realism about the sort of world we inhabit. Ephesians shows this realism by concluding with an inventory of armour for 'the evil day' (6.10ff.).

27. Cf. especially chapters 6 and 8 below.
28. This point is developed further in chapters 7 and 8 below.

5.6 Suspicion, justice and gentleness: Ephesians and politics

The singing self requires not only to be relativised, however; it also needs to be suspected. 'The corruption of the best is the worst', and the energised, united community of praise that the writer of the Letter to the Ephesians envisages sets up dynamics whose power can be disastrously perverted. It may even be that the very rhetoric of Ephesians is totalitarian. It loves to use the word 'all'. Does it not portray a group identity that is imperialist, overwhelming and intolerant of others? Does its repeated advocacy of unity not call to mind the many regimes of domination that thrive on the suppression of difference? What about those who do not share this particular vision of God and God's abundance? Is there anything to prevent this letter being the charter for a thoroughly triumphalistic Christianity? Can it inform a Christianity that relates respectfully to others in a pluralistic society? Might the singing of such a community rather resonate with those many uses of song which create confident, aggressive solidarity aimed at coercive assimilation of others or confrontation with them?

Such questions all have a political thrust to them, and in the final section of this chapter I want briefly to explore with the help of Ephesians the relation of communities of the face to politics. Farley[29] discusses the interrelation of communities of the face and the 'social', and for my purposes it is unnecessary to try to improve upon his overall mapping. Above

---

29. Farley, *Good and Evil*. The systematic shape of Farley's portrayal of the human condition integrates his most fruitful idea, the identification of the sphere of the 'interhuman'. He distinguishes three spheres of human reality, those of the individual agent, the interhuman and the social. Individuals are 'irreducible, complex and multi-dimensional' (ibid., p. 29), and Farley portrays the dimensions of historicity (in which agents are both conditioned and self-transcending), embodiment, and passions (reason is included under the 'passion for reality'). He takes care that the biological constitution of human beings is taken fully into account, while sustaining a non-reductionist argument. The social embraces language, customs, roles, norms, values, bodies of knowledge, belief systems, rituals and institutions.

Farley's distinctiveness is in discerning the third, mediating sphere of the interhuman. This can be variously described as the sphere of intersubjectivity, the interpersonal, face to face relationship, mutual reciprocity, or dialogue and empathy with one recognised as a genuine other who in turn acts towards and interprets oneself.

Farley shows how the three spheres are interdependent and coinherent, but it is important that he grants the interhuman a certain pre-eminence:

Although each of these spheres is primary in its own order, the interhuman is primary to both agents and the social because it is the sphere that engenders the criterion, the face (Emmanuel Levinas), for the workings of the other spheres (p. 29). The primacy means that there is a new principle operating in his descriptions of the human condition and of redemption, and I suggest Ephesians as a good instantiation of that.

all, he argues in some detail the case that communities of the face are at the heart of a healthy society at all levels from the local to the international, without this reducing all political discourse to interpersonal terms. In this study I am mostly bracketing out explicit examination of the political in the sense of the decision-making, organisation and governance of social groups and the relations between them. Yet issues of politics and social justice are constantly implied or presupposed in any treatment of self and salvation. Edward Schillebeeckx wrote that 'if any book lays a foundation for a political theology in the New Testament, it is Ephesians'.[30] I will not attempt that, but will take up his suggestion in relation to my main concerns.

The first remark is that the dangers of triumphalism were probably not too great for the letter's original recipients. One should probably imagine fairly small communities in Asia Minor cities that had some important features in common with modern pluralist, syncretistic societies. Ephesus was an expanding city of over 250,000, a centre for all sorts of trade, religion, philosophy, culture. If the congregations addressed were anything like those described by Wayne Meeks[31] and others then the massive affirmation of dignity that Ephesians gives was needed by those with high 'status inconsistency' and vulnerability to all sorts of threats to their identity. This is theology for unprivileged Christians. It is striking to see how it still flourishes in comparable contemporary situations.[32]

The second remark, however, is that the dangers have often been realised in Christian history. That means several things for the contemporary Christian theological interpretation of the letter. It requires facing up to and learning from the terrible history of Christian triumphalism, imperialism and so forth. With regard to Ephesians, which makes the relations of Jews and Gentiles so central, that points first of all to the so often tragic history of Christians with Jews. Ephesians could be read as a charter for 'supersessionism' in the sense of seeing Jews and Gentiles united in the church and Judaism disappearing. If Grayston is right, the

30. Edward Schillebeeckx, *Christ: The Christian Experience in the Modern World* (SCM Press, London 1980) p. 196.

31. Wayne Meeks, *The First Urban Christians: The Social World of the Apostle Paul* (Yale University Press, New Haven and London 1983)

32. See my essay, based on the interpretation of Ephesians in contemporary inner city areas of Britain, 'Transformation' in *God in the City. Essays and Reflections from the Archbishop of Canterbury's Urban Theology Group*, edited by Peter Sedgwick (Mowbray, London 1995), pp. 199–209. That whole volume might be seen as stressing the importance of 'communities of the face' as inseparable from social and political analysis and activity. It treats worship and idolatry in the essay 'Praise' by David F. Ford and Alasdair I. McFadyen, pp. 95–104.

original intention contradicts that insofar as it is a radicalising of Romans 9–11:

> What is said in Romans 11 to warn Gentile Christians against despising Jews and in Romans 15 to encourage Jewish and Gentile Christians to live joyfully and peaceably in the same community is here transformed into a basic principle of the gospel: that Gentile Christians can have access to God only if they enter into the Jewish heritage by faith. The epistle is a sustained assertion that Gentiles can benefit from the overwhelming power of God only on these terms.[33]

Yet that is a weak bulwark against misuse in later very different circumstances, and the response to the accusation that the letter encourages political abuse needs to go deeper. I would start with the ethic which it portrays. It is one of non-coercive action and speech. The recurrent 'all' is applied here too: appealing for a life to be lived 'with all lowliness and gentleness, with patience [*tapeinophrosune, praütes, makrothumia*], forbearing one another in love' (4.2). If the overflow of action and communication towards those beyond the community were to be of this quality then the boundaries would be constituted in such a way as to exclude coercive claims over others. The way militaristic language is used in the external affairs of the community in Ephesians 6 bears this out. The ethic of patience and gentleness leads on the part of the Christian community not to a strategy of aggression or imperial conquest but to a war of resistance and defence in feet shod with 'the equipment of the gospel of peace' (6.15). The aim is simply to stand. It is noteworthy that the author left out the vengeance and fury in his (or her) source, Isaiah 59.17:

> He put on righteousness as a breastplate,
>   and a helmet of salvation upon his head;
> he put on garments of vengeance for clothing,
>   and wrapped himself in fury as a mantle.

More fundamentally, the ethic itself is tied into the heart of the testimony to Jesus Christ in Ephesians. This is the most critical issue of all. Must not the 'high' christology and ecclesiology of Ephesians be intolerant and feel superior to other beliefs and communities? Here everything turns on the character of the one this community is testifying to and being conformed to. The blood, the death, the cross of Christ are prominent in the first two chapters, and the main interpretation of them is in terms of love and peacemaking. It is a common irony that the greatest oppression often takes place in the name of such things. But a strong case

---

33. Grayston, *Dying We Live*, p. 144.

can be made against blaming the corruption on what Ephesians says. To have this crucified and risen person as the location of the community's identity should, in the light of what the rest of the letter says, have consequences such as: giving testimony in ways which suffer rather than coerce; refusing to claim any overview of the extent, subtleties and surprises of the love of Christ (it surpasses knowledge – 3.19); being open to radical reconceptions of one's boundaries, comparable in significance to those the recipients of the letter were having to cope with; and, above all, giving up any idea of being in control of a *pleroma* that works in unimaginably generous, gentle and understanding ways. The high ecclesiology is a double-edged weapon for any Christian triumphalism because it means the church is the first to be judged by this ethic of love and abundance. If this were to happen according to the criteria of Ephesians the result would be devastating for a great deal of what the church has done and continues to do in its exercise of power and its forms of communication. The meanings of triumph, domination, power and strength are being redefined through this 'new human being [*kainos anthropos*]' (2.15). Ephesians offers a good deal of material for the discernment and critique of the dangers suggested by this section's opening questions.

The positive contribution of Ephesians to political flourishing might be summed up by saying that to have communities animated by such a vision and such practices greatly benefits civil society. The church envisaged in Ephesians sustains human dignity without excluding anyone; its ethic of reconciliation faces religious, racial, cultural and household issues; it advocates an array of neighbour-friendly virtues; it encourages learning and teaching; and it sponsors high quality, respectful communication as an alternative to violence. Whether such a community of the face can flourish in peace and contribute to the wider society may be a good test of the quality of a political system; and new measures might primarily be judged by the effects they have on such communities.

But what about the hard issues of power, distributive justice, criminal justice and the shaping of institutions in society? I will end this chapter by making two related points on such matters.

The first draws on an aspect of Ricoeur's thought which I only mentioned in passing in chapter 4. In *Oneself As Another* he sees the ethical intention as 'aiming at the "good life" with and for others, in just institutions'.[34] His philosophy of self therefore builds in a political dimension.

---

34. *Oneself As Another*, p. 172.

He follows Charles Taylor in seeing 'the fate of political theory' depending on the way personhood is conceived. It is vital whether persons are
regarded as complete individuals before entering society, their participation in society being contingent and in principle revocable, or whether
they are seen as having an 'intrinsic obligation to participate in the
burdens of perfecting the social bond'.[35] Ricoeur's crucial move is to
relate an ethic of the face to an ethic of justice for all, making them interdependent:

> *Equality,* however it is modulated, *is to life in institutions what solicitude is
> to interpersonal relations.* Solicitude provides to the self another who is a
> face, in the strong sense that Emmanuel Levinas has taught us to
> recognize. Equality provides to the self another who is an *each* ... [T]he
> sense of justice takes nothing away from solicitude; the sense of
> justice presupposes it, to the extent that it holds persons to be
> irreplaceable. Justice in turn adds to solicitude, to the extent that the
> field of application of equality is all humanity [original italics].[36]

His concept of just institutions in particular stresses the role of the
ethics of communication, and he might be said to draw the lines of
continuity between the communicational virtues commended by
Ephesians and the conduct of public debate about the conflicts within
and between societies. But it is in his more explicitly theological writing
that the full relevance of Ephesians is clear. In his essay on 'Love and
Justice'[37] he builds a bridge between the poetics of love's abundance,
as expressed in the hymn, and the prose of justice's equivalence, as
expressed in the formal rule. Their union in tension culminates in something like the practical wisdom for a political programme:

> It is the task of both philosophy and theology to discern ... the secret
> discordance between the logic of superabundance and the logic of
> equivalence. It is also their task to say that it is only in the moral
> judgement made within some particular situation that this unstable
> equilibrium can be assured and protected. Thus we may affirm in
> good faith and with a good conscience that the enterprise of
> expressing this equilibrium in everyday life, on the individual,
> judicial, social, and political planes, is perfectly practicable. I would
> even say that the tenacious incorporation, step by step, of a
> supplementary degree of compassion and generosity in all of our
> codes – including our penal codes and our codes of social justice –
> constitutes a perfectly reasonable task, however difficult and
> interminable it may be.[38]

35. Ibid., p. 181.   36. Ibid., p. 202.   37. *Figuring the Sacred,* pp. 315–29.
38. Ibid., p. 329.

Ephesians is about the logic of superabundance in the everyday life of a community, expressed most obviously in singing psalms and hymns and spiritual songs. Yet it is also clear that justice or righteousness is intrinsically part of this: 'Put on the new nature [*kainon anthropon*], created after the likeness of God, in justice [*dikaiosune*] and holiness' (4.24). Further, this justice is universal in its implications: 'For the fruit of light is found in all goodness and justice [*dikaiosune*] and truth' (5.9). When the institution of the household is considered, it is taken for granted that justice is a basic consideration (6.1); and in fighting evil the 'breastplate of justice' is to be put on (6.14). This is not at all surprising for an author whose Bible is full of God's passion for justice within and between nations. Psalm 85.10 comes to mind:

> Steadfast love and faithfulness will meet;
> justice and peace will kiss each other.

Ricoeur sees such meeting and kissing 'in the moral judgement made within some particular situation'; Ephesians describes a community where the practice of such judgement might be formed, and where the energy and patience for the long haul of 'tenacious incorporation, step by step, of a supplementary degree of compassion and generosity into all our codes' might be sustained in singing.[39]

The final point concerns the political relevance of the following verses:

> ... with all lowliness and gentleness, with patience, forbearing one another in love ... (Eph. 4.2)

> ... be kind to one another, tenderhearted, forgiving one another, as God in Christ forgave you. (Eph. 4.32)

This little family of virtues and practices, akin to the 'fruit of the Spirit' in Paul's letter to the Galatians (5.22f.), I will take under the heading of gentleness. That is a quality dear to Levinas (*douceur*). In Ricoeur it is embraced in his 'solicitude' and 'compassion'. In the Gospels

---

39. Jeremy Begbie convincingly relates musical improvisation to developing sensitivity to particular situations. Improvisation, he says, 'entails what the poet Peter Riley has called "the exploration of occasion". Much depends on the particularities of the specific context of performance – for example, the acoustic of the building, the time of day, he number of people present, their expectations and experience, their audible responses as the performance proceeds, and, not least, the music produced by fellow-improvisers ... Life in the Spirit ... involves a combination of faithfulness and particularising what is received in the present in anticipation of the future. This is the dynamic of musical improvisation ... [I]n improvisation we encounter an extraordinarily fruitful enacted model, where we find that disciplined fidelity to a shared tradition and a concern for singularity of circumstances are interwoven in a dynamic of patient and confident hopefulness.' ('Theology and the Arts. (2) Music' in Ford, *The Modern Theologians*, pp. 694f.)

it is the subject of a beatitude (Matt. 5.5) and of Jesus's self-description: 'I am gentle' (Matt. 11.29). In a culture of great physical, verbal and structural violence it may be that gentleness is a virtue of prophetic power. Ephesians sees gentleness at the heart of a community of tenderheartedness and forgiveness. A common alternative conception would be that there has to be toughness and even violence at the heart of an institution for it to survive and thrive, and any gentleness is an optional extra. The challenge of Ephesians, therefore, is not just to strive for Ricoeur's supplementary compassion and generosity but to try to make them constitutive.

Is that conceivable? The 'good news' of Ephesians is that they already are constitutive, however counter-intuitive that may seem. It testifies to the crucified and risen Jesus Christ as 'our peace' and to his constituting a community empowered to realise this peace in singing, suffering, patience and gentleness. It is a contingent realisation, as history clearly shows, and there are massively powerful forces against it. Yet the politics of faith and hope in this peace is one that not only patiently modifies the way society works but also generates institutions which can risk trusting that that really is the truth before God.[40]

Now having engaged with the 'word' of scripture in community I will turn to the dynamics of that 'sacrament' which is most formative of the worshipping self in Christian community.

---

40. One could gather examples of both the modification of institutions and institutional creativity along these lines.

As a significant modification I think of Broadmoor Hospital, a 'secure hospital' for the criminally insane, to which those convicted of some of the most horrendous crimes in England are sent. It has very tight security and tough 'nurses' trained in physical restraint. Part of its history in recent decades has been innovative forms of psychotherapy. A leading pioneer of this was Dr Murray Cox (1931–97) a leading authority on forensic psychotherapy (see C. Cordess and M. Cox, *Forensic Psychotherapy: Crime, Psychodynamics and the Offender Patient*, 2 vols., Jessica Kingsley, London 1996; M. Cox and A. Theilgaard, *Shakespeare as Prompter: The Amending Imagination and the Therapeutic Process*, Jessica Kingsley, London 1994). Overall, when compared with the past, the regime is an example of the introduction of a degree of gentleness, embodied in high quality therapeutic and dramatic communication, accompanied by realism about the need for security and restraint.

As an example of institutional creativity that has gentleness at its heart I think of the L'Arche Communities for the severely disabled, founded by Jean Vanier. They combine regular worship and celebration, much singing, and realism about suffering and death. One of the most striking features of the L'Arche homes I have visited is the role of touching. Gentle handling is the habitual accompaniment of ordinary living. The mutuality of touch is a basic form of communication. See David F. Ford, 'L'Arche and Jesus: What is the Theology?' (with other essays on L'Arche) in Frances M. Young (ed.), *Encounter with Mystery* (Darton, Longman and Todd, London 1997), pp. 77–88.

6

'Do this': a eucharistic self

The eucharist or holy communion or mass or Lord's supper is prob- ably the ritual most participated in and most discussed in human history. It is the principal act of worship of the majority of the billion and a half or so Christians in the world today and has some importance for most of the minority. It is a fruitful focus for a Christian theology of self and salvation partly for sheerly statistical reasons: it is rooted in the experience of most Christians century after century. But the statistics are not arbitrary; they reflect the fact that from the beginning of the church the eucharist has been intrinsic to its identity.

More specifically, the eucharist was inextricable from the earliest Christian conception of salvation. John McIntyre asks about the reason why the early church did not produce any developed definition of salvation comparable with those on christology and the Trinity, and he concludes convincingly that the main reason

> must surely be the centrality not only of a soteriological theme, but of the direct connection between the death of Christ and the forgiveness of sins, to [sic] all the *eucharistic liturgies* of the Church . . . If, further, we reflect that this understanding of the death of Christ [sc. as conveyed in the 'institution narrative' of the eucharist] was central to a liturgy practised, not just every Sunday, but more probably every time the congregation met – for the Eucharist *was* Christian worship; then we begin to realise that the atonement effected by the death of Christ was more integral to the worship-life of the church than to the thought-life of its theologians [original italics].[1]

This has generally continued to be so, though there have always been theologians who have tried to make the deep connections between their

1. John McIntyre, *The Shape of Soteriology* (T.&T. Clark, Edinburgh 1992), pp. 8, 10.

thought and the understanding and selfhood formed through eucharistic worship. An additional problem has been that, because explicitly eucharistic theology tended to emerge in response to Medieval and Reformation controversies, one danger has been that (especially in the eyes of later interpreters who are not immersed in the practice of the period when the controversy was going on) the issues concerning it have often been discussed in abstraction from the complex 'ecology' of how the eucharist actually worked as the main taken-for-granted ingredient in shaping the common-sense world of Christianity.

In this chapter I inquire into the formation of self through the eucharist. What happens to the self shaped through that worship? Simply as an inquiry about what has happened in the past and what happens around the world at present that would clearly be an impossible question to answer with anything approaching thoroughness. Most theological inquiry into what happens in the eucharist leads into discussing real presence, eucharistic sacrifice, valid ministry and so on. Those are important, but I am reluctant to forget about inquiry into actual practice. The difficulties are enormous. Eucharistic practice has been diverse from as far back as there are records – the New Testament accounts testifying to the Last Supper (no doubt reflecting the way the eucharist was celebrated in various early Christian communities) show significant differences. The sheer abundance of ways of trying to be faithful to these traditions defies description. Even if one were able to characterise the diversity of it over two thousand years, and now embracing every country in the world, there would still be the major problem of relating all that to the transformation of a particular self. One person in a particular worshipping community in one place and period is likely to have been formed through the eucharist differently at various stages of life; and through any year the content will have changed according to seasons, sermons, concerns in intercession and the manifold interplay with all the rest of the worshipper's life.

The richness and complexity of this phenomenon are a significant part of the context of this chapter. So I will start by trying to begin to do justice to it, both through some social anthropological remarks about the pervasiveness and diversity of eucharistic worship and through a theological response to that. That will be the springboard for an attempt to redescribe the eucharist in relation to some New Testament statements, without pretending that the intervening thousands of years that have generated so much eucharistic diversity have not occurred. The main concerns there will be imperatives, especially the imperative of death; and Jesus as an agent of incorporation, critical concepts being those of ordinariness, face to face relations, prophetic drama, and eucharistic time which embraces 'non-identical repetition'.[2] I will then try to do theological justice to the great New Testament surd as regards the Last Supper and eucharistic theology: their treatment in the Gospel of John. The final section will take up suggestions of earlier sections in order to develop the notion of a 'eucharistic self'. The overall aim of the chapter is to recapitulate and also develop previous chapters in relation to one fundamental practice of Christian communities. In the debates with Levinas, Jüngel and Ricoeur the notion of selfhood has in many respects been quite general. In the 'singing self' of Ephesians the sung word in worship was focussed on 'always and for everything giving thanks [*eucharistountes*] in the name of our Lord Jesus Christ to God the Father' (Eph. 5.20). Now the focus will be on the main liturgical practice through which that thanks has been expressed.

6.1 Doing justice to practice: anthropological and theological considerations

In order to sketch a context for the later part of this chapter I will take just four points about anthropological knowledge gained through fieldwork[3] and relate them to the eucharist and then make a brief theological comment.

6.1.1 The eucharistic habitus

The first is the non-verbal and habitual character of much practical knowledge. To ask participants: what is happening? may be very misleading. It is like asking experienced drivers to describe their own driving – they may offer accounts, including all sorts of rules and maxims, which are only marginally related to what good driving is actually about. Or, even more apposite, it is like asking what is going on in family life: the complexities go back generations and are embedded in

2. I am especially grateful to Catherine Pickstock for the use of the notion of non-identical repetition in relation to the eucharist: see her Cambridge University Ph.D. dissertation, 'The Sacred Polis. Language, Death and Liturgy' (1996) and 'Necrophilia: The Middle of Modernity. A Study of Death, Signs and the Eucharist' in *Modern Theology*, vol. 12, no. 4, October 1996, p. 429.
3. The anthropological points are made by Timothy Jenkins as he tries to elucidate the 'intrinsic elusive quality' of such knowledge in 'Fieldwork and the Perception of Everyday Life' in *Man*, ns, vol. 29, no. 2, June 1994, pp. 444ff.

multidimensional practices which are often adverted to with a frequency in indirect ratio to their importance.

It is hard to overestimate the importance for Christianity of the fact that the eucharist, a pivotal locus of its identity, is a corporate practice rather than, say, an ethical code, a worldview, a set of doctrines, an institutional constitution, a book, or some other distinctive feature. This connects with McIntyre's explanation as to why the early church produced so little formal doctrinal definition in relation to its main practical concern, salvation. How might the pervasive significance of the eucharist to which he points be further elucidated?

Pierre Bourdieu has tried to make sociologists and anthropologists more aware of the dangers of certain sorts of description which fail to do justice to practical modes of knowing. Neither 'objectivist' accounts, which abstract the 'rules' of a culture or ritual, nor 'subjectivist' accounts, in terms of individuals' free agency and interaction, are adequate. He tries to avoid the common dualisms here – not only objective and subjective, but 'culture' and 'personality', 'social' and 'individual', 'structuralist' and 'humanist'. A key concept is that of the 'habitus'. This is the set of dispositions (habitual ways of being and behaving, with a repertoire of predispositions, tendencies, propensities and inclinations, all shaped by structures and previous actions[4]) which structure and generate practices and representations.[5] He specially focusses on the '"art" of the *necessary improvisation*' (original italics) which defines 'excellence'[6] in living in a culture. The habitus is 'the durably installed generative principle of regulated improvisations'[7] through which the contingencies of ongoing life are responded to. As in any art, those who are best at performing it may be unreliable guides in giving an account of it.

The eucharist has, in its many variations, been a condensation of the Christian habitus. What I called above the complex ecology of how it has actually worked leads into all areas of life. Economics, power relations, and ways of perceiving, understanding and judging are woven together with the explicit themes. These dimensions are relevant to answering the question about what happens in the eucharist (as Paul in 1 Corinthians chapter 11 recognised), and often it is neither the words nor the confessed theological understandings that are most helpful in appreciating the dynamics of the celebration. Rather, one needs to follow the patterns of architecture and decoration; how and why these particular people gather in these ways; practices of welcoming or excluding; habits of presiding;

---

4. See Pierre Bourdieu, *Outline of a Theory of Practice* (Cambridge University Press, Cambridge 1977), p. 214 note 1.   5. Ibid., pp. 72ff.   6. Ibid., p. 8.   7. Ibid., p. 78.

forms of attentiveness and inattentiveness; the distribution of roles; dress, body language, music and other non-verbal symbols. And none of these might be obvious, since their practical meanings might be rooted in distant or recent history, or be expressions of an improvisation which relates in complex ways to different worshippers, or require that part of their meaning be related to the structures and habitus of the wider church and society. Such considerations complexify, even beyond the already great complexity of the theological discussions, the attempt to ask what happens to people in the eucharist. But at least they suggest why much eucharistic theology seems to miss so many of the points which an immersion in the habitus tells us should figure in the discussion. One might readily transfer to eucharistic theology Bourdieu's remark about 'the pure – because infinitely impoverished – realm of the "rules of marriage" and the "elementary structures of kinship"' which make so much anthropological theory inadequate.[8]

6.1.2 Apprenticeships

The second factor contributing to elusiveness in knowledge of social practices is 'the apprenticeships undergone by all actors'.[9] That is already implicit in the previous paragraph. Social knowledge is not had just by studying texts. To appreciate the many levels and interconnections there has to be a learning of dispositions, an involvement in which skills, perceptions, memories and desires are changed. A common problem is that of trying to short-circuit apprenticeship by taking an overall view. That makes a basic error, assuming that the social sphere is somehow transparent, accessible without the specific disciplines of 'fieldwork' which require that one play a role in the group or practice studied. Bourdieu calls this the 'synoptic illusion' and shows time and again how it falsifies the social dynamics. Instead of being like a map in which all available routes can be marked, social life is more like paths travelled and made more or less practicable by use or disuse.[10] Apprenticeship is following

---

8. Ibid., p. 70.   9. Jenkins, 'Fieldwork and the Perception', p. 444.
10. Bourdieu, *Outline of a Theory*, pp. 37f.: 'The logical relationships constructed by the anthropologist are opposed to "practical" relationships – practical because continuously practised, kept up, and cultivated – in the same way as the geometrical space of a map, an imaginary representation of all theoretically possible roads and routes, is opposed to the network of beaten tracks, of paths made ever more practicable by constant use.' Cf. p. 105: 'Just as genealogy substitutes a space of unequivocal, homogeneous relationships, established once and for all, for a spatially and temporally discontinuous set of islands of kinship, ranked and organized to suit the needs of the moment and brought into a practical existence gradually and intermittently, and just as a map replaces the discontinuous, patchy space of practical roads by the homogeneous, continuous space of geometry, so a calendar substitutes a linear, homogeneous, continuous time for practical

particular paths and learning how to negotiate them in all weathers. It is a matter of the quality of experience needed to understand and make judgements, and Jenkins suggests that good ethnography requires not only sincerity and accuracy but also experience and maturity.[11]

The eucharist is clearly a phenomenon which, in order to answer the question about what happens in it, requires apprenticeships in practical mastery rather than overviews. It is not that certain questions about it cannot be answered from the literature or from the abundant testimony of participants. The point is that such accounts in language alone are abstractions from its complex ecology. Reference to the need for apprenticeship serves at least three functions. First, it reminds any literary account of its limits and dangers. Second, it suggests what this chapter might, within these limits, aim to do – to deal with some of the literary aspects of the eucharist; to articulate with caution what accords with one's own apprenticeship, trying to relate that to the testimonies and understandings of others; to open up ways in which there can be appropriate contemporary improvisations in line with a eucharistic 'habitus'; and to relate all that to the discussion of the transformation of selves. Third, it reminds one of the wisdom of acknowledging the ways in which one might oneself have been shaped by one's own apprenticeships. There is no neutrality here, and there is no possibility of 'repeating experiments'. There have been multiple contingencies in an unrepeatable sequence along each path. My path has been through more than thirty years of Anglican eucharists of many sorts and in many contexts, combined with a theological training and with guest participation in other traditions. This issue will be discussed in a less personal way when I explore how the eucharist 'incorporates' participants. Its character as an activity which organises and transforms us means that the most fundamental questions are raised about perceptions and perspectives, desires, interests, power relations, priorities, and alternative ways of organising reality.

6.1.3 Coinherent practices
The third factor is 'the mutuality of all practices'.[12] This intensifies the second factor. Apprenticeships are complexly related to each other. To

time, which is made up of incommensurable islands of duration, each with its own rhythm, the time that flies by or drags, depending on what one is *doing*, i.e. on the *functions* conferred on it by the activity in progress.'

11. Jenkins, 'Fieldwork and the Perception', p. 445.   12. Ibid., p. 444.

take part with others in a eucharistic community over many years is to engage in a mutual shaping of lives with many dimensions. There are mutual adjustments, understandings and misunderstandings, fixing and crossing of boundaries, bodily behaviour, reactions to crises, corporate decisions and divisions, and so on. Everyone is engaged in other practices as well as the eucharist, and the interpenetration of these constantly changes the overall ecology. Power relations are especially important, overtly and covertly. These range from the role and nature of leadership and presidency through gender relations to the ways in which no individual is just him or herself but is always an embodiment of power relations between groups with a history of encounters.[13]

This mutual coinherence of practices in the eucharist is a locus of intensive exchanges in which the question of its characteristic ways of informing selves and their relations is always an issue. What is at stake is, as Bourdieu puts it (not, of course, with reference to the eucharist),

> the principle generating and unifying all practices . . . the *socially informed body*, with its tastes and distastes, its compulsions and repulsions, with, in a word, all its *senses*, that is to say, not only the traditional five senses – which never escape the structuring action of social determinisms – but also the sense of necessity and the sense of duty, the sense of direction and the sense of reality, the sense of balance and the sense of beauty, common sense and the sense of the sacred, tactile sense and the sense of responsibility, business sense and the sense of propriety, the sense of humour and the sense of absurdity, moral sense and the sense of practicality, and so on [original italics].[14]

The idea of a 'socially informed body' and 'all its senses' suits the eucharistic self well.

6.1.4 Representation in language

The final anthropological point is about 'the representational properties of language'.[15] The act of consciously adverting to an activity can distort it, and giving an account of it can 'freeze' it and allow it to be manipulated in ways that distance it from its context (for better or for worse). Language (especially in print) can also give an impression of exact repetition which is untrue to a temporal process in which such repetition does not happen. Questions about non-identical repetition will be taken up later with regard to the eucharist. The main point now is that theology

---

13. Ibid., p. 447.   14. Bourdieu, *Outline of a Theory*, p. 124.
15. Jenkins, 'Fieldwork and the Perception', p. 446.

needs to be wary of its habits of generalising about the eucharist, and the general statements of this chapter are to be read as verbal distillations of a convergence of practices, verbal and other, which can never transcend the fourfold elusiveness described by Jenkins. One of his concerns, like mine, is to do justice to everyday life, temporal, embodied and multi-levelled, and often language can only indicate how it is inadequate to the task.

More positively, the language of the eucharist needs to be recognised not only as intrinsically part of a multidimensional sign through which habitus, apprenticeships and coinherent practices are shaped, but also as itself diverse. Eucharistic language embraces many genres: praise, lament, confession, exclamation, narrative, proclamation, petition, and all the other genres of the Bible. It also unites the oral and the written, escaping many of the constrictions of both. Above all it is a language which is performed, and resists discursive overviews in a somewhat similar way to good drama.

6.1.5 The abundance of God

Besides that related to social anthropology, a second reason for paying close attention to the complex developments of eucharistic practice is more explicitly theological. It is intrinsic to Christian faith that it is true to itself only by becoming freshly embodied in different contexts. Life in the Spirit of Christ is, in Bourdieu's terms, a matter of 'necessary improvisation', and the new articulations and practices should not be seen as inessential derivatives. Theologically understood, they are testi-mony to God's creativity and abundance (though of course there can be inauthentic developments, discerning which is a controversial matter). They show the particularising activity of the Holy Spirit – a flourishing of distinctive and different realisations of the eventfulness of God. They enact in ways beyond any overview the truth of the doxology: 'Heaven and earth are full of your glory.'

It makes sense that a vision of the Kingdom of God seen in terms of inexhaustible feasting should be anticipated by a wealth of diverse forms of celebration. It also makes sense that a faith meant to be spread by respectful communication to each person and group should be able to accommodate and be enhanced by the distinctive responses of each of them in worship.

One result of the above anthropological and theological considera-tions is that the eucharist offers a superabundance of meaning. It is extravagantly 'overdetermined' in its significance. It continues to generate endless streams of devotion, practical implications, theological interpretations, music, art, architecture, mystical experiences, conversions, philosophical speculations, political ideals and, through them all, controversies, travesties and betrayals. Each major Christian doctrine can be worked out through it. Each part of the liturgy can be a lens through which the whole is understood, so that it can all be seen as visible word, as intercession, as communion or as praise. This might be overwhelming, but it can also be liberating. There can be no pretence of completeness, so it is excusable to select a few key themes for development.

6.2 Redescribing the eucharist

Bearing in mind the variations generated over two thousand years, how might some of the key elements in the New Testament eucharistic texts be thought through?

6.2.1 Imperatives

One obvious feature of the four New Testament stories of the institution of the eucharist is that imperatives run through them. Matthew has: 'Take, eat' (26.26), 'Drink' (26.27). Mark has: 'Take' (14.22). Luke has: 'Take . . . divide' (22.17), 'Do this' (22.19). Paul has: 'Do this' (1 Cor. 11.24), 'Do this' (v. 25). Whatever notion of transformation is found through the eucharist must be linked to command and obedience. Whatever notion of presence is affirmed must have the face to face authority of this person at its root.[16] The primacy of confrontational yet welcoming presence is clear in all the sources, and all the more important to emphasise because of the power of the incorporative thrust. The story is of one who while facing his disciples commands a practice which will be continued in face to face meals and looks towards the ultimate confrontation when 'he comes' (1. Cor. 11.26) or 'it is fulfilled in the

---

16. This priority of the imperative was seen particularly clearly by Martin Luther. David Dawson comments on Luther's *Confession Concerning Christ's Supper*: 'Luther moves between the extremes of idolatrizing presence and atheistic absence by invoking the notion of performance at crucial points in his argument, and by drawing on the ancient christological formulation of the Creed of Chalcedon for rules by which to think and speak with theological propriety about the character of divine presence . . . Zwingli wants to detach the imperative "Take, eat" from the declarative "this is my body." Luther insists that the statement must be taken as a whole and that priority must be given to its imperative aspect. He argues that when understood in this way, the entire utterance becomes performative – as much a deed as a word.' (*Literary Theory*, Fortress Press, Minneapolis 1995), pp. 55, 57.)

kingdom of God' (Luke 22.16).[17] The primary locus of transformation is in community with him in his irreducible otherness and in following his instruction.

This is intensified by the reference in all four sources to the covenant, with Matthew and Mark referring especially to Exodus 24, the 'blood of the covenant' ratifying the agreement of the people to obey what Moses had received on Sinai. The references to 'new covenant' in Luke and Paul evoke Jeremiah's vision of a new sort of obedience: 'I will put my law within them, and I will write it upon their hearts; and I will be their God and they shall be my people' (Jer. 31.33). What is most distinctive in this improvising on the covenant theme? It is the self-reference of Jesus: 'my body', 'my blood', 'in remembrance of me'. The obedience is tied inextricably to himself. There is a transformation of covenantal obedience, of the bonds that tie a people to God and each other. What is the nature of the change? The heart of it is to do with the way the person and message of Jesus are related. Jesus comes preaching and enacting the Kingdom of God. It is seen as obedience to his Father, pleasing his Father. In the pivotal Synoptic story of the transfiguration there is a complex, condensed message. It interweaves Moses and Elijah, resonances of Sinai, and a divine affirmation of Jesus as both pleasing God and to be obeyed. But there is also the focus on his person, his radiance. Message and person converge, and in Mark, Matthew and John the stories of the woman anointing Jesus carry this further in their focus on his body and death.[18] The Last Supper is where this knot is decisively tied. It looks to the culmination of Jesus's obedience in death and commands a sharing in his body and blood.

How does this affect the practice of obedience? It gives a particular face to the law. It makes communion with him the embracing commandment. There is an astonishing scandal of particularity, as the remembering of this person through this event becomes the context for one's vocation and the bond of one's community. I will soon move on to the enfolding, incorporative capacity of this remembering, but it is worth pausing to appreciate that particularity.

The Last Supper was a meal in the face of death. It was a situation of

---

17. The Paul–Luke tradition is especially strong on the eschatological dimension.
18. The fourth Gospel, as has often been noted, can be seen as distributing the message of the transfiguration throughout its story, and this is certainly true about the identification of person and message, most clearly seen in the Prologue and in the 'I am' sayings. Where the Synoptics have the Last Supper, John has another way of relating person and message in the footwashing and farewell discourses. This is discussed further below.

radical contingency in which complex forces and people converged on a climax in which participants could not know in advance how they would react. All were to be tested, Jesus above all. Of course the church's later remembering was of the continuation in crucifixion and resurrection, but it is extremely dangerous for the actual situation of the Last Supper to be forgotten. Kierkegaard's insistence that contemporaneity with Christ should follow the order of the story, and that one cannot have the resurrection without first passing through the crucifixion,[19] applies here too. The remembering is false if it is not connected with entering more fully into the contingencies and tragic potentialities of life in the face of evil and death. There can be no quick leap across Gethsemane and Calvary. Here are massive dislocation and disorientation, agonising loss and the demand to unlearn some of one's deepest convictions and habits. It is therefore very serious if a contemporary celebration of the eucharist dulls instead of sharpening the sense both of exposure to danger and of a God whose way of being God is to be involved in the contingencies in a shockingly complete and painful way.

This indwelling of the specific moment of the Last Supper could be explored in many ways. I will mention just one here. In *The Morals of Jesus*,[20] Nicholas Peter Harvey does full justice to the contingencies but also controversially affirms the specific way in which 'Jesus is Lord' in this situation. Scandalously, Jesus is a willing victim; he has chosen to come to Jerusalem to die. There is no sense of his simply being carried along by events. He is clear about his vocation to life through death. The various accounts describe the Last Supper as full of life – food, drink, singing, arguments, warnings, teaching, anticipation – while also being a rehearsal for death. It is life inseparable from obedience to death; an enactment of losing life in order to save it and of a grain of wheat falling into the ground in order to bear fruit. The deepest imperative is the sense of the necessity of this death.

Harvey says:

> Jesus' approach to his death as something desired, as something without which his destiny would be unfulfilled, left his friends in total disarray. They could not cope with the deathward direction of this life which they could only interpret as life-affirming in an unredeemed sense, stopping short of death. There was for them an

19. Sören Kierkegaard, *Training in Christianity and the Edifying Discourse which 'accompanied' it,* translated with an Introduction and Notes by Walter Lowrie (Princeton University Press, Princeton 1967), pp. 108ff.   **20.** Darton, Longman and Todd, London 1991.

appropriate disillusionment. They came to see the force of Jesus' searing words to the sign-seekers that the only sign that mattered was the sign of Jonah: that is to say, himself dead, Jesus in the heart of the earth. That is how he became, in being raised from the dead, the burning centre of this universe, the one in whom our cosmos finds its godward meaning, no longer bound by death.

In Jesus the human flight from reality, symptomatically expressed in the multiple forms taken by the denial of death, is put into reverse. His death unlocks in humanity our freedom to obey. Through his death the Spirit is ready to open up in us that capacity freely to embrace our vocation epitomised in the words, 'Having nothing, we possess all things.' Our surprise at those who in face of death seem to become more vibrantly alive suggests that we are slow to acknowledge this reversal, and to become alive to the capacity in ourselves to enact it.[21]

In this regard he repeatedly draws attention to Etty Hillesum in her writings from Westerbork, a transit-camp for Auschwitz.

The moment of the Last Supper, therefore, is one in which Jesus, facing death, draws his disciples into identification with his movement towards death in the interests of life. What Harvey calls Jesus's 'wild hope of human flourishing' is tied into this small, divided community and into his coming death. Jesus is sharing with them an unrepressed sense of death which allows that they too might give themselves with comparable radicality. To remember this moment is therefore to set ourselves before this face that has once been set towards Jerusalem and to identify with his death. Further, it is to be commanded in such a way that to recognise this death as 'for us' is to find that one's fundamental imperative is to improvise on it in new situations and so discover an unimaginable fulness of life through death. As Harvey says:

> I sometimes have a sense that what Jesus opened up in pursuit of this goal was so staggeringly ambitious on our behalf that we are still in part paralysed rather than empowered by the degree of exposure and risk involved. Hence, perhaps, regressive forms of slavish imitation, which keep the real opportunity and task at a distance. In the meantime the identification with him which is on offer finds its sign in the Eucharist, in which we 'celebrate the Lord's death until he comes.' Have we begun to glimpse what this might mean for our own living and dying, and for the destiny of humanity?[22]

21. Ibid., p. 93.   22. Ibid., p. 38.

6.2.2 Incorporation: ordinary life face to face

The church lives in the face of this imperative person and event, being shaped by a habitus which is continually reshaped by further improvisations. One aspect that has already begun to come clear might be called the distinctive dynamic of incorporation enacted by Jesus at the Last Supper. This is another theme so rich that it could be developed in many directions. There is an extraordinary concentration of meaning associated with it, and much recent thought about the eucharist has helpfully stressed the importance of *koinonia*, especially in its ecumenical implications.[23] I want to focus on Jesus as an agent of incorporation, with special reference to ordinary life, otherness, prophetic drama and historical time.

The Last Supper is a gathering of people who have had many meals together. It is inseparable from eating and drinking, a common language, sharing life at close quarters, being involved in the same rituals, and being part of that society at that time and place. Its being a meal in particular makes sure that it resonates with the most common and basic practices necessary for sustaining life. It evokes the whole realm of the material, the bodily, the economic, and the recurrent habits of social life which are the unavoidable accompaniments of eating and drinking in all cultures. It ensures a deep connection with ordinary patterns of repetitive behaviour, common substances, artefacts and words. Such commonplace things are not told of in narratives of events or in dramas; they are not about the individual, the personal or the unique. They are the stuff of ordinariness, of domesticity and all that constitutes 'home'.[24]

This is intensified by the use of familiar gesture (breaking bread, passing a cup) and by the immediate involvement of touch and taste,

---

23. Robert Jenson in *Unbaptized God. The Basic Flaw in Ecumenical Theology* (Fortress Press, Minneapolis 1992) summarises some of the results of ecumenical discussions as follows:
    Jesus' sacrificial act on the cross is his giving of himself *to* the Father *for* us and inseparably his giving of himself *to* us in *obedience* to the Father. What he gives is therefore communion: our communion with him, and just so our communion with the Father and with one another. Just so again, the content of this encompassing communion is our sharing in Jesus' 'own life and fate', which is to say, in his self-giving, his sacrifice. Precisely in that Jesus sacramentally gives himself to us in the bread and cup of the Eucharist, all these dialectics belong also to the event of the eucharistic meal, of his giving the bread and cup and our receiving them. The sacrament of his self-giving to us incorporates us as a communion, as the church, precisely into the communion of his sacrifice of himself and of us to the Father. (p. 40)
24. For some rich (though often quite contentious) reflection on this in relation to still life see Norman Bryson, *Looking at the Overlooked. Four Essays on Still Life Painting* (Harvard University Press, Cambridge, MA 1990).

those most intimate of senses. The words of Jesus draw extraordinary attention to the bread and wine (or cup). Those elements are drawn into the drama of the occasion with the force of paradox or of prophetic gesture – and the battle of interpretations still goes on. But, whatever the interpretation, the realm of the ordinary has been taken up and involved in the most momentous events without rejection, contrast or competition between the two. There is no middle ground needed, no mediating of the ordinary to the extraordinary. The God who is implied by the blessing of these elements is at home with matter and its routine usage as well as with the climactic drama of Jesus's life. This integrates the sphere of the ordinary with the historically significant in a way that recalls features of the cultic and of the sacrificial, and the injunction to repeat it draws the parallel further. But there is a low-key homeliness and intimacy about the Last Supper that has always acted as a resource for critique of the ritual embellishments of tradition, which yet in their turn can never as a class be ruled out as inappropriate improvisations. The main thrust is towards blessing the ordinary, and if ritual (or anything else, such as the categories of narrative, drama or 'sacramentality') threatens to function as a middle ground and develops a dynamic that fails to refer one insistently back to the transformation of the ordinary, then this critical resource can be activated.

An essential part of the homeliness is the priority of face to face relationships between those who know each other well. These, together with the ordinary routines and elements, help to give density and universality to the occasion. The specificity of what goes on in this sphere is a clue to the quality of incorporation that Jesus is realising. He and the disciples come to the meal with a history of face to face interaction in many situations. It is itself in many ways a repetition of other meals together, other occasions for eating, teaching, argument and surprise developments. All of that accumulation of events in the interpersonal sphere has been incorporating them with Jesus into a distinctive community. What we know of that Jewish milieu confirms the communal, incorporative significance of meals. David Stacey sums it up: 'Fundamentally meals stand for togetherness and reconciliation between the participants, and between the participants and Yahweh.'[25]

But this is togetherness with sharp differentiation. I have brought this

---

25. David Stacey, 'The Lord's Supper as Prophetic Drama' in *Epworth Review*, vol. 21, no. 1, January 1994, p. 68.

out already in relation to the imperatives and above all the imperative of death for Jesus. One of those present must die, and their togetherness has to incorporate that – or, rather, be incorporated into it. They are approaching something which will test the bonds of their community past breaking point. This is reflected in accompanying stories of disputes about power and honour in the community and the foretelling of Peter's denial. The massive differentiator is, however, the betrayal by Judas. This is so deeply embedded in the tradition that the betrayal is even mentioned by Paul. It is the differentiation classically called judgement.

6.2.3 Incorporation: prophetic drama

In the face of all this Jesus as an agent of incorporation performs what David Stacey calls a prophetic drama. Stacey shows how the main features of prophetic drama come together to make this category the most appropriate one for what might be conjectured to have happened at the Last Supper.[26] Prophets often responded to a divine compulsion by dramatically signifying a larger event, and in the process they used everyday, oft-repeated actions, they let ordinary objects represent something else for the purpose of the drama, they used mimetic elements, and they sometimes accompanied this with words which deepened rather than explained. There was also often an urgent, imperative meaning. It fits the Last Supper very well, and in Stacey's interpretation makes the incorporative meaning central.

There is yet another feature which is especially relevant to the action of Jesus. The prophets often involved other people unwittingly in their dramatic acts. Jesus at the Last Supper is incorporating those who will betray, deny and abandon him. He does something that can create a community of trust on the other side of the rupture, but meanwhile he himself carries the responsibility for it alone. The language of 'given for you', of representation and even substitution is appropriate. He forms a community for them without their trust or understanding. He does the trusting, obeying, suffering and dying. This lack of presumption that they have to do anything right to be the recipients of the bread and wine makes it an archimedean point of receptivity – and, therefore, of potential gratitude. It can be for whoever eats and drinks. The universality of food and drink is combined with the particularity of this person and this story. They are

---

26. Ibid.

together in the Last Supper and together in the picture of the eating and
drinking in the Kingdom of God.

6.2.4 Incorporation: eucharistic time and
non-identical repetition

In between the Last Supper and the expected consummation signified by
the Kingdom of God there is history punctuated by obedience to the
command to 'Do this'. This is eucharistic time – time understood and
shaped through the reality celebrated repeatedly in the eucharist.

Repetition is an immensely rich theme and pervades life. It occurs in
innumerable forms, and consideration of it has been a characteristically
modern way into some of the basic issues of philosophy. There are aspects
of modernity which seem fixated on identical repetition. It can be seen in
strict correspondence theories of truth and of language; in notions of the
proper meaning of a text; in the mass production of commodities; in the
endless reduplication of cultural artefacts; in bureaucratic and totalitarian concepts of authority and law; in the translatability of value into
money; in scientific knowledge as the result of repeatable experiments;
in the maintenance of racial purity; in quests for standardisation and
universal norms; in reductionist accounts of humanity, ethics, religion
and much else; and in fundamentalist interpretations of scripture or
tradition that hold out the hope of identically repeating what has been.
One way of seeing postmodernity is as a reaction against this: emphasising difference to the point of the disintegration of identities; suspecting
that all discernment of sameness is an attempt by the stronger to integrate and dominate; contextualising or relativising every apparent
universal so that it appears as particular after all; finding in every 'correspondence' what does not correspond; multiplying interpretations of
every text; and so on.

Yet those somewhat stereotypical extremes set only some of the terms
for a range of constructive responses to the phenomenon of repetition. Of
special significance to the present discussion, philosophies of knowledge, language, hermeneutics and history have found ways other than
having to choose between the polarised alternatives of strict correspondence or the abandonment of reference. Ricoeur's long-term reflection on
metaphor and analogy has produced such a 'third way'. The strongly
emphasised 'as' in 'oneself as another' requires a notion of analogy which
construes being itself in those terms. Of comparable relevance to the
eucharist, his discussion of the reference of narrative culminates, after

extended examination of both historical and fictional narratives, in replacing the concept of reference by the more embracing (but not less rigorous) concept of refiguration. Central to that is a strong emphasis on the analogical 'as' in Ranke's dictum that history is about 'the facts as they really happened'.[27] This helps to conceive of the relation of the eucharist to history. It draws on the resources not only of documents and 'traces' which testify to its origins but also on the narrative imagination and on other resources of language, tradition, gesture and contemporary life, in order to pay the debt to the past. Eucharistic performance can be seen as a complex 'standing-for' which constantly refigures in order to pay its debt of memory. Improvisation is part of this refiguring, and is part of what I will now discuss under the concept of non-identical repetition.

I start with Kierkegaard, who saw repetition as a critical concept for modern philosophy[28] and as having an intrinsic relation with the new: 'repetition properly so called is recollected forwards'.[29] He also saw it as vital to understanding time, the ethical and the Christian.[30] But with regard to my topic perhaps the most intriguing point in his elusive discussion of repetition is his comment on the story of Job. By the end of the story 'Job is blessed and has received everything *double*. This is what is called a *repetition*.'[31] The way there led through losing everything so that 'in the sense of immediacy all is lost'.[32] Then through 'a thunderstorm' it is resolved into this abundant repetition, a blessing from God.

---

27. On the one side (which might be seen as the issue of 'modern' repetition) the question is: Is the reality of the past to which history testifies repeated (or re-enacted) in the present in story form? Ricoeur wants to retain reference and documentation while rejecting the notion of identical re-enactment. History is not adequately described 'under the sign of the same' (*Time and Narrative*, vol. III, pp. 144ff.). Or, on the other side (which might be seen as the issue of 'postmodern' refusal of repetition) is the reality of the past always elusive and different from any account? Ricoeur respects the distance and strangeness of the past but argues against a 'negative ontology of the past' because 'in the last analysis, the notion of difference does not do justice to what seems to be positive in the persistence of the past in the present'. History is not adequately described 'under the sign of the "other"' (pp. 147ff.). The mediating position which he adopts is to see the referent of historical narrative 'under the sign of the analogous' (pp. 151ff.). He retains the primacy of the referential intention of history. But he comments on Ranke's expression 'the facts as they really happened': 'In the analogical interpretation of the relationship of "taking the place of" or "standing-for", the "really" is signified only through the "as"' (p. 155). Analogy retains connection with both re-enactment and taking a distance. It stands for the past while recognising that the most it can say is that it happened *like* this. This means that the activity of 'referring' is more adequately rendered as 'refiguring'.

28. Sören Kierkegaard, *Repetition. An Essay in Experimental Psychology* (Harper, New York 1964), p. 33.   29. Ibid.

30. Cf. ibid., Walter Lowrie's Introduction; and, for a perceptive comparative study of what Kierkegaard means by his concept of repetition, with special reference to temporality, similarity and difference, see Arne Melberg, *Theories of Mimesis* (Cambridge University Press, Cambridge 1995).   31. *Repetition*, p. 117.   32. Ibid., p. 118.

This 'doubling' repetition of the eucharist is perhaps best approached through the name I am using for it, 'eucharist' meaning 'thanks'. In gratitude the past is repeated in such a way that it is fruitful in a new way for the present and future. It is somewhat paradoxical: what has been completed continues. The more decisively and gloriously completed it is the more richly it can continue in repetition. In this way the good of the past can overflow into continuing life. Those people to whom we owe great gratitude never cease to evoke it, and the habit of thanks itself helps to transform our life and enrich our relationships. There is an expansive dynamic of non-identical repetition which can take into its flow new people, events and practices. Gratitude does, in fact, frequently generate surprises. The urge to correspond adequately in words, gifts, actions and even a whole way of life inspires creativity in all those spheres.

The greatest occasions for our gratitude act in our lives or the histories of our communities like what Solzhenitsyn calls a 'knot' in history.[33] A 'knot' is a time when there is a convergence of significant strands so as to affect the shape of a history decisively. In our own lives many of us can probably think of periods which were pivotal and formative. At least it makes sense to talk of some events being more important than others – marrying my wife more significant than dropping my pencil. This is true also of groups, nations and conceivably of humanity. It is, of course, possible to dispute this and to deny any narrative sense to history, and I would not want to claim any clear unitary plot.[34] It is rather a matter of using the metaphor of a 'knot' to illustrate how thanks for an event such as that remembered in the eucharist can gather strands significant for the past and the future, and how there need be no limit to its significance.[35]

33. Solzhenitsyn works out this idea most fully in his novel *August 1914. The Red Wheel 1. A Narrative in Discrete Periods of Time* (The Bodley Head, London 1989), in which August 1914 is regarded as such a 'knot' in Russian history.
34. Indeed, I see the eucharist as subversive of any clear conception of a 'metanarrative' in history. The non-identical repetition of this liturgy has endless implications and it is not possible to set a limit to its relevance to continuing history; but that is a very different matter from claiming that the plot of its story is in any direct sense the plot of universal history. The indirect sense in which it testifies to the ultimate meaning of history is in attesting to the one before whom history is judged and blessed. But life before that face is full of surprises. The eucharist (and Christian faith in general) gives no privileged knowledge of the plot of history; it encourages a great deal of agnosticism about the future together with a trust that it is ultimately eucharistic. The Johannine emphasis on the ethical thrust of the Last Supper is sometimes seen as a conscious alternative to, or demythologising of, overspecific eschatological scenarios.
35. Such 'knots' are related to by being continually refigured in thoughts, words and acts of remembrance. Ricoeur speaks of the most significant of them as:
those events that a historical community holds to be significant because it sees in them an origin, a return to its beginnings. These events, which are said to be

It can become epoch-making, as the event of Jesus did, eventually inspiring a calendar[36] used around the world.

Thanks easily modulates into praise.[37] There the greater the perfection the more repetition is evoked, classically including the repetition of the name of the one praised. To live in a divine presence inexhaustibly creative, wise, good, merciful, and so on, is to find repetition infinitely rich and surprising. It is a logic that leads Kierkegaard to say that 'repetition is always a transcendence', and also to talk of eternity as 'the true repetition'.[38] Praise is an active receptivity which is free within the dynamics of non-identical repetition. The eucharist informs that responsive freedom by orienting it on the decisive 'knot' of history and allowing for endless improvisation in gratitude and praise.[39]

But Kierkegaard wrote of blessing rather than thanks or praise. In the eucharist, to consider blessing draws us back to Jesus as an agent of

> 'epoch-making', draw their specific meaning from their capacity to found or reinforce the community's consciousness of its identity, its narrative identity, as well as the identity of its members. These events generate feelings of considerable ethical intensity, whether this be fervent commemoration or some manifestation of loathing, or indignation, or of regret or compassion, or even the call for forgiveness. (*Time and Narrative*, vol. III, p. 187)

The Last Supper, death and resurrection of Jesus are clearly 'epoch-making' in that sense. Ricoeur's argument is that such events (the one he discusses is the Holocaust) especially call for the resources of fiction (in his sense, which allows fiction a vital imaginative relation to reality) as well as of history if their singularity and 'uniquely unique' character are to be done justice to.

36. Cf. Ricoeur's exploration of the role calendars play in the connection of phenomenological, lived, 'subjective' time with cosmic, universal, 'objective' time in *Time and Narrative*, pp. 104ff. He sees two other such 'reflective instruments' operating alongside calendars, 'the idea of the succession of generations – and . . . recourse to archives, documents, and traces' (vol. III, p. 104).

The eucharist is involved deeply with all three of those 'reflective instruments'. The annual Christian calendar culminates in the events of Holy Week and Easter Sunday, which are remembered in the eucharist. It fits well the function Ricoeur ascribes to the calendar: 'It cosmologizes lived time and humanizes cosmic time. This is how it contributes to reinscribing the time of narrative into the time of the world' (p. 109). The eucharist is even more radical in its claims: it holds that the one it remembers is the one by whom the world is timed.

The realm of contemporaries, predecessors and successors is also held together through the eucharist. It reaches back through history represented in the Old Testament and the unbroken succession of celebrations over two thousand years, it reaches around the world today, and it anticipates the gathering of all peoples before God.

Finally, the eucharist is testified to in traces and in archives (defined by Ricoeur as a set of documents resulting from institutional activity), and suits well his criterion for the meaningfulness of history:

> As soon as the idea of a debt to the dead, to people of flesh and blood to whom something really happened in the past, stops giving documentary research its highest end, history loses its meaning. (p. 118)

37. On the theology of thanks and praise see further Hardy and Ford, *Jubilate*, *passim*.
38. Kierkegaard, *Repetition*, pp. 90, 126.
39. Cf. Rowan Williams on music in *Open to Judgement*, pp. 247ff.

incorporation without losing responsiveness and mutuality. Perhaps the best summary of what happens in the eucharist is: *The blessing of Jesus Christ*.[40] Blessing is a word whose biblical and traditional use enables us to maintain the priority of God without seeming to diminish humanity or creation. God blesses and is blessed, we bless and are blessed, creation blesses and is blessed, and a glorious ecology of blessing is the climactic vision of the Kingdom of God. It is perhaps the best of all ways to the theological heart of non-identical repetition. The eucharist generates a habitus of blessing and offers a hospitality which incorporates people and the material world by blessing.

This could be explored in many directions, but I will conclude this point by looking briefly at Luke's Gospel. In Luke, Jesus is blessed as a baby by Simeon (2.28, 34), in the sermon on the plain there is an ethic of blessing those who curse you (6.28), and the thanks over bread and wine at the Last Supper (which in that context means the same as blessing) are echoed by the climactic moment of the post-resurrection Emmaus story (24.30). Then Luke concludes his Gospel:

> Then he led them out as far as Bethany, and lifting up his hands he blessed them. While he blessed them, he parted from them, and was carried up into heaven. And they returned to Jerusalem with great joy, and were continually in the temple blessing God. (24.50–3)

This is not the place to consider the problems of the ascension or to compare this ending with those of the other Gospels. Luke's main point is not about disappearing feet but about the blessing by Jesus. I will improvise on this a little.

The Emmaus meal had been a rehearsal involving blessing and disappearance. That ran on into the story of Jesus emphasising the reality of his risen body by eating fish. (The risen Jesus might be taken as the Christian definition of non-identical repetition.) After that he interprets scripture in relation to himself as fulfilled, he affirms the disciples as witnesses and he promises the Holy Spirit. The blessing of the ascension gathers up all that and more into a closure which implies both absence and presence. There has been a transfer of understanding, responsibilities and promises; the continuing bodily humanity of Jesus has been affirmed; and the final blessing with pierced hands might be seen as the ultimate image of fulfilment in finitude, appropriately responded to by 'great joy' and blessing God. It is an image of life through transfer and exchange, of face to face inspiring (the fourth Gospel's partial analogue is

---

40. The genitive is both objective and subjective.

the face to face breathing of the Spirit), of fulness in being for others, of corporate vocation, of recapitulation and anticipation, and of Jesus as an agent of incorporation by blessing. The whole final chapter of Luke is a massive reinforcement of the command to 'do this in remembrance of me' (22.19), and, in the form of a final remembering, it suggests an embracing definition of what happens in the eucharist: the blessing of Jesus as the blessing of God.[41] If that 'as' is given the full ontological weight of 'being as', then the way is opened for a concept of real presence which does justice to time, event and personhood in relation to the trinitarian God.[42]

6.3 Refiguring the eucharist: the Johannine improvisation

There is a startling, provocative tension in the New Testament testimony to the eucharist. The Gospel of John has a Last Supper, including the betrayal by Judas, before Jesus's death. But there is no mention of bread and body, wine and blood – it is definitely not the story of the institution of the eucharist as told by the other Gospels or Paul. Instead there is a different action, which can also be described as a prophetic drama: Jesus washes his disciples' feet and instructs this to be repeated:

> When he had washed their feet, and taken his garments, and resumed his place, he said to them, 'Do you know what I have done to you? You call me Teacher and Lord; and you are right, for so I am. If I then, your Lord and Teacher, have washed your feet, you also ought to wash one another's feet. For I have given you an example, that you also should do as I have done to you. Truly, truly, I say to you, a servant is not greater than his master; nor is he who is sent greater than he who sent him. If you know these things, blessed are you if you do them.' (John 13.12–17)

41. Again the genitives are both objective and subjective. On 'being as' see Ricoeur, *Time and Narrative*, vol. III, pp. 154f. and *Oneself As Another*, tenth Study.

Calvin would seem to be right in interpreting the eucharist from the ascension. There was a danger that the Lutheran affirmation of the ubiquity of Christ would compromise the continuing particularity of his humanity. It also threatens the eschatological tension of presence and absence in the eucharist. Luke's image of separation from face to face encounter until seeing him 'come in the same way as you saw him go' (Acts 1.11) clearly affirms both the particularity and a mode of absence. Cf. for a most illuminating discussion of this Douglas Bryce Farrow, 'Ascension and Ecclesia. On the Significance of the Doctrine of the Ascension for Ecclesiology and Christian Cosmology' (Ph.D. dissertation, King's College London 1994).

42. Cf. Jenson, *Unbaptized God*. He analyses the huge amount of ecumenical discussion of the eucharist and related matters, and he is particularly illuminating on the need for the concept of real presence to be thought through in a way that allows notions of time, event and person to coinhere and to relate to the trinitarian God.

In addition, from chapters 13 to 17 there is much teaching, conversation and prayer which are not mentioned elsewhere, before the arrest of Jesus in chapter 18 rejoins the general direction of the other versions.

Yet it is not a matter of John ignoring the bread and body, wine and blood. He has the most radical New Testament affirmation of them in chapter 6. After feeding more than five thousand people Jesus gives some teaching in relation to himself, Moses, faith, resurrection, eternal life, bread, seeing the Father, and much else. What the listeners find most difficult is what is said about eating and drinking Jesus's flesh and blood:

> 'I am the living bread which came down from heaven; if anyone eats of
> this bread, he will live for ever; and the bread which I shall give for the
> life of the world is my flesh.' The Jews then disputed among
> themselves, saying, 'How can this man give us his flesh to eat?' So
> Jesus said to them, 'Truly, truly, I say to you, unless you eat the flesh of
> the Son of man and drink his blood, you have no life in you; he who
> eats my flesh and drinks my blood has eternal life, and I will raise him
> up at the last day. For my flesh is food indeed, and my blood is drink
> indeed. He who eats my flesh and drinks my blood abides in me, and I
> in him ... Do you take offence at this? Then what if you were to see the
> Son of man ascending where he was before? It is the spirit that gives
> life, the flesh is of no avail; the words that I have spoken to you are
> spirit and life. (John 6.51–6, 61b–63)

There is a flood of questions about the eucharist in John, and the commentators are deeply divided.[43] Did 'John' (whoever the author was) know the eucharistic traditions of the other Gospels and Paul? Or does he simply reflect the practice of some early church communities with different traditions? Did the account fall out accidentally in the course of transmission? Is he deliberately 'anti-sacramental' or at least correcting what he regards as a wrong emphasis on the eucharist? Or does he presuppose the eucharist throughout, writing his Gospel as homilies for the eucharistic setting and omitting the story of the institution at the Last Supper because that came elsewhere in the service? Are chapters 13–17 the 'final discourse of a great man' inspired by Moses in the Old Testament and other models? That would fit well with Ricoeur's idea of a momentous event eliciting 'fiction' in order to do fuller justice to its meaning. Did an editor modify John chapter 6 in order, through the final verse (v. 63)

---

43. See Barnabas Lindars, *The Gospel of John* (Marshall, Morgan and Scott, London 1972) pp. 441ff. for a survey of some of the main possibilities; C. K. Barrett, *Essays on John* (SPCK, London 1982), chapter 6; and, for a treatment of many of the broad issues, D. Moody Smith, *Johannine Christianity. Essays on its Setting, Sources and Theology* (T. & T. Clark, Edinburgh 1984) and *The Theology of the Gospel of John* (Cambridge University Press, Cambridge 1995).

quoted above, to soften the extremism of eating and drinking flesh and blood with reference to spirit and word? While bearing in mind these questions, I want to take the text of John in its present redacted form as part of the New Testament in order to draw out its significance for the eucharist today and in particular for my present theme of incorporation into eucharistic time.

One effect of John's approach is that there is a highlighting of the death and resurrection of Jesus. John 6 does this as part of a series of 'sign' narratives in chapters 5–12, each of which anticipatorily develops aspects of the meaning of the final chapters. In chapter 6 itself John

> makes striking use of his community's supper tradition to insist that faith in the life-giving Son of man means entrusting oneself to him who gave his body to suffering and death that others might have life . . . [T]here is no way of preserving eternal life for ourselves except by sharing his death in whatever corresponding way is presented to us. If that is your meat and drink, you will live for ever.[44]

The fact that chapter 6 takes place near Passover, just as chapters 13–17 do, intensifies the primary Passover typology of the eucharist (which is shared with the Synoptic traditions). In chapters 13–17 there is a long drawn-out anticipation of the death and resurrection, with preparation for its grief, its joy, and a life beyond it which yet centres on it. None of it contradicts eucharistic celebration but could be construed as an improvisatory variation upon it.

Another, closely related, effect is the focus on the quality of the 'community of the face' which is formed around Jesus. The footwashing enacts an ethos of service and hospitality, embodied in a network of welcome: 'Truly, truly, I say to you, he who receives any one whom I send receives me; and he who receives me receives him who sent me' (13.20). Judas is the antithesis of this, and it is only after he leaves that the Johannine equivalent of the Synoptic 'new covenant' is given: 'A new commandment I give to you, that you love one another; even as I have loved you, that you also love one another. By this all will know that you are my disciples, if you have love one for another' (13.34f.). This imperative is stressed time and again: it is the 'Do this!' at the heart of John's reworking of the eucharistic theme. The promised Holy Spirit 'will teach you all things, and bring to your remembrance all that I have said to you' (14.26), which in context refers especially to the new commandment. The community theme is enriched by the image of Jesus as the true vine and

44. Grayston, *Dying We Live*, p. 300.

the need to abide in him, which is again explained in terms of love: 'As the Father has loved me, so have I loved you; abide in my love. If you keep my commandments, you will abide in my love, just as I have kept my Father's commandments and abide in his love. These things I have spoken to you, that my joy may be in you and that your joy may be full' (15.9–11).

This joyful responsibility of love is then expressed as an ethos of friendship informed by the death of Jesus:

> Greater love has no man than this, that a man lay down his life for his friends. You are my friends if you do what I command you. No longer do I call you servants, for the servant does not know what his master is doing; but I have called you friends, for all that I have heard from my Father I have made known to you.' (15.13–15)

This is contrasted with the inevitable persecution they will suffer, and chapter 16 deals with questions of presence and absence inseparable from Jesus's death and resurrection. Finally, the community-building theme reaches its climax in the prayer of Jesus in chapter 17. The prayer is for their unity in love and truth and also for 'all those who believe in me through their word' (17.20). It is a community of the face which is always oriented to the facing of Jesus: 'Father, I desire that they also, whom thou hast given me, may be with me where I am, to behold my glory which thou hast given me in thy love for me before the foundation of the world' (17.24).

In what follows, even on the cross Jesus is forming community: 'When Jesus saw his mother, and the disciple whom he loved standing near, he said to his mother, "Woman, behold your son!" Then he said to the disciple, "Behold your mother!" and from that hour the disciple took her to his own home' (John 19.27). Finally, in the resurrection stories John offers an utterly face to face account of the joint transformation of the disciples into a community of forgiveness: 'He breathed on them, and said to them, "Receive the Holy Spirit. If you forgive the sins of any, they are forgiven; if you retain the sins of any, they are retained"' (20.22f.).

Besides the concentration on the cross and resurrection in relation to the building of a community of the face, John not only practises improvisation on the traditions he has received but also gives a rationale for endless further 'faithful innovation'. The Holy Spirit leads into further truth. 'But when the Counsellor comes, whom I shall send to you from the Father, even the Spirit of truth, who proceeds from the Father, he will bear witness to me' (15.26). This confidence in the accessibility of inexhaustible truth underwrites the deepening of the eucharistic moment before Jesus's death which chapters 13–17 offer. It also encourages further enrichments. These are not only in understanding, they are in action too – John has a strong concept of doing the truth. His (or his tradition's) most striking variation is the dramatic footwashing. This is the glory (in the Johannine meaning of that term, seen above all in the crucifixion) of the cross in action. But then soon afterwards there is a promise of innovation in action that goes beyond any repetition of what even Jesus has done: 'Truly, truly, I say to you, he who believes in me will also do the works I do; and greater works than these will he do, because I go to the Father' (14.12).

Here we have the heart of the Johannine contribution to a conception of eucharistic time. He refigures time by an innovative retelling of the story of the epochal event of Jesus's death and resurrection. He does this through evoking a habitus of love centred on it, which includes drawing constantly on the Old Testament. It is like a recapitulation of the main points of this chapter. There is the improvisation on a habitus and apprenticeship in a community. John sets up mutually interacting eucharistic practices by affirming not only the eating and drinking of the body and blood of Christ but also the footwashing. He extends the moment of the Last Supper over five chapters, offering a discourse whose repetitive language immerses readers, in a way comparable to liturgy, in an evocation of an ethos of friendship in God. As in my account above of the institution of the eucharist, the imperative is the embracing mood. The drama of incorporation is focussed through a prophetic action. The 'world of the text' which this helps create is one of joyful responsibility before one who breathes the Holy Spirit face to face. This is 'ethical time' which is tied into the repetitive eating of the eucharist by that climactic statement of John 6.63: 'The words that I have spoken to you are spirit and life.' Reaching further back in John it is tied into worship of the Father 'in spirit and truth' (John 4.23f.). Looking further forward, it culminates in Thomas's worship facing the risen Jesus: '"My Lord and my God!"' (John 20.28).

Within the Christian eucharistic tradition John stands as a constant interrogation of sacramental practices. He is especially subversive of any fundamentalism, whether of Bible, tradition or liturgy, which conceives of the identity of a person or community in terms of past-oriented identi-

cal repetition. He is equally resistant to innovation which does not penetrate deeper into the tradition. Above all he stands as a Levinassian figure
obsessed with the joyful responsibility of obeying the imperative to love.
The legend about him was that in his old age he repeated over and over
again: 'My children, love one another!'

6.4 Conclusion: a eucharistic self

What conception of self might be formed through habituation to the
eucharist? What sort of apprenticeship helps that self to flourish?

6.4.1 Blessed

The most embracing description is that a eucharistic self is blessed and
blesses. In earlier chapters, culminating in the previous chapter's
'singing self', I discussed coping with the abundance of God. A God who
blesses in the ways testified to in the Bible and later traditions poses the
problem of how to cope with the generosity of blessing, wisdom, truth,
love, forgiveness, compassion, beauty and so on.[45] The eucharist is the
focal Christian way of coping, and selfhood needs to be conceived in its
terms. Most images and concepts of the self are impoverished in comparison with what emerges from the abundant meaning of a celebration
which allows scope for dynamic relationship with God, other people and
creation to be conceived in such rich terms: through taste and physicality;
through drama and history; through being commanded, judged and forgiven; through multifaceted responsiveness in word and action; through
learning; through hospitality and a range of other exchanges; through
individualisation and incorporation.

The self in this dynamic relationality can be elucidated by various disciplines and described in many genres and concepts. My culminating
formal concept was that of non-identical repetition. In relation to each
Christian this recalls the blessing which is given in baptism. A eucharistic self is a baptised self in the routine of being blessed and blessing.
Baptism is the archetypical Christian sign of personal identity, non-
identically repeating Jesus's baptism, his death and resurrection, and the
baptism of every other Christian. This is the initiating sacrament of
blessing: being named and blessed in the name of the Father, Son and

---

45. Brian Gerrish's fine discussion, *Grace and Gratitude. The Eucharist Theology of John Calvin*
(T. & T. Clark, Edinburgh 1993), is superb on Calvin's appreciation of the eucharist as a
celebration of the abundant goodness of God.

Holy Spirit. It signifies the reality and availability of the abundance; it invites and initiates into a eucharistic practice in order to sustain a life of flourishing within the infinite love and joy of God.

6.4.2 Placed

A person only occupies one place at a time, and selfhood is bound up with particularity of place. Baptism and eucharist are a new placing of the self: under water (though for most this is attenuated into a few drops) and around a table. Inseparable from the water and the table are other people, the community of the face. Space is not just a container. It is refigured through matter and action, filled with the sound of words and music. The body is the primary place of convergence for action and matter: in the marking of the cross on the forehead, the giving of bread and wine to be eaten and drunk, and, for John, the washing and drying of feet. Baptism and eucharist are ways of being placed before others, and they shape a habitus of facing. Above all they are oriented towards the face of Christ.

The baptismal promise is, 'I turn to Christ', and the cross on the face responds to the face on the cross. The eucharist remembers Jesus facing his disciples at the Last Supper, and it is directed in hope towards seeing him face to face. 'Maranatha! Come, Lord Jesus!' seems to have been the acclamation of the earliest Christians, and the rich tradition of 'the vision of God' has taken up that longing for an ultimate facing. The ultimate place is, therefore, in 'the light of the knowledge of the glory of God in the face of Christ' (2 Cor. 4.6); and the transformation of self happens in that facing of faith: 'And we all, with unveiled face, beholding the glory of the Lord, are being changed into his likeness from one degree of glory to another; for this comes from the Lord who is the Spirit' (2 Cor. 3.18).

6.4.3 Timed

Baptism re-enacts the epoch-making event of Jesus Christ in its once and for all character. The eucharist 'times' history with that event; but it also relates to the timing of regular family meals, making bread, maturing wine, conversing and singing. History is punctuated with eucharists which can transfigure time through this interweaving of the ordinary and extraordinary. A self may be timed by the eucharist. This can encourage seeking wisdom about the focussing and distribution of time and energy in the other times with which the self is enmeshed – those, for example, of nature, nation, children, financial markets, television, novels, music, and business organisations. Above all, being timed by the eucharist relativises death, and liberates for the ethical, fasting and festal time of responsibility and joy before the crucified and risen Jesus.

6.4.4 Commanded

One danger of a theology of the abundance of God is what Bonhoeffer called cheap grace which generalises the truth of God's grace and applies it as a principle.[46] The main ingredient in his insistence on costly grace is obedience to the command of the living Christ. A eucharistic self is defined as being face to face (in faith, love and hope) with the one who commands that this be done in memory of him. 'Do this!' is the all-embracing command, recapitulating his teaching and example. The Johannine tradition is especially insistent on the priority of the imperative, and I have described how most of this chapter can be recapitulated through John's retelling of the Last Supper giving centrality to the 'new commandment'.

The participant in the eucharist is therefore under an obedience which has its first (and, as Judas and Peter suggest, most testing) arena in relation to those around the table. There is a particularity of obedience to be constantly discerned in the contingencies of life. The central orientation for the formation of this obedient self is towards death. The imperative is to die to self, as enacted in baptism. The self that is formed is awake to death and identified with a particular death. All repetition sets up expectation of the next repetition but also makes us sensitive to any changes. The repetition of the eucharist sets up an expectation of death, and it allows participants to have an unrepressed sense of death; yet, at the same time, because death is now inseparable from the news of resurrection, it allows for daringly faithful improvisations of new life. In the imperative of facing death (and all the sin and evil connected with it) we find the connection between the substitutionary self of Jesus Christ and the substitutionary responsibility of his followers. Baptism is, in this regard, the non-identical repetition of the substitutionary self of Jesus Christ, while the eucharist is its continuation 'under the sign of the analogous'.

That continuation is the opportunity for the rooting and flourishing of a eucharistic habitus. The imperative 'Do this!' includes a wisdom of habituation which is embodied in liturgical practices. Repetition after

---

46. See Dietrich Bonhoeffer, *The Cost of Discipleship* (SCM Press, London 1959), part one.

repetition of hearing scripture and its interpretation, of repentance, of intercession and petition, of the kiss of peace, of communion, of praising and thanking, all within a dramatic pattern that slowly becomes second nature: who can tell in advance what sort of self is being shaped year after year as these practices are interwoven thoughtfully with all the rest of life?

Yet that is hardly the point. The eucharistic habitus is a training not preoccupied with the cultivation of self but with being responsive to Jesus Christ and other people and coping with their responses in turn. The logic of this is not to become too concerned with the pattern of the eucharist, significant though that is. What will help most in acquiring the habitus? At the practical level, the answer is obvious: practice. But thought and practice are inseparable, so a further question for a theological study such as this is: what sort of thought will help most? I long to find a full anthropological study of eucharistic practice along the lines suggested by Jenkins and Bourdieu above. That, if it were theologically informed, could be a most helpful accompaniment. Yet the utterly essential matter for thought is indicated by the distinctive nature of the eucharistic habitus. Because it is oriented to Jesus Christ and to others the main energies of thought must be directed towards Jesus Christ and others. That simple principle dictates the topics of the remaining chapters: two chapters on Jesus Christ, two on other people worth being apprenticed with, and a final one on feasting.

7

Facing Jesus Christ

Jesus Christ is a person who in facing God and other people embodies the other-oriented concept of self proposed by this book. Being this person he is also faced by others, whose selves can be shaped in the encounter. The many-faceted transformation that happens in this relationship is the core of the proposed concept of salvation. Two chapters will now be focussed on the content of the relationship with special reference to the facing of Jesus Christ. The leading question underlying all the others is about how this person can be understood as pivotal for human flourishing, and at the end of the next chapter I will review the answer that has emerged.

This chapter specifically explores the idea of facing Jesus Christ. Taking the christology of Ingolf Dalferth as a starting point there is an attempt to answer two leading questions. The first concerns the recognition of the face of Christ – is this too vague a notion? That leads into two discussions, one about facing the risen Christ, the other about his historical face. The second leading question asks about power and responsibility – is this a dominating face? This is taken to the verge of Jesus's crucifixion and is then continued in the next chapter. There the meaning of the dead face of Jesus is explored, followed by a series of issues about the resurrection, idolatry and the worship of Jesus Christ.

Jesus Christ has already been a theme of this book. He has figured as a particular 'other' in a concept of selfhood which has brought Levinas and Jüngel into dialogue with Ricoeur's understanding of 'oneself as another'. This concept has then been intensified through engagement with the 'word' of the Letter to the Ephesians and the 'sacrament' of the eucharist. It has been my intention neither to develop a concept of self independently of Jesus Christ and then relate this to him, nor to attempt to read a concept of self out of some description of Jesus Christ. Neither way would do justice to the complexity and scope of what is appropriate.[1] So I have not tried to conceptualise in abstraction from Jesus Christ as if he did not exist; but nor have I pretended that there is any way of describing him that does not require the resources generated through wide-ranging considerations of selfhood such as those offered by my leading dialogue partners. So what is being attempted is an understanding of self and salvation that explores the biblical testimony to Jesus Christ with the help of scholars, philosophers, theologians and others, and that simultaneously reconceives the transformation of selfhood 'in Christ' today.

The two chapters together obviously cannot claim to be a full christology or soteriology. They take for granted a great deal that I consider to have been capably argued by others and, in line with the 'essay' genre of this book, continue the 'journey of intensification' already begun.

7.1 Facing the crucified and risen Jesus Christ

The two main interwoven themes of the present chapter have already appeared in what has been said in fragmentary ways about Jesus Christ in earlier chapters. The first is his death and resurrection as the central focus in a Christian understanding of salvation; the second is the centrality of worship for understanding self and salvation. It is worth recapitulating the main points already made.

In chapter 3 crucifixion and resurrection were at the heart of Jüngel's answer to the question: Where is God? 'God on the cross as our neighbour' was for him inseparable from the resurrection showing that 'God himself happened in this death'. But, learning from Levinas, the question was raised about the consequences of taking the face of Christ to be as integral to Jüngel's position as the death of Christ, especially as regards the concept of substitutionary responsibility. Chapter 4 attempted to conceptualise a self for whom joy is as extreme as responsibility. It drew on Jüngel's theology of joy which is inspired by the resurrection of Jesus Christ. The resurrected Christ is an intensification and even redefinition of the unity of joy and responsibility for the sake of joy.

Ricoeur's 'oneself as another' helped to articulate the notion of selfhood implied here. The final pages of chapter 4 sketched some of the implications of this selfhood 'before the face of Christ'. That suggested

---

1. In terms of the discussion of this chapter below, one reason for both those alternatives being unsatisfactory is the appropriate 'vagueness' of the face of Jesus Christ in its relating to God and all humanity.

very important issues about the person of Jesus Christ which need to be taken further in the present chapter. Jesus was seen as embodying the 'economy of the gift', the 'logic of superabundance'. The 'how much more' of the crucified and risen Jesus Christ in Romans chapter 5 was understood as a naming of God. The dynamics of 2 Corinthians 3.18, in which selves are transformed 'from glory to glory' before the face of Christ, raised sharply the issue of idolatry. Ricoeur's 'aporia of the Other' and his opening up the 'resources of singularity' can also both be focussed through the face of Jesus Christ. The result is that being transformed before this face is inseparable from conceiving him as both worshipper and worshipped, and this in turn pivots around his crucifixion and resurrection.

This theme of the particularity of Jesus Christ, who is intrinsic both to the identification of God in Christian worship and to the transformation of self in salvation, continued through chapter 5. The Letter to the Ephesians' idea of being 'in Christ' was elucidated in terms of a worship and salvation with an unlimited horizon and centring on the death and resurrection of Jesus. The culmination was in chapter 6 where the eucharist was described as a habitus, the practice of selves whose 'other' is Jesus Christ. He mediates the blessing and abundance of God; he commands 'Do this!'; he obeys the imperative of his own dying; and he incorporates people through a practice of worship which refigures time around the 'knot' of his own death and resurrection. The christological summary of this practice was: 'The blessing of Jesus Christ as the blessing of God.' In that statement the 'as' is given ontological force, Jesus blesses as God and is blessed as God. Again the interweaving of the resurrection of the crucified Jesus Christ with the theme of facing in worship was pivotal.

If I were writing a full systematic theology I would now need to work out the doctrinal implications of this facing in worship. In fact a large number of mainstream Christian theologians this century have offered doctrinal frameworks which are 'good enough' to act as support for the constructive position in this chapter. There has been an immense amount of attention paid to the death and resurrection of Jesus as central for christology, soteriology and eschatology. There has also been a range of theologies which stress the constitutive role of the death and resurrection of Jesus in the theology of God as Trinity. Distinctively Christian worship of God as Trinity, which is christocentric in the sense of Jesus Christ, crucified and risen, being its pivotal and unsurpassable disclosure, has therefore inspired (and been justified by) a great deal of theology. The 'classic' continental European theologians who (for all their differences among themselves) have been major contributors to this have included Karl Barth, Henri de Lubac, Karl Rahner, Dietrich Bonhoeffer, Hans Urs von Balthasar, Eberhard Jüngel, Wolfhart Pannenberg and Jürgen Moltmann.[2] The theological 'grammar' of those theologies (and of the many others which in this essential respect agree with them) has been well laid out by Ingolf Dalferth.[3]

Dalferth carefully shows how the resurrection of Jesus Christ leads to considering his death, his life and his person, how these involve reconceiving who God is, and how it is only then that the dimensions of the salvation which he realises can be grasped. Dalferth traces the interconnections between the 'resurrected crucified one' and questions of creation, anthropology, history, salvation, ecclesiology and eschatology, and he analyses the 'grammar' of these relations as irreducibly trinitarian. I see his achievement as a sensitive summary of the most important thrust of twentieth-century Christian systematic theology. His work can serve as a background and complement to my argument in this chapter. It does so all the more appropriately because of four further factors.

First, Dalferth has worked closely with Jüngel, to whom his book is dedicated, and the two of them agree theologically insofar as it matters for my purposes. Dalferth's thought takes up in a more systematic way many of the ideas of Jüngel which were discussed in chapters 3 and 4 above. Jüngel has not written a systematic christology, so Dalferth can act as a theological link between those remarks (which left many relevant questions 'hanging') and the present chapter.

Second, just as Ricoeur made a connection between English-language philosophy and that of continental Europe (especially Levinas), so Dalferth spans the two worlds of discourse. He is particularly influenced by Anglo-American linguistic philosophy, and in theology has been immersed in British discussions – his book opens with the debate provoked by *The Myth of God Incarnate*, and its final chapter on sacrifice argues vigorously with some British positions such as that of Stephen Sykes. He therefore offers a critical dialogue between some of the main traditions and thinkers which feed into this essay.

Third, his 'grammatical' approach ensures that the connections between issues are mapped and that attention is paid to the more technical theological discussions which my position presupposes. For example,

2. For an introduction to these and other twentieth-century theologians see Ford (ed.), *The Modern Theologians*.
3. Ingolf U. Dalferth, *Der auferweckte Gekreuzigte. Zur Grammatik der Christologie* (J. C. B. Mohr (Paul Siebeck), Tübingen 1994).

I do not follow through questions about the immanent and economic Trinity, the meaning of the various titles of Jesus, the ways different Gospels testify to Jesus, 'two natures' christology, *communicatio idiomatum*, or the epistemology of language about God. Dalferth treats all these in ways which cohere with the conclusions of this chapter.

Finally, there is a convergence which goes to the heart of my concern. Dalferth is alert to the variety of ways of picturing salvation through Jesus Christ. He describes them under four headings: political, cultic, legal, and personal.[4] He recognises the varied relevance of these for different contexts and uses, but there is no doubt that his own theology gives primacy to the personal model, with love as his central concept. When he treats soteriology he is concerned that primacy not be given to the cultic picture of sacrifice, for all its usefulness in indicating, after appropriate 'baptism', the meaning of salvation in Christ. The thrust of his emphasis on the crucifixion and resurrection, and even more of his concern that in salvation the 'person' of Christ is inseparable from his 'work', combines with the pivotal role of 'love' to make the personal model fundamental – he refers to his theology as 'personal-trinitarian thinking'.[5] Yet as most of his energy in soteriology is spent on the discussion of sacrifice he does not develop the model in fresh ways.

In the rest of this chapter I am accepting the broad lines of Dalferth's 'grammar' and his concentration on the personal but am also attempting to contribute to a reconception of the personal. Its specific point of contact with Dalferth's approach might be seen in his insistence that all theology should happen *coram deo* and *coram Christo* – which in my terms is before the face of God, of Christ. It is the fascinating issue raised by the 'of God, of Christ' which makes Dalferth's trinitarian grammar so vital, as he says in the same passage.[6] But it is also appropriate to explore the dynamics of the *coram*.

4. Ibid., S.260. The terms associated with each heading include the following: the political model – imprisonment, ransom, victory, liberation, and others; the cultic model – sacrifice, suffering, self-surrender, substitution, atonement, renewal of life, acceptance, rejection and others; the juridical model – treaty, covenant, rights and duties, transgression of the law, restitution, guilt, punishment, satisfaction, reward, pardon, indemnification, repentance, compensation, justification and others; and the personal model – community, friendship, freedom, responsibility, disappointment, injury, broken faith, deceit, forgiveness, love and others.   5. Ibid., S.303.

6. The passage reads: 'In diesem Sinn sind theologische Lehraussagen über Jesus Christus, Gott, Mensch, Welt und alles übrige keine Beschreibungen dessen, von dem sie reden, sondern Regeln, die uns anleiten, das, wovon die Rede ist, im Kontext des Heilshandelns Gottes zu bestimmen und zu verstehen, es also nicht für sich, sondern *coram deo* und damit *coram Christo* zu betrachten. Und das geschieht nach Einsicht und Erfahrung der christlichen Theologie genau dann sachgemäss, wenn es nach Massgabe der Grammatik betrachtet wird, deren Grundzüge die Trinitätslehre formuliert.' (Ibid., S.303.)

7.2 A vague face?

The most obvious problem for a theology of the face of Jesus Christ is its apparent vagueness. Nobody can see this face. We do not even have artistic or photographic evidence of it. So people might imagine any sort of face and project whatever they like on to it. It seems that our conception of the face of Jesus Christ is so 'underdetermined' by evidence that a theology focussed on it has a licence for invention.

In response it is necessary to try to suggest what sort of particularity and precision are required for theologically reliable reference to this face. Might there be an accompanying concept of vagueness which signifies not so much an impoverishment of reference as the sort of unimaginable intensity and inexhaustible abundance indicated by the term 'glory'? And might there be an historically reliable way of referring to this face? Those are the questions explored in the following two sub-sections.

7.2.1 A glorious face

With regard to the testimonies in the New Testament it is of the utmost importance that the face of Christ is not just that of an historical person who is dead and gone. The New Testament presupposes throughout that Jesus is risen from the dead.[7] How reliable that presupposition is will be discussed later in this chapter. For now the point is to try to grasp the implications of faith in the resurrection for reference to the face of Jesus Christ. To believe in him is to know that one is living before his face, in his presence. How is this *coram Christo* articulated in the various witnesses?

In Paul the key texts for this study indicate, with reference to the face of Christ, the dynamics of faith and transformation in community, the connection of these with the God of creation and the Spirit, and the relation of knowledge to glory:

> And we all, with unveiled face, beholding [or reflecting] the glory of the Lord, are being transformed into his likeness from one degree of glory to another; for this comes from the Lord who is the Spirit . . .
> For it is the God who said, 'Light will shine out of darkness,' who has shone in our hearts to give the light of the knowledge of the glory of God in the face of Christ. (2 Cor. 3.18, 4.6)

In the Gospel resurrection stories there is a strong sense of a disturbance of ordinary recognisability. In Luke, 'their eyes were kept from

---

7. The whole of Dalferth's argument is based on the irreducible primacy of the resurrection of the crucified Jesus for the New Testament and for Christianity, as indicated in the title of his book, *Der auferweckte Gekreuzigte* (The Resurrected Crucified One).

recognising him' (24.16) and 'they were startled and thought they saw a spirit' (24.37). In Matthew, 'when they saw him they worshipped him; but some doubted' (28.17). In John, Mary 'did not know that it was Jesus' (20.14) and 'Jesus stood on the beach; yet the disciples did not know that it was Jesus' (21.4). In each there are verbal and physical signs of recognition but it is clear that, while the risen one is still Jesus, he is not simply the identical person. In Ricoeur's terms, he is 'himself as another', and the other can be acknowledged as God: 'Thomas answered him, "My Lord and my God!"' (John 20.28); 'And they came up and took hold of his feet and worshipped him' (Matt. 28.9). In Mark, the Gospel most reticent about the resurrection, the news that 'you will see him' evokes a reaction in the women at the tomb which recalls awestruck worship: 'for trembling and astonishment had come upon them; and they said nothing to anyone, for they were afraid' (16.8).

This facing of Jesus as the facing of God is better seen as an intensification of facing rather than an indeterminate vagueness. The risen face of Jesus is a 'revelation' not in the sense of making him plain in a straightforward manner. Rather, what is 'unveiled' is a face that transcends simple recognisability, that eludes our categories and stretches our capacities in the way in which God does. It provokes fear, bewilderment, doubt, joy and amazement. It therefore is profoundly questioning and questionable. It generates a community whose life before this face is endlessly interrogative, and whose response to it leads into ever new complexities, ambiguities, joys and sufferings.

The resurrection stories also tie this new facing of Jesus to a facing of people without restriction: 'Go therefore and make disciples of all nations' (Matt. 28.19); '. . . repentance and forgiveness of sins should be preached in his name to all nations' (Luke 24.47); 'As the Father has sent me, so I send you' (John 21.21). The selfhood of Jesus 'as another' embraces the others of the nations as well as God.

This means that the underdetermination of this face is intrinsically connected to both the mystery of God and relationship to every other face. It is the openness of the hospitable face, the good underdetermination of not being self-contained. This face is alive with the life and glory of God, so its openness has all the capacity for innovation and surprise which belong to God. It is so oriented to others that knowing and loving this face means being called to know and love them. Its self-effacement constantly urges those who look to it that they should route their seeking the face of Christ through other people. This is the long detour of recognising Christ in others, not one of whom is irrelevant to knowing and loving him. His substitutionary responsibility creates an exchange through which each person can be related in responsibility to each other. This generates a community which can be bound together in joyful responsibility for those outside it.

Other New Testament witnesses add dimensions to this facing of the resurrected Jesus Christ. In Acts, the culmination of Peter's Pentecost sermon summarising the gospel is the resurrected Jesus 'exalted at the right hand of God' as 'both Lord and Christ' (Acts 2.33, 36) – one way of saying that to be before God is to be before this face. Stephen before his martyrdom, 'his face like the face of an angel' (Acts 6.15) and 'full of the Holy Spirit, gazed into heaven and saw the glory of God, and Jesus standing at the right hand of God' (Acts 7.55). Saul on the road to Damascus was blinded by a light from heaven and then addressed: 'Saul, Saul, why do you persecute me? . . . I am Jesus, whom you are persecuting' (Acts 9.4–5). Here the facing is intimately bound up with the facing of the community: Jesus is represented as the particular individual who speaks but is also identified with his community. The double reference to Jesus as at God's right hand and seen in other people is in line with the 'hospitable face' of Christ discussed above in the Gospel resurrection stories.

The Pastoral Epistles to Timothy and Titus are especially interesting in showing how living before the face of the risen Jesus Christ had by then become the normality of Christian living. It could be routinely appealed to – 'In the presence of God and of Christ Jesus and of the elect angels I charge you . . .' (1 Tim. 5.21; cf. 6.13, 2 Tim. 4.1). The Letter to the Hebrews has a strong theology of the exalted Jesus: 'But we see Jesus, who for a little while was made lower than the angels, crowned with glory and honour because of the suffering of death, so that by the grace of God he might taste death for everyone' (Heb. 2.9). The culmination of the catalogue of examples of faith is the lesson:

> Therefore, since we are surrounded by so great a cloud of witnesses, let us also lay aside every weight, and sin which clings so closely, and let us run with perseverance the race that is set before us, looking to Jesus the pioneer and perfecter of our faith, who for the joy that was set before him endured the cross, despising the shame, and is seated at the right hand of God. (Heb. 12.1–2)

This is the taken for granted reality of Christian faith, and, when the writer does a vivid, worship-saturated improvisation on it, the climax is the encounter with the crucified, living Jesus:

For you have not come to what may be touched, a blazing fire, and darkness, and gloom, and a tempest, and the sound of a trumpet, and a voice whose words made the hearers entreat that no further messages be spoken to them. For they could not endure the order that was given, 'If even a beast touches the mountain, it shall be stoned.' Indeed, so terrifying was the sight that Moses said, 'I tremble with fear.' But you have come to Mount Zion and to the city of the living God, the heavenly Jerusalem, and to innumerable angels in festal gathering, and to a judge who is God of all, and to the spirits of the just made perfect, and to Jesus, the mediator of a new covenant, and to the sprinkled blood that speaks more graciously than the blood of Abel. (Heb. 12.18–24)

Yet in all those writings there is also another, ultimate dimension to the facing of Jesus Christ. Hebrews calls faith 'the assurance of things hoped for, the conviction of things not seen' (Heb. 11.1). The Pastorals have the same future orientation: 'I charge you in the presence of God and of Christ Jesus who is to judge the living and the dead, and by his appearing and his kingdom . . .' (2 Tim. 4.1; cf. 1 Tim. 6.13–14). Paul's vision of fulfilment and love is captured in the phrase 'then face to face' (1 Cor. 13.12). Again and again the full facing of Christ is integral to what is ultimately hoped for and awaited. It is perhaps most vividly expressed in the First Letter of Peter, where in the context of praise of 'God the Father and of our Lord Jesus Christ' the intense joy of a faith which does not at present see the risen Jesus is imagined as surpassed 'at the revelation of Jesus Christ':

Blessed be the God and Father of our Lord Jesus Christ! By his great mercy we have been born anew to a living hope through the resurrection of Jesus Christ from the dead, and to an inheritance which is imperishable, undefiled, and unfading, kept in heaven for you, who by God's power are guarded through faith for a salvation ready to be revealed in the last time. In this you rejoice, though now for a little while you may have to suffer various trials, so that the genuineness of your faith, more precious than gold which though perishable is tested by fire, may redound to praise and glory and honour at the revelation of Jesus Christ. Without having seen him you love him; though you do not now see him you believe in him and rejoice with unutterable and exalted joy. As the outcome of your faith you obtain the salvation of your souls. (1 Pet. 1.3–9)

The final New Testament statement of this vision is in the Book of Revelation. It is shot through with Old Testament imagery from prophecy, apocalyptic and elsewhere, and evokes the ultimate facing:

> Then I turned to see the voice that was speaking to me, and on turning I saw seven golden lampstands, and in the midst of the lampstands one like a son of man, clothed with a long robe and with a golden girdle round his breast; his head and his hair were white as white wool, white as snow; his eyes were like a flame of fire, his feet were like burnished bronze, refined as in a furnace, and his voice was like the sound of many waters; in his right hand he held seven stars, from his mouth issued a sharp two-edged sword, and his face was like the sun shining in full strength.
>
> When I saw him, I fell at his feet as though dead. But he laid his right hand upon me, saying, 'Fear not, I am the first and the last, and the living one; I died, and behold I am alive for evermore, and I have the keys of Death and Hades.' (Rev. 1.12–19)

Revelation concludes with the vision of the new Jerusalem:

> Then he showed me the river of the water of life, bright as crystal, flowing from the throne of God and of the Lamb through the middle of the street of the city; and also, on either side of the river, the tree of life with its twelve kinds of fruit, yielding its fruit each month; and the leaves of the tree were for the healing of the nations. There shall no more be anything accursed, but the throne of God and of the Lamb shall be in it, and his servants shall worship him; they shall see his face, and his name shall be on their foreheads. And night shall be no more; they need no lamp or light or sun, for the Lord God will be their light, and they shall reign for ever and ever. (Rev. 22.1–5)

Seeing his face in worship is here the picture of unsurpassable joy and perfection, which for the worshippers includes a radical testing and purifying to the point of martyrdom. Such worship is integral to what for diverse Christian traditions has been the most embracing conception of the motivation in Christian living: the desire for 'the vision of God'.

What is the overall significance of this pervasive theme of the facing of the risen Jesus Christ for the problem of vagueness? His face attracts trust, adoration, love, joy, repentance, attentive listening, and ultimate hope. There is such multifaceted abundance that any notion of precision which requires an overview and appraisal is absurd. Its significance is indicated by the phrase 'the glory of God in the face of Christ': this facing is identified with the facing of God. This in turn means that it is a face which relates to every face. Any vagueness is not so much because of abstraction or generality but because of the utter particularity of this face's relating to each face. In other words indefiniteness is intrinsic to any attempt to speak of it in a way which is not context-specific, because each context is part of its definition. In this way vagueness is by no means something to defend it against: to be vague (in the sense of eluding definitions which try to avoid the richness of its infinitely particular relationships) is intrinsic to its reality.[8] The overwhelming diversity and intensity of these relationships is part of the meaning of transformation 'from one degree of glory to another' (2 Cor. 3.18).

The form of precision most appropriate to this glory is the testimony of those involved. Their stories, worship, art and wisdom, together with the shaping of their lives and communities, are, for better or for worse, the irreducibly particular witnesses to the meaning of living before this face. But their access to this face is not direct and unmediated. It relies on the testimonies of others, in the Bible and down the centuries, and also on the endless mediation through the living faces of other people. This too involves abundant particularity, recognising the face of Christ as reflected in all the faces to which (even when they are not aware of it) he relates. It also involves infinite responsibility, as the face of Christ to which believers turn directs them (if they understand rightly to whom they are looking) to those on whom he looks with love. But the heart of it all is being faced by one in whom they can 'rejoice with unutterable and exalted joy' (1 Pet. 1.8). So in practical terms this face is at the heart of an overwhelming diversity of transformations of selves in worship and in ordinary living. Intellectually it generates questions which stretch the theological mind and imagination in the spheres of all the classic doctrines.

7.2.2 An historical face

Yet all that is an insufficient answer to the question about the vagueness of this face. It does not grapple with the question which is raised both by the New Testament and by those concerned with the truth of its witness.

---

8. The logic of vagueness is one of the most important philosophical explorations to be undertaken in relation to the concept of the face. I suspect the best way forward is that proposed by Peter Ochs in *Peirce, Pragmatism, and the Logic of Scripture* (Cambridge University Press, Cambridge 1998). He summarises some of the theological implications of his appropriation of Peirce's logic of vagueness in 'Scriptural Logic: Diagrams for a Postcritical Metaphysics', *Modern Theology*, vol. 11, no. 1, January 1995, pp. 65–92. He summarises Peirce's logic of relations in which 'something means something to someone' and 'concepts inter-relate only with respect to their respective points of indefiniteness or vagueness ... The inter-relation therefore helps mutually define the concepts' (p. 77). He shows how Peirce's logic of relations leads into a logic of vagueness and a logic of dialogue. His own example of the interpretation of Exodus chapter 3 in which the name of God 'generalizes itself through its performance, which can be reiterated an indefinite number of times' (p. 82) could be transposed in terms of the face of God.

This face has an inescapable historical reference. In the New Testament, where the horizon for reference to Jesus is that of faith in his resurrection, the continuity between the person who was crucified under Pontius Pilate and the one who was resurrected is essential. Historical claims are made about him, and mainstream Christianity has always insisted on historical factuality as intrinsic to its confession of faith – as the inclusion of Pontius Pilate in its creed shows. Despite attempts to insulate faith from historical inquiry, that creed commits Christian theologians to taking historical evidence as seriously as do any others interested in the truth of the New Testament.

Historical investigation requires testimonies, which come in many forms. The historian collects them, cross-examines them and tries to make coherent sense of them. These activities give rise to wide-ranging debates about what historical truth is, whether or to what degree it is accessible, and what might be the appropriate forms of inquiry, understanding, communication and testing. These historiographical, literary and philosophical issues are not the subject of this chapter, though I do assume certain positions which will occasionally surface.[9]

Besides the general questions of historical truth and method there is the extensive field of the study of Christian origins. Here too there is no question of being able to do justice to the relevant literature, but certain scholars who have tried to do so form the background for the position that follows.[10] I want to redescribe their ways of rendering Jesus in terms of facing and salvation.

9. Of those with whom this study has engaged, the thinker most congenial on these topics is Paul Ricoeur, especially in his three-volume *Time and Narrative* where he treats at length issues of historical and fictional reference and their interrelationship. Cf. chapter 6 above, pp. 153ff.; also Fodor, *Christian Hermeneutics,* chapter 7, where I consider he does better justice to Ricoeur than to Hans Frei on the subject of historical reference.

10. The picture of Jesus that I find convincing in terms of academic historical investigation is one which draws on the work of older scholars such as Nils Alstrup Dahl, especially the posthumous book of essays, *Jesus the Christ. The Historical Origins of Christological Doctrine,* edited by Donald H. Juel (Fortress Press, Minneapolis 1991); C. K. Barrett, *Jesus and the Gospel Tradition* (SPCK, London 1967); Grayston, *Dying We Live;* and Martin Hengel, *Studies in Early Christology* (T. & T. Clark, Edinburgh 1995) and *Crucifixion in the Ancient World and the Folly of the Message of the Cross* (Fortress Press, Philadelphia 1977), in dialogue with others such as Markus Bockmuehl, *This Jesus. Martyr, Lord, Messiah* (T. & T. Clark, Edinburgh 1994); Marcus J. Borg, *Conflict, Holiness and Politics in the Teaching of Jesus* (Edwin Mellen, New York and Toronto 1984) and *Jesus: A New Vision. Spirit, Culture, and the Life of Discipleship* (Harper, San Francisco 1991); Larry Hurtado, *One God, One Lord: Early Christian Devotion and Ancient Jewish Monotheism* (Fortress, Philadelphia 1988); E. P. Sanders, *The Historical Figure of Jesus* (Allen Lane/Penguin, London 1993) and *Jesus and Judaism* (SCM Press, London 1985); G. N. Stanton, *The Gospels and Jesus* (Oxford University Press, Oxford 1989); N. T. Wright, *The New Testament and the People of God (Christian Origins and the Question of God. Volume 1)* (Fortress Press, Minneapolis 1992) and *Jesus and the Victory of God (Christian Origins and the Question of God. Volume 2)* (Fortress Press, Minneapolis 1996).

The obvious general point is that the Gospels portray Jesus primarily in his face to face relationships. Their stories are about his conversations, teaching, actions, meals, and so on. The primary perspective is that of Farley's 'interhuman' and 'communities of the face',[11] so all that has been said about that in philosophical and theological terms can be applied here. It is a perspective which chapter 6 has described in its culmination in the Last Supper. The Gospels are largely 'realistic narrative',[12] giving testimony by rendering the interaction of characters and circumstances. It is a literary form which distils some of the complexities of facing into language. It is well suited to indicating those aspects of facing which have been of most concern in previous chapters, especially responsible speech and action before God and before other people.

What about the specific character of Jesus in his facing of others? The overwhelming reality in his facing is undoubtedly God his Father. Jesus is seen as living his life and dying his death utterly with reference to God. His God is radically alive, 'not the God of the dead but of the living' (Matt. 22.32), generous and compassionate, surprising in his judging and loving. Jesus prays a great deal and teaches a way to pray which is intimate, confident, persistent, and oriented towards God's glory and God's Kingdom. He prays in solitude and teaches others to do so, a form of prayer which emphasises simply being before God.

There are also stories that seem to break the bounds of realism in order to signify his specialness to God – his baptism and his transfiguration. The latter is an intense interweaving of facings: with his three closest disciples ('and he was transfigured before them, and his face shone like the sun' – Matt. 17.2); with the archetypal biblical figures of Moses and Elijah; and, in the hiddenness of the bright cloud, with his Father who says: 'This is my beloved Son, in whom I am well pleased; listen to him' (Matt. 17.5). The baptism also emphasises the dynamic unity between Jesus and his Father: the Spirit descends on him. Jesus is a Spirit-filled person who has visions, claims the authority of God, does healings and exorcisms as signs of God's Kingdom, and calls twelve disciples representing the tribes of Israel.

---

11. See above chapter 5, p. 130.
12. For my interpretation of the significance of realistic narrative for Christian theology see Ford, 'System, Story, Performance' in eds, Hauerwas and Jones, *Why Narrative?*, pp. 191–215. That essay is indebted to Hans Frei, especially *The Eclipse of Biblical Narrative. A Study in Eighteenth and Nineteenth Century Hermeneutics* (Yale University Press, New Haven and London 1974) and *The Identity of Jesus Christ. The Hermeneutical Bases of Dogmatic Theology* (Fortress Press, Philadelphia 1975).

God is also at the centre of Jesus's concern in his final journey to Jerusalem and in his teachings, actions and conflicts there. I have already examined this from the viewpoint of the Last Supper. The story of Gethsemane is centred on Jesus's passion for the will of God. The crucifixion is told in different ways by the evangelists, but in all of them Jesus on the cross prays (or cries) to God.

Jesus's facing of others is in line with his facing of God. It is above all about communicating the good news of this God who is radically different from the God represented by most people's beliefs, fears, expectations and practices. His parables reimagine how God relates to people. His teaching is only acceptable if God really is like that. His miracles are signs of a life that God alone can offer. His meals are celebrations of God's welcome to the despised, rejected and victimised. His controversies are confrontations with those who, he says, are responsible for the victimising and despising. The overarching concern of his ministry is the Kingdom of God, which is a God-given joy and responsibility. The responsibility for it dominates his life and death. The joy of it is tasted in his feasting and in his parables, and in the response to his teaching, miracles and resurrection.

Yet none of that makes explicit the central issue about his facing. Jesus's communication of the Kingdom of God in word and action leads to a climax in which his message and his person are inextricable. The transfiguration story graphically expresses this: his face shines like the sun and there is God's command to listen to him. The Last Supper has already been described in the previous chapter as enacting this unity of person and message, and the focus on his body and blood is a dramatisation of it. In Gethsemane the will of God (and therefore the Kingdom of God) is identified with Jesus's passion and death. His resurrection (to be discussed further in the next chapter) is the seal on the union of the proclaimer and his proclamation. The logic of the story told by all four evangelists is that the fate of Jesus's message of the Kingdom of God and the fate of his person were inseparable.[13]

This is most important for his facing. It means that his particular face continues to be central as the glorious face discussed in the previous section. This face is affirmed as the face of the one who taught, ate, drank and died. The resurrection appearances are, for all their insistence on strangeness and discontinuity, still testimonies to the 'same' face – while

---

13. For a strong argument in favour of this see Frei, *The Identity of Jesus Christ*.

redefining 'sameness' through this specific non-identical repetition created through death and resurrection rather than conforming to some general category of identity.

It is this pivotal role of the face of Jesus Christ as both a significant referent of the testimonies to his historical activity and also a continuing referent of those who live and worship before his 'glorious face' that makes it a helpful focus for this chapter. The objection to its vagueness has been rejected on two grounds. First, as the glorious face of the crucified and risen Jesus Christ, it is not so much vague as superabundant in its reality as relating to God and to all people. Second, as the historical face it is testified to in diverse ways. Testimonies can always be suspected and disbelieved, but the main lines of the Gospels as outlined can be affirmed as reliable in line with the conclusions of the scholars mentioned already.

This use of 'face' and 'facing' in regard to historical testimony to Jesus Christ has some advantages which help in understanding both the importance and the limitations of biblical testimony. As argued above, the notion of facing is well suited to the main characteristic of realistic narratives, their primary focus on the perspective of the 'interhuman' rather than, say, on interiority or general overviews. But it also reminds us how abstractive even a vivid narrative is from the multifaceted intensity of facings over time. It suggests the absence of so much. It summons our imaginations to re-enact the events and make our own productions. This in turn reminds us that the authors of the Gospels were doing something similar. They received condensed accounts, oral or written, 'scripts' which were already inspiring diverse performances and which had to be edited, produced and performed for new situations and communities.[14]

The facing of Jesus Christ is an idea which can help to handle the question of the truth of such testimony in two ways. First, it implies an appropriate concept of precision for historical testimony to Jesus. This is not the precision of verbal or circumstantial detail but one suited to the complexity of facing. To do justice to this complexity involves a notion of the 'correspondence' of the testimony to what has happened, but also requires imaginative fashioning that uses 'fictional' skills. It is not surprising that there are varied accounts and even contradictions and endless discussions about what is reliable. But in the Gospels there is also,

---

14. In Ricoeur's terms they were interweaving history and fiction in the interests of truthful testimony (*Time and Narrative*, vol. III, chapter 8).

as the scholars I have mentioned argue, a remarkable amount of convergence on the sort of things that Jesus said, did and suffered. We do not have the detail of a physical face but we are allowed to imagine well enough what it was like to be before this face.

Second, that phrase 'well enough' raises the issue of the main purpose of the testimony. Its aim is not just to give interesting historical information but to enable living before this face as the face of the risen Jesus Christ. It is trying to convey a truth which has no parallel and involves both God and all humanity, but which is also inextricably tied to history. The 'well enough' evocation of Jesus's life therefore crucially includes a distinctive way of living before God and before other people, and at the same time a concentration on this particular face – the face of a baby; a face speaking, confronting, eating and drinking; a face transfigured, kissed by Judas, crowned with thorns, crying out on the cross, and dead. The continuity of the 'historical Jesus' and the 'Christ of faith' is deeply mysterious, as the coming sections will reaffirm. The idea of the face of Jesus Christ does not solve the problems or evacuate the mystery, but it does make sure that at the heart of the mystery there is a concept which is unavoidably there throughout the biblical testimony and is also rich enough to inspire appropriate thought, feeling, imagining, action and worship.

7.2.3 Visually imagining the face of Jesus Christ

At the beginning of this discussion of the vagueness of the face of Jesus Christ I raised the question of the lack of any artistic or photographic evidence for this face. In conclusion I want to look at this briefly, assuming all that has been said in between about the glorious and the historical face.

Clearly there was a particular historical face. That this face did have specific features is obvious and important, but the argument of the two preceding sub-sections has been that precision in rendering them is not necessary for theological reference. The narrative testimonies to the 'facing' of Jesus in many situations as he followed his vocation allow the reader to imagine the range and quality of his complex facing and to conceive something of what it might mean to live before this face. They shape communities of the face which are left with enough definiteness to orient them towards Jesus Christ, and with enough openness, or vagueness, to generate continuing questioning about what this implies.

But to say that visual representation is not necessary is not the same as saying that it is undesirable. This is a major issue in the history of Christianity. It raises questions that also split the world's religions, where there are those such as Hinduism with strong iconic tendencies and others such as Judaism and Islam with a deep suspicion of them. Within Christianity both strands are present, with periodic outbursts of open conflict between them, as during the eighth- and ninth-century Iconoclastic Controversy and the sixteenth-century Reformation.

The main concern in Christianity goes back to the Old Testament critique of idolatry. Those issues will be dealt with further in the next chapter. If the question of idolatry is set to one side, what about the visual representation of Jesus? It is arguable that imagining some sort of face is unavoidable. But what if that is followed through into portraying him in art or in film? It is easy to see objections. It can never be true to 'the real Jesus'. It is like 'the film of the book' which can constrict the imagination by imposing the definiteness of one face and interpretation. It leads us to imagine Jesus back there then and can never do justice to the risen, glorious face. Its focus on a past image can distract from the living mediation of the face of Christ through the faces of fellow worshippers or of the poor and needy.

Yet none of those objections can be decisive. Being true to 'the real Jesus' is not something which could conceivably have been attained even if there had been artists, photographers and camera crews to record his features and actions. Any such representation is always just one fragment of testimony in one medium at one time. What is most significant in a relationship of facing can only at best be hinted at in such ways, and the hinting is open to terrible corruption and distortion, as our contemporary media prove daily. Yet if imagining really is unavoidable it is hard to see why the best visual artists of a community should not be able to give their testimony to this person. It will of course have to be done wisely, as suits the power of the visual media. It will need whole traditions of theological and practical wisdom if it is to serve the truth of witnessing to and before the historical and glorious face of Christ. Part of that will be establishing the definitive context of worship in community and of disciplines that help to discern idolatries. That is in fact what has happened in the best schools of iconography in the Orthodox Church and in other Christian artistic settings down the centuries and today.

Perhaps the challenge now should be seen as being to inspire analogous 'iconographic' traditions in art, sculpture, architecture, cinema, theatre, television and interactive media that can try to reimagine what it might mean to do justice to the face of Jesus Christ. It is by no means necessary that these media explicitly render a face identifiable as his, and it may be that the overwhelming majority of representations will be of facings which indirectly and anonymously mediate the quality of his facing. Yet it should also not be ruled out that such media might serve worship more directly, and that one of the expressions of that service might be through inspired representations of the face of Jesus Christ. The 'negative way' of refusing such representations, or only permitting the indirect or non-representational, is not invalid. But it cannot be excluded that the 'affirmative way' of risking them has the capacity to be true to the inspiration of faith, hope and love before this face, or that an abundance of representations might be as effective a safeguard against 'fixing' this face in one interpretation or one period as is the attempted rejection of all representations.

7.3 A dominating face?

The limitless relating ascribed to the face of Christ easily gives rise to an accusation of imperialism. Surely this relational range competes with the claims of others? Is it not a recipe for continual disputes over hegemony? That has been so in many periods and places during Christian history. I discussed this theme briefly at the end of chapter 5 on Ephesians, a letter which has been especially prone to misuse in that way. The principle of the response there was that Ephesians has within itself the resources to criticise such a tendency and to offer an alternative. Likewise the face of Christ can be appealed to in domination but it can also subvert its own distortions. The question is whether universal relating must mean imperialism: might there be a non-coercive form of universality?

Levinas's ethic of facing suggests one. It resists the 'assimilation of the other to the same'; it is universal by being 'responsible in all directions', and powerful willing is subordinated to responsibility and to the practices of speaking and reasoning understood in ethical terms.[15] It enables the conception of a 'hospitable self' whose way of relating across boundaries is not that of domination but of peace. That responsibility can be radicalised in terms of sacrifice, substitution and being hostage. When

15. See above chapter 2.

such an ethic is critically related to the thought of Jüngel and Ricoeur as they bear on Jesus Christ[16] the result is a universality which can be related to this one face. It is possible to imagine this face relating limitlessly in a non-coercive way. To give content to this relating it is necessary to look again at Jesus's life, death and resurrection, this time asking about Jesus with regard to power and domination. Whereas in the previous sections the emphasis was on the resurrection (the glorious face) and the attestation to his life (the historical face), now the main focus will be on Jesus's political involvement as it led to his death.

7.3.1 Transforming a social world

The most obvious relevance of power to Jesus is his exercise of charismatic powers, as mentioned in the previous section. That, and the associated question of his authority,[17] would be a fascinating theme, but it does not reach the main point of this section. As Borg says:

> Though Jesus shared much in common with other Jewish charismatics of his time, he also differed from them in a number of ways. What distinguished him most – besides the extraordinary fact that he was crucified and became the central figure of what was to become a global religion – was his deep involvement with the sociopolitical life of his own people . . . Jesus became a national figure who undertook a mission to his own people in the midst of a cultural crisis, climaxing in a final journey to Jerusalem, the very centre of their cultural life.[18]

Jesus's concern with the society and politics of his day is one of the most controversial issues in current Christianity. In a world situation of massive poverty, violence, displacement of large numbers of refugees, and multiple forms of oppression, it is tempting for those better off and more secure to suppress or ignore the radical implications of the political Jesus. Yet, if Borg and others are correct, the historical Jesus not only was alert to the complex social, economic and political situation of his time but also shaped his message and mission to respond to it. If, therefore, there is continuity between his historical and risen face, it is important to reflect on the content of his politics. Only by doing that is it possible to live before his risen face with an appropriate political consciousness.

---

16. See chapters 3, 4, 5 and 6 above.
17. See 'The Authority of Paul', chapter 8 in Young and Ford, *Meaning and Truth in 2 Corinthians*, for a discussion of power and authority in relation to the face of Christ.
18. Borg, *Jesus: A New Vision*, p. 79.

The overwhelming reality in Jesus's politics is God and the Kingdom of God. He taught and practised a God-centred way of transformation which had radical consequences for the main features of his people's life. He reconceived Israel's identity at its heart – how God is imagined to be God – and therefore at its boundaries, and this, as the next section will discuss, meant conflict with the main political options. But more fundamental to his teaching and action was the shaping of ordinary life.

What were the implications of a life trusting that reality is in fact in the hands of a God who is shockingly hospitable to all? It means loving the poor, the sick, children, women, outcasts of all sorts, enemies, persecutors. The invitation is to imitate God:

> You have heard that it was said, 'You shall love your neighbour and hate your enemy.' But I say to you, Love your enemies and pray for those who persecute you, so that you may be sons of your Father who is in heaven; for he makes his sun rise on the evil and on the good, and sends rain on the just and on the unjust. For if you love those who love you, what reward have you? Do not even the tax collectors do the same? And if you salute only your brethren, what more are you doing than others? Do not even the Gentiles do the same? You, therefore, must be perfect, as your heavenly Father is perfect. (Matt. 6.43–8)

This has consequences in all areas of life, as the rest of the Sermon on the Mount makes clear: for how Torah is understood, for justice, anger, lust, marriage, keeping promises, responding to violence, generosity in lending and giving, receiving honour from God rather than other people, prayer, forgiveness, non-accumulation of wealth (the sharpest choice is between God and Mammon), freedom from anxiety about physical needs, not judging others, and confidently asking God for everything. All the main dimensions of the social world were reimagined before this God – Torah, wealth, status, family and other social relationships.

The exercise of power was reimagined in line with this sort of Kingdom:

> And an argument arose among them as to which of them was the greatest. But when Jesus perceived the thought of their hearts, he took a child and put him by his side, and said to them, 'Whoever receives this child in my name receives me, and whoever receives me receives him who sent me; for he who is least among you all is the one who is great. (Luke 9.46–8)

> A dispute arose among them, which of them was to be regarded as the greatest. And he said to them, 'The kings of the Gentiles exercise

lordship over them; and those in authority over them are called benefactors. But not so with you; rather let the greatest among you become as the youngest, and the leader as one who serves. For which is the greater, one who sits at table, or one who serves? But I am among you as one who serves. (Luke 22.24–7)

When Karl Barth reworked the Christian understanding of salvation in volume IV of his *Church Dogmatics*[19] one of the fundamental images through which he reimagined it was the parable of the Prodigal Son, Jesus being daringly identified with the son who goes off to a riotous life in a foreign country and then returns to the overwhelmingly generous welcome of his father. Another fundamental image was of Jesus who is 'the Lord as servant' and also 'the servant as Lord'. In volumes IV.1 and IV.2 most of the basic issues of christology, soteriology and ecclesiology are thought through in that imaginative framework of the astonishing compassion of God seen in the Prodigal's father and its consequences for the exercise of power in the world, reconceiving what lordship and service mean. That is the most comprehensive response in twentieth-century theology to the problem of whether Jesus is dominating. It affirms at length the basic 'grammar of Christology' which Dalferth[20] lays out in more formal conceptual terms. According to it Jesus's message of the Kingdom of God, in which the greatest serve and the whole social world is transformed along the lines described above, is inseparable from his person and his face. To live before this face is to be challenged by an embodiment of non-coercive power whose principles are articulated in his teaching.

7.3.2 Jesus and the religio-political options

How did this teaching find practical expression in the conflictual politics of Jesus's time?

The main lines of the situation had been laid down since 63 BC when Palestine had been annexed by Rome. There were deep tensions and antagonisms between Roman political power (and the Hellenistic culture which predated and supported it) and the social and religious world of Judaism. The responses within Judaism were varied,[21] and Jesus's behaviour in relation to four of the main options is instructive.

19. Karl Barth, *Church Dogmatics*, vols. I–IV (T. & T. Clark, Edinburgh 1936–69).
20. Dalferth, *Der auferweckte Gekreuzigte*.
21. For brief summaries with further references see Markus Bockmuehl, *This Jesus*, chapter 5, and Borg, *Jesus: A New Vision*, chapters 5–9.

In terms of power, the Zealots posed the symmetrical alternative to Rome: to become dominant by using the same violent means as the Romans in order to overcome them and their collaborators. The Zealots were probably close to the Pharisees (see below) in theology, but they opposed paying taxes to Rome and were willing to be martyred (with crucifixion the common form of execution) rather than submit to imperial authority. Jesus's response to them can be seen as a form of 'subversion from the inside'. He affirmed their radicalism – his summons to his followers to 'take up the cross' (Mark 8.34) may have borrowed their slogan; but he decisively did not follow their line on armed rebellion, taxes and attitudes to enemies. He subverted their dualisms and transformed the boundaries they drew by recommending love of enemies, turning the other cheek, and 'if anyone forces you to go one mile, go with him two miles' (Matt. 5.41) – a Roman soldier could require anyone to carry his pack for one mile. It was peacemaking centred on a God of generous compassion, and at its heart was Jesus's self-identification in calling people to himself: 'I am gentle and lowly in heart' (Matt. 11.29).

The Pharisees were perhaps the most important of the parties Jesus dealt with. They stressed the observance and study of Torah and of the oral tradition of its interpretation, and they insisted on strict rules of ritual purity together with strict tithing. They were passionately devoted to God, to prayer, fasting and love of neighbour. They were a school for many 'saints' and also for the sort of Judaism which survived the destruction of the Jerusalem Temple in 70 AD and became the main formative influence on it ever since. They had wide popular support but were not usually in positions of political power. They offered a way of living in a foreign-dominated society while being loyal to the God of Torah.

Jesus was very close to them on many issues, and even in conflicts with some of them he was often agreeing with the positions of other Pharisees (on the Sabbath, offerings in the Temple, divorce).[22] In the

---

22. Levinas is within the tradition of rabbinic Judaism and Talmudic learning begun by the Pharisees. It is striking that several of the matters about which I critically question Levinas (for example, worship, joy, petitionary prayer, love) could equally well be raised by some members of his own tradition, some of them by his own favourite thinker Franz Rosenzweig. On the Christian side there are also traditions which would on such matters be more inclined to Christian versions of Levinas's position than to mine. In terms of the community of the face the vital practice, going back to the Pharisees, is the joint study of Torah and the community of discussion generated by that. The way in which two essential social dynamics, study and worship, interact is of the greatest significance to both Judaism and Christianity (and far beyond them), but this does not seem to have been at issue between Jesus and the Pharisees.

Gospel accounts it is often hard to separate what happened in Jesus's relations with the Pharisees and what reflects later conflicts in the time of the church. But it seems clear that they had critical differences concerning the boundaries of the community, with the limits of table fellowship, for example, representing who was considered in and out. The God Jesus presented in teaching and in his own practice of table fellowship with 'tax collectors and sinners' challenged the Pharisees' boundaries and therefore threatened their way of being loyal to God in their situation. Facing the Pharisees, one might say that Jesus represented a different oral Torah, claiming the authority of God for his own teaching and practice.

The most deadly political conflict for Jesus was with a third group, the Sadducees. They were the wealthy priestly aristocracy centred in Jerusalem and its Temple. They gave exclusive authority to scripture over tradition and, unlike the Pharisees and Jesus, they did not believe in the resurrection of the body. Their power depended on collaboration with the Romans and control of the Temple. It is probable that Jesus's prophetic speech and action in relation to the Temple, which in turn threatened the Roman peace in Jerusalem, was the single most important factor in his arrest and death.[23]

The Temple was a potent symbol, in which there was a convergence of the presence of God, the worship of God through sacrifice, the priestly, prophetic and royal traditions of Israel, and the expectation of God's deliverance from foreign rule and injustice. It was no accident that Jesus's ministry culminated with his entry into Jerusalem, his 'demonstration' in the Temple, and the Last Supper at Passover time: it is possible to interpret these as the appropriate fulfilment of his teaching and actions, a 'prophetic drama' in several acts. Was he indicating the culmination of his inauguration of the Kingdom of God in his own person? Whatever the interpretation of this extraordinarily complex convergence of history, symbolism and mission, it was a dangerous initiative, subverting a delicate balance of corrupt power, and proclaiming a God who, in the interests of the prophetic vision of 'a house of prayer for all nations' (Mark 11.17), condemned the operation of the religio-political system.

The final group were the Essenes. The Dead Sea Scrolls show them to have been a radical monastic community living in the desert at Qumran on the Dead Sea. They had withdrawn from the Temple cult as being too

---

23. For a summary of recent scholarly discussions on this see Bockmuehl, *This Jesus*, chapter 3.

corrupt and saw the Pharisees as too lenient and compromising in their interpretation of Torah. Jesus has not been shown to have had links with them (the nearest possibility is that John the Baptist did), and he was in obvious contradiction of their asceticism and of their extreme separation and distinction between the holy insiders and those outside. But they did see themselves as a community of eschatological fulfilment, with a strong emphasis on prophecies in the Hebrew scriptures and on Messianic ideas. They expected God to destroy the Romans in a final battle.

This raises the questions of Jesus's eschatology and of his Messianic status, both hotly disputed areas. In the interpreters I am following Jesus offers a radical contrast to Qumran and to other options in his milieu. Again, the key to both is God and Jesus's role in relation to God.

His eschatology of the nearness of the Kingdom of God subverts the sorts of dualisms and the sort of God represented by the apocalyptic expectations of Essenes and others. James Alison's convincing recovery of Jesus's eschatological imagination stresses the two critical factors. First, at its heart was good news about God which has clear political implications:

> If your mind is absolutely quickened by the effervescent vivacity of
> God, then you can speak the sort of truth and reveal the sort of
> injustice which may well provoke people into killing you . . . [24]

Second, the key to subverting the dualisms is the criterion of the victim:

> There is then a good *prima facie* reason for thinking that the subversion
> of the apocalyptic imagination by what I have called Jesus'
> eschatological imagination is something proper to Jesus rather than
> something invented by a disconcerted early community in the face of
> the indefinite postponement of the Day. This *prima facie* evidence
> deepens somewhat when we discover that at the root of the
> subversion which Jesus was making of these dualities, the criterion of
> the victim is to be found. Jesus offers a prophetic criterion in terms of
> ethical demands that are capable of being carried out as the basis of his
> subversion of these dualities: the social duality is redefined in terms of
> the victim, so that the victim is the criterion for determining if one is a
> sheep or a goat (Matt. 25), or if one is a neighbour (Luke 10); it is the
> victims and those who live precariously who are to be at the centre of
> the new victim people, to whom belongs the Kingdom of God which is
> arriving (Matt. 5–6). No one can be surprised that this insistence,

24. James Alison, *Raising Abel. The Recovery of the Eschatological Imagination* (Crossroad, New York 1996), p. 41.

more in the line of the prophetic imagination than the apocalyptic, comes also to be subversive of the cosmic and temporal dualities. It is thus that the forgiving victim, the crucified and risen one, comes to be, himself, the presence of the kingdom in the here and now.[25]

Alison is clear about Jesus's message of the Kingdom of God being linked directly to his victimisation and death. That is also the main point about Jesus as Messiah (or Christ). He was most likely crucified as a Messianic pretender, but to accept him as crucified Messiah was to change accepted notions of the Messiah, including those of the Qumran community. It also points to the only place from which suspicion about his being a dominating face can be decisively answered: the crucifixion. The next chapter will begin there.

25. Ibid., p. 126.

8
_____

The face on the cross
and the worship of God

'When the days drew near for him to be received up, he set his face to go to Jerusalem' (Luke 9.51). Jesus's ministry as described in the previous chapter makes clear why he posed a political threat. That chapter also argued that the threat was not intended as a new form of domination or a takeover of power. But it did involve facing those in authority and included an imperative to represent his message at the centre of political and religious power. That meant going to Jerusalem, and the evidence points to Jesus deliberately and in awareness of the danger setting his face towards Jerusalem. Just as Jerusalem was the centre of his people's worshipping life, so the theme of worship in relation to Jesus himself reaches its climax in what happened to Jesus there. This chapter explores, by developing further the theme of the face, the significance of his death and resurrection for the worship of God, understood as that relationship in which there is full human flourishing with God, each other and all creation.

Mark's account of the journey to Jerusalem conveys a new sense of awe and apprehension felt by his disciples in the presence of Jesus:

> And they were on the road, going up to Jerusalem, and Jesus was walking ahead of them; and they were amazed, and those who followed them were afraid. And taking the twelve again, he began to tell them what was to happen to him . . . (Mark 10.32)

Mark places after this Jesus's saying contrasting rule among 'the Gentiles' with his practice of service. Luke's version tied that saying to Jesus's death by including it in the Last Supper; Mark makes the link to his death directly:

> For the Son of Man came not to be served but to serve, and to give his life as a ransom for many. (Mark 10.45)

This explicitly recognises the connection between what I have called the politics of Jesus and his death. It is reinforced by the events which followed. His entry into Jerusalem ('Palm Sunday') on a donkey's colt recalling a passage from the prophet Zechariah about a king of peace is described by Borg as 'a planned political demonstration, an appeal to Jerusalem to follow the path of peace, even as it proclaimed that this movement was the peace party in a generation headed for war'.[1] His demonstration in the Temple which followed was the immediate trigger for the plot leading to his execution. One after another of his exchanges and conflicts during this final period in Jerusalem raised questions about power, authority and God. The culmination of the engagement is his 'willing victimisation' and his powerlessness on the cross.

That is the point from which I will interpret his death. I have already in chapter 6 explored his death through the lens of the eucharist. Now, rather than rework and assess what Dalferth and many others have said on the crucifixion I want, in line with this book's concern, to focus on the dead face of Jesus on the cross.[2]

8.1 The dead face of Jesus: an obvious, neglected focus

All the Gospel writers lead us to imagine the moment of the death of Jesus. With variations, they graphically portray his last breath:

> And Jesus cried again with a loud voice and yielded up his spirit. (Matt. 27.50)

> And Jesus uttered a loud cry, and breathed his last ... And when the centurion, who stood facing him, saw that he breathed his last, he said, 'Truly this man was the Son of God!' (Mark 15.37, 39)

> Then Jesus, crying with a loud voice, said, 'Father, into thy hands I commit my spirit!' And having said this, he breathed his last. (Luke 23.46)

> When Jesus had received the vinegar, he said, 'It is finished'; and he bowed his head and gave up his spirit. (John 19.30)

So we are left with a dead face on the cross. If we follow the story that is unavoidable. The transition from life to death is signified by focussing on Jesus speaking and breathing for the last time, after which there is his dead face.

1. Borg, *Jesus. A New Vision*, p. 174.
2. I developed this theme in a preliminary way in 'The Face on the Cross' in *Anvil*, vol. 11, no. 3, 1994, pp. 215–25 and parts of that article are incorporated in what follows.

Given the immense significance that came to be attached to the death of Jesus, it is striking that this simple physical description lies at the heart of each of the Gospel accounts of the event. It is also noteworthy that the dead face of Jesus has not been a focus for doctrines of atonement. It would be possible to speculate about reasons for this, but it is perhaps more fruitful to pursue it constructively.

In earlier chapters I have tried to build up a case for conceiving an approach to self and salvation through the face and facing. The most direct treatment of the death of Jesus came in chapter 6 on the eucharist. That stopped short of focussing on the dead face of Jesus, but its way of concentrating on the New Testament narratives and relating them to ordinary living, to the Old Testament and to theological discussions can continue to be used. As regards the face on the cross, I assume that the case has already been made for the relevance of the theme of the face to ordinary living. But the Old Testament case has not yet been made, and, as so often in Christian theology, this seeming detour through what was Jesus's Bible proves to be the most direct route to the central issues.

8.2 *Panim*: salvation and the face

The word *panim* occurs in every strand of the Old Testament and is translated in various ways. The main translations in the King James Version are face (356), presence (75), sight (40), countenance (30) and person (20), but there are also several others. Often the word is used in such a way that the literal connotation of 'face' has been virtually forgotten, as in prepositional compounds with such meanings as 'away from', 'towards' or 'before'. But as the range of translations shows it has a rich array of references and it is associated with a great diversity of feelings, moods, intentions and dispositions.[3]

8.2.1 The Pentateuch
Right from the start in the book of Genesis *panim* is linked with sin and salvation, both in conventional prepositional constructs and in more

3. For an excellent scholarly overview of the word in the Old Testament, together with a selected bibliography, see Simian Yofre's article 'panim' in *Theologisches Wörterbuch zum Alten Testament*, edited by G. Johannes Botterweck, Helmer Ringgren and Heinz-Josef Fabry, vol. VI part 6/7, pp. 630–60. There is immense potential for further discussion of passages in which this word occurs and of the ways in which this theme connects to others in different texts and periods. My aim in what follows is limited to suggesting that potential and making a few links with the New Testament which will be strong enough to help sustain the overall argument.

deliberate usage. Adam and Eve after their disobedience 'hid themselves from the *panim* of the Lord God among the trees of the garden' (Gen. 3.8). In the second story of a primal sin there is a stronger emphasis on separation from the face of God – Cain protests that his banishment will hide him from God's face. He is given a protective mark (was it on his face?), and the story ends: 'Then Cain went away from the *panim* of the Lord ...' (Gen. 4.16). Earlier in this story Cain's anger at his rejected sacrifice is described as his face falling. The Lord promises him it will be lifted up if he does well, but instead he lures his brother far from witnesses and kills him. There is in these stories an intriguing interweaving of major themes in salvation such as the presence of God, divine imperatives, disobedience, shame, responsibility for others, sacrifice, sin and punishment; and, throughout, the face of God and the faces of human beings are key images.

Later in Genesis the key story of Jacob wrestling at Jabbok ford turns around multiple references to the *panim* of God, Jacob and Esau. It is a text that has been edited and re-edited over centuries and is made up of several layers. Von Rad says that its being reworked time after time has resulted in its containing

> experiences of faith that extend from the most ancient period down to the time of the narrator; there is charged to it something of the result of the entire divine history into which Israel was drawn ... Israel has here presented its entire history with God almost prophetically as such a struggle until the breaking of the day. The narrative itself makes this extended interpretation probable by equating the names Jacob and Israel.[4]

Jacob had wronged Esau by stealing his blessing by deception. Now Jacob hears that Esau is approaching with 400 men. He prays for God to save him and what follows can be seen as a complex story of salvation. Jacob thinks: ' "I may appease him [lit. cover his face] with the present [or blessing] that goes before me, and afterwards I shall see his face; perhaps he will accept me [lit. lift up my face]." So the present passed on before him; and he himself lodged that night in the camp' (Gen. 32.20–1 – these two verses have *panim* five times). During the night he wrestles with an assailant till dawn. He is wounded, he refuses to let go until he is blessed, he is given a new name, Israel, and he asks the stranger's name but is given his blessing. Then the whole incident is summed up: 'So Jacob called the name of the place Peniel [face of God], saying, "For I have seen God face to face, and yet my life is preserved" ' (v. 30).

4. G. von Rad, *Genesis. A Commentary* (SCM Press, London 1961), p. 320.

The context of this face to face seeing has been mortally dangerous, wounding combat. Rembrandt has a painting of the scene which interprets it profoundly. In it, Jacob (the supplanter who from birth seized his brother's heel from behind and later took his blessing behind his back and fled) is having his neck slowly and painfully turned so that he looks his opponent in the face.[5] It is salvation as the terrible struggle with a God who is content with nothing less than complete reconciliation face to face. On the cross too there is wrestling, there is wounding to the point of death, the identity of a people and of God is at stake, and there is eventual blessing. It is as if the whole drama is a way of painfully wrenching our necks to focus on this dead face as the sign of reconciliation.

Genesis chapter 33 then tells of the meeting with Esau. Jacob goes ahead and bows to the ground seven times. This is an instance of the way in which the face is a crucial register of submission and dominance. One of the main ordinary uses of face to face behaviour is to indicate power relations. Esau's response is to switch to the behaviour of peers and brothers: 'But Esau ran to meet him, and embraced him, and fell on his neck and kissed him, and they wept' (33.4). And in the conversation that follows Jacob sums up what has happened in a daring statement: '. . . for truly to see your face is like seeing the face of God, with such favour have you received me' (v. 10b). The wrestling with God and the reconciliation with Esau are clearly connected, but there is no explanation of the link, only the constantly repeated *panim*. Jacob's salvation in both is fraught with risky contingencies, with the central mystery being what happens between faces in hostile confrontation, blessing, seeing, speaking, prostrating, embracing, kissing and weeping. It even seems that the God of this story submits to such contingencies.

The climax of the Pentateuch's account of Israel's engagement with God is the giving of Torah on Mount Sinai. Exodus 32–4 is another passage with several layers of editing and many scholarly problems. It is also of immense importance for Old and New Testaments. Childs calls it 'a superb, new literary composition which went far beyond the individual elements of the earlier sources' and 'offered a profoundly theological interpretation of the meaning of the Sinai Covenant which left a decisive stamp on the entire Old Testament'.[6] The theme is again salvation and the *panim* of God, but in a very different way. While the climactic giving of the tablets of the law to Moses on Sinai is going on the people commit the

---

5. I am grateful to the Rev. Tim Naish for this and other insights in this Old Testament section.   6. Brevard S. Childs, *Exodus. A Commentary* (SCM Press, London 1974), p. 610.

most fundamental sin of making a molten image and worshipping it. There follows a classic story of intercession, judgement, repentance and renewal of the covenant. At the heart of it is communication with God. A version of the 'Tent of Meeting' tradition is given in chapter 33.7–11 which says that 'the Lord used to speak to Moses face to face, as a man speaks to his friend' (v. 11a). Then in the dialogue between the Lord and Moses the key issue is whether the *panim* of the Lord will accompany the people – it is on that that their future depends. The Lord says, 'My *panim* will go with you, and I will give you rest' (v. 14). Moses says, 'If thy *panim* will not go with me, do not carry us up from here . . .' (v. 15). Then in a dense passage Moses asks to see the Lord's glory. The Lord promises that all his goodness will pass before Moses and he will proclaim his name. He says, 'I will be gracious to whom I will be gracious, and will show mercy on whom I will show mercy. But you cannot see my face; for man shall not see me and live' (v. 20). Then he says he will put him in a cleft of rock and cover him with his hand while he passes by. So here in the same chapter we have side by side a tradition of seeing face to face and the impossibility of seeing face to face. This contrasts with the straightforward presence of the golden calf which contradicts the first commandment of Exodus 20.3: 'You shall have no other gods before my *panim*.' The question of the mediation of the salvific *panim* of God is set firmly in the centre of both the Jewish and Christian traditions by these chapters.

There is a further development to come. Exodus 34.29–35 tells of Moses coming down Mount Sinai unaware that the skin of his face shone because he had been talking with God. The rest of the passage is rather puzzling. First it says that the people were afraid to come near Moses because of this radiance. Then it says he talked with them and told them what the Lord had said to him and when he had finished he put a veil over his face. The veil was removed when he spoke with God and when he communicated what God had said to the people, then put on again. So why the veil? Commentators differ, and Paul in 2 Corinthians 3 has one much-disputed explanation[7] which is the context for the key texts of this

---

7. I now find the most persuasive interpretation of the veil in 2 Corinthians 3 to be that offered by Scott J. Hafemann in a paper to the Society for Biblical Literature Annual Meeting, New Orleans, November 1990 entitled 'The glory and the veil of Moses in 2 Cor. 3.7–14: An example of Paul's contextual exegesis of the Old Testament'. The context that Hafemann argues is being taken seriously by Paul is the idolatry with the golden calf. He convincingly gives an interpretation that does not derogate the covenant at Sinai. For the full discussion see Scott J. Hafemann, *Paul, Moses and the History of Israel: the letter/spirit contrast and the argument from scripture in 2 Corinthians 3* (J.C.B. Mohr (Paul Siebeck), Tübingen 1995).

study, 2 Corinthians 3.18 and 4.6. These chapters of Exodus are also crucial background to the Gospels' account of the crucifixion. In the Synoptics the face of Jesus on the cross is the face that has earlier been transfigured in glory while on a mountain praying and talking with Moses (Luke even says that the subject of conversation was Jesus's '"exodus", the destiny he was to fulfil in Jerusalem' – Luke 9.31 REB). In John's Gospel the glory of Jesus is intrinsic to the incarnation ('The Word became flesh and dwelt among us. We have seen his glory . . .' – John 1.14; cf. the reference to Moses in v. 17) and the climax of his glorification is on the cross.

8.2.2 Psalms and prophecy

The Pentateuch is only the beginning of this theme of *panim* in the Old Testament. I will concentrate on just two further strands which have special relevance to the crucifixion of Jesus. One will be the Psalms. The Gospel accounts of the crucifixion have many references to them, and they are also the place where there is the richest concentration on the face of God. The second will be the prophets and especially the 'Servant Songs' in Isaiah 50 and 53, which became key Christian texts for interpreting the death of Jesus.

In the Psalms the shining of the face of God is a summary statement of salvation.[8]

> Let thy face shine on thy servant;
>> save me in thy steadfast love! (Ps. 31.16)

> May God be gracious to us and bless us
>> and make his face to shine upon us,
> that thy way may be known upon earth,
>> thy saving power among all nations. (Ps. 67.1–2)

A further dimension of 2 Corinthians 4.6 is opened up by Markus Bockmuehl as an implication of his interpretation of Philippians 2.6 in '"The Form of God" (Phil. 2.6). Variations on a Theme of Jewish Mysticism', *Journal of Theological Studies*, ns, vol. 48, pt 1, April 1997, pp. 1–23. He connects 2 Corinthians 4.6 to his discussion of the theme of the body of God and Paul's links with Jewish interest in this. Paul's vision of God is christologically focussed, and the *morphe* of Christ (which Bockmuehl interprets in terms of his physical appearance) spans the time from before his historical presence to the eschatological future and indicates the meaning of divinity for Paul. The critical development at the culmination of his life, death and resurrection is the bestowing of 'the name above every name' and the evocation of universal worship.

8. In many of the examples which follow the point of the centrality of the face of God for the conception of salvation is made by the parallelism of the Psalms, the meaning of the second part of the parallel being a variation on the first.

> Restore us, O God;
>> let thy face shine, that we may be saved. (Ps. 80.3, 7, 19)

The corresponding human activity is to seek this face and live appropriately before it:

> Who shall ascend the hill of the Lord?
>> And who shall stand in his holy place?
> He who has clean hands and a pure heart,
>> who does not lift up his soul to what is false,
>> and does not swear deceitfully.
> He will receive blessing from the Lord,
>> and vindication from the God of his salvation.
> Such is the generation of those who seek him,
>> who seek the face of the God of Jacob. (Ps. 24.3–6)

That passage and many others show the centrality of the face of God to worship. The phrase is used cultically – going up to the temple could be described as seeking the face of God. So there is a strong association of the terminology with the community in worship in which its relationship with God is most concentratedly expressed. But it is also used individually and in many different settings, and indeed takes up the communal and the individual aspects of salvation in a mutually reinforcing way. A whole way of life could be summed up in these terms:

> Seek the Lord and his strength,
>> seek his face continually. (Ps. 105.4)

The desire of God meeting the desire of his people is caught in this imagery:

> Thou hast said, 'Seek ye my face.'
>> My heart says to thee,
>> 'Thy face, Lord, do I seek.' (Ps. 27.8)

It also expresses the fulfilment of desire:

> As for me, I shall behold thy face in righteousness;
>> when I awake, I shall be satisfied with beholding thy
>>> form. (Ps. 17.15)

Transposed into the New Testament's 'glory of God in the face of Christ' one can glimpse the potential for this as a key image of salvation and the worshipping self.

But there is a further dimension of this image in the Psalms which goes to the heart of the crucifixion of Jesus. This is the hiddenness of God's face and the associated themes of God's absence, rejection, forgetting, silence, remoteness and abandonment. There is uncertainty, doubt, despair and overwhelming bewilderment in relation to the face of God in its turning away and hiding.[9] The psalms of lament (which are where most references to the face of God occur in the Psalms) perhaps articulate this most vividly in their persistent questioning:

> Why dost thou hide thy face?
> Why dost thou forget our affliction and oppression? (Ps. 44.24)

> O Lord, why dost thou cast me off?
> Why dost thou hide thy face from me? (Ps. 88.14. Cf. Job 13.24)

> How long, O Lord? Wilt thou forget me for ever?
> How long wilt thou hide thy face from me? (Ps. 13.1)

These are cries from the heart, open questions which cannot be made impotent by remarking that they often coexist with or develop into praise and trust. Lament and radical interrogation of God regarding salvation maintain a persistent and untamed element of protest, doubt, bewilderment and even despair in the heart of the prayer of the tradition. This becomes a keynote of the stories of Jesus's crucifixion.

The most dramatic reference to the absence of God is in the use of the opening verses of Psalm 22 in Mark's and Matthew's accounts of Jesus on the cross:

> My God, my God, why hast thou forsaken me? (Mark 15.34;
> Matt. 27.46)

It is striking how this is answered within the psalm itself:

> . . . he has not hid his face from him,
> but has heard, when he cried to him. (v. 24)

Are we to assume this as the context for the cry from the cross? I suggest that, on the one hand, this context should not be used to soften

---

9. For an excellent study of this see Samuel E. Ballantine, *The Hidden God. The Hiding of the Face of God in the Old Testament* (Oxford University Press, Oxford 1983). He traces the theme through all the main strata of the tradition. It has links with other Ancient Near Eastern religions, and the ways in which Israel appropriated it say something about her connections with them as well as about her distinctiveness. His sensitive exploration of semantic fields, variations in different periods, Septuagint translations and their consequences, Rabbinic usages, and the broader framework of the motif of the hiddenness is accompanied by suggestions of its theological fruitfulness.

the dereliction of Jesus; but, on the other hand, it offers a way of understanding the resurrection as the salvific 'not hiding' of God's face which takes the form of the appearance of the crucified Jesus.

The other crucifixion psalms are also relevant to this. In Luke Jesus quotes Psalm 31 to his Father:

> Into your hand I commit my spirit. (v. 5)

The context of this in the psalm is trust in God as saviour in extreme affliction and rejection of the worship of idols. Again the theme of salvation and the face of God appears:

> Let your face shine on your servant;
>   save me in your unfailing love. (v. 16)

> You will hide me under the cover of your presence (*panim*)
>   from those who conspire together ... (v. 20)

> In sudden alarm I said,
>   'I am shut out from your sight.'
> But you heard my plea
>   when I called to you for help. (v. 22)

In John 19.28–9 Jesus's cry 'I thirst' and the sponge of vinegar echo Psalm 69.21, and that context includes the same theme:

> Do not hide your face from me, your servant;
>   answer me without delay, for I am in dire straits. (v. 17)

It therefore makes sense to interpret the crucifixion of Jesus in terms of salvation and the facing of God. It is in line not only with the Old Testament and the probable self-understanding of Jesus through the Psalms but also with all four Gospels.

There is a further complexity that this theme in the Old Testament helps to articulate. What is salvation *from*? The usage in the Psalms and other books shows that misery, suffering of all sorts, and death are as intrinsic to the answer as is sin or disobedience to God. In the Psalms the latter is less emphasised, but some of the prophets develop a rich theology of the hiding of the face of God as a judgement on sin. Isaiah sums up the theology perfectly:

> Behold, the Lord's hand is not shortened, that it cannot save,
>   or his ear dull, that it cannot hear;
> but your iniquities have made a separation
>   between you and your God,

and your sins have hid his face from you
   so that he does not hear. (Isa. 59.1–2)

Similar statements occur in other strands of the book of Isaiah (8.17, 54.8), Micah (3.4), Ezekiel (39.23, 24, 29) and Jeremiah (33.5). The final redaction of Isaiah in particular weaves the theme of the presence and absence of God into a prophetic theology of history that gives primacy to a radical confidence in salvation. The characteristic note is:

In overflowing wrath for a moment
   I hid my face from you,
but with everlasting love I will have compassion on you,
   says the Lord, your Redeemer. (Isa. 54.8)

That is the compassionate face at the heart of salvation. But the older stress on suffering and death continues and makes the face a suitably resonant image through which to evoke the various dimensions of that salvation which the New Testament found in Jesus Christ.

What of the hiding of the human face? There are just three instances in the Old Testament. One is of Moses at the Burning Bush: 'And Moses hid his face, for he was afraid to look at God' (Exod. 3.6). That is a further aspect of the complex Exodus treatment discussed above. The other two uses are both in the Servant Songs of Isaiah, which became so influential on Christian interpretations of the death of Jesus.

Isaiah 50.5–8a says:

The Lord God has opened my ear,
   and I was not rebellious,
   I turned not backward.
I gave my back to the smiters,
   and my cheeks to those who pulled out the beard;
I hid not my face
   from shame and spitting.
For the Lord God helps me;
   therefore I have not been confounded;
therefore I have set my face like flint,
   and I know that I shall not be put to shame;
   he who vindicates me is near.

Here the future vindication of the unprotected, shamed and assaulted face is what salvation is about, and in the meanwhile the vulnerability can be sustained in obedience.

The Servant Song in Isaiah 53 begins:

> Who has believed what we have heard?
>   And to whom has the arm of the Lord been revealed?
> For he grew up before him like a young plant,
>   and like a root out of dry ground;
> He had no form of comeliness that we should look at him,
>   and no beauty that we should desire him.
> He was despised and rejected by men;
>   a man of sorrows and acquainted with grief;
> and as one from whom men hide their faces
>   he was despised and we esteemed him not.

Here the focus is on the repulsiveness of the servant, an embodying of affliction that people cannot bear to face. The passage goes on to stress that he did not open his mouth, undergoing the violence and oppression in silence. Sin and its consequences are registered in bodies, and especially on faces, and the intercession for others involves suffering the most intense rejection in violent encounter, as the very sin that is being interceded for is acted out against the intercessor.[10] All this is held within the context of the servant who grew up before the Lord, confidence in whom was at the heart of his life and death. This living before God in suffering intercession opens up depths in the conception of salvation which have continued to inform Christian theology even when the resonances of the face have been ignored.

Overall, therefore, the Old Testament use of *panim*, as we have sampled it in the Pentateuch, the Psalms and the prophets, gives a rich, subtle and salvation-oriented background[11] for the understanding of the dead face of Jesus on the cross.

8.3 Facing the dead Jesus

It is a remarkable fact that it took Christian art about 900 years before it portrayed Jesus dead on the cross. Until then he was always represented alive, with open eyes. In the aftermath of this new development, both art

---

10. There might be a further dimension if the line 'as one from whom men hide their faces' is translated 'as if Yahweh were hiding his face from him', meaning 'it seems to the people that they see God turning his face away in anger from the suffering servant' (Ballantine, *The Hidden God*, pp. 65ff.). This note of rejection by God as well, at least in the eyes of others, would be a further dimension of suffering.

11. This has been a relatively crude summary which could be endlessly nuanced, but my soundings suggest that further investigation would not invalidate the theological interpretation suggested.

and devotion in Medieval Europe were gripped by the dead Jesus, and he has remained a theme in both ever since. Theology has been less attentive, but today a number of factors have helped to create a climate in which the theme appears fruitful and even urgent. The philosophers and theologians referred to in earlier chapters have helped to show the richness and relevance of the theme of the face in a century of terrible suffering and what Edith Wyschogrod calls 'man-made mass death'.[12] I have tried to elucidate some of the many strands that are tied together in the 'knot of history' focussed on the dead face of Jesus: the significance of the face for human life and identity; the dynamics of facing in Israel's tradition – in worship, in the wrestling of Jacob through which Israel is named, in the giving of Torah on Mount Sinai, in the prophetic conception of salvation and in the Suffering Servant of Isaiah; and the whole of Jesus's life and ministry, culminating in his transfiguration, Last Supper, betrayal with a kiss, trial and crucifixion.

All those converge on the dead face on the cross, but that is also a new factor. It confronts all the others and gives them a different context. It needs to be meditated upon in its pivotal importance for Christian testimony to self and salvation. It also needs, of course, to be related to the resurrection, which will be attempted in the next section. But there is an acute danger of not doing justice to the particular event of the death of Jesus because of its sequel, as if the resurrection were just giving in to the temptation to 'come down from the cross' (Mark 15.29–32) a couple of days late. The effect of the resurrection was in fact to focus the attention of memory on the crucifixion, as shown by the extended accounts in each of the Gospels. The relation and differentiation of crucifixion and resurrection, doing justice to the specificity of each, while also connecting them appropriately, is one of the most important tasks of Christian theology. These issues have led mainstream ancient and modern theology into a primary focus on the doctrines of the person and work of Jesus Christ and of the Trinity, and it is that tradition which I am trying to reinterpret through the theme of the face of Jesus Christ.[13]

12. Edith Wyschogrod, *Spirit in Ashes. Hegel, Heidegger and Man-made Mass Death* (Yale University Press, New Haven and London 1985).
13. Again Dalferth, *Der auferweckte Gekreuzigte*, sums up well the logic of relationship between crucifixion and resurrection and their inseparability from christology, soteriology and the Trinity. The fullest treatment of the relation of crucifixion and resurrection in the history of Christian theology is by Karl Barth in his *Church Dogmatics*. He returns to the theme again and again, especially in three extended approaches from different angles in IV.1, IV.2 and IV.3.1. Dalferth largely distils the main points of this in his 'grammar', but with a helpful development of the eschatological implications and an explicit philosophical dimension.

So what is the testimony of theological thought as it considers the dead face of Jesus? In particular, how can one respond to the leading question under discussion since the end of the previous chapter: Is this a dominating face? If this time of utter deadness is remembered, what does it signify?

An obvious, encompassing point needs to be made first. If the Gospel testimonies are to be trusted, this is the face of one who lived for God and for others, who suffered abandonment by God and others, who was humiliated and tortured to death, and who on the cross is an image of utter powerlessness. He was a disappointment to his followers, a cause of grief to those who loved him, a sign of victory for lies and violence. If, in the light of the resurrection, he comes to be acknowledged as 'Lord' (cf. Acts 2.37) there is yet no simple reversal of all that preceded. His lordship has this death, this tortured, bloody and dead face, always at its heart. To be dominated by this face is to be loved in a way which transforms our conception of what it is to be loved. It portrays a way of love whose normal fate, given the way human beings and the world are, is suffering, concealment, misunderstanding and humiliation to the point of martyrdom.

The early church wrote of this, and it has been repeatedly rediscovered through history in different circumstances. The next two chapters will study diverse examples from recent history, Thérèse of Lisieux and Dietrich Bonhoeffer. In ordinary Christian life it is represented by baptism, the sign of the cross on the forehead responding to the face on the cross. Within the New Testament the most personal articulation of it is given by Paul. Immediately following this book's key text of 2 Corinthians 4.6 on the shining of the face of Christ in our hearts, he writes of power in relation to the cross:

> But we have only earthenware jars to hold this treasure, and this proves that such transcendent power does not come from us: it is God's alone ... Wherever we go we carry with us in our body the death that Jesus died, so that in this body also the life that Jesus lived might be revealed. For Jesus's sake we are all our life being handed over to death, so that the life of Jesus may be revealed in this mortal body of ours. (2 Cor. 4.7–11)

Later in the same letter he quotes the revelation he received about his 'thorn in the flesh': 'My grace is all you need; power is most fully seen in weakness' (2 Cor. 12.8).

To have such a conception of power at the heart of a transformed selfhood is of course deeply controversial,[14] and in the past century it has been the target of special attacks, of which the most extreme has been by Nietzsche. The philosophical and theological dialogue partners I have chosen – Levinas, Jüngel, Ricoeur, Dalferth, Bonhoeffer and Edith Wyschogrod – have all engaged critically with Nietzsche and others. I am suggesting, in dialogue with them, that the face of the dead Christ, in the context of testimony to his life, death and resurrection, is the Christian touchstone for love and power.

In line with that initial, global response to the question of the significance of this dead face there are several further points.

First, it is a literal, physical face which has undergone bodily and mental death. To have this as our primary 'other' is, as was discussed in chapter 6 above, to have an unrepressed sense of death. This includes affirmation of bodiliness and finitude in ways that resist the deep-running dualisms which continually recur and are nourished above all by the body's vulnerability and mortality. One manifestation of these is to give consciousness in some form the task of sustaining continuity through death. But this is full death for Jesus, and there can be no immanent continuity across it. The only continuity is the corpse with this dead face, awaiting a resurrection which, as will be discussed below, is utterly due to God giving life in body, mind and spirit.

This face as dead matter is like a 'black hole' for all familiar and comforting images of this event. It sucks into it other reality, represented in the inexhaustible stream of metaphors, drawing on every area of creation, and their conceptual elaborations. In the personal realm it suggests, for example, reservations about what is perhaps the main contemporary overemphasis, the language of relationship. It is only in a peculiar sense that one can talk of a dead face being 'in relationship' with others. If this dead face of Jesus is intrinsic to salvation, then there is needed a radical critique of concepts of salvation which major on ideas of mutuality, reciprocity, interpersonal consciousness or communication, including 'facing'. They may indeed all be sucked into the black hole in order to be reconstituted with reserve as appropriate metaphors, but the dead face is a vital criterion of appropriateness and signifies a radical rupture at the

---

14. It was, of course, deeply controversial in Paul's own time too. Cf. Timothy B. Savage, *Power through Weakness. Paul's Understanding of the Christian Ministry in 2 Corinthians* (Cambridge University Press, Cambridge 1996), which discusses at length the background and the meaning of 'the glory of God in the face of a crucified man' (p. 188).

heart of relating.[15] The significance for relating and 'being transformed' of having the face of the crucified Jesus Christ shining in our hearts will be examined further through Thérèse and Bonhoeffer.

Yet the dead face as the face of this particular person is not simply identified with death. A usual way of conceiving death is as a general fate, an impersonal power which subsumes all persons in its unchallengeable universality. But this face is of one who has lived for God and for others and has trusted God even in death. The dead face therefore holds open the answer to the question: might the particularity of this face, dead before God, be the true universal? Might the general inclusiveness of death be challenged? Or, more precisely, might death itself be transformed by this person undergoing it?[16] Here the question of the dominating face is posed in relation to the power of death.

How is the dead face of Jesus to be understood in relation to his commitment to others which led to his death? In chapters 3 and 4 I developed Levinas's concept of substitutionary responsibility in dialogue with Jüngel, Bonhoeffer and Ricoeur. That can now be brought to bear here. The dead face resists any notion of substitution which is about replacement of the one substituted for and which therefore sponsors irresponsibility. Instead, it represents the full person of Jesus Christ, but in an absence which demands a comparable responsibility. It signifies simultaneously the ultimate carrying out of responsibility and the complete handing over of it. Before this dead face one can recognise both someone who gave himself utterly for God and for us, and also the fact that being dead is not a matter of doing anything for us: it is being dead for us, being absent for us, being one who creates by his death a limitless sphere of responsibility for us. As in Jesus's parables of masters who go away and leave stewards in charge, the dead face is the embodiment of a call to responsibility in absence. Bonhoeffer's theology of responsibility will be seen to explore this. Thérèse's homely use of the picture of Jesus asleep in the boat makes a similar point: the sleeping Jesus expects his disciples to act responsibly in faith, not wake him up. In very different contexts Bonhoeffer and Thérèse agonise over the awesome responsibil-

---

15. It would be possible to deconstruct and reconstruct with reference to the dead face of Jesus each of the traditional key metaphors through which doctrines of atonement are conceived.

16. Cf. above chapter 3 pp. 62f. where Levinas's idea of how 'the absolute singularity of the responsible one encompasses the generality or generalization of death' is discussed in relation to Jüngel's understanding of death in relation to Jesus.

ity handed over by Jesus. Bonhoeffer is having to decide whether to take part in a plot to assassinate Hitler. Thérèse, in all the complexities and pettiness of convent life, but also conscious that 'my vocation is love', is going through years of what her tradition of spirituality knew as 'desolation'. That at its heart is living in 'mortification', without 'consolation' in solidarity with and before the dead Jesus, and she summed it up in her veneration of the despised and rejected 'Holy Face' of Jesus.

In relation to this substitutionary responsibility of Jesus culminating in his death and his summoning of others to similar responsibility, the resurrection is primarily a revelation and empowering of the vocation to be forgiven freely and to live in this responsibility and call others into it. The resurrection appearances are events of reconciling forgiveness[17] and also calls to joint, expanding responsibility in the Spirit of the crucified Jesus.

That responsibility of Jesus was not only towards individuals; it was also, as the previous chapter argued, towards a whole social and political system and the power relations within it. His dead face is marked with the results of following through his responsibility to the centre of that system's power in Jerusalem. It is the face of a victim of the system, recognised as deeply subversive. To both Jews and Romans it seemed scandalous or ridiculous to venerate someone crucified, as the Christians later did. The political clash was later symbolised by their refusal, in the name of this Lord, to offer worship to Caesar's image. Still later in the eighth and ninth centuries the Iconoclastic Controversy was one of the greatest cultural and political crises in the East Roman Christian civilisation, reaching into the court, the academy, the monastery, the artist's studio and the home. One commentator on it says: 'For the Christian world, from that moment on, the theology of the face is the key to power.'[18] It is

17. For a perceptive discussion of forgiveness which goes far beyond the present work's brief references to it (though it is constantly implied in the idea of facing and being faced by Jesus) and accords well with my main points see L. Gregory Jones, *Embodying Forgiveness. A Theological Analysis* (Eerdmans, Grand Rapids 1995).

18. Marie-José Baudinet, 'The Face of Christ, The Form of the Church' in *Fragments for a History of the Human Body*, Part One, edited by Michel Feher with Ramona Nadaff and Nadia Tazi (Zone, New York 1989), p. 155. Both sides in the controversy were clear that issues of salvation and power were at stake – see Jaroslav Pelikan, *The Christian Tradition. A History of the Development of Doctrine. Vol. 2. The Spirit of Eastern Christendom (600–1700)* (Chicago University Press, Chicago and London 1974), pp. 145ff. Baudinet's contention is that, in this image-pervaded society with a strong central power, the resistance of iconophiles to the Emperor's attempt to eliminate icons of Christ (while of course keeping representations of himself) was a radical assertion of an alternative vision of power – maintaining what might be called today a separation of powers and a certain pluralism.

not appropriate to pursue this fascinating line of inquiry further. But it is clear that the face of this victim of the political and religious powers, remembered as crucified, was bound to be a continuing challenge to all other icons and images of power and authority. Even when apparently most domesticated, which is one possible interpretation of what happened in much post-Constantinian iconography, it signifies a dangerous memory. It is therefore of the utmost importance that the face is remembered not just as dead, but as violently and judicially executed.

Finally, what about this dead face and God? I have stressed the God-centred identity and mission of Jesus, and how his message, person and fate are inextricable. I have also raised the question of Jesus as both worshipper and worshipped, which will be discussed further in the next section. In preparation for that I want here to suggest how the death of Jesus is a transformation of worship.

The psalms prayed on the cross suggest that the death of Jesus be seen as worship in the fullest sense. It is the offering of all he has and is to his Father in trust that his Father's face will shine on him. The basic form of offering in Israel's worship was sacrifice, and it is no accident that the most fully developed theology of the death of Jesus in the New Testament, the Letter to the Hebrews, is conceived in terms of priesthood and sacrifice in the temple. Sacrifice is, of all the traditional images of atonement, perhaps the most congenial for my purposes in this book. It combines worship and physicality, and it goes well with substitutionary responsibility. The dead face of Christ can be read as standing for the body of the sacrificial victim.

Dalferth[19] has an excellent discussion of sacrifice in relation to the soteriological understanding of the death of Jesus, taking account of some of the vast literature on the subject. He argues carefully that it is a helpful image but should not be taken as the encompassing one. The event of Jesus Christ radically revises and supersedes the Old Testament practice of sacrifice. After Jesus, for Christians sacrifice as in the temple is no longer needed. Dalferth stresses the primacy of the person of Jesus

Christoph von Schönborn in *L'Icône du Christ. Fondements théologiques élaborés entre le Ier et le IIe Concile de Nicée (325–787)* (Editions Universitaires Fribourg Suisse, Fribourg 1976) describes the development of theology between the two Councils of Nicea (325, 787) as the emergence of the face of Christ as at the heart of the mystery of salvation. In this story apparently abstruse debates such as the use of the terms *hypostasis* and *prosopon* in christology proved critical means of sustaining the centrality of the face of Christ. As Schönborn concludes his discussion of Basil's convergence of those two terms: 'Les défenseurs des images pourront en conclure que le visage humain du Verbe incarné est paradoxalement l'expression intègre de l'hypostase du Verbe' (p. 44).
19. *Der auferweckte Gekreuzigte*, chapter 5.

Christ: he is the new covenant in person, not just in work, and is the person who is what he should be *coram deo*. The crucifixion and resurrection become the end of sacrifice and the centre of worship; sacrifice is just one of many images that help to elucidate that. The weakness in his account is its failure to do justice to the physicality that sacrifice makes unavoidable. In his concern for the word of the cross, for the activity of God through Christ and for Christ as a corporate person Dalferth does not reckon with the bodily particularity of the dead Jesus and the continuing importance of this, represented in his face. So I wish in concluding this section to accept both his way of relativising sacrificial imagery and his overall grammar of christology but to articulate this in relation to the dead face of Jesus.[20]

The dead face of Jesus can, as suggested, be connected with the body of a sacrificial victim – and that face signifies all that the Letter to the Hebrews, for example, ascribes to Jesus Christ as simultaneously High Priest and victim. The human, worshipping High Priest and the dead animal victim are both focussed through the dead face. Its deadness is the mark of a completed offering, of worship that has been perfected. At the heart of that worship has been utter trust in God in the face of death. As Hebrews in a crucial passage says:

> In the days of his earthly life he offered up prayers and petitions, with
> loud cries and tears, to God who was able to deliver him from the
> grave. Because of his humble submission his prayer was heard: son
> though he was, he learned obedience in the school of suffering, and,
> once perfected, became the source of eternal salvation for all who obey
> him, named by God high priest in the succession of Melchizedek.
> (5.7–10)

So there is one form of completion or perfection, but it calls for its perfection to be perfected in the response of the God to whom it has been offered. Utter reliance on the perfecting initiative of God in the passivity of this death (taking account of what has been said above about the particularity of this passivity and death, encompassing through their substitutionary responsibility the generality of universal death) is the heart of Jesus's worship. That initiative is what the New Testament calls the resurrection. It has already been discussed in passing, but now requires fuller consideration.

---

20. I recognise that this might have wider critical implications for Dalferth's theology, especially as regards personhood and substitution, but it is not my concern to explore those.

8.4 An idolised face?

In chapter 4 on the worshipping self Ricoeur's question arising out of his discussion of 2 Corinthians 3.18 was quoted: is an icon that is not an idol possible? He was not speaking of a work of art, but of the central concern of this chapter, the human face of Christ. Clearly Christians did come to worship Jesus Christ. He inspired in them new forms of prayer and devotion which joined him with his Father and the Holy Spirit in the basic naming of God in baptism and eucharist. The 'grammar' of Christian faith was eventually articulated as the doctrines of incarnation and Trinity, but the language was in use long before the grammar was made explicit. I will not try to encompass this vast topic – I find that Dalferth and the many Christian thinkers whose arguments he agrees with have treated this well enough for my purposes here. But they also generally agree that the Christian transformation of worship is unthinkable without the crucifixion and resurrection of Jesus. I have treated the crucifixion in relation to the face of Christ; now I will explore the resurrection with special concern for the focussing of worship on and through this crucified and risen face. First I will explain what sort of event I understand the resurrection to be.

8.4.1 The resurrection as an event than which none better or greater could be conceived

Interpretations of the testimonies to the resurrection of Jesus vary widely. Verdicts include mistaken identity, fraud, delusion, vision, mythological or symbolic interpretation of the meaning of the crucifixion, a spiritual resurrection with no implications for his dead body, a transformed physical body about the physics and chemistry of which it is appropriate to remain agnostic, and an emergence from the tomb which could have been photographed. All of these have their accompanying and informing theologies or other worldviews, and it is not my concern to try to debate them here. I will simply lay out in brief the framework for interpreting it that I find most convincing.

The main point is that the testimonies cannot be done justice to unless they are understood to be referring to a God-sized event. The whole New Testament is clear about this: the raising of Jesus from the dead is ascribed to God. One of St Anselm of Canterbury's 'names' for God was 'that than which none greater can be conceived', and St Bonaventure argued that, because of the priority of goodness over being, the 'greater' should be changed to 'better'.[21] For the New Testament the resurrection is an ultimate, eschatological event of overwhelming joy for which God is responsible. It is therefore an event than which none better or greater could be conceived. One can of course consider aspects of it by abstracting from its relation to God, or one can deny the reality of the God who is testified to, but if one wants to be talking about the same event one has to acknowledge that what is testified to is God-sized.

But who is the God involved? If this event is seen at the heart of the generation of the worship of God as Trinity then it is an event through which God is newly identifiable. For Christian theology this is the key point, and its conceivability can be approached in the following three ways.

First, the God concerned is the creator of everything and the God of Abraham, Isaac, Jacob and Moses. Perhaps the most important Old Testament name for God is Yahweh, 'I am who I am'. It is much discussed, but at least means a God who is free to act and reveal who God is in history, as the story of Moses and the Burning Bush in Exodus 3 suggests. This means that there can be further self-revelations of this God of creation and history. The resurrection of Jesus is seen as such an event. It is paralleled with creation as a comparable act of God (e.g. Romans 4.16–25); it is also seen as the culmination of Israel's history with God (e.g. Luke 24; Acts 2). So in interpreting the resurrection testimonies our whole framework for understanding the universe and history is at stake. It is clear that many rejections of the testimonies are based on presuppositions about what creation is like, what is likely to happen in history, and whether this sort of God is credible. So the largest issues of presuppositions, worldviews, ideologies and beliefs are raised. They are beyond the scope of this book, but I too of course make presuppositions in this area. Put very concisely, within a framework of basic trust in the truth of the testimonies to the resurrection I find them raising radical questions for believers as well as unbelievers, and developments in philosophy, the sciences, the arts and history have to be engaged with more thoroughly as a result. It would be odd if that were not the case with an event claimed to be as fundamental as creation. The present study attempts only a little of such engagement.[22]

---

21. For a provocative discussion of this in relation to the question of God and idolatry see Jean-Luc Marion, *God Without Being* (University of Chicago Press, Chicago and London 1991), especially pp. 73ff.
22. The multiple implications are sketched in chapter 11's final meditation, 'Feasting'.

What about Jesus in this? In the New Testament he was not seen as just the occasion for this event of God's new self-determination. He was seen as intrinsic to it. This was strikingly so in some of the earliest writings (e.g. 1 Corinthians 8.6), and by the later documents the conviction has been developed further (John 1, Hebrews 1, Colossians 1, Ephesians 1). Seeing Jesus Christ as intrinsic to who God is in creation and in the whole of history is a clear implication of New Testament faith in the resurrection.

Second, the God of the resurrection is the God of the life and death of Jesus. I have already explored this at length, especially as regards the way in which Jesus's message, person and fate were coinherent. They were coinherent in being centred on God, and their vindication was also dependent on God. As Hans Frei argued, the logic of the resurrection stories is: God acts; Jesus appears.[23] This logic, pivotal to the worshipping of Jesus, will appear again in the next section.

Just as faith in God as creator involves a complex of truth judgements inseparable from a whole worldview, so faith in the resurrection is inseparable not just from faith in God as creator but also from trust in the truth of particular testimonies. This faith is in principle falsifiable, and the witnesses are rightly subjected to endless cross-examination. Christians are those who are convinced of their reliability, which does not, of course, mean that every detail has to be believed to have taken place as recounted. Their faith, like the core concept of 'conviction' in Ricoeur's understanding of self discussed in chapter 4 above, is inseparable from trust in the truth of testimony.

Third, the logic of the resurrection accounts has a further dimension: God acts; Jesus appears; the disciples are transformed. In John's Gospel this is expressed in the risen Jesus breathing the Holy Spirit on them face to face. In Luke-Acts the giving of the Spirit is at Pentecost. 2 Corinthians 3.18 is close to the Johannine pattern: the transformation 'from glory to glory' is face to face in faith with the glorified Jesus and is ascribed to 'the Lord the Spirit'. However it is articulated, this 'second difference'[24] in the God of the resurrection is essential to the grammar of the event.[25] It is not just a point about what happens to the disciples; it is testimony to the self-distribution of God and, under the heading of the doctrine of the

23. Frei, *The Identity of Jesus Christ*, chapters 11–14.
24. See John Milbank's perceptive discussion, 'The Second Difference', chapter 7 in *The Word Made Strange* (Blackwell, Oxford 1997).
25. Cf. Dalferth, *Der auferweckte Gekreuzigte*, chapters 3, 4.

Holy Spirit or grace, it has been one of the most discussed and disputed areas of Christian theology.

In these three ways, therefore, corresponding to the later development of the members of the Trinity, the resurrection is a God-sized event, and if its full truth is to be affirmed it involves all the elements mentioned – acknowledging a God who is free to do new and self-revealing things, the God of creation and of Abraham, Isaac, Jacob and Moses; trusting the testimony of the first witnesses that Jesus Christ died and is risen; and, through and in all that, being transformed by the Holy Spirit.

8.4.2 Worship before this face

With this understanding of the resurrection, I take up where section 8.3 left off: the completed worship of Jesus Christ on the cross. This was seen as a perfection waiting to be perfected, on the analogy of praise which, the more perfect its object is, the more it tries to add to it in worship. Jesus's death is the utter differentiation of the worshipping human being from God. It simply awaits God's response and is utterly dependent on it – which is why it generated the classic Pauline, Augustinian and Lutheran doctrine of justification by faith. That response is the resurrection. What is its significance for worship?

I have summed up the resurrection's logic above as 'God acts; Jesus appears; the disciples are transformed.' The first significance of the appearance of Jesus for worship is that it is anti-idolatrous. He has confronted his own temptation to false worship and the idolatrous dynamics of his society, he has offered true worship in the form of sacrificial, substitutionary responsibility, and has completed that on the cross. From there he radically interrogates all worship and exposes any that does not unite love of God and love of neighbour. His vindication by God is therefore a confirmation of his way of facing God and others. That whole dynamic of facing is revealed as true to God. The disciples are therefore drawn into a new facing of God, each other and innumerable further people by this event.

But what about the face of the risen Jesus Christ in this new dynamic? For the lesson of anti-idolatry it is not needed at all – any sign of confirmation would do. But in fact it is intrinsic to the confirmation and continues to be so. The appearance of Jesus is the substance of God's eschatological act, of the event than which none better or greater can be conceived. The person of Jesus is the content of the anti-idolatry. But positively this means that it is possible not to be idolatrous in worshipping Jesus. He is given by God as the content of God's facing of creation. This transforms worship, as the early church testifies. More radically, the resurrection and exaltation of Jesus show that there is facing in God and there is humanity in God. The picture of Jesus 'at the right side of God' conveys this: worship addressed to God goes inseparably to Jesus too; and the Father also faces the Son, the transformative overflow of which is the Holy Spirit.

The transformation of worship is thorough. To have one person as worshipper and worshipped rules out a conception of worship in which a subject, the worshipper, is directed towards a God conceived as a separate, undifferentiated object. Getting rid of that is a major step away from idolatry. Instead, God is free to take an initiative in order to lead us into worship from our side. Jesus is God in a way which tells us how to worship God. He embodies the facing of God and the facing of humanity. So there is facing, otherness, within God. There is worship within God, a dynamic of love and glorification. The dead face is taken up as the pivotal moment of worship and glory – 'the lamb on the throne', 'the lamb slain since before the foundation of the world' (Rev. 13.8). The self of Jesus, given for others in worship of God, is the reconstitution of facing and so is saviour and salvation. In Ricoeur's terms, he is a human self *as* (in Ricoeur's fullest ontological sense) the other who is God; he is also a human self as the other who is each person he faces. Salvation for the self is therefore to be 'christomorphic' in its facing of him and 'being transformed from glory to glory'.

To worship in faith before this face is above all to be faced by him. Whatever refers us to this face – whether the faces of fellow human beings, or the imagination aroused by scripture and worship, or works of art, or joyful responsibility, or 'the face of the earth' – is seen with an iconic, not an idolatrous gaze: it leads us to 'see' Jesus Christ only to find ourselves 'more radically looked at',[26] loved, delighted in and accountable. And even 'seeing' this face in faith is to find it a self-effacing face, referring us to the face of the Father and to the faces of fellow human beings, as has been discussed in the previous chapter.[27] So worship is reconstituted into the transformation of 2 Corinthians 3.18, and our selfhood is saved by inhabiting the reality of 2 Corinthians 4.6 – our context is all creation, before the God 'who said "Light will shine in darkness"'; and our hearts overflow towards others with 'the light of the knowledge

---

26. Marion, *God Without Being*, p. 22. The phrase comes in a difficult but suggestive interpretation of 2 Corinthians 3.18.
27. See above, pp. 172ff.

of the glory of God in the face of Christ'. The event that unifies that verse is the raising of the crucified Christ by God from the darkness of death to the light of the new creation.

The worship which has most consistently and fruitfully represented all this is the eucharist, and chapter 6 can now be very briefly connected with the culmination of this one. Its understanding of Jesus Christ was summarised in the statement: 'Jesus Christ as the blessing of God'. Through Jesus Christ God blesses and is blessed. Death is denied ultimacy, life is 'timed' in a new way, a covenant community which obeys the imperative 'Do this!' is shaped, and the 'non-identical repetition' realised in the resurrection of the crucified Jesus Christ is celebrated. The eucharist is an apprenticeship in being blessed and blessing before the face of Jesus Christ through whom the face of God in the Aaronic blessing is recognised:

> The Lord bless you and keep you:
> The Lord make his face to shine upon you,
>   and be gracious to you:
> The Lord lift up his countenance upon you,
>   and give you peace. (Num. 6.24–6)

9

Love as vocation: Thérèse of Lisieux

What sort of selves are formed before the face of Christ? This and the following chapters are concerned with the transformed and transforming selves classically called 'saints'. Their lives elude general descriptions and are as differently unique as faces.

Part of trying to do justice to this abundance of particularities and their interrelations is the labour of conceptualising. Previous chapters have produced a series of conceptions that together converge on the notion of joyful responsibility to the point of substitutionary sacrifice. This has been elaborated in such terms as hospitality, love, witness, worship, singing, gentleness, the eucharist, the abundant generosity of God, an unrepressed sense of death, the shape of time, an economy of blessing, and the life, death and resurrection of Jesus Christ. Jesus has been the first specific person to be discussed in depth in the previous two chapters, and the narrative density of the testimonies to him were explored so as to add dimensions to the key concepts and also to indicate the quality of his imperative confrontation of others. This chapter looks especially at Thérèse of Lisieux and the next chapter at Dietrich Bonhoeffer, as two people whose lives were shaped through that confrontation. But first I will discuss a work on saints that connects with the discussions of some previous chapters.

9.1 Levinassian saints

The theme of imperative confrontation with saints through hagiographic testimony is central to Edith Wyschogrod's work, *Saints and Postmodernism. Revisioning Moral Philosophy*.[1] She develops many of

---

1. University of Chicago Press, Chicago and London 1990.

Levinas's lines in a direction that he did not take.[2] Her thesis is threefold: that Levinas and others summon us to place a reworked notion of altruism, in the sense of radical responsibility towards others who are suffering, at the centre of our ethics; but moral philosophy in ancient, modern or most postmodern forms is not up to the task of addressing matters that urgently call for action – 'moral theories do not result in moral actions' or in personal moral transformation;[3] so in this situation a fresh starting point is required, and she finds it in the saint whose primary trait is compassion for 'the Other' whatever the cost to the saint.

She therefore argues for a 'hagiographic ethic' to replace a theoretical one,[4] while staying in critical dialogue with Anglo-American analytic philosophy as well as with classical Western moral philosophy. In a key summary of her thesis she makes the conception of other and self the critical factor:

> The reservations expressed regarding moral theory do not preclude insightful observation into the character of other-directed existence by analytic ethicists. In mining their arguments for such insights, I show that they run into difficulty because the Other is treated as another self. The accounts that derive from this perspective develop an altruism qualified by self-interest. Recent historical events will inevitably impact differently on altruism that begins with the self as the unit of significance and altruism that takes the Other as its starting point. A postmodern altruism must appeal to radical saintly generosity, to a benevolence that will not be brought to a close. Such saintliness is not a nostalgic return to premodern hagiography but a postmodern expression of excessive desire, a desire on behalf of the Other that seeks the cessation of another's suffering and the birth of another's joy.[5]

Confronted with the stories of saints the effect is to be challenged to imitate their compassionate altruism. The verbal mood that dominates hagiographic narrative is the imperative,[6] and 'saints are "native speakers" of the language of alterity, poets of the imperative'.[7] What gives force to the imperative is not a theory or argument but the actual embodiment of compassionate responsibility.

So physicality is intrinsic to this ethic of the 'incarnate subject' in which the unit of significance is the saint's body. General meaning is

---

2. Other key thinkers for her are Heidegger, Merleau-Ponty, Derrida, Bataille and Blanchot.   3. *Saints and Postmodernism*, p. xxv.   4. Ibid., p. xxvii.   5. Ibid., p. xxiv.
6. Ibid., p. 178, in the course of a perceptive analysis of how the philosophy of Quine and Davidson suppresses both the imperative mood and reference to the Other.
7. Ibid., p. 183.

found not primarily through theory, or verbal communication, or seeing the saint as an example of a concept (even of altruism), but through the flesh. 'The saintly body acts as a signifier, as a carnal generality that condenses and channels meaning, a signifier that expresses extremes of love, compassion, and generosity. In their disclosure of what is morally possible, saintly bodies "fill" the discursive space of ethics.'[8] The key idea here is 'carnal generality', which she sees as a development of what is implicit in Merleau-Ponty and Levinas. In carnal generality 'a new mode of generality that precedes the reification of universals – goodness, justice, and so on – is exhibited'.[9] That sums up better than any other philosophical terminology the importance of the face in my previous chapters: it allows a particular person to have wide significance which is still intrinsic to one body and the detailed complexity of its story.

Wyschogrod herself also follows through the theme of the face in relation to thinkers who in an extreme way represent that suspicion of the 'dominating face' which I discussed in chapter 7 above. Gilles Deleuze and Felix Guattari, in *A Thousand Plateaus: Capitalism and Schizophrenia*,[10] deconstruct the face. For them, on the one hand it is a material surface revealing the 'black hole' of interiority; on the other, it is a fetishised commodity and an oppressive political instrument, absorbing other faces and excluding them from power: 'The face . . . is White Man himself . . . The face is Christ . . . The face is the typical European . . . The face is a politics.'[11] Wyschogrod's analysis of their position shows how it fails to do justice to the otherness of the face or to the way its vulnerability and mortality appeal for respect. Otherness and mortality are more primary than the politics of the face – 'the despotic face masks what is common to faces: the manifestation of mortality that, irrespective of race, gender, and class, is expressed in every face . . .'[12] Before the appeal in the vulnerable face of the Other saints respond with generosity and compassion. 'Faces lay claim to saints who substitute for or become the hostage of the Other.'[13]

So Wyschogrod 'thinks the unthought' in Levinas by finding the imperative of radical responsibility best embodied and interpreted in the stories of saints. In philosophical terms this has many affinities with Ricoeur's *Oneself As Another*[14] where the self is described through a

---

8. Ibid., p. 52.   9. Ibid., p. 50.   10. University of Minnesota Press, Minneapolis 1987.
11. Ibid., pp. 176f., 181, quoted in Wyschogrod, *Saints and Postmodernism*, p. 225.
12. *Saints and Postmodernism*, p. 226.   13. Ibid., p. 227.
14. Cf. especially the discussion above in chapter 4.

modified Levinassian ethic integrated with narrative identity. In theological terms it helps in conceptualising stories (and other genres) about the facing of Jesus – both Jesus facing others and them facing him – as central to a treatment of self and salvation. It also raises three major questions in relation to the course of this book so far.

9.1.1 Joy and responsibility

The first question is about joy. As we saw above, Wyschogrod in her preface sees the saint expressing 'excessive desire, a desire on behalf of the Other that seeks the cessation of another's suffering and the birth of another's joy'.[15] At the end of the book she returns to this theme:

> The saintly desire for the Other is excessive and wild. In traditional
> Christian theological language, the saint desires not only the welfare
> of the Other, the cessation of another's suffering, but also the Other's
> beatitude; not only to sit at the right hand of God oneself but to desire
> the elevation of the Other.[16]

Yet in the body of the book this is largely neglected. As in Levinas, joy is a submerged theme in her own position. The main explicit reason is her discrimination between two types of postmodern thought. There is a 'crucial fault line'[17] between them. On the one hand is the 'ecstatic' postmodernism of Deleuze and Guattari, Jean Genet, Peter Sloterdijk and Julia Kristeva. She finds in this a will to joy and ecstasy, and a desire that is at best ambiguously related to the Other and to ethics. Kristeva is 'especially disquieting'[18] in her ultimate orientation towards 'the jouissance of aesthetic quietism',[19] as exemplified in her interpretation of the facing of the Virgin Mary in the madonnas of Leonardo da Vinci and Giovanni Bellini.[20] On the other hand there is the 'differential' postmodernism of the later Heidegger, Maurice Blanchot, Jacques Derrida, Levinas and Michel de Certeau. Here she finds the ethical significance of the face, and a stress on alterity, difference, delay, fissure, break, gap, trace, spoor, and

---

15. Wyschogrod, *Saints and Postmodernism*, p. xxiv.   16. Ibid., p. 255.
17. Ibid., p. 229; cf. pp. xxiv, 192, 208, 223, 235, 244ff.   18. Ibid., p. 246.
19. Ibid., p. 249.
20. Ibid., p. 251: 'The preference for a joy beyond pleasure, for an ecstaticism that is different from solicitude, shows itself elsewhere in Kristeva's work, in her preference for the madonnas of Giovanni Bellini over those of Leonardo da Vinci on the grounds that, in the distanced look of Bellini's Virgin, "unlike the solicitude in Leonardo's paintings, [there is] ineffable jouissance" (Julia Kristeva, *Desire in Language: A Semiotic Approach to Literature and Art*, New York, Columbia University Press 1980, p. 347). The face of the Virgin is averted, the gaze is "never center[ed] in the baby" (Ibid. p. 247). It seems that there is in Bellini's madonnas "a shattering, a loss of identity, a sweet jubilation where she is not" (Ibid.).'

the restraint of desire and power in confrontation with the Other.[21] Her basic concern is that ecstatic joy cannot coexist with the terrible realities of history and must be at root irresponsible and escapist:

> To gain the pleromatic fullness of ecstasy requires a present that forgets history for the reasons discussed earlier, because who in the century of man-made mass death could attain ecstasy without amnesia?[22]

Yet over against this is her own stated concern for joy. Is it possible to have an ethically responsible joy? She affirms it briefly, but otherwise is as reticent as Levinas. The logic of her thought would seem to imply something like 'substitutionary joy' in the joy of others, which is to be distinguished from the ecstatic joy of which she is rightly suspicious. I have tried to argue for joyful responsibility which trusts the testimony to the death and resurrection of Jesus Christ. Neither she nor Levinas wants to follow that way, but I suggest that the thrust of their thinking might allow for it.

9.1.2 Worship and God

The second question is about worship and God. This is the most problematic part of Wyschogrod's book[23] as regards my position. She gives her definition of a saint explicitly in order to exclude worship from any constitutive role in the saint's selfhood:

> The English word saint as well as the Romance language equivalents derive from the Latin sanctum, dedicated or set apart for the worship of deity. Thus, in Western Christian tradition, a linguistic link connects the saints with theistic belief. I shall, however, define the saint – the subject of hagiographic narrative – as one whose adult life in its entirety is devoted to the alleviation of sorrow (the psychological suffering) and pain (the physical suffering) that afflicts other persons without distinction of rank or group or, alternatively, that afflicts sentient beings, whatever the cost to the saint in pain or sorrow. On this view theistic belief may but need not be a component of the saint's belief system.[24]

Her aim in this is to include as saints those such as 'nonbelievers or Buddhists who alleviated suffering in epidemics and wars'.[25] The saint need not be a mystic or a theist. She claims that it is possible to find con-

---

21. See especially ibid. pp. 223, 229, 235.   22. Ibid., p. 252.
23. Her position is stated in the section 'Mysticism, Theism, and Saintly Life' on pp. 34–9, and my discussion of it refers to these pages.   24. Ibid., p. 34.   25. Ibid., pp. 34f.

stitutive elements in mystical experience across religious traditions,[26] and is even more insistent that this is true of saintly experience:

> Once the distinction between mystic and saint is drawn, the saint's experience can be considered in terms of her/his actual or envisioned acts. To be sure, these are incorporated into a conceptual framework but, more important, they are articulated within a context anchored in human need and, therefore, one which remains relatively constant.[27]

The main support for her position is an analysis of the relation of the moral and the contemplative in St Teresa of Avila. There are also corroborative statements about St Catherine of Siena, about meditation and the relief of suffering in Buddhism, and about the Hasidic tradition of 'joyful worship' in which there is a distinction between the hidden contemplative holy man and the one who reveals himself and engages in communal activity.

I start from the phrase 'more important' in the previous quotation. What is its weight? She has slid from 'worship' via 'theism' and 'mysticism' to 'a conceptual framework' as what is to be differentiated from altruistic action for other people who are suffering. It is especially significant that she shifts the focus from worship to 'the saint's belief system'.[28] There is an attempt to interpret the 'actual or envisioned acts' without intrinsic reference to God. The Other is for her the human Other in need. The univocal identification of the Other in this way recalls Ricoeur's critique of Levinas at the end of *Oneself As Another*, pleading for philosophical openness to 'a certain equivocalness of the status of the Other'.[29] In chapter 4 I pressed this theologically in the direction of the worshipping self. In the light of that and the position that has been developed since, there are several problems with Wyschogrod's position.

First, from the point of view of St Teresa and the Hasidim, she seems to be reversing the order of the commandments to love God and love the neighbour. Their 'experience' in terms of their 'actual or envisioned acts' is most profoundly shaped through worship and prayer. Their bodies, which for Wyschogrod are the basic units of significance, are disciplined, energised and formed through worship. Their perception of the Other is as someone created by God in God's image. So how can acts articulated in the context of human need be 'more important' than the conceptual

26. Ibid., p. 35 on the ineffable and paradoxical.   27. Ibid., pp. 35f.   28. Ibid., p. 34.
29. Ricoeur's *Oneself As Another*, p. 355.

framework which is inextricable from loving God with all their heart, soul, mind and bodily strength? It is also puzzling why it is noted as an advantage that the context of human need 'remains relatively constant', without reference to what is the decisive constant for these saints, the constancy of God. The main problem is that she shifts from talking about worship to talking about the saint's belief system, and this leads her to leave out of account precisely the dimensions of worship which make it so complexly involved in relations with other people – its physicality, its communality and language, its transformation of how others are perceived.

In Wyschogrod's analysis of St Teresa's experiences she recognises that the moral and the contemplative have to be kept together as well as distinguished. But when she comments on Teresa's statement about the soul rejoicing in 'some good thing, in which are comprised all good things at once' she says:

> What can the fruits of this incomprehensible good thing be? Not the bliss of divine proximity, which is mixed with intense bodily pain. Rather, it must be the detachment this 'good thing' provides to do God's work . . . [T]hese special favors granted by God are interpreted as proofs that God wants to use her 'in order to help a great many people'.[30]

In Teresa there is no such disjunction ('Not . . . Rather') between divine proximity (whether blissful or painful) and the detachment needed to do God's work.[31]

The thrust of Wyschogrod's differentiation is towards a contemporary version of what the Enlightenment distinguished as 'natural' and 'revealed' religion, with the belief systems of 'revealed' religion inessential (and even possibly harmful[32]) to a healthy altruistic ethic. This can be argued for, but it should not be implied as offering an overview of all the specific religions or a privileged criterion for judging them.[33]

---

30. *Saints and Postmodernism*, p. 37.
31. For a perceptive discussion of Teresa, including an understanding of mysticism which resists the differentiation Wyschogrod attempts to make, see Rowan Williams, *St. Teresa of Avila* (Chapman, London 1991).
32. Cf. her abstraction of altruistic behaviour from 'historical contexts in which saintliness has arisen with their often deeply rooted prejudices against other claimants to transcendent truth' (ibid., p. xiv) and from any 'specific religious community' (ibid., p. xxiii). This might be no more than an ethical hermeneutic of suspicion, but in the light of the rest of the book it is more like resistance to engagement with the positive as well as negative aspects of the full context of saintliness in specific periods and communities. This comes to a head in my discussion of saintly singularity below.
33. For a historical and theological understanding of religion in line with my point see Nicholas Lash, *The Beginning and the End of 'Religion'* (Cambridge University Press, Cambridge 1996), especially chapters 1 and 4.

Wyschogrod's worshipless ethic is itself a fundamental option and it sits uneasily with Teresa and the Hasidim.

Second, from the standpoint of the reception of hagiographic narratives, what are the imperatives that are to be obeyed? Wyschogrod isolates the imitation of the saint's altruistic acts, but this mutes the challenge of saints such as Teresa and the Hasidim, which refuses to sideline questions of God. It is not that such saints, or those who hear the imperatives presented by their stories, need rule out altruistic acts by atheists, Buddhists or anyone else; nor need they be imperialistic in their claims to truth; but they do refuse to interpret any altruism apart from reference to God (a reference that may, of course, largely be a confession of ignorance about how God relates to altruism). To respond to their imperatives as they desire would be to join in 'joyful worship'; not to do this would be to miss what they see as most important and as the true spring of their altruism. How can Wyschogrod's differentiation of imperatives not seem either arbitrary or else dictated by an alternative worldview or quasi-religion? To do justice to worship-centred saints such as Teresa and the Hasidim she would have to enter thoroughly into the debate between these saints and others whose altruism is differently inspired and embodied, rather than subsuming both under the category of altruism and thereby relativising God. It is striking how little role any conception of God as the Other plays in the rest of her book.

Third, her use of a definition of saintliness to elide radical differences, and also to make disjunctions between worship and altruism that are alien to the saints themselves, seems to be in danger of weakening the potential of some of her own best insights. She champions Bakhtin's 'heteroglossia, the interplay of a novel's multiple voices',[34] resisting the 'gaze without a body',[35] or the 'panoptic gaze',[36] yet this seems in tension with her embrace of such diverse saints within her definition. She further recognises that 'it is the phenomenology of desire as exorbitance that makes the excesses of saintly lives comprehensible',[37] and that 'the Other is also an excess',[38] but she does not do justice to worship as a practice of excess or to God as Other.

The problem is perhaps sharpest of all in her brilliant analysis of the way in which the philosophies of Quine, Davidson, Husserl and others suppress both reference and mood.[39] By reference she means reference to the Other – theirs is a language without alterity:[40] but for her there is no

---

34. Wyschogrod, *Saints and Postmodernism*, p. 11.   35. Ibid., p. 51.   36. Ibid., p. 129.
37. Ibid., p. 146.   38. Ibid., p. 148.   39. Ibid., chapter 6.   40. E.g. ibid., p. 170.

Ricoeurian equivocalness leaving open the Other as referring to God. By the suppression of mood she means the imperative mood summoning to responsibility before the Other. Here there is not just a failure to grapple with responsibility before God; she also ignores the suppression of the vocative mood, that calling upon God which is the overflow of, for example, Teresa's exorbitant desire and which is the subject of so many biblical exhortations.[41]

Overall, there is a suspicion that her evenhandedness in relation to the religions springs from wrenching out of context what she defines as altruism in the saints of each religion and of none, and from an accompanying reluctance to travel the long detour of detailed involvement with the specifics of each. This leads into my third concern.

9.1.3 Saintly singularity

It is ironic that Wyschogrod should appear to engage inadequately with saintly specifics since she insists on the importance of working through detailed narratives and above all on what she calls 'saintly singularity'.[42] Yet the chief value of the book is not in its hermeneutics of particular lives. It lies rather in its conceptual creativity together with its effect (in line with her insight into the imperative force of saintly lives) of summoning readers to a fuller appreciation of hagiography. This may be no more than to say that she is writing a work of moral philosophy and not of literary criticism, scriptural commentary or historical testimony.

At the very end of her book she wrestles with 'saintliness and some aporias of postmodernism',[43] the culminating problem being that of saintly singularity. Above all she holds to the excessive character both of the suffering Other whom the saint serves and of the saint's own desire, as testified to in hagiographical narratives. These can never simply exemplify moral or other categories: saintly individuation overflows concepts and theories. The 'unthought' in her book is about what happens when involvement in the singularity of individual saints is more radical than hers. Her brief excursions into saints' lives are overwhelmed by her extended discussion of philosophical questions. This invites a rebalancing of her proportions, which this chapter and the next will attempt to do.

I therefore turn to two specific figures, Thérèse of Lisieux and Dietrich Bonhoeffer.

---

41. Cf. chapter 4 p. 81f. above on prayer as petition.
42. Wyschogrod, *Saints and Postmodernism*, pp. 235, 252ff.
43. Ibid., chapter 8, pp. 233–57.

9.2 St Thérèse of Lisieux

Thérèse Martin was born in Alençon in France in 1873, the youngest of five sisters in an extremely devout Catholic family. Her mother died when she was five and the family moved to Lisieux. Her two eldest sisters entered the Carmelite convent in Lisieux, and when she was fifteen Thérèse did so too, later to be followed there by yet another sister. She became novice mistress, and, on the instructions of her sister Pauline, who was the Prioress, she wrote the story of her life.[44] On 30 September 1897 she died of tuberculosis at the age of twenty-four. Veneration of her, assisted by the publication of her autobiography and by the energetic support of her sisters, spread rapidly. Pope Pius XI beatified her in 1923 and canonised her in 1925 after the usual thorough investigation and 'trial'. He saw her as 'the star of his pontificate'.[45] Before him Pope Pius X is said to have called her 'the greatest saint of modern times'.[46]

There are many fascinating questions about her background, her life and the subsequent veneration, and a vast and growing literature. I will concentrate on her own writings and sayings, and on three theological interpretations of her life, those of Hans Urs von Balthasar,[47] Ida Görres[48] and Constance Fitzgerald,[49] my main concern being to relate her to the themes of this study.

44. The edition I refer to is *Story of a Soul. The Autobiography of St. Thérèse of Lisieux* (ICS Publications, Washington, DC 1976).
45. Ida Görres, *The Hidden Face. A Study of St. Thérèse of Lisieux* (Burns and Oates, London 1959), a translation of *Das Senfkorn von Lisieux*, the 8th revised edition of *Das verborgene Antlitz: Eine Studie über Thérèse von Lisieux* (Herder Verlag, Freiburg im Breisgau 1944).
46. Ibid., pp. 4, 413. Hans Urs von Balthasar, *Thérèse of Lisieux. The Story of a Mission* (Sheed and Ward, London and New York 1953), p. xix, ascribes this statement to Pius XI.
47. *Thérèse of Lisieux.*   48. *The Hidden Face.*
49. 'The Mission of Thérèse of Lisieux' in *Contemporary Carmelite Women, The Way Supplement* 89, Summer 1997, pp. 74–96. Of the three, Görres is the more historical, but still theologically sensitive; Fitzgerald is more psychological, concentrating on the dynamics of Thérèse's relations with women and with God, and she is likewise theologically sensitive; von Balthasar is more singlemindedly theological. Görres and von Balthasar wrote before recent controversies about the ways in which Thérèse's writings and words were edited and arguably distorted, especially by her sister Pauline (Mother Agnes). A strong recent critique of Pauline's role, together with a new interpretation of the last eighteen months of Thérèse's life, is given by Jean-François Six in *Light of the Night. The Last Eighteen Months in the Life of Thérèse of Lisieux* (SCM Press, London 1996). Yet I find the theological points made by Görres and von Balthasar are very little affected even if all Six's arguments about the history of the manuscripts are accepted. Fitzgerald, writing in awareness of the controversy, interprets Pauline's role in a far more sympathetic light. For her, there is a relationship of mutuality and reciprocity between Thérèse and Pauline both before and after Thérèse's death. Her interpretation reads like an illustration of Ricoeur's 'self as another' and profoundly questions the concept of identity underlying Six's attempt to separate Thérèse from Pauline and accuse Pauline of distortion. ('The Mission of Thérèse of Lisieux', pp. 87f.)

9.2.1 The Holy Face

Thérèse had two 'names in religion'. The first was 'of the Child Jesus', which was given to her on her entry into the convent. The other, 'of the Holy Face', she chose for herself when she received the veil at the age of sixteen. As Görres shows, the roots of her desire for this name are deep and multiple.[50] Her sister Pauline had introduced her to it, and it had been a special devotion of the founder of the Lisieux Carmel, Mother Geneviève, who placed an image of the 'Veil of Veronica' (relating to the apocryphal story that on his way to Calvary carrying the cross Jesus had his face wiped by Veronica and this 'veil' retained the imprint of his face) in the chapel of the convent. A more powerful impetus was given by the illness of her father, to whom she was extraordinarily close, just after she entered the convent:

> The face of the person she loved most on earth was now for ever deprived of sanity and transformed into the frightful mask of living death. Added to that was the memory of her mysterious vision in childhood, in which she had seen her father walking in the garden with covered head. With the obsessiveness of grief she pondered on the meaning of this trial which had befallen so faithful a servant of God. Combined with this was her own experience of God turning away from her. All this was given form and significance in her mind by the 'bleeding Head, so wounded'. Thérèse herself says little about this. Six weeks before her death she remarked to Pauline: 'The words in Isaiah: "No stateliness here, no majesty, no beauty, as we gaze upon him, to win our hearts. Nay, here is one despised, left out of all human reckoning; bowed with misery, and no stranger to weakness; how should we recognise that face? How should we take any account of him, a man so despised" – these words were the basis of my whole worship of the Holy Face . . . I, too, wanted to be without comeliness and beauty, alone to tread the grapes, unknown to all creatures.'[51]

Fitzgerald complements this with an interpretation of Thérèse's whole life in terms of the dynamics of facing, especially between women. She convincingly explores the long-term significance of the death of Thérèse's mother when she was five;[52] of the successive displacements on

50. Görres. *The Hidden Face*, pp. 26off.   51. Ibid., pp. 26of.
52. 'Her mother's face functions as the first mirror into which Thérèse looks to discover her own precious identity which is secure and self-assured until her mother dies. In Thérèse we see very clearly the psychological dynamic by which a baby is affirmed in her mother's gaze.' (Fitzgerald, 'The Mission of Thérèse of Lisieux', p. 76.)

to her sisters Pauline and Marie, until each successively took the veil; and of the complex maturing in a succession of predominantly female settings of her capacity to be mothered and to mother others. Woven into Fitzgerald's discussion is a theological argument about how an understanding of Thérèse's development in terms of 'le regard',[53] the gaze or facing, can illuminate how her relationships with her father, mother, sisters and others are interwoven with her relationships with Mary, Jesus and God.

Thérèse was not given to extraordinary experiences and was suspicious of mystical phenomena. But the theme of facing is central to those she tells about. This was so during a serious illness and personal crisis when she was aged ten.[54] It recurs as she entered upon years of spiritual aridity: during the retreat before her Profession she prays in classic Carmelite imagery to reach 'the summit of the mountain of Love', but instead

> Our Lord took me by the hand and made me enter a subterranean way where it is neither cold nor warm, where the sun does not shine and where rain and wind may not enter; a tunnel where I see nothing but a half-veiled glow from the downcast eyes in the Face of my Spouse.[55]

In May of the year before she died, as her aridity intensified, she had a dream of the transfigured face of Anne of Jesus, who had founded Carmel in France.[56]

53. Fitzgerald notes that in the concordance for Thérèse's autobiography in French there are two columns of references for the word 'regard', and she interprets it in terms of look, gaze, face and esteem. 'The Mission of Thérèse of Lisieux', p. 77.
54. While she was praying before a statue of Mary:
> All of a sudden the Blessed Virgin appeared beautiful to me, so beautiful that never had I seen anything so attractive; her face was suffused with an ineffable benevolence and tenderness, but what penetrated to the very depths of my soul was the 'ravishing smile of the Blessed Virgin.' At that instant all my pain disappeared, and two large tears glistened on my eyelashes, and flowed down my cheeks silently, but they were tears of unmixed joy. Ah! I thought, the Blessed Virgin smiled at me, how happy I am, but never will I tell anyone for my happiness would then disappear ... It was her countenance alone that had struck me. (*Story of a Soul*, pp. 65–7)
Fitzgerald's interpretation of this as the displacement of the 'mother-face' on to Mary and the beginning for Thérèse of the '"Mamma" God' opens up a fruitful possibility for a feminist development of the understanding of the face of Christ – see 'The Mission of Thérèse of Lisieux', pp. 83f.
55. Görres, *The Hidden Face*, quoting from Letter 91.
56. She writes:
> ... I saw three Carmelites, dressed in their mantles and long veils ... In the depths of my heart I cried out: 'Oh! how happy I would be if I could see the face of one of these Carmelites!' Then, as though my prayer were heard by her, the tallest of the saints advanced towards me; immediately I fell to my knees. Oh! what happiness! the Carmelite raised her veil or rather she raised it and covered me with it. Without the least hesitation, I recognised Venerable Anne of Jesus, Foundress of Carmel in

Such experiences, together with a very close and affectionate family life in which expressions were registered with great sensitivity, followed by a convent in which nuns had long periods of silence but observed each other with close attention, made the theme of facing a constant and fruitful image. It is all related to what von Balthasar sees as crucial:

> ... that image which she placed at the centre of her entire devotion; the face of Our Lord suffering, with his eyelids closed. Her whole life in Christ is concentrated into her devotion to the Holy Face; unwaveringly she gazes upon God in the extremity of his love, gazing on his face where the eternal light seems to have been extinguished and yet is most transparent, streaming irresistibly from beneath the closed lids ... The Holy Face ... is for her the direct revelation and vision of the divine countenance ... Thérèse is never tired of returning to 'the eyes which fascinate her', of 'Him whose Face was hidden so that men knew Him not', of 'the loved unknown Countenance which ravishes us with its tears'. She gazes entranced upon those downcast eyes; everything is centred there.[57]

The face of Jesus becomes for Thérèse a way into the basic truths of faith, from God to eschatology. She sees God delighting to look upon his children, but not in a way that makes them self-conscious. The effect is to focus them on another, on Jesus alone, above all in his hiddenness and suffering, but there is also a hope for the joyful vision of God which she expressed with great confidence.[58]

The Holy Face above all was a thread through the life, death, resurrec-

---

France. Her face was beautiful but with an immaterial beauty. No ray escaped from it and still, in spite of the veil which covered us both, I saw this heavenly face suffused with an unspeakably gentle light, a light it didn't receive from without but was produced from within.

I cannot express the joy of my soul since these things are experienced but cannot be put into words. Several months have passed ... I still see Venerable Mother's glance and smile which was FILLED WITH LOVE ...

[In the course of conversing with Anne, Thérèse asks if God is content with her.] The saint's face took on an expression incomparably more tender than the first time she spoke to me. Her look and her caresses were the sweetest of answers. However, she said to me: 'God asks no other thing from you. He is content, very content!' After again embracing me with more love than the tenderest of mothers has ever given to her child, I saw her leave. My heart was filled with joy. (*Story of a Soul*, pp. 191f.)

For Fitzgerald's interpretation of this see 'The Mission of Thérèse of Lisieux', p. 90.

57. Von Balthasar, *Thérèse of Lisieux*, pp. 157–9.

58. ' "But one day in Heaven, in our beautiful Homeland, I shall look at You, and in my look You will see all I want to say, for silence is the language of the blissful inhabitants of Heaven." ... "When I am in Heaven", she declares, "I shall not imitate the Seraphim in God's presence. They cover their countenances with their wings. I will take care not to cover myself with my wings ..." ... "O ineffable bliss, when I am caught for the first time in the divine brightness of Your adorable Face".' (Ibid., p. 162.)

tion and ascension of Jesus. Jesus as a baby; as a child; asleep and smiling in a boat; on the mountain of the transfiguration; being anointed by Mary Magdalene; weeping; in Gethsemane; bloody and wearing the crown of thorns; carrying the cross; on the cross; resurrected and in heaven; and on the day of judgement: all are connected with his face. The implications of living before this face can in my terms be summed up as a life of joyful responsibility, worked out in practices of facing.

9.2.2 Practices of facing

The practices in which Thérèse's devotion to the face of Jesus Christ was expressed most obviously were those to do with worship, meditation, prayer and the liturgical year. She addressed the Holy Face in prayer, she wrote hymns and poems about it, she painted it on Mass vestments and in pictures; she meditated on it and always had its picture in her breviary and in her place in choir; when she was novice mistress she composed a form of consecration to the Holy Face for the novices to use; she specially celebrated the Feast of the Transfiguration on 6 August (focussing on the Sorrowful Face); and in her last illness she had its picture on the curtain of her bed so that she could always see it.[59]

The distinctive thing about her devotion is, however, the way in which it becomes intrinsic to the way of life resulting in the teaching for which she is best known, her 'little way'. This she described as

> ... the way of spiritual childhood, the way of trust and total surrender. I wish to ... tell [people] that there is only one thing to do here below – to strew before Jesus the flowers of little sacrifices ...[60]

The little way means recognising one's nothingness, expecting everything from God, as a little child expects everything from its father. It is a way of trust in the generosity of God at every moment and of an overwhelming desire to love and please God. This involves being constantly alert for ways of pleasing God by sacrificial love, little acts which are like petals strewn before Jesus. There can be no reckoning up of what we achieve like this, since we recognise we owe it all to God and continue to expect everything from God. Whatever the sacrifice required, God has grace enough for it. In theological terms it unites faith, hope and love; justification by grace, sanctification by grace, and vocation by grace.

Another way of summarising it is in terms of Thérèse's vocation. In a famous passage in her autobiography she describes her recognition of

---

59. See von Balthasar, *Thérèse of Lisieux*, pp. 157f.
60. Ibid., p. 220, extracted from a helpful composite quotation on the little way.

her vocation. She was overwhelmed by 'infinite desires' and longed to serve Jesus by being Carmelite, spouse, mother, warrior, priest, apostle, doctor, martyr, crusader, papal guard, prophet. This daring conception of herself in terms 'transcending the confinement of a very circum-scribed landscape, an extremely limited intellectual space, a remarkably small language; stretching even beyond the way women are socially constructed'[61] is followed by a meditation on 1 Corinthians 13 on love as the excellent way:

> I finally had rest. Considering the mystical body of the Church, I had not recognised myself in any of the members described by St. Paul, or rather I desired to see myself in them all. Charity gave me the key to my vocation. I understood that if the Church had a body composed of different members, the most necessary and most noble of all could not be lacking to it, and so I understood that the Church had a heart and that this heart was BURNING WITH LOVE. I understood it was Love alone that made the Church's members act, that if Love ever became extinct, apostles would not preach the Gospel and martyrs would not shed their blood. I understood that LOVE COMPRISED ALL VOCATIONS, THAT LOVE WAS EVERYTHING, THAT IT EMBRACED ALL TIMES AND PLACES . . . IN A WORD, THAT IT WAS ETERNAL!
>
> Then, in the excess of my delirious joy, I cried out: O Jesus, my Love . . . my vocation, at last I have found it . . . MY VOCATION IS LOVE![62]

Thérèse goes on to meditate on why this is a little way. She is a little child who 'knows only one thing: to love You, O Jesus. Astounding works are forbidden to her . . . But how will she prove her love since love is proved by works? Well, the little child will strew flowers, she will perfume the royal throne with their sweet scents, and she will sing in her silvery tones the canticle of Love.'[63] In the metaphors of flowers, petals, scents and singing she points to the practices that are at the heart of her vocation. They amount to a double discipline.

On the one hand there is her devotion to the hidden, despised face of Christ. Her experience of this was through a faith that was largely devoid of consolation year after year in the convent. She experienced rather what is classically called 'desolation', and Görres chronicles this vividly, build-ing up from hints and details a picture of continuing and devastating spiritual aridity, reaching a crescendo of intensity during her final illness

---

61. Fitzgerald, 'The Mission of Thérèse of Lisieux', pp. 90f.   62. *Story of a Soul*, p. 194.
63. Ibid., p. 196.

in doubt, temptation, abandonment, persecution by well-wishers as well as ill-wishers, and sheer physical pain and disintegration.

On the other hand there is her conduct with her sisters in the convent. Her 'special note' as a saint is 'the veil of the smile'.[64]

> Smilingly, Thérèse went through her years in the convent, graciously, guilelessly, sunnily smiling. But that smile was the most stringent instrument of her physical and spiritual penance.[65]

She took literally the Sermon on the Mount's instructions not to let a discipline that involves suffering be revealed in the face (Matt. 6.16–18). So little and larger self-denials and sacrifices for the sake of others, and minor and sometimes major physical sufferings were concealed by her smile. There was a 'veil of ordinariness' embodied in smiling regard for the other which was, for her, the only permissible way to suffer. Forty years after her death the surviving nuns from the convent always spoke first of her beautiful, radiant smile. A friend of the Prioress called her 'une âme chantante', a singing soul. She was also a good mimic, had a fine sense of humour, and regularly made the nuns laugh in recreation.

This poses a special historical problem because by definition this 'penance' was only authentic if it remained hidden. How can it emerge so strongly? Partly because she was ordered to write her autobiography and took obedience very seriously, to the point of revealing what otherwise would never have been known – chapters 10 and 11 in *Story of a Soul* are especially relevant. This was complemented by the comprehensive interrogation of her conducted by her sisters and others, especially during her final illness. There was also the evidence of her novices to whom she taught her way of the veil and often gave illustrations from her own experience.

Her smile can easily be misunderstood. It could be seen as hypocritical, a pretence of happiness and of love towards the other, or as a form of politeness which conceals. But Görres' sensitive analysis is convincing: 'To Thérèse her smile was simply honest fulfilment of her vocation.'[66] Its theological basis is clear.[67] On the one hand it springs from living before

---

64. Görres, *The Hidden Face*, p. 112.   65. Ibid., p. 305.   66. Ibid., p. 308.

67. Underwriting her theology is her understanding of the New Testament, and especially her grasp of the 'new commandment' to love one another as Christ has loved us. In chapter 10 of *Story of a Soul* she repeatedly returns to the Sermon on the Mount in order to interpret that commandment. She gives her own interpretations to the lamp on the lampstand (ibid., p. 220), not judging (p. 222), love of enemies and persecutors, giving to everyone who asks (p. 225), giving your cloak to someone who steals your coat (p. 226), going two miles with those who force you to go one (p. 227), and lending without hoping for return (p. 229). And woven into the meditation are examples of her practice of smiling.

the face of Christ – as she wrote in a poem: 'For Him I love I wish my smile to shine.'[68] She wants to smile for him and also to imitate his hiddenness. 'Beneath that smile she sacrificed things profound and valid: the basic human longing for recognition, for another's understanding look into one's own heart.'[69] On the other hand it springs from the certainty that each person is made in the image of God and that each can genuinely be delighted in – 'young Thérèse set about mastering this hidden reality of God in her fellow human beings'.[70] Appreciation of the interplay of these two dimensions calls for the detail Görres brings to bear in illuminating Thérèse's 'saintly singularity'. It also invites the more recent appropriation by Fitzgerald, who recapitulates Thérèse's history of facing in ways that do justice to the dimensions of mothering and female bonding and shows how Thérèse can inspire a spirituality alert to the concerns of feminism while at the same time oriented towards the face of Christ.[71]

9.2.3 Saving souls

Smiling might appear a somewhat precious and even trivial discipline in the light of the problems of the world. Yet Thérèse's solemn declaration about her reason for entering the convent was: 'I have come to save souls and above all to pray for priests.'[72] The two sides of that are closely linked, since she saw priesthood as primarily about the salvation of souls. But what is this salvation?

Thérèse is clear that saving souls is about love. She writes to her sister Céline that the 'one thing' is 'to love, to love Jesus with all the power of our hearts, and to save souls for Him, so that He will be loved still more'.[73] But her way was not that of 'great deeds' like those of the 'great saints'. Rather it relied on God's delight in his 'little ones' even when they can do very little: they do their little out of love for him and he does all they ask.

---

68. Görres, *The Hidden Face*, p. 309.   69. Ibid., p. 311.   70. Ibid., p. 239.

71. Her article opens up far more issues than it can explore. Among these are the way in which Thérèse's relationship with her father is to be understood (fascinating questions are raised about his being veiled in Thérèse's vision of him, and about a transcendent reciprocity with Christ who is both male and female but ultimately beyond gender – 'The Mission of Thérèse of Lisieux', p. 80), and above all about the interplay of divine and human facings as, for example, in the following paragraph:

> From one perspective, what we see Thérèse doing with the face of Christ is displacing the mother's face onto that Face. From another perspective, if we understand that the people who are gifts in our lives are the means by which the divine displaces itself on to physical reality, then the mother's face is the first displacement. In Thérèse we have a series of displacements that from the very beginning lead to the face of Jesus, even though Thérèse does not realize this. The ultimate locus *is* the face of God. This means that the degree to which we understand this reciprocity is the degree to which we experience the mystery of the incarnation even if we do not rationally comprehend this. (p. 82)

72. Görres, *The Hidden Face*, p. 139.   73. Ibid., p. 287.

She says to God: '... I am but a poor little thing who would return to nothingness if your divine glance did not give me life from one moment to the
next.'[74] The utter reliance upon God intensified during her final illness:
'We experience such great peace in being absolutely poor, in being able to
count upon nothing but God.'[75] Even the sacraments were relativised:
'Undoubtedly it is a great grace to receive the Sacraments, but if God does
not permit it, that is well too ... All is grace.'[76]

Yet the 'all is grace' is not competitive with human responsibility.
Thérèse was fascinated by the relationship of grace, obedience and works,
and her actions and teachings frequently show her transcending the
usual dilemmas. For example, she writes to Céline: 'Jesus has so incom-
prehensible, so uncompromising a love for us, that He wants to do
nothing without us; He wants us to share with Him in the salvation of
souls.'[77] That 'nothing without us' is the mysterious, 'uncompromising'
gift of responsibility. Indeed the responsibility is all the more radical
because of who gives it, and it is pictured in one of her favourite images:
Jesus asleep, either as a baby or in the boat in the storm on the Sea of
Galilee.[78] For Jesus to sleep means that one is still responsible before his
face,[79] but must take responsibility for what one does without his saying
or doing anything. This rather 'cute' image conceals years of Thérèse
experiencing no consolations that might be interpreted as his smiles. She
maintains in faith her love of him, and prays and works for herself and
others to give him joy.

Joy is a frequent topic in what she says and writes. It is primarily oriented towards others and is essentially joy in the joy of others. This is first
of all the joy of Jesus and of his Father, but inseparable from that is joy in
the joy of other people, above all in their love of each other and of God.
This is 'substitutionary joy' inseparable from substitutionary responsibility. It is therefore a joy which does not exclude suffering: on the contrary it even rejoices in suffering for God and others. Thérèse's embracing
of suffering with joy can seem scandalous to the point of being masochis-
tic if taken out of context.[80] But it fits very well Wyschogrod's description
of altruistic desire for the beatitude of the other. The further twist

74. Quoted and discussed in Six, *Light of the Night*, p. 87.
75. Görres, *The Hidden Face*, p. 373.   76. Ibid., p. 378.   77. Ibid., p. 288.
78. Cf. von Balthasar, *Thérèse of Lisieux*, pp. 216ff.
79. 'How entrancing is your smile as you sleep!' (ibid., p. 217).
80. Part of its context is Francis of Assisi's definition of perfect joy as a friar arriving at his
monastery on a snowy night and being turned away, to which Thérèse refers. Cf. Six, *Light
of the Night*, p. 79, commenting on Thérèse's letter to Abbé Belière on 26 December 1896 in
which she says that St Francis 'teaches ... the means of finding joy in the midst of the trials
and combats of life'; also p. 146.

Thérèse gives to this is that, while Wyschogrod's examples are all 'great saints', she offers a little way for 'little saints', and longs for ordinary people to be able to follow it. Wyschogrod's altruism tends to the heroic; Thérèse's is for the weak, for those who identify with her as a little child trusting utterly in God and not worrying unduly about making a major impact. Her attractiveness has partly been in her opening a way of sanctification at the heart of ordinary life, where most of the sacrifices appear 'little' but are, before God, the ways that love is multiplied and souls are shaped:

> I have no other means of proving my love for You other than that of strewing flowers, that is, not allowing one little sacrfice to escape, not one look, one word, profiting by all the smallest things and doing them through love. I desire to suffer for love and even to rejoice through love; and in this way I shall strew flowers before Your throne. I shall not come upon one without unpetalling it for You. While I am strewing my flowers, I shall sing, for could one cry while doing such a joyous action? I shall sing even when I must gather my flowers in the midst of thorns, and my song will be all the more melodious in proportion to the length and sharpness of the thorns.[81]

This little way is small enough to fit into every vocation every day, and the ultimate simplicity of its desire to suffer for love and rejoice through love is in its constant orientation to the face of Christ: 'I wish for no other joy but that of making You smile.'[82] Jesus smiles on love for God and neighbour, and incarnates both. The 'detour' of desire by way of the face of Christ brings her back to other neighbours with an altruism which is in line with that of Wyschogrod's worshipless ethic, and with a recognition of sisterhood and motherhood (as stressed by Fitzgerald) which is oriented to all people:

> I am writing about sisterly love, which gives me plenty of opportunity to practise it. Mother, love of one's neighbour is everything in this world. We only love God in so far as we practise love of our neighbour.[83]

Her way of helping to save souls is therefore to take on the joyful responsibility of trying to love them so as to open up for them the way of joyful responsibility before God. It is an imitable 'little way' which yet demands everything of whoever travels it. It is a 'lay' way, subversive of many traditional models of sanctity[84] and revising conceptions of salva-

---

81. *Story of a Soul*, pp. 196f.   82. Quoted by von Balthasar, *Thérèse of Lisieux*, p. 215.
83. Ibid., p. 4.
84. Görres, *The Hidden Face*, is especially perceptive and provocative on this, especially chapters 1, 2, 7.

tion and heaven.[85] And it is a woman's way, whose potential for women and men owes much to the lessons learnt in the 'small female space'[86] of her home and convent.

9.2.4 Selfhood beyond Gethsemane

What sort of selfhood is glimpsed in Thérèse? I have been describing her as embodying and reinterpreting key concepts of selfhood used in this and earlier chapters. Wyschogrod's ideas of altruism, 'carnal generality', desire for the beatitude of others, and hagiographic use of 'face'; the facing of Jesus Christ; the eucharistic self being abundantly blessed; Ephesians' singing self in Christ; Farley's communities of the face; Ricoeur's self as another developed in the direction of Rosenzweig's worship-centred Jewish conception of response to the injunction from the lover of the Song of Songs, 'Love thou me!';[87] Jüngel's interpretation of love and joy through the crucifixion and resurrection of Jesus; and Levinas's hospitable and substitutionary self responding to the infinite demand in the face of the other: all these are recapitulated in the testimonies by and to Thérèse. They pivot around worship and joyful responsibility before the 'Holy Face' of Jesus Christ, embodied in an ordinary life of love for others.

This is still short of adequate 'singularity', and one way of exploring further is through the significance of the different readings of Thérèse offered by those I have taken as helpful commentators on her, Görres, von Balthasar and Fitzgerald. Their writings are largely complementary of each other, and each of them in different ways convincingly replies to the main alternative interpretations. But there are some crucial divergences, which are most sharply seen between the longer works of Görres and von Balthasar.

Partly the differences between the two are a matter of the genre of each book. Von Balthasar is giving a theological interpretation of Thérèse which is concerned to place her in relation to doctrines, the celibate and married 'states of life', the official ministry of the Roman Catholic Church, patterns of holiness, and traditions of mysticism. He often finds her wanting in some of those respects: very little emphasis on the Holy

---

85. Von Balthasar, *Thérèse of Lisieux*, pp. 13ff., 148ff., 167ff.
86. Fitzgerald, with reference to Gerda Lerner's understanding of feminist consciousness, says that 'the small female space can certainly be a place of imprisonment and limitation, but it can just as well be the place which, above all, produces depth, transcendence and creativity. And this is what we see in Thérèse.' ('The Mission of Thérèse of Lisieux', p. 89.)
87. Six in *Light of the Night*, pp. 127ff. sensitively explores Thérèse's fascination with the Song of Songs.

Spirit in the Trinity, a defective appreciation of original sin, little contact with the 'objective' ministry of the church, strengths and weaknesses in relation to von Balthasar's favourite pattern of Ignatian sanctity, and less than full immersion in the 'dark night of the soul'.

Görres, on the other hand, is primarily telling a story, though with a thorough awareness of the theological issues. Since she wrote before von Balthasar, and he draws frequently on her, his major divergences from her are likely to be deliberate. The most striking thing in comparing them is how much detail von Balthasar leaves out and how profoundly this affects the portrayal of Thérèse. The form that Görres uses seems more adequate to the content. She is describing, her eye constantly alert to the significance of details, a 'micro-drama' of nuanced facings, apparently tiny decisions, hints of what is largely hidden, complex ambiguities which defy overview. In Wyschogrod's terms, it is a hagiographic style whose imperative force is constantly felt in the ordinary habits of the reader's life: its impact is on the next detail of family life or prayer life. It communicates the littleness of the 'little way' with practical power.

Von Balthasar's verdict on Görres is that she is too influenced by 'German personalism' and depth psychology.[88] He concludes:

> With a tremendous liveliness, and touches of genius, Görres pours out her criticism of the bourgeois piety prevalent in the family milieu and the reactionary convent, and of the threadbare theological teaching on the states of life. She specially criticizes the practice by which girls of seventeen to twenty had to make a choice for life between the convent and marriage. But since Görres does not introduce the distinction between the person and the mission she has to resort to depth psychology in order to bring out her heroine's greatness. This leads to obvious misinterpretations, so that in spite of her brilliant account of Thérèse's personal life and milieu Görres' work is inadequate on the theological side.[89]

It is questionable whether 'depth psychology' is the right label for Görres' patient and illuminating attention to the detail of a life.[90] 'Criticism' is also hardly the right term for her unsentimental yet understanding analysis of bourgeois piety, convent life and limited vocational possibilities. But, setting those aside, the heart of the verdict is that she fails to use von Balthasar's own key distinction between person and mission. In his other writings he has offered a typology of sainthood integrated with his doctrine of the church, and his *Theo-Drama* explains at

---

88. Von Balthasar, *Thérèse of Lisieux*, p. 276.   89. Ibid., p. 277.
90. Fitzgerald, 'The Mission of Thérèse of Lisieux', is far more indebted to such psychology.

great length his concept of mission in relation to person.[91] His theological net is cast as widely as possible and he delivers a series of negative judgements on both Thérèse and Görres. The problem is that the mesh of his net seems too large to catch the littleness of Thérèse and the theological significance of Görres' portrayal. Von Balthasar's construct of saintliness is deeply influenced by Hegel's notion of 'world-historical individuals', and his drama embraces the whole history of God with the world.[92] Within that the key to the drama is the life, death and resurrection of Jesus Christ in the context of Israel and the church. He has a lively appreciation of the dramatic roles of saints and of the varied ways in which person and mission can come together and can be in tension.

The problem in relation to Thérèse comes when he assumes something like an overview of the drama, judging her performance according to his criteria. It is not that it is inappropriate to make judgements – Görres too does so, and by no means so as always to portray Thérèse as a 'heroine'. But whereas Görres travels a lengthy 'detour through the details' in order to arrive there, von Balthasar tends to impose his categories and use the details as illustrations. For all his recognition of novelty in Thérèse there is little sense of von Balthasar's generalities concerning sanctity, church, doctrine or mysticism having been affected by Thérèse's particularities. So in spite of his eloquent recognition of the centrality of Thérèse facing the Holy Face at the heart of her mission and vocation of love, this is subsumed into something like what Levinas might call a 'totality'. Görres' method allows her to stay before Thérèse's face and transform categories accordingly. Above all it is the meaning of the face which is thus transformed through Thérèse's devotion to the Holy Face. Von Balthasar criticises Görres' 'German personalism' and her failure to distinguish person and mission; her response might be that in Thérèse's vocation of love embodied in practices of facing there is an undercutting of that distinction. It does not mean that the distinction is useless, but, applied to this person and her mission of largely hidden ordinariness, it is not illuminating. Thérèse's own account of her discovery of her vocation[93] implies as much: her yearning for the more 'heroic' missions or vocations is overwhelmed by the realisation

---

91. *Theo-Drama: Theological Dramatic Theory*, 5 vols. (Ignatius Press, San Francisco 1988–). Volume III is especially important for his understanding of mission and person.
92. J. B. Quash in '"Between the Brutely Given and the Brutally, Banally Free": Von Balthasar's Theology of Drama in Dialogue with Hegel' (*Modern Theology*, vol. 13, no. 3, July 1997, pp. 293–318) discusses some of the problems with von Balthasar's position. Quash's argument that von Balthasar does not, in his own terms, sustain a fully dramatic theology but tends to slip into 'epic' modes is in line with my point that he misses the distinctive 'mini-dramatic' mode in Thérèse and Görres.   93. Quoted above, p. 230.

that her own is more radical than any and is a presupposition of them all.

Von Balthasar's vast gallery of saints, theologians, dramatists and others are marshalled by him and assigned roles in the 'theo-drama' of history. He tries to apply the same criteria to Thérèse and to Görres' account of her, but, like Levinas's 'face' in relation to 'totality', Thérèse in her littleness and vulnerability eludes and even subverts his criteria. It is no accident that the very genesis of Görres' study of Thérèse shows a recognition of the explosive significance of her face, including its subversive potential:

> During a meeting at Burg Rothenfels, then the centre of the Catholic Youth Movement in Germany, a student showed me a small picture, like a passport photograph. 'This is the true appearance of Little Thérèse,' he said. 'Dom Willibord Verkade, the monk-painter of Beuron, discovered and published it. The Carmel at Lisieux, and a French bishop as well, protested vehemently against its publication.'
>
> A small group of young people gathered around him; the picture passed from hand to hand. In stunned silence we gazed at the familiar and yet so alien features, and someone said: '. . . Almost like the face of a female Christ.' From that August morning on I was determined to pursue the riddle of her look and her smile – so different from the honeyed insipidity of the usual representations of her. Who was Thérèse of the Child Jesus in reality?[94]

Fitzgerald's article might be seen as an extended footnote to the 'female' in the phrase 'the face of a female Christ'.

The culminating difference between Görres and von Balthasar comes in their interpretations of her death. His verdict (in which, however, there is also an agnostic note) is: '. . . Thérèse's little way leaves her at the beginning of the Passion; it confines her to the Mount of Olives.'[95]

---

94. Görres, *The Hidden Face*, p. 13.
95. Von Balthasar, *Thérèse of Lisieux*, p. 271. The whole passage reads:
    Thérèse's world remains immune from the effects of elemental evil – a fact which confirms our opinion that her night of the soul never reached the dimensions of the night of the Cross, that point where the Son is brought face to face with the sinner's absolute abandonment by God. In a sense Thérèse's little way leaves her at the beginning of the Passion; it confines her to the Mount of Olives. That is *her* mystery, which she loves and reverently worships; she herself describes it as the essence, the heart of her devotion. Once more, it is very difficult to say whether she did not go a step further during the last weeks of all, or to decide the point on the way of suffering to which her terrible last agony took her. But she drinks in full measure the chalice for which she had asked: 'The chalice is full to overflowing! No. I would never have believed it possible to suffer so much. I cannot explain it except by my boundless desire to save souls . . .' . . . With this suffering her plans of love are finally realised: 'I who have desired every form of martyrdom for myself – ah, a person has to be plunged into it to know what it means!'

Görres gives a different verdict: 'She was participating in the un-fathomable Passion of Our Lord when His Father abandoned Him.'[96] She is supported by Thérèse's own preoccupation with the death of Jesus on the cross during her final months.[97] Her dying was, in the convent setting, public and exposed – she was endlessly interrogated by the nuns, her words recorded. There was a continuing experience which Görres seems right to describe in terms of abandonment by God in the face of suffering, sin, evil, death and the demonic.[98] Above all there was the sheer physical pain, the disintegration of her body and the accompanying threat of the disintegration of her sanity, as she had seen happen to her father.[99]

Yet in all this identification there is a parallel differentiation. It is not the distinction between Gethsemane and Calvary. It is the differentiation between her own dying and that of Jesus, while yet utterly identifying with Jesus:

> I should never ask God for greater pain, for then it would be my own pain; I would have to bear it alone – and I have never been able to do anything by myself.[100]

This identification and differentiation is summed up in her being face to face in faith with the one who died for her. Von Balthasar has a continuing doubt about whether she really appreciated the depth of evil and sin, but even he acknowledges the strong statements during her final illness about contrition, forgiveness of debts, and being a sinner. Görres goes further and suggests that, alongside this sense of utter dependence on the forgiveness and mercy of God, 'in her last days Thérèse experienced a kind of judgement upon her past life and upon the testimony she had written'.[101] It was a conviction of the truth of what she had embodied and taught:

> [S]ix days before her death she looked at Pauline . . . and said: 'Now I feel it clearly: what I have said and written is true – *all of it*. It is true that I asked to suffer greatly for God – and it is true that I still desire to do so.'[102]

96. Görres, *The Hidden Face*, p. 359. Fitzgerald's verdict accords with this, 'The Mission of Thérèse of Lisieux', p. 92.
97. For example, Thérèse's response to the weird experience of one of the nuns regularly standing by her bed laughing at her was: 'Yes, it is very painful to be regarded laughingly while one is suffering – but I think Our Lord on the Cross in the midst of his torment must have been looked at in exactly that way . . .' (Görres, *The Hidden Face*, p. 379.) Görres' account brings out other elements which identify her with Calvary.
98. Ibid., especially pp. 355ff., 375f. This verdict is supported by Six's study, *Light of the Night*.   99. Görres, *The Hidden Face*, especially pp. 353f.   100. Ibid., p. 375.
101. Ibid., p. 385.   102. Ibid.

This sense of completeness within the continuing suffering is for Görres a further theological argument for the cross being the appropriate key to what she was going through. It also, of course, has more than a little of the scandal of the cross: the claim is stupendous, and Görres explores well the stark alternatives between judging this as humble recognition of what God has done through her and a shocking assertion of self-importance.

In the terms that I used in the last chapter, the self of Thérèse is most adequately understood as formed through a lifetime of facing Jesus Christ in faith. For her he is the suffering servant of Isaiah 53 and the hidden, crucified one. The resurrection is not allowed to overcome the hiddenness, and the implications for responsibility are symbolised in her devotion to the sleeping face of Jesus. Her life before him also forms and is formed through a succession of particular facings, many of them in close relationships with women.[103] I conclude with Görres that Thérèse certainly does not stop short at the agonised face in Gethsemane but in her final illness, as interpreted by Görres, facing death in the form of trusting the crucified Jesus is her final act of being for others and for God.

Thérèse exemplifies what Wyschogrod discusses in terms of carnal generality and saintly singularity, her practices of facing being the most illuminating way into her spirituality and theology. Her imperative power within an ethic shaped by testimonies to saints is inseparable from her vocative orientation to God in worship and her earthing of worship in the details of ordinary living. If she offers, as has been suggested, a spirituality for the third millennium, its secret perhaps lies in the simplicity of this compassionate face turned smiling to other faces, and able to inspire in them sensitive, daily improvisations on the theme of substitutionary joy united with substitutionary responsibility.

103. Fitzgerald writes, for example, about the 'female bonding' between Thérèse and her sister Pauline which is 'made indestructible by its openness to a transcendent Face'. ('The Mission of Thérèse of Lisieux', p. 87.)

10

Polyphonic living: Dietrich Bonhoeffer

The exploration of 'saintly singularity' could be endless, with each saint adding something fresh and throwing light on the others. The full definition of self and salvation would have to embrace every true testimony to every saint. I will add just one more in detail, someone whose life and theology resonate especially clearly with the themes of this book and who also leads those themes into new developments.

10.1 Thérèse alongside Bonhoeffer

Dietrich Bonhoeffer was born in Breslau, Germany in 1906, nine years after Thérèse of Lisieux's death. To set the two alongside each other is to be struck by many contrasts.

Both came from large, close and happy families, but Thérèse's French Catholic bourgeois environment was intensely religious and deeply hostile to 'the world' of nineteenth-century Europe, whereas Bonhoeffer's sophisticated upper-class family was immersed in secular activities and public responsibilities, and its Protestant ethos did not involve deep attachment to the church. Berlin was in many respects the cultural and intellectual capital of Europe, and Bonhoeffer's family was at the heart of this. The contrast is clearest in their respective educations. Thérèse had a few years of inadequate schooling and was never encouraged to read and think in relation to a range of subjects: the focus of her upbringing was on piety and its practices, with much of her learning happening through her older sisters. Bonhoeffer was broadly educated, investigated many subjects and disciplines, developed skills such as piano-playing to a high level, and went to two of the leading German universities. Thérèse's childhood was enclosed and protected, cut off from physical contact with 'the world' beyond the family, their employees and their visitors; her travels were confined to one well-supervised pilgrimage to Rome; and after she entered the convent at fifteen the seclusion intensified and she never left it. Bonhoeffer's home in Berlin was a centre of discussion and of meeting with participants in many areas of contemporary cultural, political, scientific and academic life. Later he travelled widely in Italy, Spain, North Africa, Eastern and Northern Europe, England and the USA.

Thérèse's vocation to be a Carmelite was completely in line with what her family wanted and encouraged; Bonhoeffer's to be a theologian and pastor was not opposed by his family but surprised them. Thérèse's upbringing was filled with ideals of Roman Catholic sanctity, mainly represented by celibate, ascetical men and women. Bonhoeffer's upbringing was disciplined but he always relished eating, drinking, smoking, and entertainments and literature that would have been seen as irredeemably worldly in Thérèse's milieu. He felt no tension between serving God and getting married, and was suspicious of the whole matter of wanting to be a saint. Their ideals of Christian living were expressed in very divergent terms, culminating in Thérèse's 'little way of spiritual childhood' and Bonhoeffer's adult Christian in a 'world come of age'. Thérèse was almost obsessively self-aware, and her self was the subject of her own constant, vigilant observation. Bonhoeffer shunned such self-examination, and even in solitude in his prison cell[1] was largely oriented towards friends, family and fellow prisoners, to prayer and study, and to issues of theology, church, culture and the future beyond the Second World War. Her arena of sanctification was family and convent; his was university, church politics, seminary living, and above all participation in the conspiracy to kill Hitler. Thérèse was glad to approach death, she longed for martyrdom and found what she recognised as a form of it; Bonhoeffer had no desire for it and was planning his marriage from his prison cell, but he found literal (though controversial) martyrdom. Thérèse eventually saw herself opening up a 'little way' for ordinary Christians; Bonhoeffer had no sense of having such an exemplary vocation.

Yet for all the contrasts the similarities might go deeper. Jesus Christ is obviously central to both. The Bible, prayer, worship and the abundance and generosity of the grace of God grip each of them. Thérèse as novice

---

1. See below p. 261 on his poem 'Who Am I?' for his own form of self-examination.

mistress experienced, in the complex, conflictual politics of her convent, the dilemmas and ambiguities of institutional responsibilities, as Bonhoeffer did in the ecclesiastical and political life of Nazi Germany and the ecumenical movement. Each was fascinated by the understanding and practice of Christian obedience and by the relation of God's grace to human action. They took the Sermon on the Mount with challenging directness: it was to be obeyed. Each had a strong sense of reserve and secrecy, which still leaves, despite the large amount of their own and others' testimony to them, a good deal of mystery surrounding them, and sustains very different interpretations. They also had a commitment to radical responsibility to and for others in response to the life, teaching, death and resurrection of Jesus Christ, realised through identification with him in his suffering, weakness and death. Each also writes with remarkable directness and authority, and their own works are supplemented by exceptionally able biographers and commentators.[2]

10.2 Thérèse and Bonhoeffer – crosslights

Thérèse and Bonhoeffer were each committed to their own tradition within Christianity. For Thérèse this was Roman Catholicism, and in particular the Carmelite tradition as renewed by St John of the Cross and St Teresa of Avila and then translated to France. For Bonhoeffer it was Protestantism, and in particular Martin Luther's theology and, three centuries later, the nineteenth- and early twentieth-century attempts (especially in Germany) to work out in theology and practice the shape of Christianity in the context of Western modernity. Those traditions were either hostile or deeply unsympathetic to each other, yet the developments of them embodied by Thérèse and Bonhoeffer open up French Roman Catholicism and German Lutheranism to each other in a new way.

2. On Bonhoeffer the unsurpassed biography is by Eberhard Bethge, *Dietrich Bonhoeffer: Theologian, Christian, Contemporary* (Collins, Fountain Books, London and New York 1977; first published in German, Chr. Kaiser Verlag, Munich 1967). Among the most helpful discussions of him are: John De Gruchy (ed.), *Bonhoeffer for a New Day: Theology in a Time of Transition* (Eerdmans, Grand Rapids 1997); André Dumas, *Dietrich Bonhoeffer: Theologian of Reality* (SCM Press, New York 1971); Ernst Feil, *The Theology of Dietrich Bonhoeffer* (Fortress Press, Philadelphia 1985); Ronald Gregor Smith (ed.), *World Come of Age* (Collins, London 1967); Charles Marsh, *Reclaiming Dietrich Bonhoeffer* (Oxford University Press, New York and Oxford 1994); Wayne Whitson Floyd Jr and Charles Marsh (eds.), *Theology and the Practice of Responsibility: Essays on Dietrich Bonhoeffer* (Trinity Press International, Valley Forge, PA 1994); R. Wüstenberg, *Glauben als Leben: Dietrich Bonhoeffer und die nichtreligiöse Interpretation biblischer Begriffe* (Peter Lang, Frankfurt 1996); and the good sections on Bonhoeffer in S. E. Fowl and L. Gregory Jones, *Reading in Communion: Scripture and Ethics in Christian Life* (SPCK, London 1991) and in Jones, *Embodying Forgiveness*.

The effect of this is to challenge each to recognise in someone deeply loyal to the other tradition a member of the 'communion of saints', and at the same time to respond to the transformative imperatives with which Thérèse and Bonhoeffer, when taken together, confront those and other traditions.

Thérèse was almost obsessively faithful to her Carmelite rule of life, but, in uniting it with her devotion to the face of Christ interpreted through the New Testament, she articulated and, even more, embodied a penetrating critique of many of the images, practices and presuppositions of holiness in that tradition. It has already emerged how her 'little way' did not conceive itself in terms of heroic sanctity or extraordinary practices and experiences. Its presupposition was the superabundance of God's grace given with a generosity that always overwhelmed her ability adequately to appreciate it or receive it. 'All is grace'[3] was a truth that radically relativised human works and made sure that they had no salvific significance – they are petals scattered for Jesus to gather and use if he wishes. It is easy to see, as both Görres and von Balthasar do, that this has clear resemblances to Luther's understanding of justification by grace alone through faith. She was as alert as he was to the temptation to self-sanctification and fought it all her life in herself and her novices.[4] Both of them have a radical understanding of good human action rooted in gratitude to God, even for the capacity to be grateful. It is also striking how Thérèse's devotion to the Holy Face resonates with Luther's recurrent theme of living *coram Deo*, before God. She takes for granted the wisdom of her Carmelite tradition, and uses the New Testament to open it up afresh to a root that goes back farther than its own historical context in the Counter-Reformation.

Von Balthasar's recognition of the Protestant affinities of Thérèse's little way leads him to say:

> Luther, brought face to face with Scripture, came to conclusions which might be considered remotely parallel to those of Thérèse: the personal certainty of salvation, the stress upon trusting *fiducia* as opposed to ascetic practices and other good works, the clear-cut preference for New Testament mercy as against Old Testament justice. And in this sense, all due reserves having been made, the 'little way' can be regarded as the Catholic answer to the demands and questions raised by Luther.[5]

3. Cf. above, p. 233.   4. Cf. Görres, *The Hidden Face*, p. 103.
5. Von Balthasar, *Thérèse of Lisieux*, p. 50.

His 'due reserves' are, however, unconvincing. They are twofold. The first is that she remains firmly rooted in her church's tradition, 'thoroughly at ease within the framework of the Church'.[6] This begs many questions – about Luther's rooting in church tradition, about her own Carmelite tradition having been partly concerned to renew the Catholic Church that Luther reformed in another way, and about whether she was 'thoroughly at ease' in that part of the church which she tried to reform, the Lisieux Carmel. His second reserve comes later when he quotes Thérèse on the lack of proportion between God's eternal rewards and our little sacrifices, and he comments:

> This lack of proportion cannot be identified with the empty dialectic
> between sin and grace characteristic of Protestantism; it is the
> Catholic truth that the relation between grace received and grace to be
> received is infinitely increasing.[7]

What he describes as a 'Catholic truth' does not seem alien to Luther; but, more important, the blanket accusation of a Protestant 'empty dialectic' is hard to sustain.

It is especially hard to justify as regards Bonhoeffer. He, like Thérèse, was fascinated by the relation of grace, freedom, sin and obedience. Whereas she took over her Carmelite tradition and never contradicted it, he did the same with Luther. But Lutheranism is questioned as profoundly by Bonhoeffer as is Carmelite holiness by Thérèse. There are three main thrusts in his interrogation.

The first is to do with the disciplines of the church as a community.[8] Bonhoeffer laid the foundations for his thought on the church in his two doctorates, *Sanctorum Communio* and *Act and Being*, but the culmination of his questioning of his own tradition came in the years he spent leading the Confessing Church seminary at Finkenwalde. There he encouraged the confession of sins, silent meditation and a form of communal living and discipline which exposed its members to accusations of betraying the Reformation.[9] More will be said about this community in the next section.

The second thrust was closely related to this: his probing of the relationship between faith and obedience in *The Cost of Discipleship*, resulting

6. Ibid.   7. Ibid., p. 186.
8. Bonhoeffer noted in his diary in 1924 that he thought he was 'beginning to understand the concept of the church' during his first encounter with the Roman Catholic Church on his visit to Italy (see Bethge, *Dietrich Bonhoeffer*, p. 39).
9. See Bethge, *Dietrich Bonhoeffer*, pp. 379ff. and Bonhoeffer's own book based on the Finkenwalde time, *Life Together* (SCM Press, London 1954).

in the formula, 'Only he who believes is obedient, and only he who is obedient believes.'[10] He united under the heading of discipleship what Reformed theologians treated under 'Faith', 'Justification' and 'Sanctification',[11] and his basic contrast was between 'cheap grace' and 'costly grace'.[12] His concept of 'the first step' of obedience in faith[13] functions in relation to the Lutheran doctrine of justification as Thérèse's scattering of petals does in relation to some traditional Roman Catholic ideas of sanctification. Each manages to open their own tradition to the riches represented by the other through a reinterpretation which appeals to scripture.

The third thrust concerns the relation of Christian faith to 'the natural', all the ordinary elements of human existence (material, social, cultural, economic, moral and so on) which are not about ultimate matters but which make up a great deal of daily life. Bonhoeffer was especially concerned that a tendency had developed in Lutheranism to emphasise the 'ultimate' of justification to such an extent that the 'penultimate' of ordinary goodness was played down. It was easy to regard all those not 'justified by faith' as equally in need of salvation, and therefore not to discriminate among them. The Nazi assault on ordinary

---

10. Bonhoeffer, *The Cost of Discipleship*, a translation of the German 'Nur der Glaubende ist gehorsam, und nur der Gehorsame glaubt' – *Nachfolge* (the German original of *The Cost of Discipleship*), edited by Martin Kuske and Ilse Tödt (Chr. Kaiser Verlag, Gütersloh 1994), S.52.
11. On this and on Bonhoeffer's basic concern to reaffirm Luther in a new context see Bethge, *Dietrich Bonhoeffer*, pp. 372f.
12. Cf. *The Cost of Discipleship*, p. 36:

Cheap grace is the preaching of forgiveness without requiring repentance, baptism without church discipline, Communion without confession, absolution without personal confession. Cheap grace is grace without discipleship, grace without the cross, grace without Jesus Christ, living and incarnate.

Costly grace is the treasure hidden in the field; for the sake of it a man will gladly go and sell all that he has. It is the pearl of great price to buy which the merchant will sell all his goods. It is the kingly rule of Christ, for whose sake a man will pluck out the eye which causes him to stumble, it is the call of Jesus Christ at which the disciple leaves his nets and follows him.

13. Cf. ibid. p. 55.

Only the obedient believe. If we are to believe, we must obey a concrete command. Without this preliminary step of obedience, our faith will only be pious humbug, and lead us to the grace which is not costly. Everything depends on the first step. It has a unique quality of its own. The first step of obedience makes Peter leave his nets, and later get out of the ship; it calls upon the young man to leave his riches. Only this new existence, created through obedience, can make faith possible.

... Although Peter cannot achieve his own conversion, he can leave his nets.

Bonhoeffer goes on to find recognition of his point in both Roman Catholic and Lutheran traditions, but in the former it is, in the sense he intends, restricted to monastic commitment, while the latter tends 'to soft-pedal it as though they were almost ashamed of it' (ibid.). There is a convergence here as Thérèse the nun offers a 'little way' to lay people and Bonhoeffer the Lutheran in 'the world' calls them into the obedience of costly grace.

goodness made such discrimination urgent, above all in the practical matter of joining with others, whether Christian or not, in defence of justice, freedom and human life. Similarly, Lutheranism had tended to distinguish church from state in a way which made it very difficult to justify the sort of opposition to the state that he considered appropriate in Nazi Germany. Bonhoeffer did not participate in the conspiracy against Hitler on the basis of some general theological or ethical argument; he recognised that it was an exceptional situation in which one had to take a free, responsible decision which also risked the guilt of doing wrong. In the ten years of resisting the Nazis until his arrest he saw the inadequacy of all the usual ethical responses, appealing to reason or principles or conscience or freedom or virtue, and concluded in January 1943:

> Only now are the Germans beginning to discover the meaning of free responsibility. It depends on a God who demands responsible action in a bold venture of faith, and who promises forgiveness and consolation to the man who becomes a sinner in that venture.[14]

This ethic of free responsibility before God above all required the right interrelation of the ultimate and penultimate, and in some of the writings that were put together to form his *Ethics* he began to think this through. The key to it is living before Jesus Christ in whom the world and God come together, avoiding the wrong radicalism (ultimacy without appreciation of the penultimate) and the wrong compromises (penultimate without the priority of the ultimate). The crucial summary statement is:

> In Jesus Christ we have faith in the incarnate, crucified and risen God. In the incarnation we learn of the love of God for his creation; in the crucifixion we learn of the judgement of God upon all flesh; and in the resurrection we learn of God's will for a new world. There could be no greater error than to tear these three elements apart; for each of them comprises the whole...
>
> As for the question of the things before the last, it follows from what has been said so far that the Christian life means neither a destruction nor a sanctioning of the penultimate. In Christ the reality of God meets the reality of the world and allows us to share in that encounter. It is an encounter beyond all radicalism and beyond all compromise. Christian life is participation in the encounter of Christ with the world.[15]

14. 'After Ten Years' in *Letters and Papers from Prison* (SCM Press, London 1971), p. 6.
15. Dietrich Bonhoeffer, *Ethics* (Collins, London 1964), pp. 130–3.

That position reconceptualises the Lutheran understanding of justification by reference to the living Jesus Christ who is identified through his life, death and resurrection, and who is set at the centre of God's involvement with the world. It is a reminting of the Lutheran *simul*, in which apparent contradictions are held together through Jesus Christ. Bonhoeffer's distinctive emphasis is on the inseparability of the full history of Jesus Christ, the love of God for the whole world, and the life of free responsibility. Intrinsic to this is the basic reality of joy.

Joy in the crucified and risen Christ is of course affirmed; but joy is most striking in what Bonhoeffer says about the right to natural life. In a way that accords with Levinas on *jouissement*,[16] Bonhoeffer writes:

> It is in the joys of the body that it becomes apparent that the body is an end in itself within the natural life. If the body were only a means to an end man would have no right to bodily joys. It would then not be permissible to exceed an expedient minimum of bodily enjoyment. This would have very far-reaching consequences for the Christian appraisal of all the problems that have to do with the life of the body, housing, food, clothing, recreation, play and sex. But if the body is rightly to be regarded as an end in itself, then there is a right to bodily joys, even though these are not necessarily subordinated to some higher purpose. It is inherent in the nature of joy itself that it is spoilt by any thought of purpose.[17]

This *simul* of joy and responsibility, tied into the life, death and resurrection of Jesus Christ, is at the heart of Bonhoeffer's conception of mature humanity. Through it he offers a constructive way through what he saw as Lutheranism's inadequacies when faced with Nazism. It generates fresh thinking and action about the relationship of justification to what is penultimate, such as the 'natural', politics and the state. Above all, in its dynamic simultaneity of ultimate and penultimate, embodied in the crucified and living Jesus Christ, it reveals the theology pervading the final period of Bonhoeffer's life. His *Letters and Papers from Prison* will in the next section be read as improvisations on these insights of his *Ethics*.

So both Thérèse and Bonhoeffer penetratingly interrogated their own traditions as they found them, and the direction of each exploration led to intersections with the other's tradition. But, as with Thérèse, it is necessary to penetrate further into Bonhoeffer's particularity before returning finally to a further intersection.

16. See chapter 2 above.   17. *Ethics*, pp. 156f.

10.3 Worship and worldliness

In order to explore further the contribution of Bonhoeffer to a conception of holy selfhood I will focus on two of his works on either side of the *Ethics*, *Life Together* (supplemented by *Prayerbook of the Bible. An Introduction to the Psalms*) and *Letters and Papers from Prison*.

10.3.1 *Life Together* – immersed in the Psalms

Life Together sprang directly out of Bonhoeffer's time living in and leading the Confessing Church's seminary at Zingst and later Finkenwalde, but also out of the rest of his broad experience and study of communities of many sorts. He was fascinated by forms of sociality – families, Lutheran parishes, the worldwide Roman Catholic Church, a Benedictine monastery, the ecumenical movement, black churches in Harlem, university seminars, weekend excursions for recreation and theology with his Berlin students, Anglican religious orders, the Quakers in Birmingham, English Presbyterian, Congregational and Methodist seminaries, Gandhian ashrams, working-class Berlin, nation states, cultural traditions, and the data and theories drawn from sociological studies. *Life Together* is the condensation of a great deal of experience and travel, and it also distils the lessons for sociality and selfhood which are discussed more academically in *Sanctorum Communio* (theology and sociology), *Act and Being* (theology and philosophy), his Berlin lectures on christology, and more exegetically in *Cost of Discipleship*. Müller and Schönherr argue for its being 'chronologically and materially in the middle' of his theology,[18] in continuity both with those earlier works and with his later writings on ethics and in prison. If that is so, then it is a crucial work for understanding him.

This conclusion is reinforced by the deliberateness with which he sat down for a concentrated period in 1938 in order to write it. He had been reluctant to publicise what went on in Finkenwalde before its dissolution by the Gestapo: the seminary had something of the status of a 'secret dis-

---

18. Gerhard Ludwig Müller and Albrecht Schönherr, 'Editors' Afterword to the German Edition' in *Dietrich Bonhoeffer Works, Volume 5. Life Together and Prayerbook of the Bible*, edited by Gerhard Ludwig Müller and Albrecht Schönherr, English edition edited by Geffrey B. Kelly (Fortress Press, Minneapolis 1996), p. 133. While I agree with their conclusion as regards the continuity, I find their account of it does not do justice either to the theme of worship or to the polyphonic, Renaissance-like richness of his 'worldliness' and celebration of *hilaritas* (see below).

cipline' of the Confessing Church, was always controversial, and could have been harmed by publicity. Bonhoeffer had given himself to the seminary, and shared his friendship, theology, prayer, money, books, even his confession of sins. It had been the culmination up to that time of his understanding and practice of Christian faith, and his account of it was written as a testimony. As such it is unique among his writings in being a deliberate statement for publication of what usually remained secret, 'among friends' or oral. It is no accident that *Life Together* has sold more copies than any other of his works: it is a confluence of the complexities of his academic work, the wisdom of several Christian traditions, a clear vision of contemporary Christian living, the experience of Finkenwalde and of Nazi Germany, and the ordinary daily life of any Christian – all expressed simply and practically. It is a public statement that resonates not only with what goes on in intimacy and secrecy (while always maintaining discretion and reserve), but also with the 'insane tension'[19] of the political setting of its production, as anti-Semitic measures grew harsher, pressure on the Confessing Church increased, and Hitler annexed the Sudetenland and then concluded the Munich agreement with Chamberlain.

The Christians whose life is described and prescribed in this book are above all worshippers, and I see *Life Together* as Bonhoeffer's wisdom in brief on the worshipping self. In earlier works he had engaged with the main Western philosophical and theological conceptions of selfhood, past and present, and Jesus Christ in his being for others and for God had become central to his understanding of humanity. The practical implication of this was a life of discipleship in community, taking the Sermon on the Mount as guidance. All of this comes together in the picture of an ordinary day whose dynamic principle is found in worshipping God. There are four basic features of this day.

The first is the pervasiveness of the Psalms. The book opens with a psalm and psalms run right through it. Bonhoeffer had become convinced that the Psalms are at the heart of Christian worship and life, and that they should be used daily. His thinking about them was expanded in the last of his writings to be published in his lifetime, *Prayerbook of the Bible. An Introduction to the Psalms* (1940).[20] There he wrote:

19. Eberhard Bethge, quoted by Geffrey B. Kelly in 'Editor's Introduction to the English Edition', *Dietrich Bonhoeffer Works, Volume 5*, p. 5. This introduction gives an account of the setting of *Life Together* in Bonhoeffer's life and works, and notes echoes of the public events in the text.   20. See *Dietrich Bonhoeffer Works, Volume 5*.

In many churches psalms are read or sung every Sunday, or even daily, according to a regular pattern. These churches have preserved for themselves a priceless treasure, for only with daily use does one become immersed in that divine prayerbook. With only occasional reading these prayers are too overwhelming for us in thought and power, so that we again and again turn to lighter fare. But whoever has begun to pray the Psalter earnestly and regularly will 'soon take leave' of those other light and personal 'little devotional prayers and say: Ah, there is not the juice, the strength, the passion, the fire which I find in the Psalter. Anything else tastes too cold and too hard' (Luther).[21]

The self that is formed through this discipline is one in community with others who have prayed and continue to pray the Psalms, and so learns the language of this large community. There is no question of being able, out of one's own experience, to identify with everything that is prayed. Essential to the learning is that we pray as a community, and from the literary form of the Psalms Bonhoeffer draws theological lessons for the otherness intrinsic to selfhood. The parallelism of the verses combines the need for the other person praying alongside and penetration to the depth of the heart through repetition.[22] Who is the person alongside? For Bonhoeffer the main theological truth of the community which prays the Psalms is that Jesus Christ is a member of it. 'He prayed the Psalter and now it has become his prayer for all time ... The Psalter is the vicarious prayer of Christ for his congregation.'[23]

This leads into the second feature of the ordinary Christian day: the reality of Jesus Christ. Just as the presence of Jesus Christ praying the Psalms mediates all Christian prayer, so Jesus Christ mediates all

21. Ibid., p. 161.
22. *Life Together*, ibid. pp. 57–8: 'Many of the Psalms were very probably prayed antiphonally by the Old Testament congregation. The so-called parallelism of the verses (*parallelismus membrorum*), that remarkable repetition of the same idea in different words in the second line of the verse, it not merely a literary form. It also has a meaning for the church and theology ... Repeatedly there are two voices, bringing the same prayer request to God in different words. Is that not meant to be an indication that the one who prays never prays alone? There must always be a second person, another, a member of the Church, the body of Christ, indeed Jesus Christ himself, praying with the Christian in order that the prayer of the individual may be true prayer. In the repetition of the same subject, which is heightened in Psalm 119 to such a degree that it seems it does not want to end and becomes so simple that it is virtually impervious to our exegetical analysis, is there not the suggestion that every word of prayer must penetrate to a depth of the heart which can be reached only by unceasing repetition? And in the end not even in that way! Is that not an indication that prayer is not a matter of a unique pouring out of the human heart in need or joy, but an unbroken, indeed continuous process of learning, appropriating and impressing God's will in Jesus Christ on the mind.'   23. Ibid., p. 55.

relationships with other people. This is the most challenging idea in Bonhoeffer's notion of Christian community: 'Because Christ stands between me and an other, I must not long for unmediated community with that person.'[24] As Bonhoeffer develops this thought in the opening chapter of *Life Together* on 'Community', he uses it to distinguish *agape* from other forms of community (not least in the church) which are shaped by emotion, self-seeking, intimate I–thou fusion, power over others, the satisfactions of piety, elitism, exclusion of the weak and insignificant, or other distortions: '"Christ between me and an other" means that others should encounter me only as the persons they already are for Christ . . . Spiritual love recognises the true image of the other person as seen from the perspective of Jesus Christ. It is the image Jesus Christ has formed and wants to form in all people.'[25] This is also true of one's relationship to oneself: there is no immediate recognition of who one is, only self-recognition before Jesus Christ. So, faced with the one who is for us and for God, daily worship sustains the self in a community of free others before Jesus Christ. Worship runs through 'the day together' in joint singing, prayer, listening to scripture, meals, work and forgiveness;[26] and through 'the day alone' in silence, meditation, prayer and intercession.[27] The double maxim is: 'Whoever cannot be alone [*allein*] should beware of community' and 'Whoever cannot stand being in community should beware of being alone.'[28] The practice of worshipping God through Jesus Christ shapes the togetherness and the aloneness, and continually opens any image of self or community up to the living Jesus Christ.

This is the context for the third feature, the radical responsibility before and for others that also pervades the day. It culminates in the fourfold service[29] of listening to others, helping others, bearing their burdens (including the consequences of their sin), and communication of 'the free word from person to person, not the word bound to a particular pastoral office, time or place',[30] together with the responsibility to confess one's sins in the presence of another member of the community which for Bonhoeffer is a special case of experiencing 'the presence of God in the reality of the other'.[31]

Yet it is striking that the fourth feature is even more insistent and pervasive: joy. The book opens with the joy of being physically face to face

24. Ibid., p. 43.   25. Ibid., p. 44.   26. Ibid., pp. 48–80.   27. Ibid., pp. 81–92.
28. Ibid., p. 82.   29. Ibid., pp. 98ff.   30. Ibid., p. 103.   31. Ibid., p. 113.

with others in community. The note of joy continually reappears: joy in small ordinary things during the day; joy in Jesus Christ; in the gift of light at the beginning of a new day; in singing together; in interceding for each other; in physical life, eating and drinking; in work; in other members of the community in their weakness and their strength; in helping others, bearing each other's burdens, and forgiving and being forgiven; in baptism; and in confession of sin to each other. The finale is the celebration of the Lord's Supper: 'Here joy in Christ and Christ's community is complete.'[32]

Life Together therefore offers another variation on the theme of joyful, worship-centred responsibility in the presence of Jesus Christ, giving special attention to the shaping of daily life with others. There were abundant possibilities for further development here, especially as regards the scope and implications of that presence in the world. We have already looked at some of those possibilities unfolding in his *Ethics*, but the most adventurous explorations took place in his prison writings.

10.3.2 Polyphonic life

In prison Bonhoeffer was in one way isolated and cast back on himself; but he was also thrown together with people he would otherwise not have met, and so it was a new stage in his involvement in the secular world. Not only that, it was an intensification of what he had described just before his arrest as 'The view from below'. He said that the years resisting Nazi rule had been

> an experience of incomparable value. We have for once learnt to see the great events of world history from below, from the perspective of the outcast, the suspects, the maltreated, the powerless, the oppressed, the reviled – in short, from the perspective of those who suffer . . . We have learnt that personal suffering is a more effective key, a more rewarding principle for exploring the world in thought and action than personal good fortune.[33]

I suggest that that 'view from below' be taken very seriously in looking at his *Letters and Papers from Prison*. If the suffering which enabled this

---

32. Ibid., p. 118.
33. *Letters and Papers from Prison*, p. 17. This was written by Bonhoeffer probably at the end of 1942 but not as part of 'After Ten Years', where it is included in the enlarged English edition of *Letters and Papers from Prison* at the suggestion of Bethge (see footnote 2, ibid., p. 17).

viewpoint really did act as an 'effective key' or 'principle for exploring the world in thought and action' then attention needs to be paid to his prison writings with this in mind. I see this principle contributing to his engagement with Christian faith in its relationship with Western civilisation since the Middle Ages. In prison he is liberated to range widely in reading and thought, and, looking steadily 'from below', he recapitulates and reconceives some of the main themes of Renaissance, Reformation, Enlightenment and more recent modernity. From the centre of the culminating disaster of Western modernity, the Nazi takeover of a sophisticated, 'Christian' nation and their use of power to create terror, wage war and commit genocide, Bonhoeffer the sophisticated, intellectual Christian rethinks faith and looks in hope to the future after the war. His authority in doing this comes in part from his years of living as one of 'the outcast, the suspects, the maltreated, the powerless, the oppressed, the reviled' – although compared to many during those years he had got off lightly until his imprisonment.[34] The convergence of faith, education, theological gifts, risk-taking responsibility, historical situation, and the time in prison, when he could both write letters and smuggle them out, together amount to an exceptional prophetic possibility whose meaning needs further exploration.

I start with one of his most striking images, that of polyphony. On 20 May 1944 he wrote to Eberhard Bethge:

> There's always a danger in all strong, erotic love that one may love what I may call the polyphony of life. What I mean is that God wants us to love him eternally with our whole hearts – not in such a way as to injure or weaken our earthly love, but to provide a kind of *cantus firmus* to which the other melodies of life provide the counterpoint. One of these contrapuntal themes (which have their own complete independence but are yet related to the *cantus firmus*) is earthly affection. Even in the Bible we have the Song of Songs; and really one can imagine no more ardent, passionate, sensual love than is portrayed there (see 7.6). It's a good thing that the book is in the Bible, in face of all those who believe that the restraint of passion is Christian (where is there such restraint in the Old Testament?). Where the *cantus firmus* is clear and plain, the counterpoint can be developed to its limits. The two are 'undivided yet distinct', in the words of the Chalcedonian Definition, like Christ in his divine and human natures.

---

34. Even his conditions in prison were comparatively humane by Nazi standards.

> May not the attraction and importance of polyphony in music consist
> in its being a musical reflection of this Christological fact and
> therefore of our *vita christiana*?[35]

This image fits well with Bonhoeffer's own life in prison. He had just become engaged to Maria von Wedemeyer before his arrest, and their correspondence shows how wholeheartedly that counterpoint was developed.[36] But there was a range of other voices too. Besides Maria, he was deeply involved in friendships and family life from prison, and in prison had a wide circle of relationships with staff and inmates. In addition to letters he wrote fiction, drama and poetry. He read history, poetry, science, novels, patristics, theology, philosophy and much else. Music was constantly on his mind. Through it all he was doing new theology and reinterpreting key historical periods – the Old Testament, the early church, the 'Christian worldliness' of the Middle Ages, the non-classicist side of the Renaissance, the Enlightenment, the nineteenth century and its aftermath. There was also a strong future orientation, looking forward to his marriage, to the reshaping of church and society after Nazism, and to the fresh theology that that would require.

There are resonances here of the Christian humanism of the late Middle Ages and its Renaissance successors. But the *cantus firmus* is rooted more in the Reformation, and especially in Luther. I have already discussed some of the ways in which he criticised Lutheranism while being passionately loyal to Luther. One key element in Luther that Bonhoeffer in prison takes further than before is the interweaving of a theology of the cross with involvement in full life in the world. He recapitulates in very different circumstances[37] Luther's immersion of doctrine in ordinary life. It is life seen from below, and so not only is 'life' a recurrent theme, but so also are death, dying, suffering and the cross. The *cantus firmus* is, in line with the development of the Lutheran *simul* that I have described occurring in the *Ethics*, 'the man for others', the incarnate, crucified and risen Jesus Christ. Once this is 'clear and plain' the counterpoint 'can be developed to its limits'.

This leads him to engage positively with the Enlightenment and its

---

35. *Letters and Papers from Prison*, p. 303.
36. Dietrich Bonhoeffer and Maria von Wedemeyer, *Love Letters from Cell 92* (HarperCollins, London 1994).
37. Cf. his approval of Kierkegaard's remark that 'today Luther would say the opposite of what he said then' (*Letters and Papers from Prison*, p. 123).

aftermath. Its emphases on maturity and human autonomy invite rede-scription in terms of contrapuntal themes which 'have their own complete independence'. In his thought about secularity, religionlessness, metaphysics, the adulthood of the world, the superfluity of God as 'working hypothesis' or as *deus ex machina*, and the unacceptability of using human sins, weaknesses and existential limitations to show the necessity of Christian faith, Bonhoeffer affirms a God who allows full human freedom and responsibility – and therefore maturity. This God is in deep continuity with Luther's God hidden on the cross:

> The God who is with us is the God who forsakes us (Mark 15.34). The God who lets us live in the world without the working hypothesis of God is the God before whom we stand continually. Before God and with God we live without God. God lets himself be pushed out of the world on to the cross. He is weak and powerless in the world, and that is precisely the way, the only way, in which he is with us and helps us.[38]

That radicalises the 'view from below' into God's viewpoint. It is affirmed by the resurrection of the 'weak and powerless' Jesus Christ which does not at all diminish human maturity: rather, the risen Christ intensifies it by giving vocations of free, suffering responsibility for the world. Here the very definition of God has been worked out through the crucifixion, and the 'before God' remains.

With what content? If a third person indicative answer is wanted, it is clear: the content is indicated by the crucified, dead Jesus. Bonhoeffer is not interested in working this out in a doctrine of God.[39] These paradoxes do not have in view any indicative definiteness. Their proximate origin is in a sustained interrogative:

> What is bothering me incessantly is the question what Christianity really is, or indeed who Christ really is, for us today. The time when people could be told everything by means of words, whether theological or pious, is over, and so is the time of inwardness or conscience – that means the time of religion in general.[40]

Not to be told everything by means of words clearly does not, for Bonhoeffer, require that he be silent. It rather leads him to articulate theology in moods which (whatever their literal grammar) are interrogative,

38. *Letters and Papers from Prison*, p. 360.
39. It is striking, however, that some of the doctrines of God most influential in recent decades have been deeply indebted to his *Letters and Papers from Prison*. Cf. Jürgen Moltmann, *The Crucified God* (SCM, London 1974) and Eberhard Jüngel, *God as the Mystery of the World*. Jüngel's is the broad direction in which I would develop a doctrine of God trying to follow through Bonhoeffer's later thought, while taking account of the reservations expressed above in chapter 3.   40. *Letters and Papers from Prison*, p. 279 (30 April 1944).

imperative, optative and, above all, vocative.[41] Let us look at each of those moods in turn.

Interrogatives pervade the *Letters and Papers from Prison*. They illustrate the image of polyphony. The *cantus firmus* question is: Who really is Christ for us today? It is at its most concentrated when it focusses on the crucified Christ, embodying the 'view from below'. This has, in terms of his own account of polyphony quoted above, become especially 'clear and plain' in prison, and it enables contrapuntal themes to be freely developed to their limits. Those themes involve questions probing the past, present and future, and call for rethinking Western civilisation and the truth and practice of Christianity within it.

Bonhoeffer himself conceives the polyphony of Christian life in terms of imperatives. The *cantus firmus* is that 'God wants us to love him eternally with our whole hearts', and the counterpoints are the imperatives of 'earthly love'. Together these make up the life of free responsibility before God, and Bonhoeffer immediately relates this to his leading question about Jesus Christ by suggesting that polyphony is a reflection of the Chalcedonian Definition's 'fully divine, fully human'.[42]

The optatives might be seen as expressions of the desiring involved in love for God and for humanity. The future orientation of Bonhoeffer's thinking in prison maintains the priority of confidence in God, notably in writing of his own future and in his practice of intercession for others. It also ranges contrapuntally over the future of friends and family, of the church, of Germany and of the modern West.

But it is the vocative mood which embraces and orients all the others. For Bonhoeffer, the question about Jesus Christ was always primarily in the form: Who are you? addressed to Jesus Christ in prayer.[43] That in turn leads to the return questioning of the questioner: Who are you?[44] Prayer and worship are the encompassing atmosphere of the prison writings,

41. One interpretation of his criticism of Barth for offering 'a positivist doctrine of revelation' might be that this 'like it or lump it' approach, laying out everything with undifferentiatedly indicative publicness, fails to give appropriate weight to the other moods. Above all, it fails to safeguard the 'secret discipline' 'whereby the *mysteries* of the Christian faith are protected against profanation' (*Letters and Papers from Prison*, p. 286 (5 May 1944). In my terms, Bonhoeffer sees Barth failing to do justice to the priority of the vocative, the worshipping address to God which is at the heart of the secret discipline. Long after Bonhoeffer's death, Barth in volume IV.3 of his *Church Dogmatics* took prayer of petition as the basic Christian ethical act, and built his final ethical writing around the Lord's Prayer. I discuss the secret discipline further below.
42. *Letters and Papers from Prison*, p. 303.
43. See Dietrich Bonhoeffer, *Christology* (Fontana, Collins, London 1966), Introduction, pp. 27–40.   44. Ibid., p. 36.

carrying on in isolation the sort of discipline that *Life Together* describes. He writes:

> I read the Psalms every day, as I have done for many years; I know them and love them more than any other book.[45]

He constantly refers to hymns, he goes over Bach's B Minor Mass 'bit by bit, in my mind',[46] there is frequent mention of prayer in many forms, and he observes the church year. Much of his poetry is in the vocative, addressed to God or others.

So worship is the fundamental imperative, corresponding to loving God with the whole heart, and inseparable from a life of responsibility in the world. His most succinct summary of this is in his May 1944 'Thoughts on the Day of the Baptism of Dietrich Wilhelm Rüdiger Bethge':

> Our earlier words are therefore bound to lose their force and cease, and our being Christians today will be limited to two things: prayer and righteous action among men.[47] All Christian thinking, speaking, and organizing must be born anew out of this prayer and action.[48]

The whole of this address is oriented to the future of the baby being baptised in the middle of a terrible war, and the note of joy sounds persistently through it:

> Music, as your parents understand and practise it, will help to dissolve your perplexities and purify your character and sensibility, and in times of care and sorrow will keep a ground-bass of joy alive in you.[49]

There joy is seen as part of the *cantus firmus*. The prison writings are shot through with joy and its analogues, sounding in the most diverse contexts. It even appears, modulated into the quality of *hilaritas*, as a criterion for intellectual and artistic greatness:

> Walther v.d. Vogelweide, the Knight of Bamberg, Luther, Lessing, Rubens, Hugo Wolf, Karl Barth – to mention only a few – also have a kind of *hilaritas*, which I might describe as confidence in their own work, boldness and defiance of the world and of popular opinion, a steadfast certainty that in their own work they are showing the world

45. *Letters and Papers from Prison*, p. 40.   46. Ibid., p. 127.
47. The German is 'im Beten und im Tun des Gerechten unter den Menschen', and the latter phrase could also be translated as 'action for justice among people'.
48. *Letters and Papers from Prison*, p. 300.
49. Ibid., p. 295. Walter H. Kemp in his essay 'The "Polyphony of Life": References to Music in Bonhoeffer's *Letters and Papers from Prison*' in *Vita Laudanda Essays in Memory of Ulrich S. Leopold* (Wilfred Laurier University Press, Waterloo 1976), pp. 137–54, argues that 'ground-bass' is a mistranslation of *Grundtun*, which he maintains should be rendered 'keynote' or 'root of chord'.

something *good* (even if the world doesn't like it), and a high-spirited self-confidence. I admit that Michelangelo, Rembrandt and, at a considerable remove, Kierkegaard and Nietzsche, are in a different category from those that I've mentioned. There is something less assertive, evident, and final in their works, less conviction, detachment, humour. All the same, I think some of them are characterized by *hilaritas* in the sense that I've described, as a necessary attribute of greatness.[50]

The day after Bonhoeffer's initial letter to Bethge about polyphony he returns to the topic in another letter, and this time speaks of pain and joy:

The image of polyphony is still pursuing me. When I was rather distressed at not being with you, I couldn't help thinking that pain and joy are also part of life's polyphony, and that they can exist independently side by side.[51]

They are together like this both in the *cantus firmus* and also in the various contrapuntal themes of the prison writings, and have their most intensive development in the context of worship, above all in the Psalms.

10.4 Bonhoeffer and holiness

What does all this mean for holiness? On 21 July 1944, on the eve of the failed attempt to assassinate Hitler, which led to the end of his theological correspondence and eventually to his execution, Bonhoeffer writes to Bethge about Christian sanctity, expressing his growing appreciation of Christianity's

profound this-worldliness, characterized by discipline and the constant knowledge of death and resurrection. I think Luther lived a this-worldly life in this sense.

I remember a conversation I had in America thirteen years ago with a young French pastor. We were asking ourselves quite simply what we wanted to do with our lives. He said he would like to become a saint (and I think it's quite likely that he did become one). At that time I was very impressed, but I disagreed with him, and said, in effect, that I should like to learn to have faith. For a long time I didn't realize the depth of the contrast. I thought I could acquire faith by trying to live a holy life, or something like it . . .

I discovered later, and I'm still discovering right up to this moment, that it is only by living completely in the world that one learns to have faith. One must completely abandon any attempt to

---

50. *Letters and Papers from Prison*, p. 229.   51. Ibid., p. 305.

make something of oneself, whether it be a saint, or a converted sinner, or a churchman (a so-called priestly type), a righteous man or an unrighteous one, a sick man or a healthy one. By this-worldliness I mean living unreservedly in life's duties, problems, successes and failures, experiences and perplexities. In so doing we throw ourselves completely into the arms of God, taking seriously, not our own sufferings, but those of God in the world – watching with Christ in Gethsemane.[52]

Translated into polyphony, that passage's *cantus firmus* is our being thrown 'completely into the arms [*ganz in die Arme*] of God', as expressed in a faith characterised by 'discipline and the constant knowledge of death and resurrection'. But that faith is only learnt 'by living completely in the world [*in der vollen Diesseitigkeit des Lebens*]' with multiple responsibilities. Polyphony is a good image for this version of Luther's *simul*: completely in the arms of God and completely in the world.[53]

There is also a third 'completely': 'One must completely [*völlig*] abandon any attempt to make something of oneself.' This is for Bonhoeffer the critical difference between his worldly holiness of faith and what the French pastor was aiming at. It pivots around the conception of holy selfhood. Bonhoeffer's refuses any image of self other than Jesus Christ – 'constant knowledge of death and resurrection' and 'watching with Christ in Gethsemane'. It is 'completely' oriented towards God and other people: it is a self *coram deo* and *coram aliis*. Most radically, it is a self which sees life 'from below', 'taking seriously, not our own sufferings, but the sufferings of God in the world'. That 'not our own' (as well as the 'oneself' that one does not attempt to make something of) does not deny the 'own' and therefore the selfhood. It simply is freed from concern or anxiety about any formation or transformation of self apart from what happens in the course of worship and responsible living in the world (or 'prayer and righteous action'). This is in line with Bonhoeffer's rejection of religion as 'inwardness', and it presses towards a conception of self that might do justice to the simultaneous double orientation to God and others.

What might that be? It is a selfhood that cannot be aimed at and therefore cannot be imagined in advance. It is the surprising outcome of faithfulness to God in the world. Because of its complete immersion in God

52. Ibid., pp. 369f.
53. The imagery of sound allows much more clearly and without inappropriate paradox for a simultaneity in which one theme can be more 'constant' while yet being in essential reciprocity with others.

and the world it can gain no overview of itself. Its selfhood is therefore something like the overall impression of a polyphonic piece in which there has been continual improvisation in the counterpoints. That impression cannot be had by the improvising musicians. In Bonhoeffer's polyphony it is only had by God.

This interpretation is confirmed by Bonhoeffer's poem 'Who Am I?' The very insistence on the title question shows Bonhoeffer concerned about selfhood. The first three stanzas give pictures of himself reflected in the views of other people:

> Who am I? They often tell me
> I would step from my cell's confinement
> calmly, cheerfully, firmly,
> like a squire from his country house . . .[54]

The following stanza speaks of 'what I know of myself', a much less flattering and more anguished picture. There is clearly no bypassing of self-examination through introspection, but the introspection reveals him 'unreservedly in life's duties, problems, successes and failures, experiences and perplexities'. He asks is he only

> restless and longing and sick, like a bird in a cage,
> struggling for breath, as though hands were compressing my throat,
> yearning for colours, for flowers, for the voices of birds,
> thirsting for words of kindness, for neighbourliness,
> trembling with anger at despotisms and petty humiliation,
> tossing in expectation of great events,
> powerlessly trembling for friends at an infinite distance,
> weary and empty at praying, at thinking, at making,
> faint, and ready to say farewell to it all?

Then he wrestles with the conflicting pictures. There is no resolution, but the radical questioning is sustained by the equivalent of throwing himself into the arms of God:

> Who am I? They mock me, these lonely questions of mine.
> Whoever I am, thou knowest, O God, I am thine.[55]

There has been no overview of self, and the double otherness of God and other people is not resolved in inwardness but is intensified there. This self is best hinted at through the sustained interrogative, the opta-

---

54. *Letters and Papers from Prison*, p. 347.   55. Ibid., p. 348.

tive yearning, the imperative responsibilities, and the final vocative of faith.

There are two further points about the conception of holiness that emerges from the letter of 21 July 1944 when taken in the context of the rest of the prison writings.

One is that it is thoroughly Jewish in its main lines, and is essentially an outworking of the twofold imperative to love God and one's neighbour. Bonhoeffer's concern to 'rejudaize' Christianity, exemplified in his constant reading of the Old Testament in prison, his immersion in the Psalms, and his insistence on the this-worldliness of Christianity, was being fulfilled in a context where he could share something of the 'view from below' which was being had by his Jewish contemporaries.

The other point is that his conception of the self before God and other people is in deep accord with that which has emerged from my study of Thérèse. I will now add some final remarks on the two.

10.5 Secrets, disciplines and abundance

I remarked above[56] that Bonhoeffer and Thérèse share a strong sense of reserve and secrecy. This will be my final approach to understanding each of them.

The most helpful theological idea in understanding Bonhoeffer's discussions of religionless Christianity in the *Letters and Papers from Prison* is given in his *Ethics*, as was introduced above: that in Christ (incarnate, crucified and risen) the reality of God comes together with the reality of the world, and that Christian life is participation in that encounter. Religion, as Bonhoeffer understands it, sets up dualisms and boundaries which are inappropriate to the reality of this world which is affirmed, judged and reconciled by God – dualisms of sacred and secular, God and the world, heaven and earth, inwardness and the public world. In *Ethics* Bonhoeffer used the dynamic concept of the penultimate and ultimate to undermine such dualisms while preserving necessary distinctions. In the letter of 30 April 1944, which initiates the discussion of who Christ really is in a religionless world, Bonhoeffer writes:

> In that case Christ is no longer an object of religion, but sometimes quite different, really the Lord of the world. But what does that mean? What is the place of worship and prayer in a religionless situation? Does the secret discipline, or alternatively the difference (which I have

56. P. 243.

suggested to you before) between penultimate and ultimate, take on a new importance here?[57]

Here 'the secret discipline' is correlated with the penultimate and ultimate. What does that mean?

The *disciplina arcani*, or 'discipline of the secret', was historically the practice in the early church which reserved participation in the later part of the eucharist, when the Nicene creed was confessed and the bread and wine were shared, to those who had been baptised. The catechists, who were under instruction before their baptism, were allowed to take part in the Bible readings, prayer and sermon in the first part of the service, but the communion was seen as a 'secret' or 'mystery' forbidden to the unbaptised. The *disciplina arcani* was therefore to do with the climactic act of worship and locus of identity (baptism linked with eucharist) in the church.

How might this transfer to 'a religionless situation'? Bonhoeffer gives several clues besides the reference to penultimate and ultimate. In relation to Barth's way of laying all doctrines out in a 'positivist' way, he speaks of protecting the '*mysteries* of the Christian faith' (original italics) against profanation by observing degrees of knowledge and significance.[58] If this and the other references already mentioned are placed alongside his later remark about a 'profound this-worldliness, characterized by discipline and the constant knowledge of death and resurrection'[59] we can draw a conclusion. The 'secret' is the hidden reality of the crucified and risen Jesus Christ, and to know this is of ultimate significance. When one participates in it one cannot live in a religious sphere separate from the world; but neither can one live without worship. As Bethge has written, in the *arcanum* Christ takes everyone who really encounters him and turns them around to face other people and the world.[60] Further, this secret cannot simply be known as a fact, a positivist datum. Becoming conformed to it (language Bonhoeffer uses in the *Ethics*) is intrinsic to knowing it truly, and that, as discussed above, will involve prayer and righteous action together. It may also mean periods of silence, recognising the inexpressibility of the mystery or the inadequacy of the accustomed words. But the silence is rooted in faith that 'all Christian thinking, speaking, and organizing must be born anew out of this prayer and action'.[61]

The fundamental confidence of Bonhoeffer here is that this mystery of

---

57. *Letters and Papers from Prison*, p. 281.   58. Ibid., p. 286.   59. Ibid., p. 369.
60. Bethge, *Dietrich Bonhoeffer*, p. 787.   61. *Letters and Papers from Prison*, p. 300.

God and the world come together in Jesus Christ is abundantly generative and life-giving beyond anything that can be imagined. Its hiddenness is as radical for him as for Luther, and is summed up in his statement
discussed above: 'God lets himself be pushed out of the world on to the
cross.'[62] Its abundance is suggested by the image of a polyphony in which
the *cantus firmus* can be enhanced by endlessly adventurous and innovative counterpoint.

To shift the focus to Thérèse of Lisieux is, as I have described in this
and the previous chapter, to cross chasms of difference, but it is also to
recognise kinship. Her devotion to the hidden, despised face of Christ
was, like Bonhoeffer's Lutheran devotion, an 'open secret' which subverted dualisms and boundaries but also required its secret disciplines.
With God she experienced years of aridity and eventually the extreme
testing of a disintegrating body, doubt, and abandonment. Before her
sisters she wore 'the veil of the smile', though her obedience to her super-
iors in the convent, who instructed her to tell her story, has allowed us to
glimpse what was behind it. But the overwhelming reality for her as for
Bonhoeffer was the abundant generosity and love of God: 'all is grace'.

In both there is an intrinsic connection between the abundance and
their reserve. Anything so rich, so full of love, joy, pain and responsibility
cannot simply be laid out for immediate inspection and comprehension.
Above all, God cannot be shared directly or comprehensively. In both
Bonhoeffer and Thérèse we find disciplines which serve the secret of the
crucified and risen Jesus Christ in his relationship to the whole of reality,
which Christians believe to be the mystery of God and of humanity
together. The generative richness of this is glimpsed through their lives,
and I have tried to suggest something of it in this and the previous
chapter. To risk a simple summary of why these two are continuingly
fruitful for so many today: Thérèse's little way is small enough to slip into
any life in which daily loving is important; Bonhoeffer's polyphony is
capacious enough to sustain interrogative, intelligent faith in a Western
civilisation shaped by the Hebraic and the Hellenic together, formed in
the last millennium by Medieval Christianity, Renaissance, Reformation,
Enlightenment, and more recent modernity, and in fundamental need of
a wisdom informed by what is seen 'from below'. An even simpler (and
riskier) verdict would be that, without excluding full harmony with each
other's theme, Thérèse's vocation is love and Bonhoeffer's is wisdom.

62. Ibid., p. 360.

Yet such assessment cannot be the last word. The reserve of each is not a secrecy which 'could tell but will not'; it is a realistic recognition of the uncontainability and incommunicability of what they are engaged with, and, even more, what they are given to embody. That embodiment, the complex testimonies to how it happened in all the messiness of history, the faces of Thérèse and Bonhoeffer on the covers of their books: these hint at the excess of their meaning over all accounts and summaries, and also at the only way which either of them would recognise as giving sufficient access to their secret – living with them in joyful responsibility before Jesus Christ.

11

Feasting

This study's exploration of self and salvation began with 'facing' and will now conclude with another meditation on 'feasting'. Hospitality has already figured in earlier chapters. It has served as an image for the self, and in the central chapters on Ephesians and the eucharist it helped in interpreting the exchanges between God, humanity and the rest of creation in the economy of salvation. I have also tried to integrate hospitality into my theological method, hosting dialogues with thinkers at whose tables I have conversed over many years.

11.1 The joy of the saints

The two most recent chapters have opened up the theme of those selves called saints who are taken as embodiments of what is meant by salvation. 'The joy of the saints' is the simplest summary of the reality of selves being saved. Their joy is in God and in what delights God.

But what about joy-destroying evil? The saints offer no conceptual solution to this, but they wrestle with reality at its darkest points and still testify to the joy of God. They open ways of joy which pass through the heart of darkness and sadness. There is no formula for this – each way is different, requiring all that each has and is. But whereas evils, sins and other dark things tend towards sameness, emptiness and death, the testimonies to Thérèse, Bonhoeffer, Serafim of Sarov and many others indicate that looking in love to God and other people transformed them in liveliness, distinctive character and attractiveness.

What about the saints facing God and each other 'at home', in peace, in the trust and confidence of mutual love? That is what happens in the feast, a time of joyful participation and exchange through food and drink, conversation, music, dance and much else. Salvation seen through the figure of feasting suggests an eschatology of selfhood.

11.2 The aesthetics of feasting

All the senses are engaged in a good feast. We taste, touch, smell, see, hear. Salvation as health is here vividly physical. Anything that heals and enhances savouring the world through our senses may feed into a salvation that culminates in feasting. From prayer for healing, and all the skills of medicine, through the accumulated wisdom of traditions of cookery, wine-making and brewing, to the experiences and habits which refine our sensual discriminations and enjoyments, the requirements for full feasting draw us deeper into appreciation of our embodiment.

The arts are elaborate refinements of embodied perception. They are woven into feasts and festivals in many ways – Homeric bards; Bach cantatas; the murals and architecture of a banqueting hall; a sculpted monument to a victory; music and dancing at a party or wedding; bands at sports events; the concerts that celebrated South Africa's transition to majority rule. The intensity of feasting rejoices in the celebratory potential of the arts and their overflow of expression which configures and refigures reality. The relaxation of feasting gives time and space for sensing differently, liberated from everyday pressures and compulsions – leisure is the basis of culture.

Are there also possibilities of transformed sensing which see with 'the eyes of the heart', hear with 'the inner ear', smell 'the odour of holiness', savour 'the sweetness of the Lord' or feel 'the touch of the Spirit'? Are these 'only' metaphors? Or is there something in the rich traditions about 'the spiritual senses' within and beyond Christianity?

Much in this book's previous chapters is an invitation to see the face of Jesus Christ with the eyes of the heart. Those who know the teachings on the spiritual senses will recognise many points of contact. This seeing has involved ethical and intellectual disciplines, counsels of detachment from idols, meditation on scripture and other texts, learning from Jesus Christ and from saints, and above all the habit of prayer and worship. Insofar as seeing the face of Christ is concerned, all this points to the basic feature of the spiritual senses: they are about the whole self in relation to God, and are far from any technique enabling the curious to inspect spiritual truths without further involvement. The pure in heart see God, and it is a purity of love to the point of being crucified.

The aesthetics of Easter feasting therefore passes through Good Friday's death of Jesus's sensing, thinking and acting. Yet the thrust of the theology of the face of Christ has not been to single out sensing (or the visual arts) as a path of danger and idolatry. The suggested (though in this book only occasionally explicit) aesthetics of the face of the crucified and risen Jesus Christ allows, for example, for the Orthodox Christian tradition of iconography. That is rooted in a rich theological tradition about the spiritual senses, and in its icons the face of Christ is characteristically set at the centre of a cross.

This could be extended to all the other arts too. What does it mean in film, literature, music, dance, theatre and other media to be creative in ways which not only acknowledge (in however implicit ways) that the first audience is Jesus Christ, but also participate in the 'ecology of blessing' which he generates? How is there new perception of matter, life, death, time and people? How can the arts contribute to transformations of daily life, public life and worship?

11.3 The ethics of feasting

Jesus went to meals, weddings and parties and had a feast-centred ethic. The images are vivid: water turned into wine; guests jockeying for places at table and being told to aim for the lower places; the invitation of a lifetime refused because of being too busy with work or family; Jesus challenging conceptions of God's acceptance by eating with the outcast and marginalised; Dives feasting while Lazarus starves at his gate; children eating messily to the delight of the dogs; a woman sinner shocking the company by anointing Jesus and being forgiven by him; the reversal of expectations as the poor, handicapped and outsiders of all sorts are welcomed at the feast of the Kingdom of God while those who thought themselves sure of a place are left out; advice about not inviting to your banquet those who will invite you back; a master sitting a servant down and serving him; the Prodigal Son welcomed back unconditionally with the best robe, a ring, shoes, the fatted calf and a celebration; Jesus's last supper, which was probably also a celebration of Passover; Jesus washing his disciples' feet; and the mysterious meals of the risen Jesus.

Jesus was immersed in the religion, economics and politics of his time, and his teaching and practice about meals and feasting were sharply relevant to his particular situation. The challenge to those who want to learn from him today is to be involved in our situations with comparable perception and sharpness, in ways that testify to the abundant generosity of God, our acceptance of it, and our imitation of it.

As millions starve, ought anyone to be feasting? Ought there not to be a long detour of working to feed everyone, postponing the feasting till that has been achieved? Or should we keep alive the hope of food for all by working for justice and, if we have food, simultaneously celebrating the goodness of God? Can we even sustain work of compassion and justice in the right spirit if we are not also having some celebratory foretaste of the Kingdom of God? Or, looking at the story of the early church in the Acts of the Apostles, in the light of the explosion of joy and gratitude that followed the resurrection and Pentecost is it not the most obvious thing in the world both to share with those in need and also to celebrate with them?

That combination of sharing and celebrating is, perhaps, the most radical of all the implications of the teaching and practice of Jesus. Feeding the hungry is not a matter of the well-fed offering handouts and getting on with their private feasting: the vision is of everyone around the same table, face to face. Even to imagine sitting together like that gently but inexorably exposes injustice, exploitation, sexism, hard-heartedness, and the multiple ways of rejecting the appeal in the face of the other. Once we have started doing it in little ways, the implications for politics, economics and church life never cease ramifying. Remission of actual debt becomes inseparable from the forgiveness of sins, and idolatry of money is seen as an inhibitor of everyone's joy.

Finally, what about the ethics of exclusion? At many points in previous chapters I have tried to follow the gaze of Jesus across divisive boundaries and have interpreted his life, death and resurrection as his taking on of limitless responsibility towards other people. The feast of the Kingdom of God is described (and acted out) by him as generously inclusive beyond anyone's wildest dreams. That is the main point: the free, surprising love of a God who can be utterly trusted to judge truthfully and then decide far more compassionately than any of the rest of us. There is also a sharp note of exclusion, but it is one that follows from the inclusiveness. The excluded are those who cannot bear God's generosity and will not imitate it. The Prodigal Son's older brother is the archetype, complaining against his father welcoming his brother home with a party, and perhaps (the ending is significantly left open) refusing to join in the celebrations. He is matched by those who complain about Jesus eating with tax-collectors and sinners, by those who presume to know where

God draws lines between the invited and uninvited or the acceptable and unacceptable, and by those who harden their hearts against the poor, sick, handicapped, hungry, prisoners, children, and others in need. These poor, sick and needy are at the centre of the feast as the honoured guests, and to reject them is to exclude oneself from their host's presence. The other side of this is that to seek them out is to relate to their host too, as the parable of the sheep and the goats says (Matthew chapter 25).

Of contemporary issues of exclusion, one of the most sensitive for Christians is that of other religions. It is not possible to do more than touch interrogatively on this vast, many-sided topic, but it is an appropriate conclusion for a meditation on the ethic of feasting before the face of Christ.

What does it mean to realise that those of other faiths (and none) are before the face of Christ? Christians have no overview of how the relationship with them is carried on, or what happens from either side. This ethic therefore begins in agnosticism. Yet Christians need to try to imagine what the implications might be of Jesus being guest as well as host in relation to Mohammed, the Buddha and other founders and their followers. What might be involved in hospitality between religious communities that might give substance to such imagining? What are appropriate anticipations of the feasting of the Kingdom of God? What ethic of communication of the gospel is in line with the face on the cross? How can conversations engaging with crucial matters of meaning, truth and practice be sustained? What new shapes of Christian and other communities might there be if imaginative hospitality helped to generate honest confrontations and new understanding? Where do Christians fall into the temptation of being less generously welcoming than God? How can they come to realise their Christian self 'as another' – Jew, Muslim, Hindu, Buddhist, atheist or whatever? And what happens when guests and hosts become friends?

11.4 The metaphysics of feasting

It sounds pretentious or at least unacceptably anthropomorphic to talk of feasting as fundamental to the way reality is. But if a God of love and joy, communicated in Jesus Christ, is that than which none better or greater can be conceived then, recognising the analogical uses of 'feasting' (not at all grudgingly – analogy, as Ricoeur argues, is intrinsic to an adequate, multifaceted ontology), it is appropriate to speak like that. The meta-

physics of feasting is first of all about the reality of that God who transcends all our categories; then about the 'logic of superabundance' which
might be discerned in creation and history; and finally about the orientation of the divine economy that is appropriately described in, among
other ways, the figure of feasting.

The resource and 'currency' for exchange in that economy is the life,
truth and love of God. It is a trinitarian metaphysic, giving priority to the
doctrine of God in conceiving 'being' or 'reality'. Yet it is never able to rest
in its knowledge of God or of creation – there is infinite stretching of
heart and mind in trying to do justice to a God who is complexly and
interestingly involved in the whole of creation and history. The metaphysics of feasting is especially concerned with the abundance of the
truth and wisdom of God and of creation. How can that be savoured more
fully? What are the structures and dynamics of a universe which is created
to culminate in feasting? How do the natural and human sciences, the
scholarly disciplines, philosophy, the arts, and various cultures and religions testify to this? How can joy in truth and wisdom be fulfilled if we do
not feed on such courses?

For this metaphysics the danger to which Levinas alerts us is that of a
new totality. Feasting, however, allows for his ethical pluralism of being.
There is no overview of all those encounters and conversations, but the
feast can enact the union of substitutionary joy in the joy of others with
substitutionary responsibility.

11.5 The hermeneutics of feasting

To envisage the ultimate feasting is to imagine an endless overflow of
communication between those who love and enjoy each other. It
embraces body language, facial expressions, the ways we eat, drink, toast,
dance and sing; and accompanying every course, encounter and artistic
performance are conversations taken up into celebration. We can
imagine a 'great feast of languages' (Shakespeare), with cultures and
traditions in conversation. There can be a pluralism without divisiveness
– there is only a limited number of exchanges any guest can take part in,
and nobody needs to know what is going on in every conversation.
Aesthetics, ethics and metaphysics converge in this performance that is
'infinitely communicative' (Traherne).

It is a *'fête du sens'*, a feast of meaning, into which all aspects of
hermeneutics feed: immersion in language, being shaped by it and

shaping it; appreciation of many styles, figures, genres and contexts; labours in study and in debates over the sense, reference and application of texts and other communications; sensitivity to nuance, irony, humour and play. Pervading all is the significance of silence, reticence and mystery, in recognition of the inexhaustible abundance of meaning and an inexpressibility which yet continually invites further speech.

11.6 The spirituality of feasting

At this point intellectual indigestion threatens! That is the danger in listing contents of menus. It is now time to leave those necessary abstractions, generalisations and immense questions which might form the agendas of many books. The art of spirituality is to settle on one menu. It is about how particular communities and their members work out a specific feast-centred shape of living.

For this study, Christian vocation can be summed up as being called to the feast of the Kingdom of God. The salvation of selves is in responding to that invitation. The book's themes of joy and responsibility here come together in the most complete way: the responsibility to respond to an invitation into joy. The book's menu of a limited number of dialogues, themes and saints has focussed on a theology of the face of Jesus Christ leading into a spirituality of feasting before that face. So now let us conclude by trying to savour the joy of that feast in more vivid ways through a painting, a set of meditations and a poem.

11.6.1 Pure joy

Raphael's altarpiece for the church of San Giovanni in Monte, *The Ecstasy of St Cecilia with Sts Paul, John the Evangelist, Augustine, and Mary Magdalene*[1] (Fig. 2), was painted early in the sixteenth century, and it distils a rich Western Christian tradition about the joy of the saints. The picture stands out as a classic in the Italian Renaissance tradition of portraiture, drawing on it to depict people who are both ordinary and transformed; and at the same time it reaches back through the Middle Ages to Augustine and the New Testament for a conception of spiritual change culminating in the vision of God.

The five saints portrayed each represented radical spiritual trans-

---

1. In the Pinacoteca Nazionale, Bologna. In this meditation I am chiefly indebted to the discussion of the painting in Thomas Connolly, *Mourning into Joy. Music, Raphael, and Saint Cecilia* (Yale University Press, New Haven and London 1994).

Raphael, *The Ecstasy of St Cecilia with Sts Paul, John the Evangelist, Augustine, and Mary Magdalene*.

formation. The conversions of Paul and Augustine were the most famous in Raphael's tradition. John the Evangelist was known as the disciple who was above all renewed by love, and so immersed in it that eventually he simply repeated again and again: 'Little children, love one another!' Mary Magdalene was the prostitute who repented out of love for Jesus, and was transformed from great sinner to being specially loved and loving. Cecilia herself, the central focus of the painting, was, according to the stories about her,[2] strongly associated with the transition from sadness to joy, symbolised above all by singing continually in her heart (as in Ephesians 5.18–20). She was a key figure in conceiving the whole Christian life in these terms, sadness being associated with sin and turning in repentance, and pure joy being the final state of blessedness enjoying the vision of God. So Raphael has connected with Cecilia's ecstatic joy at the heavenly music four archetypal images of salvific transformation into intimacy with God.

The gazes of the five saints, none in the same direction as any other, are intriguing to interpret. Do they symbolise the dimensions of love in Ephesians chapter 3, Paul looking into the depths, John and Augustine to either side into the breadth, Mary Magdalene straight ahead into the length, and Cecilia upwards to the height?[3] I suspect so, but each also has its own fascination. Paul looks down at the discarded instruments of worldly music, including the sounding brass and tinkling cymbal of 1 Corinthians 13.1 – there are delights that do not harmonise with love. John and Augustine seem to be looking across at each other, the only face to face interaction – though it is possible that John is looking at Mary Magdalene. Mary is herself looking straight out at the viewer of the painting, inviting us into this community of joy.

At the centre is the gaze of Cecilia. Her expression is lively, peaceful, utterly attentive and somehow light – radiant and not at all heavy, yet at the same time solemn. She is looking past the heavenly choir, obviously at God to whom they are singing. She is letting go of an *organetto*, symbolising the 'mixed music' of joy and sadness which is the best that can be sustained in this life. Connolly links the discarded instrument with contemporary pictures of the penitent King David with his harp cast aside. Then, drawing on scriptural and other phrases which appear in the liturgies and stories of St Cecilia, he draws together key themes of this book in his climactic description:

2. On their doubtful historicity see ibid., especially chapter 2.
3. For an argument in favour see ibid., chapter 8.

In his painting of Cecilia, Raphael has carried to its logical conclusion the inherent comparison of this David, his 'joy turned to mourning,' to the musical Cecilia in whom the flux of these two passions has been reversed. Her eyes are upon the Lord, and there strike upon the ears of her heart the 'sound of the banqueter' in the everlasting holiday of the divine presence.[4]

The song is one of the supreme images of joy in the Christian theology and spirituality upon which Raphael drew, and all the saints in the painting are associated with both music and the contemplation of the vision of God. The moment caught by the painting is one in which the five saints are silent, and even Cecilia has ceased singing and playing. Another supreme image of joy is the smile, as exemplified in Dante's Beatrice. Her smile, increasingly radiant as she reflects higher circles of heaven, encourages Dante and communicates her joy to him; but at the final circle before the vision of God there is a rapture beyond smiling. Connolly concludes his book with an inspired speculation about Cecilia's intriguing expression:

> And if the *organetto* that hangs silent and forgotten in her hands tells us that she has ceased to sing, here in her new world of divine vision, can we suppose that she has also – and again, like Beatrice in a higher joy – just ceased to smile?[5]

11.6.2 Infinite felicity

I have approached the extreme of joy through considering Levinas's extreme of responsibility. In Thomas Traherne (1637–74) we find a movement in the other direction. Like Levinas he is fascinated by the idea of the infinite, but what grips him most deeply is what he calls the 'study of felicity'.

Raphael had painted *The Ecstasy of St Cecilia* in an Italy vibrant with Renaissance developments in the arts, literature, scholarship, religion, philosophy, trade, science, technology and exploration. He had recapitulated a spirituality of holy joy and presented it in contemporary artistic form as an altarpiece before which the Roman Mass could be celebrated as it had been for centuries. It was a peaceful and profound integration of old and new.

Traherne lived a century and a half later, after the Reformation had divided Europe. His was a century of devastating religious wars between Catholics and Protestants in Europe and a civil war in England, whose

4. Ibid., p. 246.   5. Ibid., p. 261.

aftermath he himself faced as he coped with the dilemmas of being a clergyman under Cromwell's Commonwealth and later under the restored monarchy. It was also a century of major scientific advances, especially in England, and he was well-educated and deeply interested in the transformations of worldview which were happening. His response in his theology and spirituality drew on the Greek and Latin classics, on the scriptures, on major Christian writers of the early church and Medieval periods, and on the Reformation, and his distinctive meditative style owes much to that inspired by Augustine and systematised by Medieval thinkers such as Bonaventure.[6] But while he, like Raphael, recapitulates a great deal from the past, there is also a world of difference. He is having to rethink his faith and practice after the Reformation and Counter-Reformation, Galileo, Cromwell and the founding of the Royal Society; and his spirituality does not have Raphael's context of unbroken ecclesiastical tradition, religious orders specialising in prayer and contemplation, and widely accepted practices of veneration of saints, spiritual direction and penance.

One common theological response was to strengthen the defences of faith and try to ensure that what was of value from the past could survive in the new situation. Traherne has that latter concern, but he does not go about it defensively. Instead he meets the new enlarged horizons with an even larger one – a fresh conception of the infinity of God in interaction with creation, in which the new scientific discoveries play a part. He responds to confidence in human thought and pride in human freedom not by detracting from humanity but by stretching his thinking in order to do justice to God as well as to all that is known about the world, and by revelling in the risk God takes in allowing the completion of creation to rely on human freedom. He is impatient with 'divines and schoolmen' who have interpreted the image of God in humanity far too constrictedly, leaving out the most wonderful aspects of God.[7]

Above all, in typical seventeenth-century style, he finds one great principle. His is felicity. This is his key term in a family that includes joy, delight, pleasure, happiness, beauty, bounty, enjoyment, blessing, amiableness, satisfaction, contentment, peace, sweetness, treasure, goodness, and many more; and all of them are closely intertwined with love.

6. Cf. Louis L. Martz, *The Paradise Within: Studies in Vaughan, Traherne, and Milton* (Yale University Press, New Haven and London 1964).
7. See Thomas Traherne, *Select Meditations*, edited by Julia Smith (Fyfield Books, Carcanet Press, Manchester 1997), p. 75.

He concludes his Second Century with a summary statement:

> The amiableness of virtue consisteth in this, that by it all happiness is either attained or enjoyed. Contentment and rest ariseth from a full perception of infinite treasures. So that whosoever will profit in the mystery of Felicity, must see the objects of his happiness, and the manner how they are to be enjoyed, and discern also the powers of his soul by which he is to enjoy them, and perhaps the rules that shall guide him in the way of enjoyment. All of which you have here, GOD, THE WORLD, YOURSELF, ALL THINGS in Time and Eternity being the objects of your Felicity, God the Giver, and you the receiver.[8]

Traherne celebrates felicity in one aspect after another, connects it with all parts of creation, all dimensions of human life, all branches of learning and science, all virtues and all theological doctrines, and orchestrates all that as an instruction in the rules that can guide in enjoyment of God, the world, yourself and all things. In the form of a spirituality, his meditations offer an aesthetics, ethics, metaphysics, hermeneutics and theology of what he calls felicity and I am discussing under the figure of feasting.

What is this felicity? Traherne describes it in his Third Century:

> In discovering the matter or objects to be enjoyed, I was greatly aided by remembering that we were made in God's Image. For thereupon it must of necessity follow that God's Treasures be our Treasures, and His joys our joys. So that by enquiring what were God's, I found the objects of our Felicity, God's Treasures being ours. For we were made in His Image that we might live in His similitude ... Now God's Treasures are His own perfections, and all His creatures.
>
> The image of God implanted in us, guided me to the manner wherein we were to enjoy. For since we were made in the similitude of God, we were to enjoy after His similitude. Now to enjoy the treasures of God in the similitude of God, is the most perfect blessedness God could devise. For the treasures of God are the most perfect treasures, and the manner of God is the most perfect manner. To enjoy therefore the treasures of God after the similitude of God is to enjoy the most perfect treasures in the most perfect manner. Upon which I was infinitely satisfied in God, and knew there was a Deity because I was satisfied. For in exerting Himself wholly in achieving thus an infinite Felicity He was infinitely delightful, great and glorious, and my desires so august and insatiable that nothing less than a Deity could satisfy them.

8. Thomas Traherne, *Centuries* (Mowbray, London and Oxford 1985), p. 106.

The spectacle once seen, will never be forgotten. It is a great part of the beatific vision. A sight of Happiness is Happiness. It transforms the soul and makes it Heavenly, it powerfully calls us to communion with God, and weans us from the customs of this world. It puts a lustre upon God and all His creatures and makes us to see them in a Divine and Eternal Light.[9]

There Traherne outlines his basic conception of transformation by joy into God's image, which involves a new relationship with all creation as well as with God.

God loves to be enjoyed, so let us do so! That is the theme which is repeated in many variations and sometimes wild and daring improvisations. Could anything be more obvious or simple? Traherne delights in the logic of this divine superabundance:

By infusing grateful principles, and inclinations to thanksgiving He hath made the creature capable of more than all worlds, yea, of more than enjoying the Deity in a simple way: though we should suppose it to be infinite. For to enjoy God as the fountain of infinite treasures, and as the giver of all, is infinite pleasure: but He by His wisdom infusing grateful principles, hath made us upon the very account of self-love to love Him more than ourselves. And us, who without self-love could not be pleased at all, even as we love ourselves He hath so infinitely pleased, that we are able to rejoice in Him, and to love Him more than ourselves. And by loving Him more than ourselves, in very gratitude and honor, to take more pleasure in His felicity, than in our own, by which way we best enjoy Him. To see His wisdom, goodness, and power employed in creating all worlds for our enjoyment, and infinitely magnified in beautifying them for us, and governing them for us satisfies our self-love; but with all it so obligeth us that in love to Him, which it createth in us, maketh us more to delight in those attributes as they are His, than as they are our own. And the truth is, without this we could not fully delight in them, for the most excellent and glorious effect of all had been unachieved. But now there is an infinite union between Him and us, He being infinitely delightful to us, and we to Him. For He infinitely delighteth to see creatures act upon such illustrious and eternal principles, in a manner so divine, heroic, and most truly blessed; and we delight in seeing Him giving us the power.[10]

A similar logic of mutual intensification in joy is found between people. Self-love is both affirmed and transcended when we realise that

9. Ibid., pp. 141f.   10. Ibid., p. 190.

joy in the joy of others enhances our own joy – and even more so when others realise that too. The self that is doing the loving and enjoying is transformed in this process.

Traherne's response to God and to his own time has something of the awe-inspiring dimensions of the Letter to the Ephesians and the gazes of Raphael's saints. It also has the ordinary everydayness of Levinas's *jouisse-ment* and of the Reformation emphasis on a spirituality for all believers. Traherne reflects that God's generosity has made occasions of joy universally accessible:

> A daily joy shall be more my joy, because it is continual. A common joy is more my delight because it is common. For all mankind are my friends, and everything is enriched in serving them.[11]

Traherne's theology and spirituality have hardly begun to be done justice to, partly for the understandable reason that most of his works were lost until this century. The *Centuries*, from which most of my quotations so far have come, were first published in 1908, and new discoveries are still taking place. Among those in recent decades have been the *Select Meditations* found in 1964, the *Commentaries of Heaven* in 1982, *The Ceremonial Law* in 1996, and the most substantial discovery of all in 1997 by Jeremy Maule in the Library of Lambeth Palace of four new works in manuscript. I conclude with a taste of one of the latter, entitled 'The Kingdom of God', in which Traherne overflows in praise of love with an ecstasy of words to match St Cecilia's silence:

> O the wonderfull excellencie of L O V ! How Great! How Marvellous it is! How ineffable, how high and Transcendent! How like unto G O D; how neer unto Him! Without lov he could never be satisfyed, never Glorious. Lov is a flaming temple, of Infinit Sence, and Brightness, Capacity, met to entertain the King of Glory: A Fountain of benefits; The Soul of Gratitude; The End of Rewards, the most tender concern; the attainment of honors, the bent and Appetite of evry Creature; the Work of Reason; the Sinke of Union in all Combinations; the Salt and swetness of all conditions; the marrow of prosperity; the Joy of Poverty; and the pith of Glory. The Mother of Peace, the Sphere of repose, the Shield of Safety, the Bullwark of Security, the Root of fidelitie, the mine of Friendship, the tree of Life, the Beauty of Holiness; the Spring of delights, the Puritie and Quintessence of Pleasure, and Prais, the Sun of heaven; it causeth all the Summer

---

11. Ibid., p. 175. Cf. p. 214: 'Knowing the greatness and sweetness of Love, I can never be poor in any estate. How sweet a thing is it as we go or ride or eat or drink, or converse abroad to remember that one is heir of the whole world, and the friend of God!'

there; the Constellation of Virtues; the Sea of happiness, the only harbor, the Ground of Content, the crown of Glory; without which there would be no Glory, no enjoyment, no felicitie.[12]

11.6.3 All God's Chillun Got Rhythm

The last dish is a poem by Micheal O'Siadhail. It takes us away from church buildings and ministers into the black slave culture of the southern United States and its descendants in big city slums. Jazz gives one of the great musical testimonies to what heaven might mean. But it challenges most notions of heaven too. It opens us up to almost impossible blends of suffering and joy, freedom and intensity, repetition and surprise, ravelling and unravelling. In 'Both' and 'Vertigo', successive poems in a series of 'Variations',[13] Lady Jazz is 'making everything her own' by being hostess to their rhythms and there are hints of the sort of universe this implies.

Both

Cotton picking or dogging around Chicago slums,
Those *Basin Street Blues*, *Never No Lament*,
Get Happy, whirl and muddle or bewilderment,
And there in the banal the jazz still hums.

Swing! Brother, Swing! Shoe Shine Boy.
Out There. Back in Your Own Backyard.
Dancing in the Dark. Bye Bye Blackbird.
Big Butter and Egg Man. Stompin' at the Savoy.

Before-the-beat, around-the-beat, passion's tone,
Just on and on swamping up those rhythms,
Afro, Creole or Latin, the Baptist hymns,
Even marches, she's making everything her own.

Someday Sweetheart. Bird of Paradise.
Nobody Knows. All God's Chillun Got Rhythm.
Garden of Souls. A Love Supreme.
Embraceable You. Smoke Gets in Your Eyes.

---

12. Thomas Traherne, 'The Kingdom of God' (Lambeth Palace MS 1360), chapter 32, folios 306, 306v, transcribed by Jeremy Maule. I am grateful to Dr Maule for the transcription and for our continuing communication about the manuscript, its significance and the thought of Traherne.
13. Micheal O'Siadhail, *Our Double Time* (Bloodaxe Books, Newcastle upon Tyne 1998) pp. 91–102.

Ordinary down-to-earthness, so heaven-minded,
Both how it is and how we must refuse it.
The body breaks against the crying spirit.
This gaiety where all ends are open-ended.

> Vertigo

To the end the jazz, pulse of surprise, off-chance,
Raveller and unraveller of tunes, wooer of margins,

Song of the servant, cotton-picker's rhythmic urge,
Whatever in evolution will always choose the verge.

Was Plato mad to dream up some infinite perfection,
Musics of fulness where the rhythm and tune are one?

Pure need of memory and of aim? A hunch? A guess?
Still this becoming, my finite rhapsody of process.

I grow older and it seems the silence that surrounds
Each tone is keener, the intensity between the sounds.

Love's moment so infinite and perfect in the flux.
Have I begun to understand something of that paradox?

A vibrato at the music's brim, my gift and privilege.
Lady Jazz, I'm your brinkman still dizzy at the edge.

There is a glimpse of 'love's moment so infinite and perfect in the flux', but there are also 'whirl and muddle or bewilderment', hunches, guesswork, intense silences, finiteness, paradox and dizziness. Passions, desires, styles, sufferings and 'ordinary down-to-earthness, so heaven-minded' are all taken up into transformations. The tone is interrogative and 'all ends are open-ended'. But what gaiety! And at the heart of it the ultimate juxtaposition:

> *A Love Supreme.*
> *Embraceable You.*

Bibliography

282   Alison, James. *Raising Abel. The Recovery of the Eschatological Imagination* (Crossroad, New York 1996).

Ballantine, Samuel E. *The Hidden God. The Hiding of the Face of God in the Old Testament* (Oxford University Press, Oxford 1983).

Balthasar, Hans Urs von. *Theo-Drama. Theological Dramatic Theory*, 5 vols. (Ignatius Press, San Francisco 1988).

Thérèse of Lisieux. The Story of a Mission (Sheed and Ward, London and New York 1953).

Barrett, C. K. *Essays on John* (SPCK, London 1982).

Jesus and the Gospel Tradition (SPCK, London 1967).

Barth, Karl. *Church Dogmatics*, vols. I–IV (T. & T. Clark, Edinburgh 1936–69).

Baudinet, Marie-José. 'The Face of Christ, The Form of the Church' in *Fragments for a History of the Human Body*, Part One, ed. Michel Feher with Ramona Nadaff and Nadia Tazi (Zone, New York 1989).

Begbie, Jeremy. *The Sound of God* (Cambridge University Press, Cambridge forthcoming).

'Theology and the Arts. (2) Music' in David F. Ford, *The Modern Theologians. An Introduction to Christian Theology in the Twentieth Century*, 2nd edition (Blackwell, Oxford 1997).

Bethge, Eberhard. *Dietrich Bonhoeffer: Theologian, Christian, Contemporary* (Collins, Fountain Books, London and New York 1977; first published in German, Chr. Kaiser Verlag, Munich 1967).

Bockmuehl, Markus. '"The Form of God" (Phil. 2.6). Variations on a Theme of Jewish Mysticism', *Journal of Theological Studies*, ns, vol. 48, pt 1, April 1997, pp. 1–23.

This Jesus. Martyr, Lord, Messiah (T. & T. Clark, Edinburgh 1994).

Bonhoeffer, Dietrich. *Christology* (Fontana, Collins, London 1966).

The Cost of Discipleship (SCM Press, London 1959).

Ethics (Collins, London 1964).

Letters and Papers from Prison (SCM Press, London 1971).

Life Together (SCM Press, London 1954).

Bonhoeffer, Dietrich, and Maria von Wedemeyer. *Love Letters from Cell 92* (HarperCollins, London 1994).

Borg, Marcus J. *Conflict, Holiness and Politics in the Teaching of Jesus* (Edwin Mellen, New York and Toronto 1984).

Jesus: A New Vision. Spirit, Culture, and the Life of Discipleship (Harper, San Francisco 1991).

Bourdieu, Pierre. *Outline of a Theory of Practice* (Cambridge University Press, Cambridge 1977).

Brook, Peter. *The Shifting Point. Forty Years of Theatrical Exploration 1946–1987* (Methuen, London 1989).

Brueggemann, Walter. *Theology of the Old Testament. Testimony, Dispute, Advocacy* (Fortress Press, Minneapolis 1997).

Bryson, Norman. *Looking at the Overlooked. Four Essays on Still Life Painting* (Harvard University Press, Cambridge, MA 1990).

Childs, Brevard S. *Exodus. A Commentary* (SCM Press, London 1974).

Connolly, Thomas. *Mourning into Joy. Music, Raphael, and Saint Cecilia* (Yale University Press, New Haven and London 1994).

Cordess, C., and M. Cox. *Forensic Psychotherapy: Crime, Psychodynamics and the Offender Patient*, 2 vols. (Jessica Kingsley, London 1996).

Cox, M., and A. Theilgaard. *Shakespeare as Prompter: The Amending Imagination and the Therapeutic Process* (Jessica Kingsley, London 1994).

Dahl, Nils Alstrup. *Jesus the Christ. The Historical Origins of Christological Doctrine*, ed. Donald H. Juel (Fortress Press, Minneapolis 1991).

Dalferth, Ingolf U. *Der auferweckte Gekreuzigte. Zur Grammatik der Christologie* (J.C.B. Mohr (Paul Siebeck), Tübingen 1994).

Dawson, David. *Literary Theory* (Fortress Press, Minneapolis 1995).

Deleuze, Gilles, and Franz Guattari. *A Thousand Plateaus: Capitalism and Schizophrenia* (University of Minnesota Press, Minneapolis 1987).

Derrida, Jacques. *Writing and Difference* (University of Chicago Press, Chicago 1978).

Dumas, André. *Dietrich Bonhoeffer: Theologian of Reality* (SCM Press, London 1971).

St Ephrem the Syrian, *Hymns on Paradise*, Introduction and translation by Sebastian Brock (St. Vladimir's Seminary Press, Crestwood, NY 1990).

Farley, Edward. *Good and Evil. Interpreting a Human Condition* (Fortress Press, Minneapolis 1990).

Farrow, Douglas Bryce. 'Ascension and Ecclesia. On the Significance of the Doctrine of the Ascension for Ecclesiology and Christian Cosmology' (Ph.D. dissertation, King's College London 1994).

Feil, Ernst. *The Theology of Dietrich Bonhoeffer* (Fortress Press, Philadelphia 1985).

Fitzgerald, Constance. 'The Mission of Thérèse of Lisieux', *Contemporary Carmelite Women, The Way Supplement* 89, Summer 1997, pp. 74–96.

Floyd, Wayne Whitson, Jr and Charles Marsh (eds.). *Theology and the Practice of Responsibility: Essays on Dietrich Bonhoeffer* (Trinity Press International, Valley Forge, PA 1994).

Fodor, James. *Christian Hermeneutics. Paul Ricoeur and the Refiguring of Theology* (Clarendon Press, Oxford 1995).

Ford, David F. 'L'Arche and Jesus: What is the Theology?' in *Encounter with Mystery*, ed. Frances M. Young (Darton, Longman and Todd, London 1997).

Barth and God's Story. Biblical Narrative and the Theological Method of Karl Barth in the Church Dogmatics (Verlag Peter Lang, Frankfurt am Main, Berne 1981).

'Before the Face of Christ. Thérèse of Lisieux and Two Interpreters', *The Way*, vol. 37, no. 3, July 1997, pp. 254–62.

'Concluding Reflection: Constructing a Public Theology' in *Dare We Speak of God in*

Public? The Edward Cadbury Lectures, 1993–94, ed. Frances Young (Mowbray, London 1995).

'The Face on the Cross', *Anvil*, vol. 11, no. 3, 1994, pp. 215–25.

'Hosting a Dialogue: Jüngel and Levinas on God, Self and Language' in *The Possibilities of Theology: Studies in the Theology of Eberhard Jüngel*, ed. John Webster (T. & T. Clark, Edinburgh 1994).

A Long Rumour of Wisdom. Redescribing Theology (Cambridge University Press, Cambridge 1991).

'On Being Theologically Hospitable to Jesus Christ: Hans Frei's Achievement', *Journal of Theological Studies*, ns, vol. 46, pt 2, October 1995, pp. 532–46.

'On Substitution' in *Facing the Other. The Ethics of Emmanuel Levinas*, ed. Sean Hand (Curzon, Richmond, Surrey 1996).

The Shape of Living (Fount/Harper Collins, London 1997).

'System, Story, Performance: A Proposal about the Role of Narrative in Christian Systematic Theology' in *Why Narrative? Readings in Narrative Theology*, ed. Stanley Hauerwas and L. Gregory Jones (Eerdmans, Grand Rapids 1989).

'Theology and Religious Studies at the Turn of the Millennium', *Teaching Theology and Religion*, vol. 1, no. 1, November 1998.

'Transformation' in *God in the City. Essays and Reflections from the Archbishop of Canterbury's Urban Theology Group*, ed. Peter Sedgwick (Mowbray, London 1995).

Ford, David F. (ed.). *The Modern Theologians. An Introduction to Christian Theology in the Twentieth Century*, 2nd edition (Blackwell, Oxford 1997).

Ford, David F., and Alasdair I. McFadyen. 'Praise' in *God in the City. Essays and Reflections from the Archbishop of Canterbury's Urban Theology Group*, ed. Peter Sedgwick (Mowbray, London 1995).

Fowl, S. E., and L. Gregory Jones, *Reading in Communion: Scripture and Ethics in Christian Life* (SPCK, London 1991).

Frei, Hans. *The Eclipse of Biblical Narrative. A Study in Eighteenth and Nineteenth Century Hermeneutics* (Yale University Press, New Haven and London 1974).

The Identity of Jesus Christ. The Hermeneutical Bases of Dogmatic Theology (Fortress Press, Philadelphia 1975).

Gerrish, Brian. *Grace and Gratitude. The Eucharistic Theology of John Calvin* (T. & T. Clark, Edinburgh 1993).

Gibbs, Robert. *Correlations in Rosenzweig and Levinas* (Princeton University Press, Princeton 1992).

Görres, Ida. *The Hidden Face. A Study of St. Thérèse of Lisieux* (Burns and Oates, London 1959) (a translation of *Das Senfkorn von Lisieux*, the 8th revised edition of *Das verborgene Antlitz: Eine Studie über Thérèse von Lisieux* (Herder Verlag, Freiburg im Breisgau 1944)).

Grayston, Kenneth. *Dying We Live. A New Enquiry into the Death of Christ in the New Testament* (Darton, Longman and Todd, London 1990).

Grout, Donald Jay. *A History of Western Music* (Dent, London 1978).

Gruchy, John De (ed.). *Bonhoeffer for a New Day: Theology in a Time of Transition* (Eerdmans, Grand Rapids 1997).

Hafemann, Scott J. 'The glory and the veil of Moses in 2 Cor. 3.7–14: An example of Paul's contextual exegesis of the Old Testament', Paper for the Society for Biblical Literature, Annual Meeting, New Orleans, November 1990.

Paul, Moses and the History of Israel: the letter/spirit contrast and the argument from scripture in 2 Corinthians 3 (J.C.B. Mohr (Paul Siebeck), Tübingen 1995).

Suffering and Ministry in the Spirit: Paul's defence of his ministry in II Corinthians 2:14–3:3 (Eerdmans, Grand Rapids 1990).

Hardy, Daniel W. *God's Ways with the World* (T. & T. Clark, Edinburgh 1996).

Hardy, Daniel W., and David F. Ford. *Jubilate. Theology in Praise* (Darton, Longman and Todd, London 1984; US edition: *Praising and Knowing God*, Westminster Press, Philadelphia 1985).

Harvey, Nicholas Peter. *The Morals of Jesus* (Darton, Longman and Todd, London 1991).

Hengel, Martin. *Crucifixion in the Ancient World and the Folly of the Message of the Cross* (Fortress Press, Philadelphia 1977).

Studies in Early Christology (T. & T. Clark, Edinburgh 1995).

Hurtado, Larry. *One God, One Lord: Early Christian Devotion and Ancient Jewish Monotheism* (Fortress Press, Philadelphia 1988).

Jenkins, Timothy D. 'Fieldwork and the Perception of Everyday Life', *Man*, ns, vol. 29, no. 2, June 1994.

Jenson, Robert. *Unbaptized God. The Basic Flaw in Ecumenical Theology* (Fortress Press, Minneapolis 1992).

Jones, L. Gregory. *Embodying Forgiveness. A Theological Analysis* (Eerdmans, Grand Rapids 1995).

Jüngel, Eberhard. *God as the Mystery of the World* (Wm. B. Eerdmans, Grand Rapids, 1983). *Theological Essays II*, ed. John Webster (T. & T. Clark, Edinburgh 1995).

Kelly, Geffrey B. Editor's Introduction to the English Edition, *Life Together and Prayerbook of the Bible (Dietrich Bonhoeffer Works, Volume 5)* (Fortress Press, Minneapolis, 1996).

Kemp, Walter H. 'The "Polyphony of Life": References to Music in Bonhoeffer's *Letters and Papers from Prison*, in *Vita Laudanda Essays in Memory of Ulrich S. Leopold*, ed. Erich Schultz (Wilfred Laurier University Press, Waterloo 1976), pp. 137–54.

Kierkegaard, Sören. *Repetition. An Essay in Experimental Psychology* (Harper, New York 1964)

Training in Christianity and the Edifying Discourse which 'accompanied' it, translated with an Introduction and Notes by Walter Lowrie (Princeton University Press, Princeton 1967).

Kristeva, Julia. *Desire in Language: A Semiotic Approach to Literature and Art* (New York, Columbia University Press 1980).

Lash, Nicholas. *The Beginning and the End of 'Religion'* (Cambridge University Press, Cambridge 1996).

Easter in Ordinary. Reflections on Human Experience and the Knowledge of God (SCM Press, London 1988).

Levinas, Emmanuel. *Collected Philosophical Papers* (Kluwer Academic Publishers, Dordrecht/Boston/London 1993).

De Dieu qui vient a l'idée (Vrin, Paris 1982).

Difficult Freedom. Essays on Judaism (Johns Hopkins University Press, Baltimore 1990).

Entre Nous: Essais sur le penser à l'autre (Bernard Grasset, Paris 1991).

The Levinas Reader, ed. Sean Hand (Blackwell, Oxford 1989).

Otherwise Than Being or Beyond Essence (Martinus Nijhoff, The Hague/Boston/London 1981).

Totality and Infinity: An Essay on Exteriority (Duquesne University Press, Pittsburgh 1969).

Lincoln, Andrew T. *Ephesians* (Word, Dallas 1990).

Lincoln, Andrew T., and A. J. M. Wedderburn. *The Theology of the Later Pauline Letters* (Cambridge University Press, Cambridge 1993).

Lindars, Barnabas. *The Gospel of John* (Marshall, Morgan and Scott, London 1972).

Llewellyn, John. *Emmanuel Levinas. The Genealogy of Ethics* (Routledge, London 1995).

Lowe, Walter. *Theology and Difference. The Wound of Reason* (Indiana University Press, Bloomington and Indianapolis 1993).

Marion, Jean-Luc. *God Without Being* (University of Chicago Press, Chicago and London 1991).

Marsh, Charles. *Reclaiming Dietrich Bonhoeffer* (Oxford University Press, New York and Oxford 1994).

Martz, Louis L. *The Paradise Within: Studies in Vaughan, Traherne, and Milton* (Yale University Press, New Haven and London 1964).

McIntyre, John. *The Shape of Soteriology* (T. & T. Clark, Edinburgh 1992).

Meeks, Wayne. *The First Urban Christians: The Social World of the Apostle Paul* (Yale University Press, New Haven and London 1983).

Melberg, Arne. *Theories of Mimesis* (Cambridge University Press, Cambridge 1995).

Milbank, John. *The Word Made Strange* (Blackwell, Oxford 1997).

Moltmann, Jürgen. *The Crucified God* (SCM, London 1974).

Müller, Gerhard Ludwig, and Albrecht Schönherr. 'Editors' Afterword to the German Edition', *Life Together and Prayerbook of the Bible (Dietrich Bonhoeffer Works, Volume 5)* (Fortress Press, Minneapolis 1996).

Nyamiti, Charles. *Christ as our Ancestor: Christology from an African Perspective* (Mamba Press, Gweru 1984).

Ochs, Peter. 'Scriptural Logic: Diagrams for a Postcritical Metaphysics', *Modern Theology*, vol. 11, no. 1, January 1995, pp. 65–92.

   Peirce, Pragmatism, and the Logic of Scripture (Cambridge University Press, Cambridge 1998).

O'Siadhail, Micheal. *Our Double Time* (Bloodaxe Books, Newcastle upon Tyne 1998).

Pelikan, Jaroslav. *The Christian Tradition. A History of the Development of Doctrine. Vol. 2. The Spirit of Eastern Christendom (600–1700)* (Chicago University Press, Chicago and London 1974).

Peperzak, Adriaan. *To the Other. An Introduction to the Philosophy of Emmanuel Levinas* (Purdue University Press, West Lafayette, IN 1993).

Pickstock, Catherine. 'Necrophilia: The Middle of Modernity. A Study of Death, Signs and the Eucharist', *Modern Theology*, vol. 12, no. 4, October 1996.

   'The Sacred Polis. Language, Death and Liturgy' (Cambridge University Ph.D. dissertation, 1996).

Rad, G. von. *Genesis. A Commentary* (SCM Press, London 1961).

Ricoeur, Paul. *Figuring the Sacred. Religion, Narrative, and Imagination* (Fortress Press, Minneapolis 1995).

   Oneself As Another (University of Chicago Press, Chicago and London 1992).

   The Symbolism of Evil (Harper & Row, New York 1967).

   Time and Narrative, 3 vols. (University of Chicago Press, Chicago and London 1984, 1985, 1988).

Rosenzweig, Franz. *The Star of Redemption* (University of Notre Dame Press, Notre Dame and London 1985).

Sanders, E. P. *The Historical Figure of Jesus* (Allen Lane/Penguin, London 1993).

   Jesus and Judaism (SCM Press, London 1985).

Savage, Timothy B. *Power through Weakness. Paul's Understanding of the Christian Ministry in 2 Corinthians* (Cambridge University Press, Cambridge 1996).

Schillebeeckx, Edward. *Christ: The Christian Experience in the Modern World* (SCM Press, London 1980).

Schnackenburg, Rudolf. *Der Brief an die Epheser* (Benziger Verlag, Zurich, Einsiedeln, Cologne; Neukirchener Verlag, Neukirchen-Vluyn 1982).

Schönborn, Christoph von. *L'Icône du Christ. Fondements théologiques élaborés entre le Ier et le IIe Concile de Nicée (325–787)* (Editions Universitaires Fribourg Suisse, Fribourg 1976).

Six, Jean-François. *Light of the Night. The Last Eighteen Months in the Life of Thérèse of Lisieux* (SCM Press, London 1996).

Smith, D. Moody. *Johannine Christianity. Essays on its Setting, Sources and Theology* (T. & T. Clark, Edinburgh 1984).

The Theology of the Gospel of John (Cambridge University Press, Cambridge 1995).

Smith, Ronald Gregor (ed.). *World Come of Age* (Collins, London 1967).

Smith, Steven G. *The Argument to the Other* (Scholars Press, Chico, CA 1983).

Solzhenitsyn, Aleksandr, *August 1914. The Red Wheel 1. A Narrative in Discrete Periods of Time* (The Bodley Head, London 1989).

Stacey, David. 'The Lord's Supper as Prophetic Drama', *Epworth Review*, vol. 21, no. 1, January 1994.

Stanton, G. N. *The Gospels and Jesus* (Oxford University Press, Oxford 1989).

Stern, J. P. *On Realism* (Routledge and Kegan Paul, London 1973).

St. Thérèse of Lisieux. *Story of a Soul. The Autobiography of St. Thérèse of Lisieux* (ICS Publications, Washington, DC 1976).

Thiselton, Anthony C. *Interpreting God and the Postmodern Self. On Meaning, Manipulation and Promise* (T. & T. Clark, Edinburgh 1995).

Traherne, Thomas. *Centuries* (Mowbray, London and Oxford 1985).

'The Kingdom of God' (Lambeth Palace MS 1360), transcribed by Jeremy Maule.

Select Meditations, ed. Julia Smith (Fyfield Books, Carcanet Press, Manchester 1997).

Webster, John. 'Eberhard Jüngel' in *The Modern Theologians. An Introduction to Christian Theology in the Twentieth Century*, ed. David F. Ford, 2nd edn. (Blackwell, Oxford 1997).

Eberhard Jüngel, An Introduction to His Theology (Cambridge University Press, Cambridge 1986).

Westphal, Merold. 'Levinas, Kierkegaard and the Theological Task', *Modern Theology*, vol. 8, no. 3, July 1992.

Williams, Rowan. 'Keeping Time. For the Three Choirs Festival' in *Open to Judgement. Sermons and Addresses* (Darton, Longman and Todd, London 1994).

St. Teresa of Avila (Chapman, London 1991).

Wright, N. T. *Jesus and the Victory of God (Christian Origins and the Question of God, Volume 2)* (Fortress Press, Minneapolis 1996).

The New Testament and the People of God (Christian Origins and the Question of God, Volume 1) (Fortress Press, Minneapolis 1992).

Wüstenberg, R. *Glauben als Leben: Dietrich Bonhoeffer und die nichtreligiöse Interpretation biblischer Begriffe* (Verlag Peter Lang, Frankfurt 1996).

Wyschogrod, Edith. *Saints and Postmodernism* (University of Chicago Press, Chicago and London 1990).

Spirit in Ashes. Hegel, Heidegger and Man-made Mass Death (Yale University Press, New Haven and London 1985).

Yofre, Simian. 'panim' in *Theologisches Wörterbuch zum Alten Testament*, ed. G. Johannes Botterweck, Helmer Ringgren, Heinz-Josef Fabry, vol. VI, part 6/7 pp. 630–60.

Young, Frances M., and David F. Ford. *Meaning and Truth in 2 Corinthians* (SPCK, London 1987; Eerdmans, Grand Rapids 1988).

Index of scriptural references

Genesis
3:8 194
4:16 194
32:20–1, 30 194
33 195
33:4, 10b 195

Exodus
3:6 201, 211
20:3 196
24 146
32–4 195
33:7–11, 14, 15, 20 196
34:29–35 196

Numbers
6:24–6 215

Psalms
13:1 199
17:15 198
22:1 128, 199
22:24 199
24:3–6 198
27:8 101, 198
31:5 128, 200
31:16 197, 200
31:20, 22 200
44:24 199
67:12 197
69:17, 21 200
80:3, 7, 19 198
85:10 135
88:14 199
105:4 198

Isaiah
8:17 201
50:5–8a 201

53 201
54:8 201
59:1–2 200–1
59:17 132

Jeremiah
31:33 146
33:5 201

Ezekiel
39:23, 24, 29 201

Micah
3:4 201

Matthew
5:5 136
6:16–18 231
6:43–8 185
11:29 136, 187
17:2, 5 178
22:32 178
26:26, 27 145
27:6 128, 199
27:50 192
28:9, 17, 19 172

Mark
8:34 187
10:32, 45 191
14:22 145
14:26 129
15:29–32 203
15:37, 39 192
16:8 172

Luke
2:28, 34 156
6:28 156

9:31 197
9:46–8 185
9:51 191
22:17, 19 145
22:24–7 186
23:46 128
24 211
24:16 172
24:30 156
24:37 172
24:50–3 156

John
1 212
1:14 197
4:23f 161
6 158–9
6:63 161
13–17 158–9
13:12–17 157
14:26 159
19:28–9 200
19:30 192
20:14 172
21:4 172
21:21 172

Acts
2 211
2:33, 36 173
2:37 204
6:15 173
7:55 173
9:4–5 173

Romans
4:16–25 211
5 101–2, 168
9–11 132

1 Corinthians
8:6   *212*
11   *140*
11:24, 25, 26   *145*
13:1   *274*
13:12   *174*

2 Corinthians
3   *196*
3:18   *24, 102, 163, 168, 171, 197,*
      212, 214
4:2   *103*
4:6   *24, 103, 163, 171, 197, 214*
4:7–11   *204*
12:8   *204*

Galatians
5:22f   *135*

Ephesians
1:3   *118*
1:7   *114, 118*
1:10   *107, 114, 120, 123*
1:12   *118*
1:19f   *118, 124*
2:5–6   *114*
2:6   *116, 119*
2:7   *114*
2:8, 13ff, 15   *114*

2:18   *119*
2:21   *116*
3   *274*
3:4–6   *114*
3:14–21   *112, 118*
3:16   *124*
3:19   *113, 133*
3:20   *122–3*
3:21   *122*
4:2   *124, 132, 135*
4:11, 14   *109*
4:15   *109, 124*
4:24, 32   *135*
5:2   *124*
5:8–21   *108–9*
5:9   *135*
5:16, 17   *125*
5:18   *124, 125, 128, 274*
5:27   *120*
5:30   *122*
6:1   *135*
6:4, 9   *120*
6:10–20   *122*
6:11–16   *119*
6:14   *135*
6:15   *132*

Philippians
2:6   *197*

Colossians
1   *212*

1 Timothy
5:21   *173*
6:13   *173, 174*

2 Timothy
4:1   *173, 174*

1 Peter
1:3–9   *174*
1:8   *176*

Hebrews
1   *212*
2:9   *173*
5:7–10   *209*
11:1   *174*
12:1–2   *173*
12:18–24   *174*

Revelation
1:12–19   *175*
13:18   *214*
22:1–5   *175*

Index

abandonment 204, 231, 239, 264
Abraham 40, 211
absence 206
  of God 46, 56, 57, 97, 104, 199
  see presence and absence
abundance 4, 10, 44, 85, 112, 115, 117, 120, 133,
    134, 242, 263, 272
  of God 113, 116, 130, 144–5, 164, 168
Adam 114, 194
aesthetics 268, 277
Alison, James 189
altruism 217, 222, 223
  altruistic desire 233–4
analogy 5, 50, 58, 77–9, 94, 95, 152–3, 164,
    270
Anglicanism 142, 249
Anne of Jesus 227
Anscombe, Elizabeth 87
Anselm of Canterbury 113, 210
anthropology, social 138, 139–45, 165
apocalyptic 189
apprenticeship 141–2, 144, 161, 215
Aristotle 42, 90, 94
art 182, 202, 267
atheism 31, 35, 36, 54, 55, 57, 81, 145, 223, 270
  atheist self 60–1, 75
atonement 137, 193, 206, 208
attestation 5, 8, 87, 89, 91, 92, 94, 96, 154
  and worship 101
  see witness; testimony
Augustine of Hippo 11, 127, 213, 272, 274, 276
Austin, J. L. 87
authority 145, 178, 188, 208
autonomy 92–3, 100, 256

Bach, Johann Sebastian 258, 267
Bakhtin, Mikhail 223
Ballantine, Samuel E. 199, 202

Balthasar, Hans Urs von 169, 225, 228, 229,
    233, 235–6, 244
baptism 100, 119, 162–3, 164, 204, 210, 246,
    263
  of Jesus 178
Barrett, C. K. 158, 177
Barth, Karl 53, 69, 81, 169, 186, 203, 257, 258
Basil the Great 208
Bataille, Georges 217
Baudinet, Marie-José 207
Begbie, Jeremy 3, 7, 120, 121, 126, 135
Belière, Abbé 233
Bellini, Giovanni 219
Bernanos, Georges 89, 90
Bethge, Eberhard 243, 245, 250, 253, 254, 263
Bible, *see* scripture
Blanchot, Maurice 217, 219
blessing 4, 10, 99, 109, 115, 117, 153, 155–7,
    162–3, 168, 215, 268, 277
  of eucharistic elements 150
blood of Christ 146, 149, 179
Bockmuehl, Markus 177, 186, 197
body 8, 44, 87, 95, 103, 124, 143, 163, 179, 202,
    205, 239, 248
  of Christ 146, 158, 209
  of the saint 217–18, 221
Bonaventure 113, 210–11, 276
Bonhoeffer, Dietrich 2, 5, 6, 11, 68–9, 86, 164,
    169, 207, 241–65, 266
  poetry 258, 261
Borg, Marcus J. 177, 184, 186, 192
Botterweck, Johannes 193
Bourdieu, Pierre 140, 143
Brock, Sebastian 29
Brook, Peter 4
Brueggemann, Walter 127
Bryson, Norman 149
Buber, Martin 54, 65

Buddhism 88, 220, 223, 270
Bultmann, Rudolf 53

calendar 155
Calvin, Jean 157, 162
Catherine of Siena 221
Catholicism 48, 241–2, 243, 245, 246, 249, 275
Cecilia 11, 274, 279
Cézanne, Paul 22
Chalcedon, Council of 145, 254, 257
Childs, Brevard S. 195
Christianity 8, 130, 137–9, 144, 177, 181, 210,
    246, 254, 262
  and atheism 54
  Christian humanism 255
  see identity, Christian
christology 64, 78, 104, 132, 186, 249
church 7, 24, 109, 112, 114, 115, 120, 126, 127,
    133, 230, 236, 245
Colossians, Letter to 111, 114, 115, 119
communication 3, 19–20, 55, 92, 108, 109,
    112–17, 122, 126, 132, 134, 144, 252, 270–1
  deceptive 21
  with God 196
communion 149, 246
  of saints 243
  see eucharist
community 5, 24, 42, 80, 99, 100, 129, 136,
    146, 198, 245, **250–3**, 274
  of the face 23, 24, 116, 121, 130–1, 133, 159,
    160, 163, 178, 181
  of praise 119, 130
compassion 67, 217, 218, 269
completion 115, 209
Confessing Church 245, 249–50
confession of sins 245, 246, 250, 252
Connolly, Thomas 272, 274–5
conscience 8, 89, 91, 93–4, 96, **103–4**, 247
conviction 89, 93, 95, 96, 101, 212
Cordess, C. 136
Counter-Reformation 244, 276
covenant 100, 146, 159, 195–6, 209, 215
Cox, Murray 136
creation 1, 36, 46, 48, 50, 51, 66–7, 98, 205, 211,
    214, 276
Cromwell, Oliver 276
cross, crucifixion 10, 46, 57, 62–3, 128–9,
    132–3, 147, 177, 179, 180, 195, 199–200,
    209, 240, 247, 255, 263
  word of 56, 71, 79, 80
  see death of Jesus

Dahl, Nils Alstrup 177
Dalferth, Ingolf 6, 10, 166, 169–70, 186, 203,
    208–9, 210
Dante Alighieri 25, 80, 120, 275
Davidson, Donald 87, 217, 223

Da Vinci, Leonardo 219
Dawson, David 145
death 8, 10, 39, 43, 45, 62–3, 102, 104, 164,
    200, 203, 266
  of God 53, 64
  of Jesus 3, 53, 64, 78, 114, 118, 119, 137, 146–8,
    159, 160, 178, **192–3**, **202–8**, 237, 239
De Certeau, Michel 219
De Gruchy, John 243
Deleuze, Gilles 218, 219
De Lubac, Henri 169
depth psychology 236
Derrida, Jacques 30, 217, 219
Descartes, Réné 33, 37, 86, 89
desire 3, 8, **39–43**, 60, 93, 100, 175, 198, 219,
    223, 230, 257, 281
'desolation' 207, 230–1
disciplina arcani 5, 257, 262–3
domination 122, 130, 133, 166, 183–4, 204, 206
drama 150, 237–8
  prophetic 139, 151–2, 157, 188
Dumas, André 243

ecclesiology 132–3
economics 12, 140, 268
election 48, 66
energy 124, 135
enjoyment 3, 8, 30, 33, **34–6**, 40, 42, 44, 47,
    60, 76, 91, 267, 277
Enlightenment 11, 21–2, 222, 254, 255–6
Ephesians, Letter to 5, 9, 86, **108–36**, 184
Ephrem the Syrian 7, 25–9
Esau 194–5
eschatology 115, 146, 168, 189–90, 203, 211
  of selfhood 267
Essenes 188–9
eternity 43, 155
ethics 37–9, 40–2, 50, 62–3, 133–6, 183–4,
    217–19, 267
  and imagination 88
  and prayer 81, 257
  and speech 109–10
  see feasting, ethics of; gentleness, ethic of
eucharist 9, 10, 80, 86, 100, **137–9**, 210, 215,
    253, 263
  and social anthropology 139–45
  in New Testament 145–62
  eucharistic self 143, 162–6, 235
event 61, 64, 87, 210
  epoch-making 155, 163
evil 31, 57, 93, 120, 147, 164, 237, 266
expiation 50, 52, 65–6

Fabry, Heinz-Josef 193
face, facing 4, 7, 8, **17–29**, 33, 34, 44, 46, 47,
    50, 51, 265, 269
  and body 95, 202

of Christ 9, 10, 13, 24–5, 62–3, 70, 74, 103–4,
   128–9, 148, 163, 166, 170, **171–83, 210–16,**
   228, 230, 232, 264, 267, 272; dead face of
   Christ 166, **192–3,** 195, 197, **202–8,** 270
of conscience 103–4
of God 128–9, 193–202
in Levinas 37–9, 69–70, 79
in Ricoeur 92, 96
in Wyschogrod 219
see community of the face; Holy Face
face-to-face 139, 150, 156, 178, 196
faith 56, 57–8, 61, 68, 71, 75, 108, 129, 173–4,
   194, 206, 212, 214, 246, 259
   biblical 85–6
Farley, Edward 32, 36, 39, 116, 130, 178
Farrow, Douglas Bryce 157
feasting 4, 11, 25, 80, 107, 144, 179, **266–81**
   ethics of 268–70
Feher, Michel 207
Feil, Ernst 243
felicity 275–80
feminism 227, 232
Fichte, Gottlob 86
fiction 100, 180
film 182, 268
Fitzgerald, Constance 225, 226, 230, 232, 235,
   236, 239
Floyd, Wayne Whitson 243
flourishing 4, 10, 107, 148, 163
Fodor, James 82, 86, 98, 177
footwashing 159, 161
Ford, David F. 6, 32, 52, 73, 104, 116, 117, 126,
   131, 135, 136, 155, 169, 178, 184
forgiveness 100, 117, 136, 160, 185, 207, 239,
   246, 253, 269
Foucault, Michel 45
Fowl, S. E. 243
Francis of Assisi 233
freedom 19, 38–9, 47, 61, 66, 77, 155, 185, 245,
   247, 256, 276
   God's 71, 211
   see responsibility, free
Frei, Hans 12, 177, 178, 212
Freud, Sigmund 45, 127
friendship 90, 91, 94, 160, 161, 250, 255, 270,
   279
fulness (*pleroma*) 113, 119, 156
fundamentalism 152, 161

Galileo 276
gaze 226, 227, 274
gender 7, 12, 21, 143, 232
generality, carnal 5, 218, 240
   see body of the saint
generosity 102, 135, 162, 185, 218, 244
   of God 178, 229, 242, 263, 269, 279
Genet, Jean 219

Géneviève, Mother 226
genre 2, 98, 111, 112, 144, 219, 235, 272
Gentiles 115, 119, 121
gentleness 25, 35, 40–1, 42, 124, 132, 135–6
   ethic of 25, 44
Gerrish, Brian 162
Gethsemane 129, 147, 179, 228, 239, 260
Gibbs, Robert 30, 49, 69–70
glory 24, 52, 113, 214, 279
   of God 74, 104, 112, 128–9, 178, 196
   of Jesus Christ 24, 103, 163, 171, 175, 179,
      197
God 5, 8, 10, 24–5, 37, 46, 48–9, 54–65, 78,
      98–9, 114, 128
   and life of Jesus 178–9, 185, 208
   and resurrection 210–13
   Father 113, 115, 121, 128, 146, 178, 208, 210,
      214
   vision of 175, 197, 228, 272–5
   Yahweh 211
   see abundance of God; face of God; glory of
      God; Trinity
God as the Mystery of the World 53, 57, 60, 76
goodness 39, 40, 42, 48, 60, 62, 246
   of God 46, 196, 278
   the 'good life' 90–1, 133–4
Görres, Ida 225, 226, 230, 231, 232, 233, 235,
      236–40, 244
Gospels 86, 116, 178, 180–1, 188
grace 89, 102, 109, 117, 164, 196, 213, 229, 233,
      242–5, 246
gratitude 100, 123, 124, 151, 244, 269
Grayston, Kenneth 110, 118, 131, 159, 177
Grout, Donald Jay 125
Guattari, Felix 218, 219

habitus 10, 161
   eucharistic 139–41, 164–5, 168
Halevy, Jehuda 59
Hand, Sean 32, 48
Hardy, Daniel W. 7, 73, 120, 155
Harvey, Nicholas Peter 147–8
Hasidim 221, 223
Hauerwas, Stanley 116, 178
healing 12
Hegel, G. W. F. 64, 237
Heidegger, Martin 31, 36, 53, 83, 94, 217, 219
Hengel, Martin 177
Herbert, George 116
hermeneutics 13, 82, 86, 88, 271–2, 277
   of suspicion 45, 81
hiddenness
   of Christ 228, 232, 240, 263–4
   of God 256
hilaritas 249, 258, 259
Hillesum, Etty 148
Hinduism 182, 270

history 51, 59, 114, 152, 153, 211–12, 220, 253
   Jesus Christ and 176–81
   of Christianity 131
   theology of 201
Hitler, Adolf 242, 247, 250, 259
holiness 259–62
Holocaust, *see* Shoah
Holy Face 207, **226–9**, 235, 244
home 40–1, 235
hospitality 5, 8, 25, 33, 41, 42, 47, 266, 270
   and eucharist 156
   and face of Christ 172, 173
   hospitable self 30, 44, 127, 128, 183, 235
   of God 129, 185
Hurtado, Larry 177
Husserl, Edmund 8, 31, 32, 86, 223

icons, iconography 102, 182, 208, 214, 268
   iconoclastic controversy 182, 207
idem and *ipse* 87, 89, 94, 95, 100
identity 7, 47, 84, 87, 117, 127, 161, 195, 226
   Christian 2, 5, 112, 133, 137, 140, 162, 263
   early Church 131
   narrative 219
   social 108
idolatry, idols 5, 8, 10, 25, **46–9**, 85, 98, 99,
   102, 145, 168, 182, 196, 200, 211, 213–14,
   267, 268
   self without idols 37, 45–72, 86
imagination 3, 18, 88, 90, 100, 153, 180, 181–3,
   214
imperative 10, 60, 74, 90, 93, 97, 139, 164, 194,
   217, 223, 257, 262
   and eucharist 145–6, 148
   of death for Jesus 146, 151
   of love 127, 159
improvisation 5, 9, 79, 100, 109, 111, 119, 120,
   124, 125, 135, 140–2, 144, 148, 164, 261
incarnation 49, 50, 66, 71, 78, 197, 247
incorporation 10, 139, 145, 149–57, 168
infinity, infinite 4, 37, 39, 40, 44, 46, 48, 52,
   75, 276, 279, 281
institutions 23–4, 90, 92, 93, 97, 119, 133, 134,
   136
intercession 202, 257
interhuman 130
interrogative mood 256–7, 261, 263, 281
Islam 182, 270
Israel 127, 194

Jacob 194–5, 211
jazz 280–1
Jenkins, Timothy 139, 141, 142, 143, 144
Jenson, Robert 149, 157
Jesus Christ 2, 5, 10, 46, 53, 113, 116, 117, 122,
   166–90, 202–15, 242, 247–8

and Christian community 251–2
and eucharist 145–6, 156–7
and psalms 128–9
event of 57, 59
God of 11, 169
life of 9, 176–81, 184–90
obedience 146–8, 151, 209
Son 214
see cross; death of Jesus; face of Jesus
   Christ; glory of Jesus Christ;
   resurrection
Job 153
John the Baptist 189
John of the Cross 243
John the Evangelist 11, 274
John, Gospel of 139, 157–62
Jones, L. Gregory 116, 178, 207, 243
joy 12, 128, 174, 211, **219–30**, 233–5, 248,
   252–3, 258–9, 269, 274
   Jüngel's theology of 73, 74–6
   of the saints 266–7
   substitutionary 220, 233, 240, 271
   see enjoyment; felicity; responsibility,
   joyful
Judaism, Jews 8, 30–2, 48, 75, 108, 115, 119,
   121, 125, 129, 131–2, 182, 262, 270
   at time of Jesus 186–90, 207
   rabbinic tradition 187, 199
Judas Iscariot 151, 164, 181
judgement 3, 39, 48, 151, 154, 178, 196, 200,
   229, 239, 247
   moral 134–5
Juel, Donald H. 177
Jüngel, Eberhard 2, 6, 32, 36, 45–6, 49, 53–72,
   73–82, 85, 94, 96, 97, 167, 169, 184, 256
justice 24, 48, 51, 64, 90, 93–4, 131, **133–6**, 185,
   247, 256
justification 3, 53, 102, 114, 229, 246, 248
   by faith 67, 213

Kant, Immanuel 42, 81, 86, 90, 92–3
Kemp, Walter H. 258
kenosis 65, 104
Kierkegaard, Søren 47, 147, 153, 255, 259
Kingdom of God 144, 146, 152, 156, 178, 179,
   185, 188–90, 268, 269, 272, 279
Kristeva, Julia 219
Kuske, Martin 246

lament 129, 144, 199
language 17, 37–8, 39, 40, 41, 44, 45, 50–2,
   76–9, 222, 251, 271–2
   and eucharist 143–4
   as address 53
   event (*Sprachereignis*) 55
L'Arche communities 136

Lash, Nicholas 54, 58, 222
Last Supper 129, 138, 146–8, 150, 151, 161, 163, 179, 268
law 65, 146
    see Torah
Lerner, Gerda 235
Lessing, Gotthold 258
Levinas, Emmanuel 2, 6, 8, **30–44**, 45–9, 49–52, 100, 134, 135, 162, 183, 187, 206, 248, 271, 275
    and Jüngel 53–72, 73–82
    and Ricoeur 83–5, 87–97
    and Wyschogrod 217, 218, 219
    influence 11
Lincoln, Andrew 108, 111, 117
Lindars, Barnabas 158
'little way' 229–30, 234, 236, 242, 244, 246
Llewellyn, John 36, 41
Lowrie, Walter 147, 153
love 8, 11, 25, 46, 98, 120, 205, 207, 214, 218, 274, 276, 281
    and Thérèse of Lisieux 133, 228, 230, 234
    Dalferth's theology 170
    erotic 42
    in John's Gospel 159–60
    Jüngel's theology 64–5, 79–82
    of enemies 187
Luther, Martin 64, 145, 157, 213, 243, 251, 256, 258, 259
    Lutheran *simul* 248, 260
    Lutheranism 243, 244, 245, 246, 248, 249

McFadyen, Alisdair I. 7, 131
McIntyre, John 137
Mandelbaum, Allen 25
Marion, Jean-Luc 211, 214
marriage 119, 120, 122, 185, 242
Marsh, Charles 243
Marshall, Bruce 7
Martin, Céline 232, 233
Martin, Pauline 225, 226, 227, 239, 240
Martz, Louis L. 276
Marx, Karl 45
Mary, mother of Jesus 219, 227
Mary Magdalene 11, 228, 274
Maule, Jeremy 279–80
media 18, 182, 268
medieval period 138, 203, 272, 276
Meeks, Wayne 131
Melberg, Arne 153
memory, *see* remembrance
Merleau-Ponty, Maurice 217, 218
Messiah, messianism 189–90
metanarrative 154
metaphysics 53, 256, 270–1, 277
    see ontology

Milbank, John 212
mission 236, 237
modernity 57, 152, 243, 254
Moltmann, Jürgen 156, 256
Moses 146, 178, 195–6, 201, 211
motherhood 227, 232
Müller, Gerhard Ludwig 249
music 7, 11, 123, 267, 274, 279–80
    see jazz
mystery 56, 71, 109, 114, 172, 243, 257, 263, 272
mysticism 220–1, 235

Nabert, Jean 83–4
Nadaff, Ramona 207
Naish, Tim 195
narrative 87–8, 98, 100, 144, 152–3, 154
    hagiographic 217, 224
    realistic 178, 180
natural, the 246–8
    'natural religion' 55, 222
Nazism 31, 76, 243, 246–7, 248, 254
necessity and non-necessity 55, 59–60, 71, 75, 98–9
    and death of Christ 147
New Testament 65, 77, 138, 176, 231, 244, 272
Nicea, Councils of 208, 263
Nietzsche, Friedrich 45, 86, 89, 205, 259
Nyamiti, Charles 104

obedience 125, 145, 146, 164, 201, 231, 233, 243, 245–6
Ochs, Peter 176
Old Testament 111, 112, 155, 161, 182, 189, **193–202**, 208, 211, 254, 262
Oneself as Another 84–97, 127, 133–4, 218
ontology 34, 38, 49, 50–1, 58
    and christology 168
    of death 63
    of the self 90, 94–7
    see metaphysics
'ontotheology' 53, 55, 56, 66, 67
optative mood 93, 96, 257, 261–2
ordinariness, ordinary living 3, 33, 67, 110, 116–17, 119, 139, 144, 185, 279, 281
    and eucharist 149–51, 163
    and Thérèse of Lisieux 231, 234–5
    in Bonhoeffer's thought 69, 250, 255
Orthodox Church 182, 268
O'Siadhail, Micheal 11, 280–1
other, the 8, 37–9, 41–3, 69–70, 95–6, 219–20
    assimilation to the same 35, 47–8, 62, 183
    otherness 62, 95, 97, 214, 251
    see separation
Otherwise than Being 31, 48, 50, 58, 62, 74, 76, 90
overflow 4, 39, 58, 74, 112–13, 115, 118, 224, 267

panim 193–202
Pannenberg, Wolfhart 55, 169
parables 77, 179, 270
    Prodigal Son 186, 268, 269
pardon 42–3
Parfit, Derek 88
particularity 19, 20, 24, 58, 101
    and christology 60, 65, 169, 209
    and death 63
    and face of Christ 171, 175–6
    and saints 216
    and the face 60, 92
    scandal of 59, 146
passivity 5, 48, 49, 61, 66–7, 71, 74, 83, 92, 94,
    100, 118, 209
Passover 159
patience 135, 136
Paul 11, 24, 86, 102, 108–10, 115, 118, 119, 171,
    213, 230, 274
    Pauline tradition 114, 115, 117
peace 24, 136, 183, 233
Peirce, Charles S. 176
Pelikan, Jaroslav 207
penance 231
Pentecostalism 126
Peperzak, Adriaan 33, 51
Peter 164, 246
petition 81, 257
Pharisees 187–8
phenomenology 8, 13, 32, 36, 53
philosophy 50, 96, 211, 271
    analytic 82, 87, 217
    and theology 53, 249
    linguistic 169
    moral 217
Pickstock, Catherine 139
Pius X, Pope 225
Pius XI, Pope 225
place 163
pluralism 37, 47, 59, 62, 131, 271
politics 3, 12, 90, 102, 120, 130–1, 133, 136, 207,
    218, 248, 268
    and Jesus 184–90, 191–2
polyphony 4, 12, 98, 101, 128, 249, **254–9**,
    260–1, 263
postmodernism 112, 152, 153, 216, 219, 224
power 10, 124, 130, 133, 143, 166, 184–6, 205,
    208, 220, 252
    powerlessness 204
praise 81, 98, 100, 109, 115, 118, 144, 155, 213
prayer 5, 81, 110, 112, 118, 178, 185, 229, 242,
    251, 257, 258, 267
presence 56, 94, 193
    and absence 46, 57, 58, 71, 104, 156, 160, 201
    eucharistic 138, 145, 146
    of Christ 171, 251

of God 50, 155, 252, 274
promise 98, 100, 128
prophecy 52, 60, 98
    see drama, prophetic
Protestantism 48, 241, 243, 244, 275
Psalms 76, 80, 86, 98, 101, 112, 122, **126–9**,
    197–9, 208, 250–1, 258, 262
psychotherapy 136

Qumran 188–9
Quash, J. B. 237
Quine, Willard van Orman 217, 223

race 20, 21
Rad, Gerhard von 194
Rahner, Karl 69
Ranke, Leopold von 153
Raphael Santi da Urbino 11, 272–5
reason 38, 39, 47, 92, 247
recognition 93–4, 100, 101, 166, 172, 232, 252
reconciliation 114, 133, 195
redemption 50, 114, 117, 130
Reformation 11, 137, 182, 245, 254, 255, 275,
    276, 279
relationship 205
religion, religions 5, 12, 45, 49, 182, 224, 256,
    262, 268, 270
Rembrandt 90, 195, 259
remembrance 153, 203, 208
    eucharistic 146, 147, 148, 153
Renaissance 11, 249, 254, 272, 275
repentance 100, 196, 246, 274
repetition, non-identical 5, 123–4, 129, 139,
    143, **152–7**, 164, 180, 215
representation 34, 35, 38, 40, 45, 47, 51–2, 95,
    104
    and the face 21–3, 37
    of face of Christ 181–3
reserve 243, 250, 264–5
responsibility 2, 12, 35, **37–9**, 40, 47–8, 51–2,
    66–7, 88–9, 93, 118, 122, 217–19, 233, 252
    free 247, 248, 257
    joyful 5, 161, 173, 214, 220, 229, 234–5, 265
    of Jesus 129, 179
    substitutionary 59–60, 69, 167, 173, 206–9,
    213, 233, 240, 271
resurrection 11, 43, 62, 75, 78, 114, 118, 128,
    147, 159, 160, 164, 169, 203–4, 207, 209,
    210–13, 237, 240, 256, 269
revelation 37, 48, 98, 103, 207, 222, 228
    self-revelation of God 55, 211
Ricoeur, Paul 2, 4, 6, 8, 32, 42, 73, 78, **82–104**,
    129, 152, 157, 158, 168, 169, 172, 177, 180,
    184, 210, 212, 214, 221, 270
Riley, Peter 135
Ringgren, Helmer 193

ritual 149, 150
Roman Empire 186–90, 207
Rosenzweig, Franz 30, 32, 42, 76, 91, 96, 97,
    99, 127, 187
Royal Society 276

Sabbath 187
sacraments 136, 162, 233
sacrifice 3, 4, 52, 63, 65, 100, 138, 169, 183, 194,
    208–9, 229, 234
Sadducees 188
saints, sainthood 9, 11, 187, **220–4**, 237–8, 241,
    259, 276
    joy of 266–7
    saintly singularity 5, 224, 240
salvation 1, 3, 4, 5, 7, 8, 31, 49, 126, 137, 140,
    168, 169–70, 193, 200–1, 205, 272
    and worship 98
    as health 1, 267
    in Psalms 197
    Thérèse's understanding of 232–5
sanctification 229, 234, 256
Sanders, E. P. 177
Savage, Timothy B. 205
Schillebeeckx, Edward 131
Schnackenberg, Rudolf 111
Schönborn, Christoph von 208
Schönherr, Albrecht 249
sciences 38, 152, 211, 271, 276
    natural and human 36, 120
    social 51, 82, 249
scripture 79, 82, 97, 98, 107, 136, 156, 242, 246,
    267
Searle, John Roger 87
secrecy 243, 249, 262
    see disciplina arcani
secularity 256
Sedgwick, Peter 131
self, practice of 99
self-esteem 89, 90–1, 93–4, 95, 100
senses 19, 143, 149–50, 267
separation 34, 35, 37, 40, 61–3, 65, 74, 95
Serafim of Sarov 266
Sermon on the Mount 185, 231, 243, 250
Servant Songs 201–2, 240, 281
Shoah 12, 31, 76, 148
Shusani, Mordechai 70
silence 77, 126, 202, 263, 272, 275, 279, 281
sin 7, 102, 164, 193, 194, 236, 239, 245, 256,
    266, 274
singing 4, 9, 112, 116–17, 135–6, 230, 231, 234,
    253, 274
    singing self 109, 120–9, 235
Six, Jean-François 225, 233, 235
Sloterdijk, Peter 219
smile 227, 228, 231–2, 234, 275

Smith, D. Moody 158
Smith, Julia 276
Smith, Ronald Gregor 243
Smith, Steven G. 60
Solzhenitsyn, Alexandr 154
Song of Songs 92, 96–7, 120, 254
soteriology 4, 53, 63, 168, 170, 186
    of abundance 113, 114, 117, 119, 120
soul 19, 50, 234
Spinoza, Benedict 94
Spirit, Holy 103, 113, 115, 121, 125, 128, 144, 148,
    159, 160, 178, 207, 210, 212, 214, 236
spirituality 272, 276, 277, 279
Stacey, David 150, 151
Stanton, Graham N. 177
state 248, 249
Stern, J. P. 116
Strawson, P. F. 87
subject, subjectivity 8, 35
substitution 4, 5, 8, 45, 46, 52, 59, 60, **65–70**,
    76, 96, 103, 119, 153, 183
    substitutionary self 69, 74, 164, 235
    see joy, substitutionary; responsibility,
        substitutionary
suffering 38, 49, 91, 95, 103, 129, 151, 200–1,
    204, 217, 224, 228, 231, 233, 239, 253, 260,
    280
superabundance 5, 9, 98, 101, 103, 134–5, 144,
    178, 244, 271, 277
    superabundant self 117
supersessionism 131
Swinford, Nigel 3
Sykes, Stephen 169

Taizé community 126
Talmud 53, 187
Taylor, Charles 134
Tazi, Nadia 207
Temple 188, 192, 198, 208
Teresa of Avila 221, 222, 223, 224, 243
testimony 5, 22, 83–4, 86, 96, 100, 101, 128,
    142, 178, 203, 210, 239, 250, 266
    and history 177, 180
    to Jesus Christ 54, 59, 114, 132, 167, 176
    see attestation; witness
thanks 4, 109, 115, 154
Theilgaard, Alice 136
theism 220
theology 2, 8, 12–13, 45, **49–57**, 66
    Christian 1, 31–2, 85
    constructive 6, 8
    eucharistic 141
    New Testament 52
    philosophical 8
    political 131
    systematic 1, 52, 168, 169

Thérèse of Lisieux 2, 5, 11, 86, 207, **225–40**, 241–8, 264, 266
  relations with women 225, 226–7, 234–5, 240
time 10, 18, 23, 36, 42–3, 51, 88, 123, 141, 153
  ethical 161
  eucharistic 5, 139, 155, 159, 161, 163–4
Time and Narrative 88
Tödt, Ilse 246
Torah 64, 116, 185, 187, 195
totality, totalisation 31, 37, 46, 47–8, 51, 62, 64, 70, 237
Totality and Infinity 31, 34, 39, 42, 43–4, 47, 90
Tracy, David 1
tradition 111
Traherne, Thomas 11, 271, 275–80
transcendence 42, 48, 51, 52, 71, 78, 112, 155
Transfiguration 146, 178, 179, 180, 228
transformation 171, 176, 222, 274, 277, 281
  and life of Jesus 185
  eucharistic 142, 145, 146, 150, 154
  of boundaries 118, 121
  of categories 237
  of Jesus' disciples 160, 212–13
  of self 2, 25, 74, 75, 103, 115, 126, 138, 168, 204–5, 260
  of sensing 267
  of time 123
  of worship 208–9, 210, 214
Trinity 7, 54, 71, 78, 128, 157, 168, 203, 213, 236, 271
trust 61, 68, 82, 89, 91, 151, 199, 200, 211, 229
  epistemology of 89
truth 89, 101, 108, 212, 239
  'doing the truth' 161

ultimate and penultimate 246, 247, 248, 262–3
universality
  ethical 59, 90, 92, 96, 183
  of eucharist 150, 151
  of God's Word 24
  of justice 135
  of responsibility 60

of the face 19
Urban Theology Group 131

Vanier, Jean 136
vagueness 166, 171, 175, 176, 180
'Veil of Veronica' 226
Verkade, Dom Willibord 238
virtue 247
vocation 11, 50, 80, 146, 148, 156, 207, 229, 230, 231, 234, 272
  Jesus' 147
vocative mood 224, 257, 258, 261
Vogel, Heinrich 68

Webster, John 32, 52, 53, 67
Wedderburn, A. J. M. 108
Wedemeyer, Maria von 255
Westphal, Merold 47
will 39
Williams, Rowan 123, 124, 155, 222
wisdom 11, 117, 164, 182, 250, 264, 277
  wisdom literature 98
witness 5, 22, 33, 38, 50, 51–2, 73, 212
  witnessing self 60
  see attestation; testimony
worldliness 260, 262, 263
worship 2, 3, 25, 45, 79, 81, 85, 96, 107, 116, 122, 161, 173, 182, 187, 198, **213–15**, **220–4**, 229, 235, 242, 252–3, 258, 263, 267
  and Jesus Christ 168
  worshipping self 4, 5, 8, 9, 10, 32, 73, 82, **97–104**, 127, 128, 129, 198, 250
  see eucharist
Wright, N. T. 177
Wüstenberg, R. 243
Wyschogrod, Edith 11, 203, **216–24**, 233, 235, 236
Wyschogrod, Michael 60

Yofre, Simon 193
Young, Frances 12, 32, 104, 117, 136, 184

Zealots 187
Zwingli, Ulrich 145